THE SERMON ON THE MOUNT AND MORAL THEOLOGY

In this volume, William Mattison demonstrates that virtue ethics provides a helpful key for unlocking the moral wisdom of the Sermon on the Mount. Showing how familiar texts such as the beatitudes and petitions of the Lord's Prayer are more richly understood, and can even be aligned, with the theological and cardinal virtues, he also locates in the Sermon classic topics in morality, such as the nature of happiness, intentionality, the intelligibility of human action, and the development of virtue.

Yet far from merely placing the teaching of Aristotle in the mouth of Jesus, Mattison demonstrates how the Sermon presents an account of happiness and virtue transformed in light of Christian faith. The happiness portrayed is that of the kingdom of heaven, and the habits needed to participate in it in the next life, but even initially in this one, are possible only by God's grace through Jesus Christ and lived in the community that is the Church.

William C. Mattison III is Associate Professor of Theology at the University of Notre Dame with a joint appointment in the Alliance for Catholic Education. He spent ten years at The Catholic University of America, where he served as interim Dean of the School of Theology and Religious Studies. He is the author of *Introducing Moral Theology: True Happiness and the Virtues* (2008), along with numerous articles and edited volumes.

THE SERMON ON THE MOUNT AND MORAL THEOLOGY

A Virtue Perspective

WILLIAM C. MATTISON III

University of Notre Dame

CAMBRIDGE
UNIVERSITY PRESS

One Liberty Plaza, 20th Floor, New York, NY 10006, USA

Cambridge University Press is part of the University of Cambridge.

It furthers the University's mission by disseminating knowledge in the pursuit of education, learning, and research at the highest international levels of excellence.

www.cambridge.org
Information on this title: www.cambridge.org/9781107171480
10.1017/9781316761342

© Cambridge University Press 2017

First published 2017

Printed in the United States of America by Sheridan Books, Inc.

A catalogue record for this publication is available from the British Library.

Library of Congress Cataloging-in-Publication Data
NAMES: Mattison, William C., III, 1971- author.
TITLE: The Sermon on the mount and moral theology : a virtue perspective / William C. Mattison III, University of Notre Dame.
DESCRIPTION: 1 [edition]. | New York : Cambridge University Press, 2017. | Includes index.
IDENTIFIERS: LCCN 2016044612 | ISBN 9781107171480 (Hardback : alk. paper)
SUBJECTS: LCSH: Sermon on the mount–Criticism, interpretation, etc. | Christian ethics–Biblical teaching. | Virtue.
CLASSIFICATION: LCC BT380.3 .M385 2017 | DDC 241.5/3–DC23
LC record available at https://lccn.loc.gov/2016044612

ISBN 978-1-107-17148-0 Hardback

For my sons,
Billy and Jack,
with all of my love

CONTENTS

ACKNOWLEDGMENTS

This book was conceptualized in 2009 and over the course of the ensuing six years a great many people made it possible in a variety of ways. I should begin by acknowledging a more remote inspiration for this book, the late Fr. Servais Pinckaers, O.P., who in my estimation is the most impactful post–Vatican II Catholic moral theologian. Not only has his work been enormously formative on me as a theologian, especially when I was fortunate enough to study with him from 2000 to 2001, but his chapter on the Sermon on the Mount in his *Sources of Christian Ethics* provides a "charge" for this book.

In 2008 I attended the Society for the Study of Christian Ethics' meeting in Cambridge on the Sermon on the Mount. Though at that point I had no plans to write this book, I delivered a paper on the Lord's Prayer and the virtues that is the basis for Chapter 6 this book. I am grateful to The Catholic University of America and Msgr. Kevin Irwin for support in attending this conference. I am also grateful to Gregory LaNave's assistance in publishing the article that arose from that paper in *The Thomist*. Finally, I am grateful to *The Thomist* for giving permission to use portions of that article in the final chapter of this book.

The next step in the development of this book came through a paper and later article on the beatitudes. For their suggestions on this project, I am grateful to Craig Steven Titus and especially Jean Porter, whose formative influence on me made this book possible in the first place. I am also grateful for Matthew Levering's assistance in publishing that article in *Nova et Vetera*. Finally, I am grateful to *Nova et Vetera* for permission to use portions of that article in the first chapter of this book.

I taught doctoral seminars on the Sermon on the Mount three times between 2009 and 2012. I am grateful to the students in those classes for how much I learned from them. I am also grateful for the series of graduate student research assistants who helped me to research and edit this book, including Siobhan Benitez Riley, Ben Safranski, Nick Hladek, James Pearce,

Andrew Whitmore, and Fr. Rodrigue Constantin. Luke Briola and Matthew Martin provided a particularly large amount of research and editorial assistance.

The third time I taught that doctoral seminar on the Sermon on the Mount I co-taught it with Fr. Frank Matera. This was a literally invaluable experience for me. Matera's biblical scholarship is unsurpassed, and this book would be much diminished without his influence. I am particularly grateful for his own book that grew out of our course, *The Sermon on the Mount* (Liturgical Press, 2013).

Though conceptualized as early as 2009 and relying on two articles published beforehand, the bulk of writing for this book occurred between 2012 and 2015, while holding various administrative positions at the School of Theology and Religious Studies at The Catholic University of America. I am very grateful to Dean Fr. Mark Morozowich for the research support and teaching release he granted me during this period to enable me to continue writing. And no one made that writing more possible than my friend and colleague, Associate Director of the Undergraduate Program Catherine Graveline. The time and perseverance I needed to write this book would not have been possible without her constant supportive encouragement, administrative prowess, and joyful leadership for our undergraduates.

In the summer of 2015, four friends and colleagues in the field agreed to do extensive manuscript reviews of this text: Patrick Clark, David Cloutier, David Elliot, and Barrett Turner. Their input was invaluable, as each of them made tangible improvements to this projects. I am enormously grateful for their assistance, but especially for their friendship.

I am grateful to The Catholic University of America which provided several "grants-in-aid" to support this research. I am grateful to Georgetown University's Department of Theology and former Chairs Terry Reynolds and Fr. Christopher Steck, SJ for hospitality in providing a secluded office to write much of this text. Thanks especially to Bill Werpehowski whose office it most commonly was! Beatrice Rehl at Cambridge University Press has been enormously helpful, and I am grateful for the suggestions from two anonymous reviewers from that press.

On a more personal level, I'm eternally grateful for my parents Joan and Bill Mattison, who made my vocation as a theologian possible with all of their love and support. And of course I am most grateful for my wife Courtney, whose love and companionship are perhaps the greatest gift in my life.

Finally, I not only thank, but dedicate this book to, my beloved sons Billy and Jack. I wrote this book as a contribution to scholarship in moral theology but also to help bring the Sermon on the Mount more to forefront of formation in the Catholic faith. Billy and Jack are the people I most have in mind for the crucial mission of forming people in the faith. And they are the people who will continue that mission after me. The Sermon on the Mount offers the Lord's guidance on how to live a life of grace-enabled virtue, a life of true happiness. Billy and Jack have taught me a great deal already about living such a life, and they will continue to teach me even more so as they grow to be men. I dedicate this book to them with all my love, to boys growing into men whom I admire more each day.

INTRODUCTION

Augustine called the Sermon on the Mount the "charter of the Christian life," complete in all the precepts that constitute the Christian life.[1] Thomas Aquinas regarded the Sermon as the written form of the new law of Christ.[2] Throughout the Christian tradition, commentaries on the Sermon are central to the moral thought of giants such as Augustine, Luther, and Bonhoeffer. Yet with too few exceptions, the Sermon has surprisingly garnered little attention from contemporary Christian ethicists and moral theologians. One broader goal of this project is an attempt to restore the Sermon on the Mount to a more prominent place in moral theology and in Christian formation more generally.

One of the most important developments in moral theology and Christian ethics has been a return to prominence of the role of virtue. Yet again with few exceptions there has been little sustained attempt to demonstrate how a virtue ethic is thoroughly rooted in Scripture. Indeed, it is even assumed that a virtue-centered approach to morality is actually non-scriptural.[3] Another broader goal of this project is to demonstrate not only that a virtue ethic is compatible with Scripture, but also that there is an illuminating convergence between the Sermon on the Mount and a virtue-centered approach to morality. Matthew did not read Aristotle, but it is extraordinary how closely the text of the Sermon matches up with the conceptual resources of virtue ethics.

---

[1] Augustine, *The Lord's Sermon on the Mount*, trans. John Jepson, S.S. (New York: Paulist Press, 1948), i.1.1.

[2] Thomas Aquinas, *Summa Theolgia* (New York: Benziger Bros., 1948), I–II 108, 3.

[3] For an example of this latter affirmation in recent biblical scholarship, see Hans Dieter Betz, *The Sermon on the Mount: A Commentary on the Sermon on the Mount, including the Sermon on the Plain (Matthew 5:3–7:72 and Luke 6:20–49)* (Minneapolis, MN: Fortress Press, 1995), 97. As further evidence of general neglect, consider that virtue is practically non-existent in what are arguably the two most important late twentieth-century books on Scripture and ethics, namely, Richard Hayes's *The Moral Vision of the New Testament* (New York: Harper Collins, 1996) and Frank Matera's *New Testament Ethics: The Legacies of Jesus and Paul* (Louisville, KY: Westminster John Knox, 1996).

The thesis of this book is that the Sermon on the Mount is fruitfully read with the questions and concerns of virtue ethics in mind. In other words, a virtue-centered approach to moral theology helps us to understand better the ethical guidance in the Sermon on the Mount. Yet the moral guidance offered in Matthew 5–7 is not simply Aristotle from the mouth of Jesus Christ. The complementary thesis of this book is that the Sermon on the Mount specifies and illuminates a virtue-centered approach to morality. In short, there is a convergence between the Sermon on the Mount and a virtue-centered approach to morality.

The tasks of this introduction are threefold. I first contextualize this project in relation to other bodies of scholarship in order to both situate it in relation to them and show the need for it given the lacunae in those bodies of scholarship. Second, I explain the rationale for the organization of this book's chapters and provide a brief overview of their content. Third and finally, I attend to some methodological issues that are helpful to have addressed before the ensuing chapters.

I. CONTEXTUALIZING THIS BOOK

In order to contextualize this project in contemporary scholarship and the tradition more broadly, it would help to situate it in relation to three distinct theological literatures. The first is the tradition of commentary on the Sermon on the Mount. Given the claims above by Augustine and Thomas Aquinas about the importance of the Sermon for life in Christ, it should be unsurprising that there is such a vast amount of commentary on the Sermon in the Christian tradition, whether it be focused on the Sermon or address the Sermon in the larger context of commentary on Matthew or the gospels.[4] Books on the Sermon and/or extended treatments of these three chapters in Matthew are ubiquitous in the writings of important figures throughout the Christian tradition. Books on the Sermon on the Mount continue to be written by biblical scholars today. The tradition of commentary on the Sermon on the Mount is enormous, and it continues today.

The second body of literature is on virtue ethics. In scholarship on moral theology and Christian ethics, one of the more seismic shifts over the past few decades has been the resurgence of virtue ethics. This rise has been well

---

[4] To provide some sense of the amount of commentary, Hans Dieter Betz reports Adolf von Harnack's quip that exegesis merely on Mt 5:17 and simply by Patristic authors could easily fill an entire book. See his *The Sermon on the Mount*, 175. Warren Kissinger's *The Sermon on the Mount: A History of Interpretation and Bibliography* (Metuchen, NJ: Scarecrow Press, 1975) comes closest to providing a comprehensive overview of that tradition, though in his opening lines he reports Jaroslav Pelikan's claim that "the history of the exposition of the Sermon on the Mount has not yet been written," and if it were to be done it would be "a massive historical enterprise" (1).

documented, with early pioneers such as Elizabeth Anscombe and Josef Pieper paving the way for philosophers such as Alasdair MacIntyre and theologians such as Stanley Hauerwas among Protestants and Servais Pinckaers, O.P. for Catholics.[5] Philosophical and theological accounts of virtue are ubiquitous today in moral thought, requiring any self-proclaimed virtue ethicist to situate him or herself as to the particular strand of virtue ethic endorsed (a topic addressed below). Nonetheless, despite the prominence of virtue ethics in recent Christian moral thought, there is surprisingly little attention given to its relation to Scripture in general, and to the Sermon in particular. This lacuna sets the stage for this book.

The third body of literature concerns the relationship between Scripture and ethics, both understood more broadly than the Sermon and virtue ethics, respectively. In Catholic moral theology, the degree of disconnect that had developed between Scripture and ethics is evident in the oft-cited Vatican II claim that moral theology should be "nourished more on the teaching of the Bible."[6] The late twentieth century saw a surge in scholarship on Scripture and ethics, from both Protestant and Catholic ethicists.[7] Particularly noteworthy are the two monographs on the topic from scripture scholars Richard Hayes and Frank Matera.[8] Though the volume of this scholarship has subsided, important works continue to appear on this interrelationship.[9]

Given the existence of these three robust bodies of scholarship, the absence of sustained attention to a virtue-centered approach to morality in

---

[5] For one such account of the rise in attention to virtue in moral theology and Christian ethics, see David Cloutier and William C. Mattison III "Review Essay: The Resurgence of Virtue in Recent Moral Theology," *Journal of Moral Theology* **3**.1, *Virtue* (Jan. 2014): 228–59. See also Jonathan Sanford's *Before Virtue: Assessing Contemporary Virtue Ethics* (Washington, D.C.: The Catholic University of America Press, 2015).

[6] See *Optatem Totius*, 707–724 in Austin Flannery, O.P., ed., *Vatican Council II: The Conciliar and Post Conciliar Documents* (Collegeville, MN: Liturgical Press, 1975), 16. For an example of one pre–Vatican II herald of the importance of being more firmly rooted in Scripture, Bernard Haring, see James F. Keenan, S. J. "Bernard Haring's Influence on American Catholic Moral Theology," *Journal of Moral Theology* **1**.1 (Jan. 2012): 23–22.

[7] Examples include Bruce C. Birch and Larry L. Rasmussen, *Bible and Ethics in Christian Life* (Minneapolis, MN: Augsburg, 1989) and William Spohn, *What Are They Saying about Scripture and Ethics?* (Mahwah, NJ: Paulist Press, 1995). For a sampling of positions on this question see Charles Curran and Richard McCormick, eds., *Readings in Moral Theology No. 4: The Use of Scripture in Moral Theology* (Mahwah, NJ: Paulist Press, 1984).

[8] See the Richard Hayes and Frank Matera volumes cited above.

[9] Examples include William Spohn, *Go and Do Likewise: Jesus and Ethics* (Bloomsbury, 2000); Allen Verhey, *Remembering Jesus: Christian Community, Scripture and the Moral Life* (Grand Rapids, MI: Eerdman's 2005); Richard Burridge, *Imitating Jesus: An Inclusive Approach to New Testament Ethics* (Grand Rapids, MI: Eerdman's, 2007); Robert Brawley, ed., *Character Ethics and the New Testament: Moral Dimensions of Scripture* (Louisville, KY: Westminster John Knox, 2007); and, Joel Green and Jacquelyn Lapsley, eds., *Dictionary of Scripture and Ethics* (Grand Rapids, MI: Baker Academic, 2011).

relation to the Sermon on the Mount is striking. With the very few exceptions noted in the following paragraph, the Sermon on the Mount does not feature prominently in either recent moral theology and Christian ethics, or recent work on Scripture and ethics.[10] As to recent scholarship on morality, despite the fact that the Sermon is universally recognized as the most lengthy and obviously ethical discourse by Jesus, it is largely absent from moral formation, be it in everyday raising of children and ongoing faith formation, or in the halls of academia where scholars of moral theology and Christian ethics are trained.[11] As to the literature on Scripture and ethics, attention to virtue is virtually non-existent in that surge of scholarship at the close of the twentieth century. Some more recent work on Scripture and ethics has begun to attend to both virtue and the Sermon. But the literature on Scripture and ethics does not yet reflect the level of depth and sophistication that has been reached in the recent resurgence of research on virtue in moral theology and Christian ethics. A lack of attention to virtue is perhaps less surprising in recent biblical scholars who are not trained moralists (much as this author is no trained biblical scholar). Yet there can even be found in recent biblical scholarship an assumption that a virtue approach to morality is antithetical to a biblical ethic.[12]

Though the lack of scholarship described above is real and significant, it is not complete.[13] There are some excellent recent books that are close kin to this book as to their subject matter. It is worth pausing to mention two of

---

[10] In addition to the following, note must be made of the Pontifical Biblical Commission document *The Bible and Morality: Biblical Roots of Christian Conduct* (Rome: Liberia Edictrice Vaticana, 2008). Obviously the general task of that document precludes a focus on either the Sermon or virtue. Indeed, the term "virtue" used in the technical sense appears just sixteen times in this 200-plus page document (4, 40, 43, 44, 47, 65, 104, 106, 109, 129, 133, 137, and 156). Nonetheless, there is an important role for virtue described in this account of the Bible and morality. Though at times (rightly) insisting a biblical morality is not simply a list of laws and virtues (4, 156), the term virtue is also used to describe life in Christ in general (43, 133); in reference to the example Christ offered to us in His life (44); to name the theological virtues (65); to describe the relationship between the "human virtue" of wisdom "potentially discoverable in all cultures" and Christian faith (104); and, in the most frequent and sustained use of the term, in the context of the beatitudes (e.g., "a whole list of fundamental dispositions and virtues is to be found in the beatitudes," 47).

[11] Anecdotally, throughout my seven years of graduate formation in moral theology, never was I required or offered to devote significant attention to the Sermon on the Mount. I myself confess, despite teaching moral theology to college students for over ten years and writing a commonly used textbook on moral theology, that I do not (yet) rely on the Sermon as a foundation in my introductory course on moral theology/Christian ethics.

[12] See, for example, Betz, *The Sermon on the Mount*, 97: "[T] attitudes, actions, and thoughts demanded [in the Sermon on the Mount] are different from what the Greeks would call 'virtues.'"

[13] For several important articles on the Sermon on the Mount and ethics, see *Studies in Christian Ethics* 22.1 (2009). This excellent collection features prominent moralists and is the fruit of a 2008 conference at Cambridge on the Sermon on the Mount.

them not only to recognize their important contributions (as will be done throughout the chapters that follow) but also to contextualize this project in relation to them. By far the closest kin to this project is Servais Pinckaers, O.P.'s *The Sources of Christian Ethics*.[14] The present book can be rightly understood as an attempted expansion of Pinckaers's brief chapter there on the morality of the Sermon.[15] The Thomistic moral theology of virtue articulated by Pinckaers is, as addressed below, the methodology adopted here in terms of virtue ethics.[16] The second book, comparatively impactful in the Protestant world of Christian ethics, is Glen Stassen and David Gushee's *Kingdom Ethics*.[17] This entire book is focused on the Sermon, and virtue features prominently in their approach to morality, so in these senses the book is quite similar to this one. Yet *Kingdom Ethics* differs from this book in terms of its organization, which includes several initial chapters on methodology followed by chapters organized topically, most often by specific ethical issues. Furthermore, Stassen and Gushee's approach to virtue ethics differs significantly from the one here.[18]

Despite the very important contributions made by these works, there is clearly a lacuna in recent scholarship as to examining the Sermon on the Mount with a virtue-centered approach to morality. In this book, I attempt to address that gap. More than simply fill a void, I make the further claim that examining the Sermon from the perspective of a virtue-centered approach to

[14] Servais Pinckaers, O.P. *The Sources of Christian Ethics* (Washington, DC: The Catholic University of America Press, 1996).

[15] Given the importance of Pinckaers to post–Vatican II Catholic moral theology, there is a sense in which all post-conciliar moral theology is a continuation of an agenda set by his work. For an analysis of his thought in the context of the post–Vatican II renewal of Catholic moral theology, see Craig Steven Titus, "Servais Pinckaers and the Renewal of Catholic Moral Theology" *Journal of Moral Theology* I.1 (Jan. 2012): 43–68.

[16] Another excellent book in Catholic moral theology closely related to this one is Daniel Harrington, S. J. and James Keenan, S. J.'s *Jesus and Virtue Ethics: Building Bridges between New Testament Studies and Moral Theology* (Sheed and Ward, 2005). Though they include a chapter on the Sermon, their focus is on the gospels more broadly. Also worthy of mention is Yiu Sing Lucas Chan's *The Ten Commandments and the Beatitudes* (Lanham, MD; Sheed and Ward, 2012). This book contains an overview chapter on virtue ethics and Scripture, and its focus on the beatitudes is obviously pertinent to this book. Chan tragically passed away suddenly as this book was completed. R.I.P.

[17] The complete title is *Kingdom Ethics: Following Jesus in Contemporary Context* (Illinois: Intervarsity Press Academic, 2003)

[18] Two other recent books warrant mention here. Dale Allison's *The Sermon on the Mount: Inspiring the Moral Imagination* (New York: Herder & Herder, 1999) also focuses on the Sermon and ethics, and like the present book is organized by the textual order of the Sermon. Yet virtue ethics does not feature prominently. Finally, Charles Talbert, who edits the series where Allison's book appears, wrote *Reading the Sermon on the Mount: Character Formation and Decision-Making in Matthew 5–7* (Grand Rapids, MI: Baker Academic, 2006). This excellent book is also organized by the Sermon's textual order and does feature character and virtue prominently, though its approach to virtue ethics differs from that offered here.

morality reveals a noteworthy convergence. In other words, a virtue perspective enables one to ascertain more fully the moral guidance offered in the Sermon. Conversely, the Sermon on the Mount specifies and perfects a virtue-centered approach to morality. It is hoped that by making this case I can: contribute to theological scholarship; do moral theology that is robustly "nourished more on the teachings of the Bible" as called for by the Second Vatican Council; and perhaps most importantly, contribute to the restoration of the Sermon on the Mount to a prominent role in Christian moral formation.[19]

II. ORGANIZATION OF THIS BOOK

How is this book organized, and why was that organization chosen? One friend who reviewed this manuscript suggested a possible tension in the structure of the book. Is this book a sort of "ethics commentary" that follows the text in order and identifies the moral relevance of passages sequentially? Or is it a more constructive argument about what a virtue-centered approach to morality looks like that is rooted in the Sermon on the Mount?[20] This book is in some ways both, but clearly more the latter than the former. The problem is that these two endeavors suggest different organizations, the first driven by textual order of the Sermon and the second a topical order based on central features of virtue ethics. Despite my claim that this book is more the latter, the organization I have chosen is the former. Why so?

First, the "downsides" of the order I have chosen. I have always been concerned that a monograph organized in the order of the sections of the Sermon could be misperceived as a work of biblical scholarship. As noted above, I am not a biblical scholar, and this is not a work of contemporary biblical scholarship. I hope biblical scholars benefit from the arguments offered here as I most certainly have from biblical scholarship, but this book is not a work of that genre. Furthermore, treating the Sermon in basic textual order can lead to a tendency to "run through" what classical commentators and contemporary biblical scholars say about this text rather than marshaling that thought toward the constructive argument that this book makes. I have been attentive to avoiding that temptation, but I likely have been less successful on some passages than others.

So why nevertheless organize this book by chapters that follow the order of the Sermon and organize chapters to *generally* follow the text of the Sermon? Moral theologians have long been accused of proof texting Scripture to

---

[19] The term "restoration" invites question as to whether or how the Sermon played such a role in the past. That primarily historical question is worthy of study but cannot be undertaken here.

[20] My thanks to David Cloutier for raising this question.

support arguments that are in actuality generated by other (non-scriptural) commitments. That charge could of course be leveled here as well. The decision to follow the order of the text of the Sermon reflects a commitment to have the constructive argument offered here be as accountable as possible to the Scripture, not only to more sporadically chosen verses, but to the very organization and structure of the Sermon itself. That is one reason why the book is organized as it is, and also why I take so seriously the organization of the Sermon and the constitution of its various components as having significance (e.g., the beatitudes, antitheses, and petitions of the Lord's Prayer). The very organization of the Sermon on the Mount is offered in support of this book's thesis that there is noteworthy convergence between the Sermon on the Mount and a virtue-centered approach to morality, and therefore I have chosen to respect that organization by the structure of the book.

This claim of course rests on some account of what the structure of the Sermon on the Mount actually is. There are many explanations of the organization of the Sermon throughout the tradition of commentary. To name just two noteworthy examples: Augustine famously organized the Sermon into seven sections that align with the beatitudes.[21] Thomas Aquinas divides the Sermon into three sections: first, Jesus promises reward (5:3–16); second, Jesus sets down precepts (5:17–7:6); and third, Jesus teaches how someone can attain the observance of these precepts (7:7–29).[22] Yet there is actually remarkable commonality in contemporary biblical scholarship as to the overall structure of Matthew 5–7.[23] The Sermon begins with a section on the beatitudes that concludes with the salt and light metaphors. It then contains what might be called the "main part," beginning with 5:17 and concluding with 7:12. Contemporary scholars virtually unanimously recognize the *inclusio* formed by these two verses based on the repeated phrase "law and the prophets." There is then a final part of the Sermon which follows 7:12, namely, 7:13–29.

As for the subdivision of the "main part," again we find virtual unanimity. The four verses in 5:17–20 on fulfillment of the old law are regarded as introducing the ensuing six antitheses in 5:21–48, with which they form one

---

[21] Augustine, *The Lord's Sermon on the Mount.* For a helpful summary of Augustine's organizational schema, see Betz, *The Sermon on the Mount,* 46.

[22] Thomas Aquinas, *Commentary on the Gospel of Matthew 1–12* (Rochester, NY: The Aquinas Institute, 2013), 403.

[23] For examples of the organization of the Sermon on the Mount along the lines offered in the ensuing sentences, see Robert Guelich, *The Sermon on the Mount: A Foundation for Understanding* (Waco, TX: Word Books, 1982), 39; Betz, *The Sermon on the Mount,* 50–66; Ulrich Luz, *Matthew 1–7: A Commentary* (Minneapolis, MN: Augsburg, 1989), 212; and W. D. Davies and Dale C. Allison, *The Gospel According to Saint Matthew, Vol. I: Matthew 1–7,* International Critical Commentary (Edinburgh, Scotland: T. & T. Clark 1988), 63.

unified section. Next, the readily evident structured parallelism of 6:1–18 leads scholars to regard these verses as another unified section. Finally, the remaining verses in the main part 6:19–7:12 can be grouped together. There is far less agreement on how these verses fit together, and frequently it is assumed that they fit together only by default, that is, as the verses left over in the main part until 7:12. Against this assumption Chapter 4 offers a case for how these verses are indeed coherently structured. However, it is still the case that 6:19–7:12 are commonly treated together in contemporary biblical scholarship.

Therefore, in contemporary biblical scholarship there are evidently five sections of the Sermon on the Mount. These sections correspond to the first five chapters of this book. This book concludes with a sixth chapter on the Lord's Prayer, which is of course found at the center (6:7–15) of the middle section of the Sermon (6:1–18). There are several reasons to "pull out" the Lord's Prayer and treat it separately in its own chapter. First, contemporary biblical scholarship indicates in various ways the unique function of these verses in the organization of the Sermon.[24] Most noteworthy is Ulrich Luz's chiastic view of the structure of the Sermon, with the Lord's Prayer as the centerpiece and very heart of the Sermon.[25] Second, the crucial importance of the Lord's Prayer in the life of Christian discipleship, along with the enormous tradition of commentary on the prayer, warrants distinct treatment of these verses. Finally and more substantively, Chapter 6 offers a constructive argument about the Lord's Prayer and its relationship to virtue that is in some ways a climactic conclusion to the thesis of this book.

In summary, the division of the Sermon into sections that correspond with the six chapters in this book is well supported in the tradition of commentary on the Sermon on the Mount. And as indicated above, we will find that this commonly recognized organization of the Sermon provides further support for this book's thesis for illuminating convergence between the Sermon and a virtue-centered approach to morality. How do these chapters unfold?

Chapter 1 (Mt 5:1–16) focuses mainly on the beatitudes. It makes a case that the classic virtue ethics' claims that morality is about happiness, and that happiness is an activity, can help us better understand the beatitudes. To make this claim in the terms of contemporary biblical scholarship, the beatitudes are best understood both ethically and eschatologically. Equipped with the questions and concerns of virtue ethics as to the role of happiness in morality and the connection between moral activity and happiness, this chapter mines the tradition of commentary on the beatitudes in order to

---

[24] See, for example, Guelich on how the petitions of the Lord's Prayer govern the ensuing verses 6:19–7:12 (*Sermon on the Mount*, 363–81). This argument (and its origins) is addressed in Chapter 4.

[25] Luz, *Matthew 1–7*, 212.

elucidate the moral guidance offered in the beatitudes. The scriptural text in turn informs common claims of classical virtue ethics, so in this chapter we see the method of the book perfectly exemplified. The chapter also concludes with an examinations of the role of suffering in the life of discipleship, the centrality of Christ, and the inextricable link between Christology and ecclesiology, particularly evident in 5:13–16.

Chapter 2 (Mt 5:17–48) examines in detail Christ's teaching in the antitheses about how the new law fulfils the old law. Granting that that the *telos* of old law and new law alike is happiness, this chapter makes an implicit argument about the compatibility of law and virtue. More explicitly, it adopts a virtue-centered approach to morality to argue that Christ's moral teaching in these verses "fulfills" the law (5:17) by depicting activity that is in greater conformity to the *telos* of the law, and thus called more "perfect" or complete (5:48).

Chapter 3 (Mt 6:1–6, 16–18) examines a crucial topic in any virtue ethic, namely, intentionality. A first-person perspective is central to the teleological view of human action endemic to classical virtue ethics, but it raises questions about the intelligibility of immediate actions and long-term goals, as well as the relationship between the two. This chapter argues that a virtue-centered approach to morality not only converges with the moral guidance offered in these verses, but such an approach is also illuminated by the scriptural text, mainly through the notions of "hypocrisy" and "reward" as well as the practical guidance offered there on the development of virtue.

Chapter 4 (Mt 6:19–7:12) analyzes a set of verses commonly grouped together by default due to the clear transitions in 6:19 and 7:12. It argues that a virtue-centered perspective reveals a clear order to these verses, centered around the (spatially centered) verse "Seek first the kingdom of God and his righteousness" (6:33). These verses address classic virtue ethics themes, such as the singularity of the final end and its impact on everyday activities with particular attention to relations with others. Once again I argue that the Sermon, far from merely relating insights of classical ethics, presents an ethic convergent with classical virtue yet thoroughly transformed by faith in our heavenly Father. This faith in a God of provident gratuity shapes our engagement with temporal goods and our relations with others.

Chapter 5 (Mt 7:13–29), which forms an *inclusio* with 5:1–16, similarly addresses the relationship between activities in this life and our ultimate destiny in the next. While the opening of the Sermon presents an account of such activity as continuous in the life and the next, these warning verses employ different metaphors to depict how such activity may fail to be continuous with eternal reward.

Chapter 6 (Mt 6:7–15) is a concluding chapter focusing on the Lord's Prayer, the spatial and thematic heart of the Sermon and a perfect microcosm of the central thesis of this book. The chapter mines the tradition of commentary for how the Lord's Prayer has been understood, structurally and substantively. It then offers a constructive proposal about the alignment of the seven petitions of the Lord's Prayer with the three theological and four cardinal virtues, an interpretation in some ways readily continuous with the tradition (e.g., Augustine) and yet in other ways novel.

III. METHODOLOGY OF THIS BOOK

The thesis of this book is that there is ready convergence between the Sermon on the Mount and a virtue-centered approach to morality, and that the former further illuminates the latter. This introduction is an appropriate place to pause to address two methodological questions. What "virtue-centered approach to morality" is employed here? And how is the meaning of the Sermon on the Mount ascertained? This section then concludes with a methodological reflection on this book's strategy of positing alignments between portions of the text and other groupings from the Christian tradition.

A. WHICH VIRTUE ETHICS?

Turning first to virtue ethics, it was noted above how virtue ethics is burgeoning today, to the extent that it is necessary to state what sort of virtue ethics approach one adopts. Approaches to virtue ethics vary significantly. Not only can they be philosophical or theological, but even within these commitments different authors employ the language of virtue in various ways influenced by figures such as Aristotle, Cicero, Hume, and Kant among others. "Virtue ethics" is not a monolithic approach, and so one must ask, "Which virtue ethic?" This project offers no attempt to delineate the significant differences in these approaches, much less make a case for the superiority of one approach over others. Nonetheless since the approach to virtue employed here is as "positioned" as any other, it is necessary to acknowledge that position. In this book, I rely on a Thomistic (and therefore quite Aristotelian) *ressourcement* (meaning in continuity with the Patristics) virtue approach to morality.[26] That means there are commitments on certain topics reflected in this book that may not be shared by other "virtue ethicists." These topics include, for instance, the singularity and function of the last end, the role of intentionality in human activity, and the distinctive role of prudence in relation to the other virtues. The virtue-centered approach to morality here also rests on certain theological claims

---

[26] Thank you to David Elliot for this description of the approach to virtue employed here.

that would be dismissed by secular approaches to virtue ethics. For instance, I rely heavily on distinctions between theological and moral virtue, as well as between acquired and infused virtue. My approach can of course also be contested by other Christian approaches to virtue. For example, a Jonathan Edwards based account of charity would differ from the one offered here in terms of its relation to natural virtue, or its account of divine causality. Again, the worthy endeavor of delineating and adjudicating these different approaches to virtue cannot be undertaken here. I simply acknowledge the particular approach to virtue adopted in this book, and I express a hope that this book may help prompt that more comparative endeavor (especially with regard to the Sermon on the Mount) in future scholarship.

Given the approach to virtue adopted in this book, which concerns and questions of a virtue-centered approach to morality are brought to an examination of the Sermon? These are addressed in more detail in each chapter as they arise. Yet a few general such questions can be identified here, with no claim that they are unique to the Thomistic *ressourcement* approach to virtue adopted here.

What is happiness?
What is the relationship between human activity and happiness?
What role does intentionality play in rendering human action intelligible, and in forming habits and character in human agent?
How are virtues (or vices for that matter) formed?
Is there one last end of a human life, and how does it function?
Why and how is prudence so central to the virtuous life, and how does it relate to other virtues?

My argument is that all of these questions, and more, are addressed by the Sermon on the Mount. Therefore, having them in mind while reading the Sermon can help us better appreciate the moral guidance offered therein.

B. AUTHORITATIVE VOICES ON THE SERMON

Having addressed the methodological question of "which virtue ethic," we now turn to the methodological question of accessing the meaning of the Sermon. Throughout this book, I make extensive appeal to authoritative authors in the Christian tradition to help understand the meaning of different passages. This requires some explanation since the authors relied upon vary across time period (Patristic, Medieval, Reformation, contemporary), East and West, and Catholic and Protestant, as well as their bases and levels of authority. From my own Catholic perspective, Scripture is of course foundationally authoritative, as interpreted by the tradition of the Church. There are some facets of the tradition that are particularly authoritative, such as the Fathers of the Church (e.g., Augustine, Ambrose, John

Chrysostom, Nyssa) and even the Angelic Doctor Thomas Aquinas.[27] There are also Protestants, such as Martin Luther and John Calvin, whose "authority" is not ecclesial for Catholics, but rather derives from any wisdom they impart in commenting on the Scriptures. The same may be said of the contemporary thinkers found in this book, including biblical scholars but also moral theologians and Christian ethicists.

Throughout this book, I appeal to all of these different sorts of "authority" quite freely in conjunction with one another, and this requires two caveats. First, though I offer no extended argument as to the varying sorts of authority here, that is not to be taken as an implicit claim that there is no difference of authority in these thinkers, nor taken as some sort of "levelling out" of all authorities relied on here. The sources and levels of authority of, for instance, Gregory of Nyssa, Luther, and Pope Benedict XVI are not the same. Second, though I rely on many of these figures, often in conjunction with one another, to make particular points in support of the theses of this book, that is not a claim that the thinkers at hand either agree with one another more broadly, or agree with the theses of this book. Examination of the differences in moral thought of the various figures appealed to here, including the differences in how they view Scripture, is an important project. Indeed, how these similarities and differences are evident in their thinking on the Sermon is particularly interesting.[28] Yet no such arguments are offered here. Nor do I claim that even the more "heavily relied upon" thinkers (e.g., Thomas Aquinas) affirm the broad conclusions offered here. How can appeal be made to such a variety of figures while avoiding using their words as mere "proof text?"

Though the best explanation will come in the ensuing chapters, the brief answer offered here is that the broader claims about the convergence of the Sermon and virtue ethics rely on more basic building blocks which are the verses in the Sermon. So for instance, though Thomas Aquinas, Luther, and Robert Guelich surely have importantly different views of Scripture, morality, and the beatitudes (let alone different levels and bases of authority), they each affirm quite similar things about what sort of activity is referenced by Jesus in

---

[27] There are other ecclesial authorities contained herein, most notably Pope Benedict XVI. But by his own account, his book on Jesus should not be afforded the authority of his papal office, but rather that of a theologian. See *Jesus of Nazareth, Vol. I: From the Baptism in the Jordan to the Transfiguration* (San Francisco: Ignatius Press, 2008), xxiii.

[28] For fine examples of precisely this endeavor, see Jeffrey Greenman, Timothy Larsen and Stephen Spencer, eds., *The Sermon on the Mount Through the Ages* (Grand Rapids, MI: Brazos press, 2007) and Tore Meistad, *Martin Luther and John Wesley on the Sermon on the Mount* (Lanham, MD: Scarecrow Press, 1999). For an example of an analysis of commentary on the Sermon by Augustine, Chrysostom, and Luther with a focus on rhetoric, see Jaroslav Pelikan, *Divine Rhetoric: The Sermon on the Mount as Message and as Model in Augustine, Chrysostom, and Luther* (Crestwood, NY: St. Vladimir's Seminary Press, 2001).

Mt 5:4, "blessed are they who mourn." In order to make my case about the beatitudes depicting human activity that is constitutive of happiness, some sense of the activity called "mourning" must be grasped. These three thinkers may not share common visions of the relationship between the first and second parts of each beatitude or the role of the beatitudes as a whole in the Sermon. No such claim is made here. But they do indeed each claim that Jesus means by mourning what is described here as recognition of one's own sinfulness and the courageous willingness to face and endure suffering in this life. Thus I appeal to these authorities to help make more immediate claims, even if they do not use that same understanding of mourning to go on to make the broader claims affirmed here.

A word is also in order as to which thinkers are deployed in such a manner in this book. With all of the above caveats about differing sources and levels of authority, the most persistently cited theologians in the ensuing chapters are Augustine, John Chrysostom, Thomas Aquinas, Martin Luther, John Calvin, Dietrich Bonhoeffer, Servais Pinckaers, O.P., and Glen Stassen and David Gushee. The main contemporary biblical scholars are Robert Guelich, Hans Dieter Betz, Ulrich Luz, and William Davies and Dale Allison. As to the theologians, although other figures could be chosen (and at times are cited herein, e.g., Ambrose) the importance of these figures' writings on the Sermon on the Mount and/or a virtue-centered approach to morality means that the omission of these figures in any survey would be at least as problematic as others.[29] As for the contemporary biblical scholars most frequently used in this book, the two most cited scholarly monographs on the Sermon in recent decades are clearly those of Robert Guelich and Hans Dieter Betz, and so I use these contemporary biblical scholars augmented by others I have found particularly helpful (e.g., Ulrich Luz, W. D. Davies, and Dale Allison). In the world of contemporary biblical scholarship, the books of these scholars on the Sermon on the Mount are as important or more so than those of any other contemporary biblical scholars.

C. A WORD ON ALIGNMENTS

Before concluding this section on methodology, a word is in order on the various alignments offered in this book between portions of the Sermon on the one hand, and other (most commonly virtue-based) prevalent groupings in the Christian life on the other hand. For instance, in Chapter 1 I offer an

---

[29] As evidence for the importance of the pre-twentieth-century commentators chosen here, all commentaries mentioned by Betz or Guelich in their treatments of the history of commentary are addressed here. See Guelich, *The Sermon on the Mount*, 14–21 and Betz, *The Sermon on the Mount*, 107–109.

argument about how the beatitudes can be aligned with the seven (three theological and four cardinal) virtues. I make a comparable argument in Chapter 6 with regard to the petitions of the Lord's Prayer. Indeed, the chapters of this book as a whole make a case for how the five sections of the Sermon that govern the book's first five chapters can be aligned with these seven virtues.

While I fully defend these different alignments, I'd like to offer two qualifications so they are properly understood. First, though as mentioned below I think there may be something deeply important at stake in the making of such alignments, it is also the case that the central thesis of this book about the convergence between the Sermon on the Mount and a virtue-centered approach to morality is not dependent on such alignments. In other words, that central argument can stand even if one does not accept the arguments offered as to particular alignments.

Second, as will be substantiated in the chapters that follow, such alignments are rampant in the tradition of commentary, and indeed continue (though far less frequently) in biblical scholarship today. So this endeavor is hardly unprecedented in the tradition of commentary. Yet whenever it occurs, never is there a claim that one *only* understands the passage of the Sermon at hand in light of said alignment. Though arguments about alignments and the structural claims upon which they rely are necessarily detailed endeavors, they should not be thought as reductive endeavors. In other words, such an alignment is neither a necessary nor a sufficient way to understand the text. Nonetheless, while such alignments ought not be regarded as rigid equivalences much less reductions, there is something true and beautiful about such correspondence that prompts a brief note to end this introduction.

Given these qualifications, why do I offer such alignments in this book? I propose two reasons. First, I claim that such alignments can be illuminating. For instance, having the seven virtues in mind can help us better understand parts of the Sermon (e.g., beatitudes and petitions) on the one hand, and on the other hand the parts of the Sermon enrich our understanding of the virtue at hand. This cannot simply be averred, but rather needs to be substantiated. I leave it to my reader to determine how well substantiated such alignments are when they arise in this book. These alignments are certainly accountable to standard scholarly standards.[30] What I can suggest here is a possible reason for that mutual illumination. Given the status of Scripture as inspired revelation, I trust there is a rationale for the text's canonical form. So when we encounter some set (of beatitudes, petitions,

---

[30] I am grateful to one anonymous peer reviewer who suggested I recognize that these alignments are not sealed off from such scholarly standards, "to make clear that we have not entered a peer-review no fly zone!"

antitheses, for example), it is reasonable to ask why *this* set. One answer is that the set offers, possibly even comprehensively, the fundamental parts of something, such as the activities of happiness or way the old law is fulfilled by the new. If there is another set that purportedly comprehensively accounts for something (in other words, the seven virtues as encapsulating the Christian moral life), it should not be surprising that the two sets can be aligned in some way. And the endeavor of aligning them may help us better understand one by the other.

Second, despite these caveats and the fact that my alignments may appear to some readers as quaint or even numerologically or organizationally compulsive, these alignments are included because they indicate something about the beauty of Scripture and the unity of the truth.[31] The convergence between the Sermon and the virtues can be argued academically on the plane of textual analysis or intellectual history. Yet it is also an indication of a deeper truth in play here. The synergy between Scripture and the tradition of the virtues "breaks open a new space for apprehending and contemplating the beauty of the wisdom that is present in these words." It points to a deeper wisdom about the beauty of Scripture and the way it draws us into contemplation of and relationship with the Author of Scripture who is Author of all. I said above that the further goals of this project are to restore the Sermon to a prominent place in moral formation and contribute to a moral theology more robustly nourished by Scripture. But surely the ultimate end of this project, as of all things, is the joyous and communal contemplation of God that constitutes eternal happiness. If reflections on alignments or indeed any of the arguments in this book can contribute to that end in the lives of readers in even a small way, this book will surely have achieved its ultimate end.

---

[31] In what follows, I am heavily and gratefully indebted to Patrick Clark, to the extent that the quotation in this paragraph is from personal correspondence with him.

1

THE BEATITUDES AND HAPPINESS:

The Christological and Ecclesiological Vision of Matthew 5:1–16

*When he saw the crowds, he went up the mountain, and after he had sat down, his
disciples came to him.*

He began to teach them, saying,

Blessed are the poor in spirit, for theirs is the kingdom of heaven.

Blessed are they who mourn, for they will be comforted.

Blessed are the meek, for they will inherit the land.

Blessed are they who hunger and thirst for righteousness, for they will be satisfied.

Blessed are the merciful, for they will be shown mercy.

Blessed are the clean of heart, for they will see God.

Blessed are the peacemakers, for they will be called children of God.

*Blessed are they who are persecuted for the sake of righteousness, for theirs is the
kingdom of heaven.*

*Blessed are you when they insult you and persecute you and utter every kind of evil
against you (falsely) because of me.*

*Rejoice and be glad, for your reward will be great in heaven. Thus they persecuted
the prophets who were before you.*

*You are the salt of the earth. But if salt loses its taste, with what can it be
seasoned? It is no longer good for anything but to be thrown out and trampled
underfoot.*

You are the light of the world. A city set on a mountain cannot be hidden.

*Nor do they light a lamp and then put it under a bushel basket; it is set on a
lampstand, where it gives light to all in the house.*

*Just so, your light must shine before others, that they may see your good deeds and
glorify your heavenly Father.*[1]

A chapter on the beatitudes could not be a more fitting way to begin this
book on the Sermon on the Mount and virtue ethics, and not simply because
the beatitudes fall at the start of the Sermon. All classical treatments of ethics

---

[1] Matthew 5:1–16, New American Bible, revised edition (used throughout this book).

begin with reflection on happiness. And what do we have at the start of the Sermon? Lo and behold a miniature treatise on happiness. Section 1 of this chapter defends the claim that the beatitudes are about happiness.

But of course claiming the beatitudes are about happiness is the start of a discussion, not the conclusion of one. This claim raises more questions than it answers. For instance, what is the nature of happiness? What is the relationship between the characteristics of people called "blessed," and the "reward" (5:12) promised to them? When does the reward promised in the beatitudes occur? Why are there a set of beatitudes (rather than, for instance, just one), and what can we learn about happiness from the beatitudes coming as a set to start off the Sermon? These are the questions this chapter addresses after the opening argument that the beatitudes are about happiness.

The second section represents the most constructive argument of the chapter and introduces a theme that is crucial to the rest of this book. Assuming happiness is what all persons seek, classical reflection on happiness immediately turns to how happiness can be obtained, and in particular what human activities and qualities lead to happiness. It is argued here that the beatitudes present what I call an "intrinsic" relationship between the characteristics of the blessed and the rewards they attain. Making this case depends first on explaining what exactly is meant by an intrinsic relationship. It is really an explication of the standard Aristotelian and Thomistic claim that happiness is an activity. Happiness is an activity, and thus what are enjoined as leading to eternal reward are activities that are constitutive of happiness. This section then turns to the history of Christian interpretation of the beatitudes, including representative contemporary biblical scholarship, to substantiate this claim.

The third section addresses some ramifications of this claim. Two in particular are addressed. First, "when" do the rewards of the beatitudes occur, now or in the future, in this life or the next? Next, what do the beatitudes *as a set* tell us about eternal happiness, the activities that constitute it, and how we can progress toward that fullness of life?

Before proceeding to the ensuing verses, a brief transitional – though in fact pivotal – psection examines two themes too often neglected in moral theology yet which are prevalent in these verses and are also more easily understood from a virtue-centered approach to morality. The first is the (literally) crucial place of suffering in the life of discipleship. The second is the centrality of Jesus Christ for these opening verses, for the Sermon as a whole, and for the life of discipleship. The following chapter contains a more extended treatment of the person of Jesus Christ and the Sermon, but for reasons explained below an emphasis on the centrality of Christ is necessary in this chapter.

The fourth section is an examination of Mt 5:13–16, those verses that can seem to teeter precariously between the beatitudes and the ensuing verses on the fulfillment of the law, but which are actually pivotal for both the beatitudes and indeed the rest of the Sermon. These verses reveal the ecclesial character of the Sermon, and in particular, the beatitudes. Disciples of Christ must remain true to their calling (in other words, be salt), and radiate that witness to those around them in mission (in other words, be light), endeavors which are inextricably bound to one another. These verses also reveal the essential link between Christology and ecclesiology, not only conceptually but in the life of discipleship.

The conclusion takes on a task that is present in some way in each chapter of this book, namely, explaining how the verses treated in the chapter at hand can be understood in relation to one of the theological or cardinal virtues. Based on the preceding arguments, this part of the Sermon is understood in light of the theological virtue of faith. It is through the gift of faith, a virtue that is always Christological and ecclesial, that the vision of happiness depicted in the beatitudes can be known, lived, and witnessed.

I. THE BEATITUDES ARE ABOUT HAPPINESS

The straightforward claim of this first section is that the beatitudes are about happiness. This claim is substantiated in three ways, which are treated together: a) by the linguistics of the text itself; b) by the text's context among other texts of the same genre; and c) by the text's interpretation by authoritative figures in the Christian tradition.

For reasons documented by recent thinkers such as Servais Pinckaers, O.P., the topic of happiness is too frequently divorced from modern discussions of morality.[2] Hence it is not surprising that we rarely hear "happy" as the opening word of each of the beatitudes, given that they are located at the start of the Sermon on the Mount, which Augustine once called the "charter of the Christian life."[3] However, the Greek *makarios* is appropriately translated as either blessed or happy. The most common English translation is "blessed." In their surveys of English translations, Robert Guelich and Hans Dieter Betz both acknowledge the preponderance of "blessed" but also claim that "happy" is as accurate a translation.[4] Robert Louis Wilken examines the use in Aristotle of both *makarios* and another Greek term for happiness commonly associated with virtue ethics – *eudaimonia* – and concludes that

---

[2] See his *Sources of Christian Ethics*. See also Alasdair MacIntyre's *After Virtue* (Notre Dame, IN: University of Notre Dame Press, 1981) for a parallel argument in moral philosophy concerning the eclipse of language of virtue and happiness.

[3] See Augustine's *The Lord's Sermon on the Mount*, trans. John Jepson (Westminster, MD: Newman Press, 1956), I.1.1

[4] See Robert Guelich, *The Sermon on the Mount: A Foundation for Understanding* (Waco, TX: Word Books, 1982), 66 for a brief survey of various translations in English. See also Hans Dieter Betz, *The Sermon on the Mount* (Minneapolis, MN: Fortress Press, 1995) 92.

the two terms are used synonymously.[5] Ulrich Luz affirms this claim. He says that "*Markarios*, can hardly be distinguished any longer from *eudaimonia* and means 'happy' in the fullest sense of the term."[6] Speculating on why we so frequently hear the translation "happy," Luz goes on to claim

> But the translation "happy" sounds somewhat banal, and it obscures the eschatological character of the promises in the second clauses. The traditional interpretation as "blessed" ... evokes in a much too unilinear way associations with the beyond: in German "the blessed" is a common designation of the dead.... In short, there is no ideal translation in German [or English].[7]

Luz's observation that the beatitudes should be taken to refer neither to the "banal" present, nor in a "unilinear" way to the "beyond," is prescient for the argument of Section 2 in this chapter. But for now it is sufficient to note his conclusion that the opening word of each beatitude can be as appropriately translated "happy" as it can be translated "blessed."[8]

This conclusion is not surprising given the historical context of the beatitudes. Consider first the context of classical culture. Greek and Roman treatments of ethics *are* discussions of what constitutes happiness, including attention to what is sought that procures happiness, and what sort of qualities (in other words, virtues) and activities on the part of persons are involved in the seeking and possession of happiness. That the nature of happiness is *the* question for how to live a good life is taken for granted in classical culture, even if what constitutes such happiness is contested.[9] For example, both Aristotle and Cicero focus important works on ethics on the question of happiness.[10] Wilken considers this classical context in his work on Gregory of Nyssa's homilies on the beatitudes:

---

[5] Robert Louis Wilken, "Gregory of Nyssa, *De Beatitudinibus*, Oratio VIII: 'Blessed are Those Who Are Persecuted for Righteousness' Sake, for Theirs Is the Kingdom of Heaven (Mt 5,10)," 243–54 in Drobner and Viciano, eds., *Gregory of Nyssa: Homilies on the Beatitudes* (Leiden: Brill, 2000), 244–45. See also Terrence Irwin's treatment of the topic in Aristotle, *Nicomachean Ethics*, ed. Terrence Irwin (Indianapolis, IN: Hackett, 1999), 318. See also Julia Annas's *The Morality of Happiness* (Oxford: Oxford University Press, 1993), 44.

[6] Luz, *Matthew 1–7*, 232.   [7] Ibid.

[8] The claim here is that *markarios* can be appropriately rendered "happy." Whether "blessed" is still preferable, given a common superficial (or "banal") connotation of happiness to mean "feeling good," is a legitimate question. Of course happiness, or *eudaimonia* as used in the context of virtue ethics, does not connote such a superficial notion of happiness. As the term "happiness" is used in virtue ethics, the beatitudes are "about happiness." Nevertheless, for the sake of consistent usage of the New American Bible revised edition, "blessed" is used here.

[9] For a helpful treatment of classical ethics from the perspective of happiness, see Julia Annas's The Morality of Happines.

[10] See Aristotle's *Nicomachean Ethics*, Books I and X on happiness. See also Cicero's *On Moral Ends*, ed. Julia Annas (Cambridge: Cambridge University Press, 2001).

For if one reads Gregory after being schooled in ancient writings that address how one is to live, for example Aristotle's *Nicomachean Ethics* or Seneca's *De beata vita*, or even Augustine's early work by the same name, it is apparent that "happiness" was a key term in ancient moral philosophy. Its appearance in the beatitudes would have triggered associations in the mind of ancient readers that are foreign to moderns unschooled in the eudaimonistic ethics of the ancient world.[11]

As Wilken notes, for anyone schooled in classical culture, the beatitudes would have been understood in the context of the enduring question of how to live a good - that is, happy - life.

This was precisely how the text was understood by early Christian thinkers. Augustine begins his sermons on the beatitudes with the observation that "clearly you couldn't find anyone who doesn't want to be happy,"[12] revealing that Augustine understood the beatitudes as responding to the universal human longing for happiness.[13] In the opening lines of his homilies on the beatitudes, Gregory of Nyssa describes the beatitudes in the terminology used to delineate human happiness. Gregory claims "*markarios* as I understand it, is something which includes every concept of goodness, and from which nothing answering to good desire is missing."[14] Gregory clearly understands the beatitudes in the context of the perennial inquiry into the nature of human happiness.

Finally, contemporary biblical scholars affirm not only that those schooled in classical thought would hear the beatitudes in this context of the question of happiness, but also that those formed by the Scriptures would similarly hear the beatitudes in such a manner. In the words of Guelich, "Judaism offers the more immediate background" for the literary form beatitude. He goes on to contextualize the beatitudes in the Scriptures by offering over forty citations of the literary form in both the Old and New Testaments.[15] Betz claims that the Matthean beatitudes stand in the tradition of Wisdom

---

[11] Robert Louis Wilken, "*De Beatitudinibus*, Oratio VIII," 243. For an excellent treatment of the beatitudes in not only Gregory but also Augustine, see Michael Dauphinais, "Gregory of Nyssa and Augustine on the Beatitudes," *Nova et Vetera* 1 (2003): 141–63.

[12] Augustine, *Sermons III (51–94)*, trans. Edmund Hill, O.P. (New York: New City Press, 1991), 53.1.

[13] See also Augustine's *The Lord's Sermon on the Mount*, I.1.3.

[14] Gregory of Nyssa, *Gregory of Nyssa: Homilies on the Beatitudes*, ed. Hubertus Drobner and Albert Viciano (Leiden: Brill, 2000), "Homily I on the Beatitudes," 24. (Further references to this text are given by homily number, followed by section number, with page in this volume in parentheses.) See also VI:2 (67) and IV:7 (55–56).

[15] See Robert Guelich, *The Sermon on the Mount*, 63. The classic study of the Jewish context of the Sermon as a whole is W. D. Davies's *The Setting of the Sermon on the Mount* (Cambridge: Cambridge, University Press, 1964). For more on the literary form beatitude, see also Betz, *The Sermon on the Mount*, 97–105; Davies and Allison, *The Gospel According to Saint Matthew*, 431–34.

literature.[16] In regard to the question of the relationship between the beatitudes and the entire Sermon on the Mount, Betz notes that beatitudes are commonly placed at the start of some didactic text, a dynamic he points out not only in the work of Epicurus, but also in Psalm 1.[17]

In sum, the beatitudes are appropriately understood within the context of ethical writings on happiness. Their origin and literary form reveal such a context in Jewish and classical sources. Furthermore, early Christian exegetes understood the beatitudes in precisely this context of the question of happiness.

If the beatitudes are appropriately understood in the content of classical ethical reflection on happiness, this is a source of inquiry, not the conclusion of it. It prompts perennial questions germane to virtue ethics, which essentially concerns the qualities (in other words, virtues) and activities of persons that direct them toward fulfillment or flourishing (in other words, happiness). What is ultimate happiness, and how is it related to the common worldly understandings of happiness? Is it attainable, and if so is it attainable in this life? How can one live toward attaining it? What does Jesus Christ have to do with ultimate happiness? These are the sorts of questions a virtue ethics inquiry into the beatitudes asks. Although answering all of these questions is beyond the scope of this chapter, the following section addresses one such question: what is the relationship between the promised happiness and the characteristics that the text identifies of those who receive this happiness?

II. THE BEATITUDES: THE RELATION THEY POSIT BETWEEN QUALIFYING CONDITION AND REWARD

Each of the beatitudes posits some connection between what might be called a "qualifying condition" (e.g., being meek), and some reward (e.g., inheriting the earth).[18] What is the nature of the relationship between the qualifying

---

[16] Betz, *The Sermon on the Mount*, 94. See also Gerald Friedlander, *The Jewish Sources of the Sermon on the Mount* (New York: Ktav Publishing House, 1969).

[17] Betz, *The Sermon on the Mount*, 104 and 59. See also Pope Benedict XVI, *Jesus of Nazareth* (New York: Doubleday, 2007), 71 for the beatitudes' root in Jewish Scriptures, including explicit reference to Psalm 1.

[18] These terms are adopted here for the sake of precision, mainly because the term "beatitude" can be used to refer to each entirety, or just to what is called here the "qualifying condition." In this essay, "beatitude" refers to the whole, each consisting of a "qualifying condition" and a "reward." The term "reward" can have the unfortunate connotation of "earned on one's own," as if God's grace were unnecessary. This connotation leads one contemporary biblical scholar, even while consistently using the term "reward", to say "reward *horribile dictum*" (Luz, *Matthew 1–7*, 246). None of the commentators surveyed here would hold such a view, nor would this author. This issue is addressed in more detail in Chapter 3 given the prominence of the term reward in those verses.

conditions on the one hand, and the rewards on the other? The text makes it clear that those characterized by certain qualifications are or will be happy, yet how or why this is the case is not as evident.[19] The argument of this section is that the beatitudes are best understood as presenting an intrinsic connection between the qualifying conditions and rewards. This claim is a crucial theme for the rest of the book. In order to make this argument, I first explain what is meant by an "intrinsic connection." Then I examine each of the beatitudes to determine how the qualifying condition and reward are best understood as intrinsically related. This section typifies the methodology of this book, in that the conceptual resources of virtue ethics are mined and brought to bear on the Scripture, which in turn specifies and extends classical virtue ethics.

A. DEFINING "INTRINSIC RELATION" AND ASCRIBING IT TO THE BEATITUDES

Happiness as understood in virtue ethics may be described simply as the attainment or possession of the greatest good.[20] This engenders questions on two levels as to the meaning of happiness, namely, identification of the greatest good and explanation of how it is attained.[21] Though this chapter on the beatitudes focuses primarily on the attainment of happiness, the beatitudes also address the "content" of happiness, in other words, the greatest good. They do so first by identifying the greatest good as the kingdom of heaven. The kingdom of heaven is named in the first beatitude as attained by those called "happy" (5:3). It is the kingdom of heaven that is attained in all the beatitudes, as indicated by the *inclusio* formed by the

---

[19] For an example of someone turning immediately from the recognition that the beatitudes are about happiness to questions of virtue and how to live to obtain such happiness, see Gregory of Nyssa, *Homilies on the Beatitudes* I:2 (24).

[20] For examples of this fundamental claim, see Augustine, *Way of Life of the Catholic Church*, I.3: "We must possess our supreme good, then, if we intend to live happily." See also Thomas Aquinas, *Summa Theologiae* I–II 3, 1 ad. 2: "Happiness is called man's supreme good, because it is the attainment or enjoyment of the supreme good."

[21] Those well versed in virtue ethics will see in this paragraph the influence of Aristotle's *Nicomachean Ethics* i.7. Here I am particularly influenced by Fr. Servais Pinckaers, O.P., who wrote frequently about the distinction between what he calls the "objective" and "subjective" meanings of happiness, relying especially on Thomas Aquinas, *Summa Theologiae* I–II 2, 8–3, 2. See his "Aquinas's Pursuit of Beatitude: From the *Commentary on the Sentences* to the *Summa Theologiae*" and "Beatitude and the Beatitudes in Thomas Aquinas's *Summa Theologiae*," 93–114 and 115–129, respectively, in John Berkman and Craig Steven Titus, eds., *The Pinckaers Reader* (Washington, DC: The Catholic University of America Press, 2005), at 100–102 and 121–123, respectively and *Saint Thomas D'Aquin, Somme Théologique: La Béatitude* (Paris, Cerf, 2001), 234. See also William C. Mattison III, "Beatitude and the Beatitudes in the *Summa Theologiae* of St. Thomas Aquinas," *Josephenum Journal of Theology* 17.2 (2010): 233–49.

repetition of "theirs is the kingdom of heaven" in the eighth beatitude (5:10). Thus the beatitudes name the greatest good sought by and attained by those called "happy" in each of the beatitudes.

Yet the beatitudes do not simply assert that the greatest good is the kingdom of heaven. They reiterate again and again reasons why it is the greatest good. Classical reflection on happiness offers several conditions characterizing the greatest good. For example, the greatest good is self-sufficient, not the path to any other (therefore higher) good.[22] Perhaps most famously, the greatest good cannot be lost.[23] The beatitudes offer little by way of explaining why the kingdom of heaven surpasses all other goods, though some such reflection is found in Chapter 3 and Chapter 4 on "reward" and "treasures," respectively.

What the beatitudes do offer is an explanation of how the kingdom of heaven meets another classical condition for the greatest good, namely, that it satisfies completely all human desire. True happiness completely satisfies all human desire precisely because it is attainment of a good that is greatest.[24] The beatitudes depict this satisfaction, and do so repeatedly in the second through seventh beatitudes (5:4–9). Those called happy attain the kingdom of heaven, which satisfies all that they long for: they are comforted, inherit the earth, are satisfied, receive mercy, see God, and are children of God. Why the beatitudes offer this set of characteristics to describe the complete satisfaction of human desire is addressed in a later section of this chapter on the beatitudes as a set. For now, it suffices to conclude that the beatitudes present the kingdom of heaven as the greatest good in which happiness consists, and they present that greatest good as satisfying all human desire.

Classical reflection on happiness not only consists of identifying the greatest good that fulfills the human longing for happiness, but it also consists of identifying what constitutes the attainment of that happiness. Despite the common (although varied) recognition that certain states of affairs befall a person with no relation to their deliberate activity,[25] the shared assumption in classical ethics is that happiness "involves my activity: it is not a thing or state of affairs that others could bring about for me."[26] This is the classic claim that happiness is an activity, rather than simply some state of affairs in which one finds oneself.[27] And since virtues are stable dispositions to activity that is constitutive of happiness, the virtuous life is a life oriented toward happiness.

---

[22] Aristotle, *Nicomachean Ethics* i.7. Thomas Aquinas, *Summa Theologiae* I–II 2, 4.

[23] Aristotle, *Nicomachean Ethics* i.9–10. Thomas Aquinas, *Summa Theologiae* I–II 5, 4.

[24] Aristotle, *Nicomachean Ethics* i.7. Thomas Aquinas, *Summa Theologiae* I–II 2, 8.

[25] The influential recent treatment of this topic is Martha Nussbaum's *Fragility of Goodness* (Cambridge: Cambridge University Press, 1986), esp. 290–372 on Aristotle.

[26] Julia Annas, *The Morality of Happiness*, 36–37.

[27] See Aristotle's *Nicomachean Ethics* i.7 and Thomas Aquinas, *Summa Theologiae* I–II 3, 2.

If happiness, presented in the beatitudes as the kingdom of heaven, entails human activity so that it is something in which we participate, rather than something that simply happens to us, then it is reasonable to inquire as to the relationship between our activity now in anticipation of the kingdom of heaven, and the activity of the kingdom. The beatitudes address precisely this question in depth. They depict not only what happiness is (the kingdom of heaven), but also the activity of happiness. My main thesis is that the beatitudes are best understood as presenting an "intrinsic relationship" between their qualifying conditions and rewards.

What marks an intrinsic relationship can be summarized by the phrase "continuity of activity." Two related features characterize "continuity of activity." First, the qualifying condition entails some *activity* on the part of the person rather than simply a state in which one finds oneself. Second, such activity is continuous with, indeed constitutive of or a participation in, the state of reward. Therefore, the state of reward is at least partially constituted by, or includes, the activities that qualify one for it. Such an intrinsic relationship is described by Herbert McCabe, O.P. in the following manner:

> In the tradition from which I speak, which we may call the tradition of Aristotle, understood with the help of [Thomas] Aquinas, it is thought proper to praise those actions and dispositions that lead to and are *constitutive* of that human satisfaction in which happiness consists. . . . [H]appiness is not just the *result* of praiseworthy action; it is *constituted* by praiseworthy action.[28]

McCabe distinguishes this tradition from consequentialist thought.[29] Both are concerned with achieving happiness. Yet McCabe rightly claims that in the case of consequentialism, the happiness achieved is not necessarily (at least partially) constituted by the activity that leads to it, but simply "results" from such activity. Therefore, activities that are incompatible with happiness can be justified if they result in happiness (but of course cease before its attainment).[30]

---

[28] *The Good Life: Ethics and the Pursuit of Happiness* (New York: Continuum, 2005), 5–6, emphasis in original. For a more recent defense of this claim, see Julia Annas's *Intelligent Virtue* (Oxford: Oxford University Press, 2011), 6, 146–52.

[29] McCabe, *The Good Life*, 6. See also Julia Annas, *The Morality of Happiness*, 37. She says the claim that happiness is an activity "goes some way toward explaining the almost complete absence in ancient theories of anything resembling consequentialist ideas. . . . These are ruled out right from the start by the fact that they have no essential [here, 'intrinsic'] connection to my activity." She notes that though people commonly think the Epicureans to be consequentialist in this sense, in actuality they are not. The only such "hedonists" among the ancients, she claims, are the Cyrenaics, who for this reason function as a foil to the various other ancient theories of ethics throughout her book.

[30] At the other end of the spectrum, Stoic ethics affirms that virtuous activity is wholly constitutive of happiness. Hence the well-known Stoic claim that the virtuous man would be fully happy "on the rack" (in other words, while tortured).

This perennial question in virtue ethics, namely, the relationship between happiness and virtue, is addressed at the end of the final chapter in this book through the Lord's Prayer. The task for this section is to establish a necessary claim for that treatment, namely, that the beatitudes present an intrinsic relation between their qualifying conditions and rewards. Such a relationship is marked by activity in the qualifying condition, and continuation of that activity in the reward. To the contrary, what would mark an *extrinsic* relationship would be either the claim that the qualifying condition was not concerned with a person's activity, or the claim that even if it were, that activity would in no way continue in the state of reward. Such an approach toward the beatitudes would affirm either that what qualifies those described as blessed or happy has nothing to do with their activity, or that even if human activity does qualify one for reward it is not continuous with activity in the state of reward.

To understand better the difference between an intrinsic and extrinsic relationship between qualifying condition and reward, consider the following beatitude: "Blessed are they who mourn, for they will be comforted." This is a challenging example. Pinckaers comments, "Let us be honest. Among all the beatitudes there is none like this one for flying in the face of common sense."[31] Here it seems that what qualifies one for reward is simply the experience of suffering that prompts mourning; in other words, it is a state in which one finds one's self rather than any activity.[32] It also seems that what characterizes the state of reward (comfort) is a cessation of the qualifying condition (mourning). There is certainly a relationship between the two, since the beatitude reads "blessed are they who mourn, for they will be comforted." But it appears to be an extrinsic relationship for two reasons. First, what qualifies one for reward is a situation in which one finds oneself rather than some activity on the part of the person. Second, the happiness promised seems to be a reversal or at least cessation of the qualifying condition. Despite this *prima facie* or "everyday" interpretation, the argument of this section is that each beatitude, including this most challenging one, presents an intrinsic relationship between qualifying condition and reward. What is rewarded is some activity described in the qualifying condition, and that activity continues in some important way in the state of reward.

B. EXAMINING PARTICULAR BEATITUDES

The previous part has gathered some resources from a virtue-centered approach to morality concerning the importance of human activity in the

---

[31] Pinckaers *The Pursuit of Happiness*, 77.

[32] More precisely, since mourning is an activity, the qualifying condition may seem to be a state of affairs in which one finds oneself that prompts mourning.

attainment of happiness. This is quite relevant for the beatitudes, since in each one we read how certain people are "happy" and why that is so. Classical virtue ethics suggests we should seek in the beatitudes descriptions of activities that are constitutive of happiness. That is the task of this section, to examine the meaning of each of the qualifying conditions and rewards. I rely on a sample of renowned commentators on the beatitudes throughout the Christian tradition, along with a sample of contemporary moralists and biblical scholars. Based on this review, I claim that the qualifying conditions are intrinsically related to the rewards, although the various beatitudes are amenable to this analysis in varying ways, a topic addressed in Section 3. I approach this argument through the methodology outlined in the Introduction, with all the caveats noted there. First a brief word is in order on the number of beatitudes.

How many Matthean beatitudes are there?[33] The answer to this seemingly simple question is not at all obvious. Commentators treat the number of beatitudes as ranging from 7 to 8 to 9.[34] Nine statements (Mt 5:3–12) begin with "Blessed are ... " Yet the final one is noticeably distinct in saying "Blessed are *you*..." (Mt 5:11–12) and hence has consistently been treated distinctly. Commentators ranging from Gregory of Nyssa to John Chrysostom to Luther to Benedict XVI have thus treated the beatitudes as a set of eight. Of the eight beatitudes beginning "Blessed are *they*" (Mt 5:3–10), the repetition of the reward "theirs is the Kingdom of heaven" in the first and eighth has led many to also treat the eighth beatitude distinctly. Hence there is a tradition starting with Augustine, continuing with Thomas Aquinas and other medieval theologians, that counts the beatitudes as seven, with the eighth beatitude as a sort of summary and recapitulation of the first eight.[35] The

---

[33] The focus of this chapter is obviously the Matthean beatitudes given the context in a book on the Sermon on the Mount. No claims are made here about the relationship between Matthew's and Luke's sets of beatitudes, although occasional references are made to Luke's beatitudes where commentators surveyed here connect the two sets. Although I suspect that the even the starker language of the Luke 6 beatitudes can be understood via an "intrinsic relationship," I do not make that argument here. For examples of recognizing the continuity between the two evangelists' beatitudes see not only Ambrose (*Treatise on the Gospel of St. Luke*, 61) but also Davies and Allison, *The Gospel According to Saint Matthew*, 444 and Stassen and Gushee, *Kingdom Ethics*, 38.

[34] As Betz notes, some even break up Mt 5:11 and 12 to number ten. For his review of arguments for seven, eight, nine, or ten beatitudes in biblical scholarship, see *The Sermon on the Mount*, 108–109.

[35] As Thomas Aquinas claims, "The eighth beatitude is a confirmation and declaration of all those that precede. . . . The eighth beatitude corresponds, in a way, to all the preceding seven" (*Summa Theologiae* I–II 69, 3 ad. 5). For this view in Augustine, see *The Lord's Sermon on the Mount* I.3.10 and I.4.12. Pinckaers affirms this approach in his *Sources of Christian Ethics*, 145–46. Note that none of these theologians deny that Mt 5:10 (or 5:11–12) is a beatitude. The claim is simply that the eighth beatitude serves a different role than the other seven. For an example of someone who counts eight beatitudes but treats the eighth as adding no significant progression to the first seven, see Gregory of

main argument given for this sevenfold count of the beatitudes is the repetition of the same reward in both the first and eighth.[36] The sevenfold interpretation is adopted here, not only due to the reward repetition but also for reasons addressed below having to do with progression within the beatitudes and their alignment as a set with other sets. As with the methodology for interpreting the content of the beatitudes, this claim is not uncontested, but certainly defensible.

1. "BLESSED ARE THE POOR IN SPIRIT, FOR THEIRS IS THE KINGDOM OF HEAVEN" Determining whether or not any beatitude offers an intrinsic relationship between qualifying condition and reward requires specifying who is called blessed in each qualifying condition. First, then, who are the "poor in spirit?" This beatitude has consistently been understood to refer to the humble. John Chrysostom is among those who answer this question directly: "What is meant by the 'poor in spirit'? The humble and contrite of mind."[37] Though many modern commentators claim material possessions are relevant, they emphasize some activity of the poor in spirit in their state of material want, such as refusing to seek ultimate comfort in

Nyssa, *Homilies on the Beatitudes,* VIII. For recognition in contemporary biblical scholarship of the distinctiveness of the eighth beatitude and thus the legitimacy of attending to the first seven as a set, Davies and Allison claim: "An *inclusio* is thus formed between the first and eighth beatitude. Its function is to mark the beginning and end of the formally similar beatitudes, that is beatitudes 1–8, which are then followed by a ninth that is different in form. The *inclusio* also implies that the promises in beatitudes 2–7 are all different ways of saying the same thing, namely, 'theirs is the kingdom of heaven,' the promise of the first and eighth beatitudes" (*The Gospel According to Saint Matthew,* 460). See also Guelich, *The Sermon on the Mount,* 93; Luz, *Matthew 1–7,* 241–242; and Betz, *The Sermon on the Mount,* 142–146.

[36] See Betz, *The Sermon on the Mount,* 109–10. Another argument, one addressed later in this chapter, is that this eighth beatitude describes the suffering that accompanies the people described in all the previous beatitudes. Thus there are arguments concerning both the qualifying condition and the reward in support of numbering seven beatitudes. For an example of a commentary where the rewards of the first and eighth beatitudes are interpreted as distinct, see Ambrose, *Treatise on the Gospel of St. Luke,* 61.3–5 (p. 205). Citations to this text are from *Traité sur l'Évangile de S. Luc,* Vol. I (Paris: Cerf, 1956), with standardized numbering from the Latin text followed by page number from this edition. Though this is Ambrose's commentary on *Luke's* gospel, in treating the beatitudes of Luke 6 Ambrose also examines the Matthean beatitudes.

[37] John Chrysostom, Homily XV.2 (41). References to Chrysostom's Homilies on Matthew given here are from Jaroslav Pelikan, ed., *The Preaching of John Chrysostom* (Philadelphia: Fortress Press, 1967). The reference includes homily, section, and in parentheses the page number from this edition. For further interpretation of the poor in spirit as meaning humility, see Augustine, *The Lord's Sermon on the Mount* I.1.3 and I.3.10, respectively. See also Augustine, *Sermons III* (51–94), 53A.2. See also Ambrose, *Treatise on the Gospel of St. Luke* 60.2 (205); Thomas Aquinas *Summa Theologiae* I–II 69, 3 and *Commentary on the Gospel of Matthew,* 415; Stassen and Gushee, *Kingdom Ethics,* 38–39; Pinckaers, *The Pursuit of Happiness,* 41; Benedict XVI, *Jesus of Nazareth,* 75; and Guelich, *The Sermon on the Mount,* 73.

temporal possessions.[38] This qualifying condition may of course be more prevalent in the material poor, but it does not simply equate to a state of material poverty.

The second step in establishing an intrinsic relationship between qualifying condition and reward is affirming that the activity specified in the qualifying condition continues in the reward. In most cases that is evident once the qualifying condition is well described. In this first beatitude, there is continuity of activity between the qualifying condition and the state of reward since humility characterizes those who enjoy eternal happiness.[39] Being humble and refusing to cling to material possessions as the source of happiness are not simply prerequisite conditions for reward, but enduring characteristics of possession of the kingdom of heaven.[40] Thus the reward here is not a simple reversal of material poverty. It is a continuation, indeed culmination, of a life of humility and freedom from possession by possessions.

2. "BLESSED ARE THEY WHO MOURN, FOR THEY WILL BE COMFORTED" As noted above, this second[41] beatitude appears most obviously to suggest an extrinsic relationship between qualifying condition and reward, since it would seem both that mourning is simply something that happens to someone, and that it is wholly discontinuous with the comfort and happiness promised as reward.[42] Yet commentators most consistently

---

[38] See, for example, Pope Benedict XVI, *Jesus of Nazareth*, 76–77; Guelich, *The Sermon on the Mount*, 75; and, Betz, *The Sermon on the Mount*, 114. Betz goes so far as to delineate the similarities and differences between Greek philosophy (esp. Socrates) and the Sermon on the Mount and considers poverty of spirit as intellectual insight (117–18). The interpretation of poverty of spirit in a manner not limited to a state of material want certainly dominates pre-twentieth-century commentaries. See Luther, *The Sermon on the Mount* in *Luther's Works* 21, 12, 13, and 17. (Given the absence of internal text divisions, references to this text are given by page number in this edition.) Dietrich Bonhoeffer, *The Cost of Discipleship* (New York: Collier Books, 1963) 120. See Thomas Aquinas, *Summa Theologiae* I–II 69, 3 and *Commentary on the Gospel of Matthew*, 416. Stassen and Gushee, *Kingdom Ethics*, 38. Pinckaers, *The Pursuit of Happiness, God's Way: Living the Beatitudes* (Staten Island, NY: Alba House, 1988), 42–46. Guelich, *The Sermon on the Mount*, 67–72.

[39] As noted below, the "kingdom of heaven" is the most general term for the state of eternal reward, a destiny that is further elucidated in the second through seventh beatitudes. See Luz, *Matthew 1–7*, 235; Davies and Allison, *The Gospel According to Saint Matthew*, 460. For more on the Matthean sense of kingdom of heaven, see Guelich, *The Sermon on the Mount*, 77–79.

[40] Luther claims the spiritually poor "depend upon an imperishable, eternal possession, that is, upon the kingdom of heaven." Described in this way it is evident how this activity of dependence upon God persists in the kingdom. See Luther, *The Sermon on the Mount*, 16. See also Stassen and Gushee, *Kingdom Ethics*, 39.

[41] The beatitude concerning those who mourn comes third in some manuscript traditions, after the beatitude concerning the meek. For more on this issue of ordering, see Guelich, *The Sermon on the Mount*, 80–82.

[42] Guelich appears to offer such an interpretation in *The Sermon on the Mount*, 80–81. See also Luz, *Matthew 1–7*, 235.

interpret this beatitude as a stark recasting of worldly understandings of happiness, not a simple reversal of a condition antithetical to happiness. There are two predominant strains of interpretation as to what is meant by "those who mourn." This first is that the mourning is over one's sins. Though affirmed by many commentators, this interpretation is beautifully described by Gregory of Nyssa who contrasts the blessed mourning over one's sins with the contented inability of some to even be aware of their own sinfulness. He likens the one who mourns to an injured person who begins to feel pain in his previously paralyzed limb. "When the soul becomes aware of what is bad and bewails the life of evil," it is a crucial early step toward full recovery.[43] In this interpretation, although mourning is surely suffered, it is the suffering entailed in the activity of an honest and searching awareness of one's actions, which in this life entails a mournful repentance of one's sins.

The second consistent line of interpretation – and one commonly endorsed by the same people who endorse the first – is of mourning as refusing to find relief in worldly comforts. Luther contrasts simple suffering from the "mourning" of this beatitude, saying, "a man is said to mourn and be sorrowful – not if his head is always drooping and his face is always sour and never smiling; but if he does not depend on having a good time and living it up, the way the world does."[44] In both of these related interpretations, mourning is understood not as simply a state in which one finds oneself, but rather what ensues from an activity. That activity is an honest and searching awareness of reality even when bitter, including the refusal to shield one's self from that reality in worldly comforts.

Given these two consistent interpretations of what constitutes the activity in the qualifying condition, the continuity of activity is more evident. In the comfort of eternal reward, what ceases is not the honest and searching awareness of reality even when painful and difficult, but rather the painfulness and difficulty of that reality. In other words, even though there is a great change between a state of mourning and a state of comfort, what changes is not what commentators identify as the activity of the qualifying condition. Being a person who faces reality even when difficult, of course only with the

---

[43] Gregory of Nyssa, *Homilies on the Beatitudes* III:2 (40). See also Augustine, *Sermons III (51–94)*, 53A.8; Ambrose, *Treatise on the Gospel of St. Luke*, 55.1–2 (203); Chrysostom, *Homilies on Matthew* XV.4 (43–44); Thomas Aquinas, *Commentary on the Gospel of Matthew*, 422; Pinckaers, *The Pursuit of Happiness*, 76; Stassen and Gushee, *Kingdom Ethics*, 39.

[44] Luther, *The Sermon on the Mount*, 19. See also Augustine *The Lord's Sermon on the Mount* I.2.5; Thomas Aquinas, *Summa Theologiae* I–II 69, 3 and *Commentary on the Gospel of Matthew*, 422; Bonhoeffer, *The Cost of Discipleship*, 121; and Guelich, *The Sermon on the Mount*, 80. Indicating that one of the main sources of worldly comfort is a refusal to face painful realities that engender suffering, Pinckaers claims this beatitude "invites us first of all to be fully human: not children, to be amused with pretty stories and shielded from painful and disturbing sights, but adults who dare to look reality in the face" (*The Pursuit of Happiness*, 78).

assistance of God's grace, is precisely what qualifies one to enjoy the true and lasting comfort of the kingdom of heaven. It always entails mourning in this life (though not all mourning in this life is indicative of such activity). One remains this sort of person even in comfort when occasions to mourn are no longer present.[45] The activity of facing reality even when painful, and refusing to find solace in worldly comforts, is itself the very sort of activity that enables one to "seek comfort in God alone."[46] This activity is not reversed but continues in the state of reward.

3. "BLESSED ARE THE MEEK, FOR THEY WILL INHERIT THE LAND" Who are the meek? The English term meek is often associated with being servile or passive. Stassen indicates that this is an erroneous assumption when he claims, "A meek person is thought of as a doormat on which others wipe their feet, and who is timid and fears what others will think. 'But nothing could be more foreign to the Biblical use of the word.'"[47] The Greek *praiais*[48] (and Vulgate Latin *mitis*) were understood to refer to, in the words

[45] The claim that one "remains a certain sort of person" is an indication of both the abiding importance of habits (which qualify a person) and the continuous yet importantly different sorts of activity that arise from the same habits in this life and the next. There is a tradition of reflection on this question beginning at least with Augustine's engagement with Cicero's claim that the cardinal virtues do not persist in the next life. Augustine claims they do indeed even while their acts differ due to the important differences between this life and the next. See Augustine's *The Trinity* (New York: New City Press, 1991), xiv, 12. Reflection on this is rampant throughout the medieval period due to Peter Lombard's treatment of it in his *Sentences* b. III d. 33 q. 1 a. 4. Thomas Aquinas offers further developments on this matter. See *Summa Theologiae* I–II 67, 1 and especially *Disputed Questions on Virtue* q. 5 a. 4. One key part of this position is explaining how habits, always defined by the acts to which they incline one, can persist when those acts seem so different due to the lack of difficulties in heaven. As noted below, in a Thomistic framework the beatitudes describe activities not habits (though of course activities proceeding from habits), yet the similarity is that activity can be formally the same (in "root") even while evidently different in the next life. The broader question of the continuities and differences between virtuous activities in this life and the next awaits rigorous treatment in moral theology and Christian ethics today.

[46] For this phrase see John Calvin, *Commentary on a Harmony of the Evangelists Matthew, Mark, and Luke, Vol. I* (Grand Rapids, MI: Eerdmans, 1956) Mt 5:4 (261). (Pages numbers given to this edition in parentheses.) The entire quotation suggests an intrinsic relationship between qualifying condition and reward:

Now nothing is supposed to be more inconsistent with happiness than mourning. But Christ does not merely show that mourners are not unhappy. He shows that their very mourning contributes to a happy life by preparing them to receive eternal joy and by furnishing them with excitements to seek true comfort in God alone.

Calvin's claim that "their very mourning *contributes* to a happy life" indicates the continuity marking an intrinsic relationship.

[47] Stassen & Gushee, *Kingdom Ethics*, 40, citing Clarence Jordan, *Sermon on the Mount* 24–25. See also Pope Benedict XVI, *Jesus of Nazareth*, 80.

[48] For more on the Hebrew word or words that likely "stand behind" the Greek terms for "poor" and "meek" in Mt 5:3 and 5, see Guelich, *The Sermon on the Mount*, 66–75.

of Augustine, "those who yield before outbursts of evil and do not resist evil, but overcome evil with good," while "those who are not meek struggle and contend for earthly things."[49] Hence the qualifying condition praised here is not being subjugated or passive, but rather being mild with regard to occasions of anger.[50]

As to the meaning of "they will inherit the land," there is divergence in the tradition as to what is meant by this reward, and in particular whether it refers to an earthly or heavenly reward.[51] More importantly for this section on the intrinsic relation between the qualifying condition and reward, it is clear that regardless of whether the land is understood as temporal and/or eternal, the meek do not inherit it as a reversal of the activity that qualifies them for it but as a continuation, even intensification, of their meekness. Indeed, it is one's very meekness, not a cessation of it, that enables one to possess what is referenced by "land." Luther explains it this way:

> "He [Christ] teaches us that whoever wants to rule and possess his property, possessions, house and home in peace must be meek, so that he may overlook things and act reasonably, putting up with just as much as he possibly can."[52]

Once again we see how a beatitude's qualifying condition is an activity that persists in some form in the promised reward.[53]

4. "BLESSED ARE THEY WHO HUNGER AND THIRST FOR RIGHT-EOUSNESS, FOR THEY WILL BE SATISFIED" The fourth beatitude seems to require the least analysis here. It is more evident that hungering and thirsting is an activity, and it is not surprising that there is continuity

---

[49] Augustine, *The Lord's Sermon on the Mount* I.2.4. See also Gregory of Nyssa, *Homilies on the Beatitudes* II:2 (34); Luther, *The Sermon on the Mount*, 36. Calvin, *Harmony of the Evangelists*, Mt 5:5 (261–62); Bonhoeffer, *The Cost of Discipleship*, 122.

[50] Thomas Aquinas claims this beatitude is an antidote to being led away by one's irascible passions. See *Summa Theologiae* I–II 69, 3. He also equates *mitis* to *mansuetudo*, the latter being the classical virtue that moderates anger (*Commentary on the Gospel of Matthew*, 419). See also Ambrose, *Treatise on the Gospel of St. Luke*, 54.5 (203) and Pinckaers, *Pursuit of Happiness*, 61, 65–66.

[51] See Augustine, *The Lord's Sermon on the Mount* I.2.4 where Augustine understands the land to refer to the "stability of an undying inheritance" and says it is the life and rest of the saints, meaning those in heaven. Gregory says the use of an earthly image is given for our aid [*Homilies on the Beatitudes* II.2 (33)], but it is clearly not earthly land that is promised (34). Yet as seen below others understand it to refer also to possession in this life. For a treatment of the interplay between both senses, see Pope Benedict XVI, *Jesus of Nazareth*, 82–84.

[52] Luther, *The Sermon on the Mount*, 24. See also Calvin's claim regarding ferocious people that "while they possess all, they possess nothing" (*Harmony of the Evangelists*, Mt 5:5 [262]). See also Augustine, *Sermons* III (51–94), 53.2.

[53] See Pinckaers, *Pursuit of Happiness*, 71 for a discussion of how the reward of the meek is also possession of one's self.

between the activity of longing for righteousness (or literally "justice"[54]) and its attainment. But why are those who hunger and thirst for justice rewarded? As with those who mourn, one might be tempted to read this beatitude as executing a simple reversal, such that those who are satisfied by justice are those who hungered and thirsted for it simply because they suffered injustice.[55] But again, this is not how the qualifying condition is consistently understood in the tradition. Rather, the hungering and thirsting of the qualifying condition is a longing for and pursuit of justice rather than a suffering of injustice (though the latter will likely occur due to the former).[56]

As for the reward of being satisfied, this beatitude is the first among those examined so far to have a less obvious discontinuity between the qualifying condition and reward. There is still discontinuity, as evident by the contrast between hunger/thirst and satisfaction. However, there is clear continuity between the person striving for justice and enjoying justice in the state of eternal reward. Furthermore, there is a consistent claim in the commentary tradition that hungering and thirsting for righteousness is actually the beginning of its possession.[57] Gregory of Nyssa devotes the most extensive treatment to the relationship between the longing for justice and its satiation.[58] Gregory claims the terms "hunger and thirst" indicate the earnestness of the craving; yet he also contrasts the hunger and thirst for justice with that for food and drink. Hunger and thirst for food and drink are not only predicated upon lack, but they are also diminished once satisfied. Yet "satisfaction" of the hunger and thirst for justice leads not to a cessation of but a further sharpening of the appetite.[59] There is appetitive activity in this possession (which may also be called enjoyment) that is continuous with the hunger and thirst to the extent that desire entails some anticipatory possession. Gregory

---

[54] Despite the common English translation righteousness, this word is understood in both the history of commentary and in contemporary biblical scholarship to be equally well translated as justice. See, for example, Guelich, *The Sermon on the Mount*, 84–87. Gregory in fact expands the sense of this term to include all of the virtues, and says it even refers to a longing for the Lord himself (*Homilies on Beatitudes* IV.6 [52–55]).

[55] Stassen and Gushee observe that those who have experienced injustice may be particularly attuned to the justice promised in this beatitude (*Kingdom Ethics*, 42). See also Calvin, *Harmony of the Evangelists*, Mt 5:6 (263). Reminiscent of the poor in spirit, it is not the experience of suffering injustice that is the qualifying condition here but (in this case) the hunger and thirst for justice. See also Guelich, *The Sermon on the Mount*, 87 and Pinckaers, *The Pursuit of Happiness*, 91–93.

[56] See Bonhoeffer, *The Cost of Discipleship*, 124; Luther, *The Sermon on the Mount*, 28; Thomas Aquinas, *Summa Theologiae* I–II 69, 3.

[57] See Augustine, *The Lord's Sermon on the Mount* I.2.6 and Luther, *The Sermon on the Mount*, 28.

[58] For a very helpful article on precisely this topic, see Luis Francisco Mateo-Seco, "Gregory of Nyssa, *De beatitudinibus*, Oratio IV: 'Blessed are those who hunger and thirst for righteousness for they will be satisfied' (Mt 5:6)," pp. 146–63 in Drobner and Viciano, eds., *Gregory of Nyssa: Homilies on the Beatitudes* (Leiden: Brill, 2000).

[59] Gregory of Nyssa, *Homilies on the Beatitudes* IV.6 (53–55).

says, "We must still try to find that justice, which is already enjoyed by the one that desires it in the anticipation of what is promised."[60] In a baldly intrinsic claim about the relationship between qualifying condition and reward, Gregory says "its [virtue's] happiness is coextensive with its operation."[61] In these words, we see affirmed the consistent claim that the qualifying condition is an activity, and one that is continuous with the state of reward. Gregory does not of course claim that nothing further is attained in the satisfaction of the yearning for justice. Yet there is clearly continuity of activity between qualifying condition and reward.

5. "BLESSED ARE THE MERCIFUL, FOR THEY WILL BE SHOWN MERCY" As in the fourth beatitude, the continuity between the qualifying condition and reward of the fifth beatitude may seem readily apparent. Those who are merciful are rewarded with mercy. Could it be interpreted with a connotation of reversal, as if to suggest that those who show mercy, although they do not receive that mercy in the present, will in the future? And could it imply a cessation of the qualifying condition, such that if one shows mercy now, one will receive it later and can stop having to show it?[62] As for the qualifying condition being an activity, Stassen is particularly helpful: "Mercy is about an action; specifically, generous action that delivers someone from need or bondage."[63] Although it may be accompanied by sentiment (e.g., "pity"), it is not primarily something that happens to a person but rather something which someone does, or exercises.[64]

As to the continuity between qualifying condition and reward, a challenge to the thesis of an intrinsic relationship between them is the suggestion that one can cease to show mercy since at the time of reward one can simply receive it.

---

[60] Gregory of Nyssa, *Homilies on the Beatitudes* IV.2 (49). See also IV.6 (55). For a comparable dynamic in Thomas Aquinas, whereby what is longed for is already attained in a limited sense, see his depiction of our hope for happiness, *Summa Theologiae* I–II 5,3, ad. 1,

[61] Gregory of Nyssa, *Homilies on the Beatitudes* IV.6 (55).

[62] For both intrinsic and extrinsic ways to interpret this beatitude (without using these terms), see Pinckaers, *Pursuit of Happiness*, 114.

[63] Stassen and Gushee, *Kingdom Ethics*, 43. Augustine also emphasizes the active nature of mercy in saying it is "those who come to the aid of the needy" (*The Lord's Sermon on the Mount* I.2.7). Guelich claims "*merciful* refers to the act of judging" (*The Sermon on the Mount*, 89, emphasis in original).

[64] Gregory of Nyssa also recognizes this emotional component by calling it a "misery" but says it is a "*voluntary* misery" prompted by other people's ills, a "loving self-identification with those vexed by grievous events." See Gregory of Nyssa, *Homilies on the Beatitudes* V.3 (59). See also Bonhoeffer: "As if their own needs and their own distress were not enough, they take upon themselves the distress and humiliation and sin of others" (*The Cost of Discipleship*, 124). For more on the role of sentiment in mercy, see Pinckaers, *Pursuit of Happiness*, 116–17. See also Calvin, *Harmony of the Evangelists*, Mt 5:7 (263) and Luther *The Sermon on the Mount*, 30.

Again Gregory is particularly helpful in explaining the continuity. First, Gregory claims mercy is born of "loving self-identification" with others, and thus it is an activity that surely continues when one is shown mercy in eternal reward. Second, Gregory describes the final judgment in the context of mercy and claims that "the person is his own judge, giving verdict upon himself by his judgment of inferiors."[65] In other words, the standard with which one shows mercy to others is the standard that one summons for one's own judgment. Guelich observes, "In this Beatitude God's mercy to be experienced at the final judgment belongs already to the merciful and furnishes the basis for their behavior toward others."[66] This notion of consistency of standards of judgment, which are actively employed in judgments of justice, is addressed further in Chapter 4 on judging. For now, it suffices to note that when the merciful are shown mercy, they are evidence of the continuity of activity in the consistent standard of merciful justice that they rely upon with regard to others, and which will be shown to them.

6. "BLESSED ARE THE CLEAN OF HEART, FOR THEY WILL SEE GOD" Despite a common contemporary association of "purity" with an absence of disordered sexual desire, the interpretation of the "clean of heart" (frequently translated "pure of heart") with direct reference to sexual desire is nowhere to be found in the commentators surveyed here.[67] Rather, "purity of heart must involve integrity, a correspondence between outward action and inward thought. ... More succinctly, purity of heart is to will one thing, God's will, with all of one's being and doing."[68] Thus being clean of heart not only entails the integrity of interior and exterior continuity[69] but an integrity that is directed toward God alone, whereby one's will is conformed to God's will.[70] This is why those who do good deeds "to be seen by others" (Mt 6:1–18) are a favorite example among commentators of those who are not clean of heart.[71] That being clean of heart is an activity rather than simply some state (as of, say, ritual purity[72]) is clear in the commentary tradition.

---

[65] Gregory of Nyssa, *Homilies on the Beatitudes* V.7 (64).

[66] Guelich, *The Sermon on the Mount*, 89.

[67] Despite the preponderance of the "pure in heart" translation, "clean of heart" is retained here for the sake of consistency.

[68] Stassen and Gushee, *Kingdom Ethics*, 45, citing Davies and Allison, *The Gospel According to Saint Matthew*, 456.

[69] See Calvin, *Harmony of the Evangelists*, Mt 5:8 (264). See also Guelich, *The Sermon on the Mount*, 90.

[70] See Luther, *The Sermon on the Mount*, 34. See also Bonhoeffer, *The Cost of Discipleship*, 125.

[71] See, for example, Augustine's correlation of this beatitude with Mt 6:1–18 (*The Lord's Sermon on the Mount* II.1.1). See also Stassen and Gushee, *Kingdom Ethics*, 44–45 for this connection.

[72] Contemporary commentaries frequently contrast being clean of heart with merely ritual purity. See, for example, Pinckaers, *Pursuit of Happiness*, 131, and Stassen and Gushee, *Kingdom Ethics*, 44.

The reward of "seeing God" is so entrenched in Scripture as a depiction of eternal life as to require little explanation from the commentators. Gregory of Nyssa's words are particularly relevant to the thesis of this book when he describes seeing God as "possessing what one beholds" and says that such a possession constitutes full happiness.[73] As interesting for this chapter is the striking continuity between being clean of heart and seeing God. Though the text is clear that the clean of heart *will* see God (future tense), commentators consistently explain that it is *by way of* being clean of heart that one is able to see God.[74] Being clean of heart is not simply an activity that qualifies one for reward but then ceases when the reward is achieved. It is constitutive of the reward as an activity that is necessary for the activity of the reward. In sum, being clean of heart not only is rewarded by seeing God but enables one to see God.[75]

7. "BLESSED ARE THE PEACEMAKERS, FOR THEY WILL BE CALLED CHILDREN OF GOD" It is common for hearers of the beatitudes today to assume the "peacemakers" are those who work for reconciliation among fractured parties, particularly in political contexts. This interpretation is found throughout the commentary tradition.[76] Yet equally common among commentators is an understanding of the peace spoken of here as a condition of a person's soul. Augustine interprets peace in this sense most forcefully, claiming that "they are at peace with themselves who quell all the emotions of

---

[73] See Gregory of Nyssa, *Homilies on the Beatitudes* VI.2 (67).

[74] Augustine claims that being clean of heart gives us "heart eyes" to see God, and that being clean of heart is what enables people to see God. See Augustine, *Sermons* III (51–94), 53.6 and *The Lord's Sermon on the Mount* I.3.10, respectively. Pinckaers describes purity as the "necessary condition" for seeing God (*Pursuit of Happiness*, 132). Pope Benedict XVI claims "the heart – the wholeness of man – must be pure, interiorly open and free, in order for man to be able to see God" (*Jesus of Nazareth*, 93). That Pinckaers and Pope Benedict XVI both understand the relationship between qualifying condition and reward intrinsically is evident when Pinckaers says purity is the "bearer of light" that enables us to see God (*Pursuit of Happiness*, 139) and Pope Benedict writes "the organ for seeing God is the heart" (*Jesus of Nazareth*, 92). Benedict also emphasizes the importance of "social ethics" (94) for becoming clean of heart.

[75] After claiming that "the cultic setting of being accepted into the presence of God becomes the basis for the eschatological hope of 'seeing God,'" Guelich clearly indicates continuity between qualifying condition and reward: "The focal point of one's life, the singleness of purpose, the object of one's loyalty and commitment – namely, God himself and his claim upon the individual – reach their ultimate fulfillment by the ultimate acceptance into God's presence" (*The Sermon on the Mount*, 91).

[76] Chrysostom emphasizes how the peacemakers "unite the divided, reconcile the alienated" (*Homilies on Matthew*, XV:7). Thomas Aquinas says it concerns one's relations with one's neighbors (*Summa Theologiae* I–II 69, 3; see also *Commentary on the Gospel of Matthew*, 438). Luther claims that being a peacemaker is being "a reconciler and mediator between your neighbors" (*The Sermon on the Mount*, 43). See also Stassen and Gushee, *Kingdom* Ethics, 45

their soul and subject them to reason."[77] Like others who recognize this meaning of peacemaking, he not only claims that both senses are important but also that they are related to one another.[78] Despite subtle differences of emphasis as to the primary locus of peacemaking, all commentators insist that peacemaking is an activity, or as Bonhoeffer describes it, not simply having peace but making it.[79]

As in the previous beatitude we have a reward in being "called children of God" that has extensive scriptural basis as a depiction of eternal life. More interesting, however, is the near constant emphasis on continuity of activity between peacemaking and being called children of God in the commentary tradition even when explained in different ways. In terminology consonant with that of this chapter, Gregory of Nyssa claims "the very work for which he promises such a great reward is itself another gift," and that "the chief thing that gives happiness is peace."[80] Peacemaking is not simply an activity that extrinsically qualifies one to become children; it is something that intrinsically qualifies one for the reward as constitutive of that reward.

The first section of this chapter established that the beatitudes are "about happiness." This is not an end of conversation about the beatitudes, but a beginning, since that claim invites further questions about happiness. Perhaps the most fundamental question about that happiness is addressed in this second section. What constitutes happiness, and what is the relationship between those called "happy" and the "reward" received? This section's survey of a tradition of commentary on the beatitudes demonstrates that

---

[77] *The Lord's Sermon on the Mount* I.2.9. See also Gregory of Nyssa, *Homilies on the Beatitudes* VII.3 (78); Thomas Aquinas, *Summa Theologiae* I–II 69, 4; Luther, *The Sermon on the Mount*, 39; Pope Benedict XVI, *Jesus of Nazareth*, 85.

[78] See *Sermons* III (51–94), 53A.12. Thomas Aquinas makes the same claim in *Commentary on the Gospel of Matthew* (438).

[79] *The Cost of Discipleship*, 127. See also Pinckaers, *The Pursuit of Happiness*, 145–48 and 161. Guelich claims "*peacemaking*, therefore, is much more than a passive suffering to maintain peace . . . " (*The Sermon on the Mount*, 92, emphasis in original). Luz says that peacemaking "means something active, not just readiness for peace" (*Matthew 1–7*, 241).

[80] Gregory of Nyssa, *Homilies on the Beatitudes* VII.2 (77–78). Augustine equates being a child of God with being peaceful when he says "the children of God are peaceful for the reason that no resistance to God is present" (*The Lord's Sermon on the Mount* I.2.9). See also *The Lord's Sermon on the Mount* I.3.10 where Augustine claims that contemplation of truth which is wisdom, and which marks a soul at peace, "effects a likeness to God." For a similar claim in Thomas Aquinas, see *Commentary on the Gospel of Matthew* (439). Calvin speaks of the God of peace accounting us children "*while* we cultivate peace" (*Harmony of the Evangelists*, Mt 5:9 [265], emphasis added). Bonhoeffer claims we are children of God as partners in Christ's work of reconciliation (*The Cost of Discipleship*, 127). Pinckaers claims that peacemakers "win the name of sons of God because they bring to the world the peace and reconciliation which can only come from Him – we can even say, the peace which is God" (*Pursuit of Happiness*, 162). Pope Benedict XVI summarizes, "The seventh beatitude invites us to be and do what the Son does, so that we ourselves may become 'sons of God'" (*Jesus of Nazareth*, 85).

happiness is understood in that tradition as at least partially constituted by activity. It is not simply something that happens *to* us, or a place we find ourselves. It is something in which we *participate*. What qualifies those called "happy" to receive their reward is (grace-enabled) activity. Furthermore, that activity does not cease in the attainment of reward but is continuous with reward. This means that the reward also entails human activity, activity which is importantly continuous with the activity of the qualifying condition even while importantly different given the heavenly context. As McCabe notes in the quotation earlier in this chapter, injunction to activity that is constitutive of happiness is perhaps the defining characteristic of a virtue approach to ethics and moral theology. Keeping this in mind enables us to see better the moral importance of the beatitudes. Though not explicitly using the language of this chapter, the tradition of commentary on the beatitudes is rife with claims that serve as the building blocks of the argument of this chapter. Hence this opening chapter provides a perfect example of the thesis of this book, namely, that a virtue-centered approach to moral theology can help us better understand the Sermon on the Mount.

This book also affirms the converse of that thesis, namely, that the Sermon on the Mount not only exemplifies but further illuminates a virtue-centered approach to moral theology. Jesus is not simply a teacher of Aristotle. In this section, we also see this claim substantiated. While fleshing out the rich meaning of each of the beatitudes is a task for an entire book and cannot be offered here, the beginnings of that account are evident. Happiness is consti- tuted by not any old activity, but humility, meekness, mercy, peacemaking, and so on. Christ the Lord (and Teacher) presents a vision of true human happiness that in many ways upends worldly conceptions of happiness. Despite the centuries old tradition that the Sermon on the Mount with its opening beatitudes is a "charter of the Christian life," the beatitudes are far too infrequently utilized a source of moral reflection. They are read (in the Catholic Church) on All Saints Day, memorized by children in religious education, and cherished as consolation in trying times. Yet if the claims of this section are accurate, they are also a depiction of the truly happy life according to Jesus Christ, and are invaluable for guiding the everyday lives of believers.

III. RAMIFICATIONS OF THE INTRINSIC RELATIONSHIP BETWEEN THE ACTIVITIES OF THE QUALIFYING CONDITIONS AND THE ACTIVITIES OF HAPPINESS ATTAINED

Having established that the beatitudes present an intrinsic relationship between their qualifying conditions and their rewards, here I address how the claims of the previous section contribute to two perennial questions about the beatitudes, namely "when" the rewards of the beatitudes occur and why there is a set of beatitudes. Doing so will help to illuminate how the beatitudes guide us in this life even as they point toward the next.

A. ESCHATOLOGY AND ETHICS: "WHEN" DO THE BEATITUDES' REWARDS OCCUR?

The first question where we see the impact of the previous section's conclusions concerns the "when" of the beatitudes. *When* does the reward depicted in the beatitudes occur? It is commonplace in twentieth-century biblical scholarship to draw a distinction between the beatitudes understood eschatologically and ethically.[81] The beatitudes are understood as eschatological promises when they are seen as promises of God's future deliverance, made possible by God's grace, and particularly targeted toward those who are suffering and in need of deliverance. They are understood ethically when they are seen as exhorting certain activities in the present, often understood as paths to future reward and at times labeled "entrance requirements"[82] to the kingdom. This distinction is traced back to different Old Testament and inter-testamental uses of the literary form beatitude,[83] and is also adopted by ethicists who rely on contemporary biblical scholarship.[84] Biblical scholarship, especially with findings gleaned from form criticism and redaction criticism, has important contributions to make to the question of the nature of the relationship between God's eschatological promises and the ethics of discipleship in this life. What does the analysis of this chapter have to contribute to this discussion?

A common assumption in biblical scholarship is that Luke's (earlier) beatitudes are properly eschatological, and that Matthew has "ethicized" the beatitudes through redaction.[85] Even if recognizing the "initial plausibility" of this view, the biblical scholars whose work is used here do not concur with this reading of the Matthean beatitudes.[86] Yet they contest it in noticeably different ways, which may be seen in how they employ the eschatological/ethical distinction.

---

[81] See Guelich, *The Sermon on the Mount*, 64–66 and 109–111. Though Guelich is primarily relied upon here, see also Betz, *The Sermon on the Mount*, 96–97 and Davies and Allison, *The Gospel According to Saint Matthew*, 439–40.

[82] For this term, see Guelich, *The Sermon on the Mount*, 109; Davies and Allison, *The Gospel According to Saint Matthew*, 439.

[83] See Guelich, *The Sermon on the Mount*, 64–65; Betz, *The Sermon on the Mount*, 97–105; Davies and Allison, *The Gospel According to Saint Matthew*, 431–34.

[84] See Stassen and Gushee, *Kingdom Ethics*, 33.

[85] Guelich describes this assumption well (*The Sermon on the Mount*, 65–66 and 109). See also Davies and Allison, *The Gospel According to Saint Matthew*, 439.

[86] Luz may be the exception. See *Matthew 1–7*, 243.

Some biblical scholars surveyed here deny Matthew's ethical subversion of Luke's eschatological beatitudes by instead claiming that for Matthew the beatitudes are also eschatological rather than ethical. In the words of Guelich, "instead of ethics swallowing up eschatology in Matthew we have just the reverse."[87] Though the opposite of the "ethicization" view, it similarly assumes Matthew's beatitudes are either ethical or eschatological. Part of the problem here may be a dichotomization of command and grace, with the former associated with ethics and the latter with eschatology. For instance, Davies and Allison claim that the beatitudes are "first of all blessings, not requirements."[88] They proceed to observe that the beatitudes are about God's grace as opposed to God's commands, and claim that the treatment of commands begins only after the beatitudes (at Mt 5:17). Such a view reveals a dichotomization between command and grace, and consequently ethics and eschatology.

But of course ethics and eschatology need not be dichotomized, and thus the universally affirmed eschatological function of the beatitudes need not exclude their ethical function as well. Betz affirms that the beatitudes have "eschatological as well as this-worldly implications," and unlike Guelich claims that it is "a fundamental mistake to favor either their future aspect of promise or their present pronouncement."[89] Rather, he says, "the beatitude has a close relationship to morality and ethics. By revealing a new way of life, the beatitude affects moral behavior and demands an ethical awareness."[90] Again revealing the connection between one's stance on the beatitudes as simply ethical or eschatological on the one hand and one's view of the relationship between law and grace on the other, Betz rightly notes that the activity exhorted by the beatitudes must "not be confused with 'works of the law' in the Pauline sense. They do not 'earn' salvation."[91] Ulrich Luz reveals an accurate understanding of the relationship between grace on the one hand, and ethics (or commands, or human activity) on the other, when he claims that the commandments (and here he mentions being poor in spirit, meek, merciful, and so on) are in an important sense gifts of the gospel.[92] In sum, the gratuitous eschatological promise offered in the beatitudes need not preclude an initial participation in that promise – of course possible only through God's grace – in the way one lives in this life.[93]

---

[87] *The Sermon on the Mount*, 111.

[88] *The Gospel According to Matthew*, 440 (see also 466).

[89] Betz, *The Sermon on the Mount*, 96 (see also 97 and 110).

[90] Betz, *The Sermon on the Mount*, 97.   [91] Betz, *The Sermon on the Mount*, 97.

[92] Luz, *Matthew 1–7*, 245–46.

[93] Due to some unfortunate negative associations Betz has with the term virtue, he will not associate the beatitudes with virtues, but he does say "taken together the Beatitudes circumscribe a way of life of the faithful disciple of Jesus." Betz, *The Sermon on the Mount*, 97. It is noteworthy that this part of Betz's work is endorsed here as describing a

What does the analysis of the beatitudes offered in this essay have to contribute to this discussion? Clearly it affirms the latter position, that the beatitudes are best understood as both ethical exhortations that guide action in this life preceding full entrance into the kingdom as well as descriptions of the eschatological deliverance offered by God and only fully and known in the end times.[94] If the *eschaton* as eternal happiness is marked by activity that is continuous with, or intrinsically related to, activity in this life, then there can be no dichotomization between eschatology and ethics. Ethics is eschatological to the extent that it is oriented toward the *telos*/happiness of the *eschaton*, and enjoins activity that is already in a limited sense a participation in that destiny. Eschatology is also ethical, to the degree that its ultimate happiness and deliverance entail human (obviously grace-enabled) activity, activity which is continuous with the (also grace-enabled) activity of this life that is a limited albeit constitutive foretaste of that ultimate destiny. Once the beatitudes are understood in the context of happiness, and the relationship between their qualifying conditions and rewards is understood intrinsically, it is easier to see how the happiness they present is thoroughly ethical and thoroughly eschatological, how the kingdom toward which they point and in which we participate is both already and not yet.[95]

B. WHY A "SET" OF BEATITUDES?

The previous part on eschatology and ethics can hopefully help the beatitudes to play a more prominent role in moral theology. In this part, I turn to another perennial question in the study of the beatitudes in order to see how the conclusions of the first two sections might contribute to answering that question, and to further identify how the beatitudes can be more prominently featured in moral theology. The question for this part is: why is there a "set" of beatitudes? Commentaries on the beatitudes have consistently stressed that the reward described in them is one, despite the fact that it is described in different ways. In other words, the beatitudes do not describe different destinies for seven (or eight, or nine) different groups of people. They offer many images of the one reward (in other words,

---

proper understanding of the relationship between ethics and eschatology, and yet this very same page is cited in the Introduction as where Betz claims that Sermon is not about "virtue." Clearly the problem here is Betz's inadequate understanding of how virtue ethics can be (and indeed has been for Augustine and Thomas Aquinas among others) compatible with Christian commitments as to the necessity of (what in the Thomistic tradition is called cooperative as well as operative) grace.

[94] This interpretation is even suggested by the verb tense of the beatitudes, which is both present tense in the first and eighth (another argument for *inclusio* and counting seven beatitudes) and future tense in the second through seventh.

[95] See Benedict XVI, *Jesus of Nazareth* on how the beatitudes are both eschatological promises (71–72) and also a "road map for the Church" and "directions for discipleship" (74).

eternal happiness), and many descriptions of the people who qualify for that reward.[96] In the words of Thomas Aquinas:

> All these rewards are one in reality, eternal happiness, which the human intellect does not grasp. Hence it was fitting to describe it by means of various goods known to us, and fittingly proportioned to the merits [qualifying conditions] to which those rewards are assigned.[97]

Thomas Aquinas assures us that having a set of beatitudes helps us to understand what are called here the qualifying conditions and rewards. Surely we can affirm this claim and appreciate why there is a set of beatitudes rather than simply one. But this still leaves unaddressed the question: why *these* beatitudes, in *this* number and in *this* order?[98]

1. TRADITIONAL EXPLANATIONS OF THE SET OF BEATITUDES
Regardless of whether or not we see the beatitudes as about happiness, and even regardless of how many beatitudes we count, the simple fact that there are numerous beatitudes prompts the question "why?" Commentators have offered three common answers to this question. First, the beatitudes offer a progression in the human journey toward God. The seminal Patristic commentaries approach the beatitudes precisely in this way. In the words of Gregory of Nyssa, "I think the arrangement of the Beatitudes is like a series of [ladder] rungs, and it makes it possible for the mind to ascend by climbing from one to another."[99]

Another strategy for addressing this question is to align the beatitudes with some other grouping. The basic insight here is, if these beatitudes are Jesus's own synopsis of happiness and fullness of life, then it is fitting that there should be correspondence between this set and other sets recognized in the Christian tradition. Ambrose aligns them with the four cardinal

---

[96] See Augustine, *The Lord's Sermon on the Mount* I.4.12: "the one reward, the kingdom of heaven, is designated variously." See also *Sermons* III (51–94), 53.9 where Augustine says of the different beatitudes that "all these are the same people" (70). See also Chrysostom, Homily XV.7 (48–49) and Davies and Allison, *The Gospel According to Saint Matthew*, 460.

[97] Thomas Aquinas, *Summa Theologiae* I–II 69, 4 ad. 1, trans. mine. See also *Commentary on the Gospel of Matthew*, 420.

[98] As Ambrose claims, "Come Lord Jesus, teach us the order of your beatitudes, for it is not without order that you have taught [them]" (*Treatise on the Gospel of St. Luke*, 52.1–2 [202]).

[99] Gregory of Nyssa, *Homilies on the Beatitudes* II.1 (32). See also Augustine *The Lord's Sermon on the Mount* I.4.10 and Ambrose, *Treatise on the Gospel of St. Luke*, 60.1–12 (204–205). John Chrysostom does not focus on progression in great detail but does mention how there is order to the set, and how one makes way for the next (Homily XV.9, 52). For more in depth inquiry into this theme of ascent, see Michael Dauphinais, "Gregory of Nyssa and Augustine on the Beatitudes." See also Betz, *The Sermon on the Mount*, 108 on this theme and even its warrant by contemporary biblical scholarship.

virtues.[100] For his part, Augustine sees the beatitudes as aligned with not one but two other groupings from the tradition, namely, the seven gifts of the Holy Spirit and the seven petitions of the Lord's Prayer.[101]

Finally, there is also precedent in the tradition for interpreting the set of beatitudes as containing sub-groupings. Ambrose counted eight Matthean beatitudes and saw them as comprised of four groups of two, each group corresponding to one of the four cardinal virtues.[102] Thomas Aquinas, references Ambrose's grouping but posits a grouping of his own. Thomas Aquinas reflects classical ethical thinking on happiness when he observes that candidates for happiness are threefold: sensual pleasures and external goods, the active life, and contemplation. The beatitudes may be sub-grouped into the first three, the next two, and final two beatitudes, which correspond to sensual pleasures/earthly goods, the active life, and the contemplative life, respectively.[103] Division of the set of beatitudes into sub-groups continues today, though generally on different grounds.[104]

2. CONTRIBUTION TO EXPLANATIONS OF THE BEATITUDES AS A SET: INCREASING CONTINUITY OF ACTIVITY What contribution does this chapter offer to the question of why *this* set of *these* beatitudes? It was noted in Section 2 that although all seven beatitudes present an intrinsic relationship between qualifying condition and reward, *how* they do so differs with different beatitudes. That claim may now be further explained. The beatitudes may be placed into three sub-groups that describe how the qualifying conditions are variously (although always intrinsically) related to the rewards.[105] The sub-groups are treated here in reverse order.

Consider the final two beatitudes: "Blessed are the clean of heart, for they will see God," and "Blessed are the peacemakers, for they will be called

---

[100] Ambrose aligns Luke's four beatitudes with the four cardinal virtues, and he claims that Matthew's eight beatitudes (four of which he sees as the same as Luke's) may be grouped into four sets of two, with each group corresponding to a cardinal virtue. See *Treatise on the Gospel of St. Luke*, 62.1–68.3 (206–207).

[101] Augustine, *The Lord's Sermon on the Mount* I.4.11. For more on strategies of alignment, including these two mentioned, see Betz, *The Sermon on the Mount*, 106–107.

[102] Ambrose, *Treatise on the Gospel of St. Luke*, 62.1–68.3 (206–207).

[103] See Thomas Aquinas, *Summa Theologiae* I–II 69, 3 and 4. See also his *Commentary on the Gospel of Matthew*, 414.

[104] See Lutz, *Matthew 1–7*, 226 and 230 (as well as Guelich, *The Sermon on the Mount*, 93 and Betz, *The Sermon on the Mount*, 110) for a division of the eight beatitudes of Mt 5:3–10 into two groups of four. Davies and Allison also recognize this division into two groups of four (*The Gospel According to Saint Matthew*, 429), but they argue for a three groups of three structure (431).

[105] Though concerns with groupings and progression are less common in contemporary readings of the beatitudes than they were in pre-modern commentaries, biblical scholar Betz claims "there is good reason to look further in this direction" (*The Sermon on the Mount*, 105–108). This chapter endeavors to do just that.

children of God." In seeing God and being children of God, we have climactic rewards that seem more than any others in the beatitudes to fully represent eternal happiness. "Seeing God" is so embedded in Scripture and tradition as constituting eternal life that commentators who see the beatitudes as a progression have struggled to explain how any beatitude could follow this one.[106] Being children of God suggests precisely the sort of adoption, kinship, and communion that constitutes eternal union with God. Gregory of Nyssa understood this reward to mean the very deification that is the ultimate destiny of the human person.[107] In sum, though the rewards of all of the beatitudes refer ultimately to the same reward, the rewards of the last two beatitudes stand out as climactic in their depiction of that reward.

What of the qualifying conditions for these final two beatitudes? More specifically, are they or their relationship to their rewards distinct from earlier beatitudes? The answer is yes. In both cases what qualifies one for reward is a condition that will not only remain in that state of reward, but will remain most closely *to its current form* in that state of reward. If peace is understood as a person's interior integration and harmony as well as harmonious relations with others, which together constitute true and ultimate peace, the kingdom of heaven is indeed marked by precisely this peace in and among its citizens as children of God. If cleanness of heart is rightly understood as single-minded focus on God, including seeing all else in truth as it is ordered to God (and acting accordingly), then cleanness of heart is a most continuous foretaste of what it means to see God as described in the reward. In both instances, there is not only an intrinsic relationship (in other words, continuity of activity) between qualifying condition and reward, but also a "least lacking" continuity.[108] How such continuity may be present but more lacking in different ways is evident in the remaining beatitudes.

Next consider the fourth and fifth beatitudes: "Blessed are they who hunger and thirst for righteousness, for they will be satisfied" and "blessed are the merciful, for they will be shown mercy." In these beatitudes (as in all others) the qualifying conditions are intrinsically related to the rewards. The continuity here is evident since the justice and mercy longed for and shown is present in the kingdom of heaven. Yet there is also in these two beatitudes more evident discontinuity between the activity of those who qualify for reward and the activity of the reward itself. Those who hunger and thirst for

---

[106] Gregory of Nyssa, *Homilies on the Beatitudes*, VI.2 (67).

[107] Gregory of Nyssa, *Homilies on the Beatitudes* I.2 (25) and VII.1 (77). See also Betz, *The Sermon on the Mount*, 110.

[108] In making a very different point than this chapter, Davies and Allison recognize that the sixth and seventh beatitudes stand out in relation to the rest by how easily the qualifying conditions can be turned into imperatives: "be clean of heart," and "be peacemakers" (*The Gospel According to Saint Matthew*, 439).

justice are not now satisfied.[109] They hunger and thirst for what they lack. The same holds true for mercy. Though the mercy lauded as the qualifying condition is present in the state of reward, the occasions presenting a need for the exercise of such mercy – toward others and indeed toward themselves – are present now in a manner they will not be in the full arrival of the kingdom. In both of these beatitudes, then, there is continuity as well as greater discontinuity between the activity of the qualifying condition and the activity of the reward.

Finally, consider the first three beatitudes. In these beatitudes, the reward promised seems least continuous with the current state of those who qualify for it. Indeed, these are the beatitudes that prompt the aforementioned "everyday" understanding of the beatitudes as simple reversals. Even granting the consistent interpretation of poor in spirit as referring to humility, the contrast between the terms poor and kingdom is obvious. The same contrast is evident between mourning and comfort, and being meek and inheriting the land. There is indeed a sort of reversal here, in that those possessing the qualifying conditions evidence a lack that is a direct result of possessing those qualifying conditions, a lack that will be rectified at the time of reward. Thus the argument of this chapter on continuity of activity should in no way be taken as a denial of the deliverance that God promises people, especially those who suffer, in the kingdom of heaven. Nevertheless, there is continuity in the people even when their state of affairs changes markedly. So the humble (often the material poor) who forgo security other than God ultimately have the kingdom of heaven. Those who mourn their sin and refuse to take solace in worldly comforts attain the comfort of eternal joy in union with God. Those who are meek in refusing to self-assertively protect or seize ultimately obtain true inheritance. Who they are and their activities remain continuous in both states, even in these beatitudes of evident contrast. Yet there is indeed a reversal as to their condition.

What conclusions can be drawn from this as to why there is a set of beatitudes? Reminiscent of the quotes from Thomas Aquinas and Ambrose above, it is reasonable to assume some purpose in there being a set of various beatitudes. The argument of this chapter suggests that one such purpose is presenting the various ways that the qualifying conditions are intrinsically related to eternal reward. There are three identifiable sub-groups within the set of seven beatitudes, each of which suggests a distinct sort of intrinsic relationship. The first three beatitudes suggest ways which the lacks endured by those possessing the qualifying conditions, lacks that exist precisely *because* of those qualifying conditions, will be reversed. This is true even as

---

[109] See Thomas Aquinas's *Commentary on the Gospel of Matthew*, 423 where he distinguishes the fullness of justice available only in the next life with true but incomplete justice in this life.

the activity of the qualifying conditions remain continuous.[110] The second two beatitudes show greater continuity, but still evidence lacks, namely, the need for full justice and the occasions to exercise mercy. Yet these lacks are described as incomplete, rather than something needing to be reversed. Finally, the last two beatitudes show the greatest continuity between qualifying condition and reward. Of course, these last two beatitudes do not claim that the peacemakers and clean of heart have obtained eternal reward.[111] Yet there is least discontinuity between the activities of being clean of heart and peacemaking in this life and eternal reward in which those very activities participate.

Therefore, this chapter's central constructive argument does support sub-grouping the seven Matthean beatitudes of 5:3–9. The traditional sub-grouping closest to the interpretation offered here is that of Thomas Aquinas. In fact, the argument offered here provides further support for Thomas Aquinas's sub-grouping. Thomas Aquinas, of course, claims that the central activity of eternal happiness is the beatific vision, which is contemplation. Thus in his own sub-grouping, beatitudes six and seven are most obviously constitutive of eternal happiness since he aligns them with contemplation. The fourth and fifth beatitudes are grouped by Thomas Aquinas as representing the active life. The active life can be distinguished from contemplative life in a variety of ways, such as will as distinct from intellect, or practical cooperation with others as distinct from (also communal) speculative intellectual activity. In any case such activity is is indeed constitutive of eternal reward even while not the most central activity of that reward.[112] The first three beatitudes are grouped by Thomas Aquinas as representative of the sensual life. Though well-ordered sensuality is of course constitutive of eternal happiness, that activity is even more removed from the central activity of the *eschaton*. Indeed, in the truly (though of course incompletely) happy this-worldly life enjoined by Christ, it is in our engagement with sensual goods that we will experience greatest discontinuity between our state of affairs now and that in the *eschaton*, even while there is continuity of activity. Thus the interpretation offered here further buttresses Thomas Aquinas's understanding of how the beatitudes are sub-grouped.[113]

---

[110] This thesis is distinct from, though reminiscent of, the claim throughout the Christian tradition that the cardinal virtues remain in heaven, though in a different manner due to differences in that state. See Augustine's *On the Trinity* XIV.12 and the extended medieval discussion due to Peter Lombard's treatment of this question in his *Sentences* III d. 33 q. 1 a. 4.

[111] Thomas Aquinas emphasizes the future tense of the rewards in these two beatitudes. See *Commentary on the Gospel of Matthew*, 407.

[112] See Thomas Aquinas, *Summa Theologiae* I–II 3,4.

[113] As should be evident from the depiction of these three sub-groups, the same argument supports an understanding of the beatitudes as a progression. The three groups offer depictions of qualifying conditions that are all continuous with the activity of eternal reward, but entail states of affairs in this life that are increasingly continuous with that

3. FURTHER CONTRIBUTION TO EXPLANATIONS OF THE BEATI-
TUDES AS A SET: ALIGNMENT WITH VIRTUES Before concluding this
section on the beatitudes as a set, one final constructive proposal is offered as
to why the beatitudes are a set, and why they are *this* set of *these* beatitudes in
this order. This one concerns not progression or sub-grouping but rather
alignment of the set of beatitudes with another set found in the Christian
tradition. It is admittedly a more speculative proposal than the argument of
Section 2 which is rooted in basic claims in virtue ethics and the history of
commentary on the beatitudes. It is offered not with the assumption that one
only understands the beatitudes with this alignment in mind. Instead, it is
offered under the assumption that if the beatitudes are a purposeful set that
is in some manner a complete or comprehensive depiction of the life of
discipleship, then it should not surprise us if they are fittingly aligned with
some other set in the tradition that is used to present a complete or
comprehensive depiction of the life of discipleship. My argument here is
that the beatitudes are fittingly aligned with the three theological and four
cardinal virtues.

Though I would argue that the proposal here is thoroughly Augustinian in
spirit given his alignment of the beatitudes with petitions of the Lord's Prayer
and gifts of the Holy Spirit, and thoroughly Thomistic given his use of the
theological and cardinal virtues to depict the *reditus* that is the life of
discipleship, neither of these thinkers nor anyone else I have encountered
in the tradition offers the alignment proposed here.[114] The alignment is
rooted in the argument of Section 2. Once we understand the seven beatitudes as depictions of activities constitutive of eternal happiness, we can
more clearly understand the distinct activities that together constitute true

---

eternal reward. No further account is offered here as to the details of that progression,
particularly as to progression within sub-groups. There is fascinating room for further
reflection here, for instance on mercy as completing justice in group two. Or, granting
the below constructive argument as to the alignment of beatitudes with virtues, it would
be fruitful to reflect on how fortitude comes after temperance or charity after prudence.
It is hoped this book prompts precisely such work.

[114] For sure the closest alignment in the tradition, as noted above, is Ambrose's alignment of
the four cardinal virtues with the eight beatitudes (two of the latter for each virtue). No
reflection is offered here on the commonalities and dissimilarities between these alignments of virtues with beatitudes. Note also that it was commonplace in the medieval
period to assume that the beatitudes themselves *were* virtues. So when medievals speak of
seven virtues, they most commonly mean not the theological and cardinal virtues but
rather poverty in spirit, mournfulness, meekness, and so on. Like the argument here, this
closely ties together the beatitudes and virtue, though it is importantly different in
equating the beatitudes with the virtues of life in Christ rather than aligning them with
the three theological and four cardinal virtues. For a contemporary example of this
common medieval equation, see Stassen and Gushee, *Kingdom Ethics*, 37–54. For an
argument on why the beatitudes are not themselves habits but rather activities (that
proceed from habits), see Thomas Aquinas, *Summa Theologiae* I–II 69, 1.

happiness. That claim alone invites comparison to the virtues. After all, virtues are simply stable dispositions to activity that is constitutive of happiness.[115] But once the exact nature of activity of each of the beatitudes is discerned in the tradition of commentary, such an alignment with these seven virtues is even more obvious.

This proposal can be summarized by a chart aligning the beatitudes and theological/cardinal virtues.[116] Note that while the various depictions of reward (eternal life) are fittingly aligned with their specific qualifying condition and of course include activity on the part of the person, the following argument will rely mainly on the activities depicted in the qualifying conditions.

FAITH	poor in spirit
TEMPERANCE	mourn
FORTITUDE	meek
HOPE	hunger/thirst for righteousness
JUSTICE	merciful
PRUDENCE	clean of heart
CHARITY	peacemakers

In the following paragraphs, I briefly explain the basis for each alignment. Reminiscent of Section 2, I draw heavily on both contemporary biblical scholarship as well as the tradition of authoritative commentaries on these verses. Though no one in either of these traditions of thought makes the alignment presented here, thinkers commonly describe the beatitude at hand in ways that support the alignment offered here.

As with any such attempt, some alignments are quite obvious and the connection strong. Others are less so, appearing "forced" and driven by the effort to align. At first glance, the alignment of the poor in spirit with faith may seem forced. But once it is recalled that the poor in spirit are the

---

[115] For an exquisite statement of the connection between the beatitudes, virtue, activity, and law, see Thomas Aquinas, *Commentary on the Gospel of Matthew*, 411: "Likewise note that the acts of virtues are those about which the law commands; moreover the merits [called here "qualifying conditions"] of the beatitudes are the acts of the virtues; and therefore all those things which are commanded and are contained below are referred back to these beatitudes." This latter phrase, referring to the antitheses of Mt 5:21-48, supports the thesis of Chapter 2.

[116] The descriptions of the three theological and four cardinal virtues referenced here are necessarily brief. The following books give extended treatments to each of these virtues, unsurprisingly with heavy reliance on Thomas Aquinas due to his use of these seven virtues in the *Secunda Secundae* of the *Summa Theologiae*: Josef Pieper, *Faith, Hope, Love* (Ignatius Press, 1996) and *The Four Cardinal Virtues* (Notre Dame, IN; University of Notre Dame Press, 1966); Stephen Pope, ed., *The Ethics of Aquinas* (Washington, DC: Georgetown University Press, 2002); Romanus Cessario, O.P, *The Virtues, or the Examined Life* (Continuum Press, 2002); William C. Mattison III, *Introducing Moral Theology: True Happiness and the Virtues* (Brazos Press, 2008).

humble, the connection is more evident. It is through the theological virtue of faith that we reverently know the truth about who God is, and God's relationship with humanity and plan for all creation.[117] What does this virtue of reverent intellectual comprehension have to do with humility? The humble are precisely those who "know their place," a place that is simultaneously creaturely and subordinate to the God of the universe, yet also invaluable and cherished by the living, loving Lord of all.[118] They know it is God, not themselves, who is the center of all that is.[119] In this part, I will have to rest content in explaining the basis of the alignment and refrain from any richer spiritual reflection on the interrelationship of faith and humility. Yet it is fitting that faith be aligned with the first beatitude on humility since both are fundamental to the life of discipleship, pillars on which that life is built.

Mourning is correlated to temperance in this account. Those who mourn are willing to face reality as it is, be it their own sinfulness or the suffering that so commonly surrounds us.[120] This facing of reality involves sadness and aversion. The temperate person is one who *accurately* experiences (and acts upon) sadness and aversion – and also delight and desire – on occasions when these are fitting responses. A common reason for the inordinate partaking of sensual delights is the desire to rest in or find comfort as escape from the sorrows that befall us. The temperate person refuses this, as does the person willing to mourn.[121] The concupiscible appetite of the temperate person also responds accurately to surrounding reality, whether in pleasure/delight or in sorrow/mourning.[122] Hence the happy who mourn well are temperate.

---

[117] Augustine says "there could be no more felicitous beginning of blessedness whose ultimate goal is wisdom" (*The Lord's Sermon on the Mount*, I.1.3). The humility of the poor in spirit is inextricably bound to an accurate grasp of the whole of reality that is wisdom.

[118] Stassen and Gushee claim that the humble not only regard themselves as lowly but more importantly recognize who God is (*Kingdom Ethics*, 38–39). Betz goes so far as to say the crux of being poor in spirit is "an intellectual insight into the human condition," with the attitude accompanying that insight being humility (*The Sermon on the Mount*, 115). For more on human persons as both creaturely and yet a cherished part of God's creation, see Chapter 4.

[119] Guelich says the kingdom of heaven that the poor in spirit receive "connotes God's desire to stand at the center of our lives," coming by an invitation "to recognize God as God" (*The Sermon on the Mount*, 100).

[120] This connection to suffering prompts Pinckaers, without offering a complete alignment such as that here, to associate this beatitude with the virtue of courage. See Pinckaers, *Pursuit of Happiness*, 78–84.

[121] Betz (citing Bultmann) claims those who mourn "are not led astray by [the world's] charms" (*The Sermon on the Mount*, 123). Augustine claims initially there is a "sting of sadness" when people turn to God rather than rejoicing in worldly delights (*The Lord's Sermon on the Mount*, I.2.5).

[122] Though he does not follow the alignment offered here, Thomas Aquinas does claim that the beatitude concerning those who mourn is best understood as acting well with regard

Meekness is perhaps most easy to align with a virtue, namely, fortitude. As depicted above, the meek are those who resist evil well, namely "those who yield before outbursts of evil and do not resist evil, but overcome evil with good."[123] Meekness is being mild with regard to occasions of anger.[124] The virtue of fortitude is understood as moderating aggression, or the irascible appetite. The meek person is precisely the one with fortitude.

Given that the term "righteousness" is correctly translated justice, it may seem most obvious to align the fourth beatitude with justice.[125] That would not be erroneous, and it serves as a reminder that what Jesus is depicting in the beatitudes is not only one reward (eternal happiness) but also one unified life in all of its distinct yet interrelated activities. In the tradition of virtue ethics, this integration is acknowledged in various accounts of the connectivity of the virtues.[126] So we should expect there to be "overlap" in this alignment between the various virtues and the beatitudes' specification of the different activities constituting happiness. But the fourth beatitude is aligned here with hope since this theological virtue is a longing for complete happiness. As Augustine says, this beatitude refers to those who "love the true and unshakeable good."[127] The object of hope is God as our complete

---

to the concupiscible passions. See *Summa Theologiae* I–II 69, 3 as well as *Commentary on the Gospel of Matthew*, 406. Though he does not explicitly mention the concupiscible appetite, it is surely implied in the very next article when Thomas Aquinas claims "men seek consolation for the toils of the present life, in the lusts and pleasures of the world. Hence Our Lord promises comfort to those that mourn" (*Summa Theologiae* I–II 69, 4). Temperance is for Thomas Aquinas the virtue that governs the concupiscible appetite.

[123] Augustine, *The Lord's Sermon on the Mount* I.2.4. See also Gregory of Nyssa *Homilies on the Beatitudes* II:2 (34); Luther, *The Sermon on the Mount*, 36; Calvin, *Harmony of the Evangelists*, Mt 5:5 (261–62); Bonhoeffer, *The Cost of Discipleship*, 122.

[124] Thomas Aquinas claims this beatitude is an antidote to being led away by one's irascible passions. See *Summa Theologiae* I–II 69, 3. He also equates *mitis* to *mansuetudo*, the latter being the classical virtue that moderates anger (*Commentary on the Gospel of Matthew*, 419). See also Ambrose, *Treatise on the Gospel of St. Luke*, 54.5 (203) and Pinckaers, *Pursuit of Happiness*, 61, 65–66. Betz also describes the opposite of meekness as "untamed anger" (*The Sermon on the Mount*, 126).

[125] Thomas Aquinas connects this beatitude to the cardinal virtue justice. See *Commentary on the Gospel of Matthew*, 427. There he also speaks of perfect and imperfect justice, noting that the perfect justice for which we long is not possible in this life. He says satisfaction of this hunger is in "seeing God through his essence," when "nothing remains to be desired" (428). These claims are clearly evocative of hope.

[126] For an outstanding recent account of the connectivity of the virtues, including various Christian and pagan formulations of it as well as a defense of it in response to contemporary challenges esp. from the social sciences, see Andrew Kim, "Thomas Aquinas on the Connection of the Virtues," PhD diss., The Catholic University of America, 2013.

[127] Augustine, *The Lord's Sermon on the Mount*, I.2.6. Guelich confirms the same: the righteousness for which they long is primarily "the eschatological gift of the new relationship with God brought about by the presence of God's redemptive work in the Kingdom" (*The Sermon on the Mount*, 102). As Guelich notes (102–103) and any worthy vision of hope affirms, this eschatological goal is not neglectful of but in continuity with justice in this life.

happiness, and surely that attainment is marked by righteousness, or justice, both in the state of affairs that pertains and in the persons who participate in that state of affairs.[128] Therefore, those who hunger and thirst for righteousness are those who hope. Those who hunger and thirst will be satisfied, yet as Gregory maintains the attainment changes their appetite, which is "sharpened."[129] Their appetites are activated in enjoyment of the satisfaction rather than the longing of what is desired but not fully present. Similarly those who hope no longer yearn for complete happiness once it is attained. Yet they do continue to enjoy that for which they hoped. Thus both in the ultimate goal of the longing and in the changing dynamics of attainment, there is fitting correspondence between the fourth beatitude and hope.

The merciful are aligned here with the virtue of justice. Justice and mercy are commonly contrasted, which is a mistake. They are united in their aim, which is proper order or right relationship among persons. As will be seen in Chapter 4 on Mt 6:19–7:12, true justice entails consistency of standards, such that "the measure with which you measure will be measured out to you" (Mt 7:2). This consistency is referenced in the beatitude on mercy, where we hear that the merciful will be shown mercy. Yet mercy fittingly complements – even perfects – justice. Mercy is not mainly a feeling; it is active restoration.[130] As Guelich notes, though mercy can be directed toward those in need more generally, primarily

> The merciful are those who reflect God's acceptance of the unworthy, the guilty, and the ones in the wrong, because the merciful themselves, conscious of their own unworthiness, guilt, and wrong, have experienced God's forgiving and restoring acceptance through the message of Jesus Christ.[131]

Mercy aids the restoration of right relationship that is the object of justice. Thus mercy can never subvert justice, but the merciful can reach out first to those in need of healing, as we see so consistently not only in the gospels but in the whole of salvation history. Mercy is exemplified in the father's loving acceptance of his prodigal son (Lk 15). It is seen in Christ's encounter with the woman caught in adultery, who is loved compassionately by Jesus even as

---

[128] The object of hope is God, but in a twofold manner, namely, as "object" of our complete happiness (in other words, in whom our complete happiness is found) and as cause of our happiness in making it possible. See Thomas Aquinas, *Summa Theologiae* I–II 17, 1, 4, and 5.

[129] Gregory of Nyssa, *Homilies on the Beatitudes* IV.6 (53–55). There is dire need in moral theology for further reflection on the human activity that is joyful resting in attainment. In Thomistic terms, the appetitive movements of joy and delight are distinct from desire. If the claims of this chapter regarding the continuity of activity between this life and the next are true, further reflection is necessary on the moral importance of joy, if you will. For a person's appetitive powers to be active in the *eschaton*, in other words, for a person to truly participate in complete happiness, such joyful resting is necessary.

[130] See Stassen and Gushee, *Kingdom Ethics*, 43.

[131] Guelich, *The Sermon on the Mount*, 105. See also Betz, *The Sermon on the Mount*, 133.

He instructs her to "go and sin no more" (Jn 8). It is the very action of God the Father in the Son Jesus Christ, who loved us first (1 Jn 4:9–10, 19) and died for us while still sinners (Rom 5:5–8). Thus the fifth beatitude is aligned with the virtue of justice since both are oriented toward the (re)establishment of right relationship. Indeed, this alignment can even serve as a source of wisdom on the perennial challenge of understanding the relationship between justice and mercy.

As noted above the clean (or pure) of heart are those who are single-minded, who are integrated. They lack hypocritical or ulterior motives, choosing their acts always with the further end of love of God.[132] They "see God," fully in the time of reward, but also even now in their particular choices. It is the cardinal virtue of prudence that disposes one to do the activity of practical decision-making, or choosing, well. Prudence is commonly associated with seeing things rightly, enabling one to subsequently choose well.[133] The clean of heart, cleansed of adulterating desires that distort their perception of reality and subsequent decision-making, seek God in all things and thus attain an integrity of life unified in its orientation toward God. They see things truthfully. Betz evidences how central and permeating this virtue is when he says of purity of heart that it is "a virtue of fundamental importance," a "virtue that underlies all ethical attitudes in the SM [Sermon on the Mount]."[134] He and other biblical scholars note the clear echo of Ps 24:3–4 here: "Who will go up to the mountain of the Lord? Who may stand in his holy place? One who has clean hands and a pure heart, who has not set his mind on what is false." As noted above, being clean of heart not only qualifies one to "see God" in the kingdom, but is constituted by having a "sound eye" now.[135] The clean of heart particularly evidently "see God" even now in their activity before eternal reward. That single-mindedness of choosing well granting the further end of union with God makes this beatitude fittingly aligned with prudence.[136]

Finally, the seventh beatitude on the peacemakers who will be called children of God is aligned here with charity. Charity is the theological virtue whereby we love God above all else and others in God. Guelich claims

---

[132] See Davies and Allison, *The Gospel According to Saint Matthew*, 456 and Guelich, *The Sermon on the Mount*, 106.

[133] Chapter 4 explores in greater detail the impact of an accurate grasp of the final end on practical decision-making.

[134] Betz, *The Sermon on the Mount*, 136. Betz never uses the word prudence, though he does describe the foundational importance of this "virtue," in both Greek and Jewish thought.

[135] For the connection between the clean of heart and the "sound eye" see Betz, *The Sermon on the Mount*, 137 and Augustine, *The Lord's Sermon on the Mount*, I.2.8. As seen in Chapter 4, the sound eye of Mt 6:22–23 is a clear depiction of prudence.

[136] It might also be noted that the distinct status of these last two beatitudes correlates with the distinct statuses of prudence and charity (in the Thomistic tradition) as charioteer of and form of the virtues, respectively.

peacemaking as "nothing short of the love commandment itself."[137] He is joined by other contemporary scholars who regard love of enemies, one of the hallmarks of the theological virtue of charity, as essential to peacemaking.[138] If peace is the reconciliation between God and humanity and between fractured human parties that is ultimately made possible through Christ, it is the virtue of charity whereby that friendship with God and others in God is established and maintained.[139] Furthermore, in the same way that being adopted children of God through Christ is – with seeing God – understood in the tradition as the essence of eternal happiness, charity is the greatest theological virtue, the one that remains even as faith and hope pass away. Thus for their corresponding activities, and for their enduring nature as constitutive of eternal reward, the activity of the seventh beatitude and charity are aligned together here.

It was stated above with regard to the survey of the Christian tradition's interpretations of the beatitudes' activities that this chapter could only hope to name those activities and would defer to future work to plumb the riches of the beatitudes as depictions of true happiness. The same must be said here with regard to alignment of beatitudes and virtues. This suggested alignment is proposed as a starting point for further reflection on the correspondence of these two sevenfold sets as encapsulating the Christian life of discipleship.[140] Nonetheless, that more spiritual and in this case speculative endeavor is briefly reviewed here since it is made possible by Section 2's argument about the beatitudes as depictions of activities constitutive of happiness, an argument that naturally invites connections to the virtues. It is hoped that this argument will prompt more of the reflection begun rather inchoately here.

TRANSITION: HAPPINESS, SUFFERING, AND JESUS CHRIST

Before turning from the beatitudes to the following section on salt and light, some attention is warranted to those two beatitudes in the three verses (5:10–12) that have not been examined as included in the above set of seven beatitudes. It is far from some pre-modern fascination with the number

---

[137] Guelich, *The Sermon on the Mount*, 107.

[138] Guelich, *The Sermon on the Mount*, 106–107. See also Stassen and Gushee, *Kingdom Ethics*, 45 and Luz, *Matthew 1–7*, 241.

[139] Indeed, Thomas Aquinas claims that being called children of God "pertains to the union of love" (*Commentary on the Gospel of Matthew*, 408). Thomas Aquinas cites 1 Jn 3:1 to support this connection between love and being children of God: "Behold what manner of charity the Father has bestowed upon us that we should be called, and should be, the sons of God."

[140] Surely part of that further work has to be the better integration of the gifts of the Holy Spirit with the argument of this chapter, a task with clear precedents in the tradition.

seven that warrants distinct treatment of the seven beatitudes. While these three concluding verses do contain what are properly termed beatitudes due to their literary form with the characteristic opening "Blessed are," they play a distinct role in this opening section of the Sermon. The connection between the eighth and ninth beatitudes is obvious. Both concern the suffering of those called blessed. Yet they are also readily connected to the salt and light verses, a connection that may be less obvious but is frequently observed by scholars. Guelich notes how the eighth beatitude's present tense refers not only back to the first beatitude, but also ahead to 5:13–16 ("you *are*").[141] Both Luz and Betz observe that the "you" of 5:11–12 connects this last beatitude to 5:13–16 where Jesus says "*you* are [salt, light]."[142] Betz claims there is such continuity between the ninth beatitude and the salt and light verses that all that is missing in the latter is the term "blessed."[143] In short, these verses are pivotal, connected to both the preceding beatitudes and the ensuing verses on salt and light.

How are the eighth and ninth beatitudes to be understood given the "set of seven" interpretation offered here? As noted above, they are certainly beatitudes. There are literary reasons (the recapitulation of reward in 5:10 and shift to second person in 5:11–12) to treat these distinctly from the previous seven. That said, what role do they play? These verses serve as a helpful reminder that even though the beatitudes are "about happiness" as argued above, the life of discipleship that constitutes true happiness is always in this life accompanied by suffering. That suffering is not constitutive of eternal happiness; this is another reason why these final beatitudes are rightly treated distinctly.[144] Yet the life of true happiness to which Jesus beckons in the beatitudes always involves the cross in this life.[145] As stated later in Matthew's gospel and beyond, the servant is not greater than the master (Mt 10:24; also Lk 6:40, Jn 13:16, and Jn 15:20). As Jesus suffered in living out the beatitudes, so too will His disciples. Jesus warned as much, not only in these beatitudes, but in his repeated injunctions to His followers to take up the cross and follow Him (Mk 8:34, Mt 10:38 and 16:24, and Lk 9:23 and 14:27).[146]

---

[141] Guelich, *The Sermon on the Mount*, 122.

[142] Betz, *The Sermon on the Mount*, 155. Luz, *Matthew 1–7*, 249.

[143] Betz, *The Sermon on the Mount*, 155. See also Thomas Aquinas, *Commentary on the Gospel of Matthew*, 446–57. In Thomas Aquinas's typically intricate textual subdivision, he groups 5:11–12 with 5:13–16.

[144] See Thomas Aquinas, *Commentary on the Gospel of Matthew*, 443: "However this persecution does not make one happy, but rather the cause of it does" ("*ipsa autem persecutio non facit beatum, sed eius causa*," trans. mine). See also 447. See also Luz, *Matthew 1–7*, 242.

[145] For an example of a comparable interpretation in contemporary biblical scholarship, see Luz, *Matthew 1–7*, 252–53. There he claims that 5:3–10 depicts "Christian virtues" and 5:11–12 (really 5:11–16) the suffering entailed in living them.

[146] The beatitudes thus contain a paradoxical element found in many of these "take up the cross" passages. These latter are almost always accompanied by Jesus's claim that in

These beatitudes thus serve as a vivid reminder that living in a manner constitutive of eternal happiness is always accompanied by suffering in this life.[147]

The repeated reference here to Christ in the context of the beatitudes provides occasion to address an essential topic for any examination of the beatitudes, namely, the importance of Jesus Christ. More sustained treatment of the centrality of Jesus for the Sermon on the Mount is reserved for the next chapter, but it could just as easily be placed here. It should be obvious in one sense that Jesus is central for the Sermon in general and the beatitudes in particular. After all, He is the wise teacher, the self-postured rabbi, who delivers the words of Mt 5–7.[148] While this is true, the preceding reflection on suffering and taking up the cross indicates that Jesus is not only a teacher in words, but in his life. The servant is not greater than the master, and the master lived the persecution vividly depicted in Mt 5:10–12. Indeed, Jesus lived out each and every one of the beatitudes. It was mentioned at the start of this chapter that the beatitudes are too infrequently the focus of moral and spiritual reflection on the life of discipleship. In moral theology, too often the same may be said for reflection on Jesus as a font of moral wisdom, which – when even addressed – can be reduced to identifying his more obviously moral injunctions such as the love commandments. Yet Jesus not only taught the path of true happiness in the beatitudes, but He embodied it. Indeed, one could say that in the beatitudes we have the most autobiographical words in

---

losing our lives we find them (Mk 8:35; Mt 10:39 and 16:25; and Lk 9:24). Just as the cross is not an end in itself in these passages but rather a path to new life, so too the suffering entailed in living the beatitudes is also not an end in itself.

[147] As is repeatedly the case in this chapter on the beatitudes, this topic invites rich spiritual reflection that cannot be offered here. The immediate topic is the importance of suffering in the life of discipleship. Some suffering is borne from our weakness, as when we perceive humble and obedient discipleship as suffering due to the persistence of our old, sinful selves, which do indeed need to die. This self-surrender is perceived by us as suffering but is actually constitutive of life in Christ. Yet there is also suffering "from the outside" if you will, referenced here as "persecution," that is not constitutive of life in Christ but an endured necessity of discipleship in a broken world. This is the suffering referenced in 5:10–12 through the term "persecute," and the sort endured by Christ who of course knew not the suffering of the first sort borne from sin (Hebrews 4:15). For another recognition of the common neglect of suffering in moral theology as well as the start of such attention, see Servais Pinckaers, O.P., *The Sources of Christian Ethics*, Washington, DC: The Catholic University of America Press, 1995, 24–27. Pinckaers claims that attention to suffering has no place in a morality dominated by obligation, so it is fitting that it is addressed in his book promoting a morality of happiness and in this chapter enjoining the same.

[148] It is common in both pre-modern and contemporary biblical scholarship to observe that Jesus adopts the posture of the rabbi in Mt 5:1–2 where he sits down, His disciples come to Him, and He begins to teach them. See, for example, Augustine, *The Lord's Sermon on the Mount*, I.1.2; Davies and Allison, *The Gospel According to Saint Matthew*, 424; Guelich, *The Sermon on the Mount*, 52; Pope Benedict XVI, *Jesus of Nazareth*, 65.

all of the gospels.[149] A further fruit of this chapter's argument on the beatitudes' depictions of true happiness is a richer way to understand the *sequela Christi*, the following of Christ whose life is the very incarnation of the eternal happiness offered humanity as a partaking in the divine nature (2 Pet 1:4).

IV. SALT AND LIGHT: A CHRISTOLOGICAL ECCLESIOLOGY

The focus of this chapter has obviously been on the beatitudes, and rightly so. But that should not be taken to indicate that the four verses on salt and light are unimportant, or that their place in the Sermon text between the more well-known beatitudes and antitheses renders them of lesser significance.[150] To the contrary, just as the beatitudes are rightly understood as thoroughly Christological in the manner just described, these verses are best understood as utterly ecclesiological. For this reason, Guelich calls these verses no mere "parenthesis" but rather a "pivot" with a "much larger role within the Sermon."[151] They demonstrate the inherent link of Christology and ecclesiology. Guelich notes that it is a common Matthean theme to follow treatment of who Jesus is with a commissioning of His disciples, as in Mt 10 following Mt 5–9 and the "great commissioning" (Mt 28:19–20) following the presentation of the "resurrected, vindicated, and exalted Lord" (Mt 28:16–18).[152] These verses thus remind us that there is no Christology without ecclesiology, and that ecclesiology must be rooted in Christology.[153]

Hence these pivotal verses are thoroughly ecclesiological, illuminating what it means to be the community of disciples called by Christ. In the Catholic tradition, Vatican II's reflections on the Church attended explicitly to both the *ad intra* and *ad extra* facets of ecclesiology.[154] In other words,

---

[149] See Pope Benedict XVI, *Jesus of Nazareth*, 74: "The beatitudes present a sort of veiled interior biography of Jesus, a kind of portrait of his figure."

[150] For an example of this unfortunate assumption, see Davies and Allison, *The Gospel According to Saint Matthew* (471) who label these "transitional," shifting the focus in the Sermon from the "blessed future" (5:3–12) to the "present life" (5:17ff.). Not only do they dichotomize ethics and eschatology in the manner described above, but they at least imply these verses are less important in themselves.

[151] Guelich, *The Sermon on the Mount*, 129.

[152] Guelich, *The Sermon on the Mount*, 130. See also Betz, *The Sermon on the Mount*, who says these verses are "theologically based on the beatitudes" and describe "what the community for which the SM was composed regarded as their role and task in the world . . . [a] role and task not as their own invention but as the commission issued by Jesus himself" (155).

[153] The ecclesial status of these verses is also evident in Thomas Aquinas's *Commentary on the Gospel of Matthew*, as he understands these verses to speak of the apostles (450, 456) and "those who teach the very teaching of the apostles" (446).

[154] For an illuminating account of the origin of the use of the *ad intra/ad extra* distinction with regard to Vatican II, including its first use in a December 1962 speech by Cardinal

ecclesiology is about both who the Church is in its identity and how the Church relates to the world as its mission, two topics that while distinct are inextricably bound together. Guelich indicates these complementary facets of ecclesiology when he claims: "Whereas the salt metaphor warns the disciple to take one's calling seriously, the light metaphor describes positively one's role as a disciple in the world."[155] The salt and light verses are best understood as ecclesiological injunctions in both *ad intra* and *ad extra* senses.[156]

"You are the salt of the earth." Despite the claim here that 5:13 is helpfully understood in an ecclesiological *ad intra* sense, the point of the Church's "saltiness" is to season the earth. The genitive "of the earth" here is objective not subjective; the earth is the target, not origin, of the Church as salt.[157] The possible meanings of "salt" in this context are manifold, as evident in both contemporary biblical scholarship and traditional commentary.[158] Betz summarizes the basic meaning of the metaphor by saying this refers to being a "seasoning and fertilizing agent" in our engagement with "the earth."[159] Guelich notes that salt not only seasons the bland but also purifies and preserves.[160] Thus any *ad intra* ecclesiological reflection must emphasize that ecclesial identity cannot be separated from mission to "the earth."

That said, after the initial metaphor, the explanatory sentence describes not the dynamics of that witness, but rather the importance of remaining "salty," presumably ultimately for the sake of that mission. "If salt loses its taste, with what can it be seasoned? It is not good for anything but to be thrown out and trampled underfoot." Though never unconcerned with mission, the Church must be true to its identity in order to witness well.

Suenens, see Joseph A. Komonchak, "The Struggle for the Council during the Preparation of Vatican II (1960–1962)," in *History of Vatican II*, vol. 1, ed. Giuseppe Alberigo and Joseph A. Komonchak (Maryknoll: Orbis Press, 1995), 249. This distinction has become commonplace in interpreting the documents of the Council as a whole.

[155] Guelich, *The Sermon on the Mount*, 128. Though he speaks of an individual disciple here, on the very next page he describes the ecclesiological importance of these verses, and thus his comment here should also be understood communally. See also Betz, *The Sermon on the Mount*, 155, where he claims that 5:13 addresses the "status" of the community, and 5:14–16 its "task."

[156] Though the only grammatically parenetical verse is 5:16 in its use of the imperative, Betz notes that these verses are "simultaneously descriptive, declarative, and determinative or imperative" (155).

[157] See Guelich, *The Sermon on the Mount*, 121. See also Davies and Allison, *The Gospel According to Saint Matthew*, 473.

[158] Davies and Allison survey a wide range of possible (closely related) meanings of salt before concluding that despite his variety of possibilities the basic meaning is still "obvious" (*The Gospel According to Saint Matthew*, 472–73). For an example of a premodern survey of the meanings of salt, see Thomas Aquinas, *Lectura*, 451.

[159] Betz, *The Sermon on the Mount*, 160. A proper use of salt, it should be noted, enriches a food's own flavor rather than overwhelms that flavor with the taste of salt. There is surely much to reflect upon in the use of a salt metaphor for mission and identity.

[160] Guelich, *The Sermon on the Mount*, 126.

Hence this verse is the perfect hinge between the beatitudes and the even more explicit injunction to mission in the ensuing verses. The salt of the earth is the community of disciples called the Church, and it retains its taste and is thus able to fulfill its mission to "the earth" when it remains rooted in the source of its life, Jesus Christ. And the way it does so is to live the life of true happiness, the activities of which are depicted in the beatitudes and most importantly in the life of Jesus.[161]

"You are the light of the world." The ensuing "light of the world" verses shift the emphasis *ad extra* to the Church's mission illuminating the world. As with the previous verse, identity and mission are inextricably bound. After all, Jesus says "your light must shine" through the performance of "good deeds."[162] But the focus here is that this be done "before others, that they may see your good deeds and glorify your heavenly Father" (5:16).[163] The city and lamp images emphasize

---

[161] Davies and Allison claim that what functions as salt (and light) is not Torah as written law or temple as place of worship, but rather a people (*The Gospel According to Saint Matthew*, 471–72). There is a sense in which people are prior to teaching. Further research on this topic is warranted. There are possible points of continuity with the classic Thomistic claim that the new law is first and foremost the grace of the Holy Spirit through Christ, and only secondarily a written law. What has this to do with the Sermon on the Mount? Affirming Augustine's observation that the Sermon is the charter of the Christian life, Thomas Aquinas identifies the Sermon as the written sense of the new law. See *Summa Theologiae* I–II 106, 1 and 108, 3–4.

The priority of persons to teaching raises the topic of exemplarity, worthy of far more in-depth research though a note will have to suffice here. Exemplarism is the claim that the most basic point of departure in morality is not a single or set of principles, but rather a person or persons. Moral exemplars are not just examples of (logically prior) moral principles, but the basis of morality. A clear forerunner in this field is Linda Zagzebski. See her "Exemplarist Virtue Theory," *Metaphilosophy* 41.1–2(2010):41–57. See also James Van Slyke, Gregory Peterson, Kevin Reimer, Michael Spezio, and Warren Brown, eds., *Theology and the Science of Moral Action: Virtue Ethics, Exemplarity, and Cognitive Neuroscience* (New York: Routledge, 2012). See Patrick Clark, "The Case for an Exemplarist Approach to Virtue in Catholic Moral Theology," *Journal of Moral Theology* 3.1 (2014):54–82, at 56 for a review of the history of exemplarism. There are obvious possibilities here for a more thorough understanding of Christ as the foundation of moral theology, and it is simply suggested here that this part of the Sermon on the Mount is a fine scriptural basis for further exploration of that claim.

Regardless of the adequacy of exemplarism as moral theory, surely the importance of moral exemplars more colloquially understood (in other words, role models) is undeniable, and thus it is fitting in a book arguing the value of reading the Sermon in hand with virtue ethics that the opening treatise on happiness is followed immediately by a reflection on the importance of (and an injunction toward) personal (individual and communal) witness.

[162] Luz claims that such a focus on good deeds is characteristically Matthean. For Matthew, "the person is constituted by, and lives by, his or her deeds" (Luz, *Matthew 1–7*, 252).

[163] It is common in both pre-modern and contemporary commentaries to pause to reconcile this injunction with the Mt 6:1–18 repeated injunctions to do good deeds "in secret." The compatibility of course is due to the fact that here the deeds are done so that people glorify our heavenly Father, whereas in Mt 6 they are done "to be seen by others." See, for example, Augustine, *The Lord's Sermon on the Mount*, II.1.3–4; Augustine, *Sermons* III

this missionary focus of the life of discipleship. As Guelich states, "we might properly call this section the disciple's mission in the world."[164] That mission is accomplished by "good deeds," which Guelich describes as "basically a life of discipleship that includes both word and deed."[165] Foreshadowing the conclusion of the Sermon, there is emphasis here on deeds rather than just words.[166] In a line that is a veritable encapsulation of the claims of this chapter, including its claims on the continuity of activity in this life and the next as depicted in the beatitudes, and its claims about the connections between the (Christological) beatitudes and (ecclesiological) salt and light verses, Guelich claims: "since this life and conduct of good deeds are characteristic of life in the new age of salvation (Jer 31:31), they bear witness to God's eschatological activity on behalf of humanity."[167] By living the ethical and eschatological life in Christ depicted in the beatitudes (and exemplified by Christ), the Church maintains its Christocentric identity and gives (Christ's) light to the world.[168]

CONCLUSION

The opening verses of the Sermon on the Mount immediately establish the authority of Christ (5:1–2), and based on that authority set forth a vision of true happiness that is not only taught by Christ but exemplified by Christ. In this chapter, I argue that the beatitudes are best understood in the context of classical ethical reflection on happiness. They further illuminate that discourse in virtue ethics by the particular vision of happiness presented, a vision ascertained here through a review of the tradition of commentary on the beatitudes. As recognized most notably by St. Augustine, the beatitudes set the program for the rest of the Sermon and arguably the entire life of discipleship. They portray true happiness as (grace-enabled) activity that begins in this life even as it is only complete in the next. They depict growth in discipleship, and speak to the place of suffering in that life. They are fittingly examined in line with another traditional and comprehensive way to depict the good life, namely, the theological and cardinal virtues. The pivotal

---

(51–94); 54.1–2; Guelich, *The Sermon on the Mount*, 279 and 301–302; Davies and Allison, *The Gospel According to Saint Matthew*, 478.

[164] Guelich, *The Sermon on the Mount*, 126.

[165] Guelich, *The Sermon on the Mount*, 125.

[166] Guelich, *The Sermon on the Mount*, 129. See Mt 7:13–27.

[167] Guelich, *The Sermon on the Mount*, 129. See also Luz, who says that good works receive their content from the preceding beatitudes and from the following antitheses (*Matthew 1–7*, 252).

[168] In commenting on the light verses, Thomas Aquinas addresses the objection that only Christ is the Light by saying "that light is essentially only Christ, but the apostles are called light illuminated, that is, by participation, as the eye is light illuminating and nevertheless illuminated" (*Commentary on the Gospel of Matthew*, 456).

salt and light verses evidence the connection between Christology and ecclesiology, and the inextricable connection between the Church's self-identity and its missionary focus.

Most chapters in this book do not align different verses of their section of the Sermon with different virtues as this one has. But each chapter does address how that section of the Sermon might be helpfully understood in relation to one of those seven virtues. The verses in this opening section of the Sermon are aligned here with the theological virtue of faith.

A central topic in this chapter is true happiness. There is an account of happiness and human flourishing presented in the beatitudes, an account whose authority is established not only through the persuasiveness and coherence of the happiness portrayed, but also and especially through the authority of Jesus who teaches and exemplifies it. The account offered here is in many ways accessible to unaided human reason. Yet it is also a vision that invites the assent of belief that is the act of the grace-enabled virtue faith.[169] As evidenced in the tradition of commentary, the true happiness that is the kingdom of heaven is a supernatural destiny of communion with God, the grasp of which (let alone the attainment of which) transcends the capacities of unaided human reason. It is possible to apprehend and live this life in Christ only through the grace of Christ, offered through the ecclesial community and fittingly so since the life offered as true happiness is a partaking in the divine communion of persons as the communion of saints.

As faith (and the humility that is so emblematic of it) is the cornerstone of the life of discipleship, the Sermon begins with a presentation and injunction to a life of true happiness that Jesus's hearers are invited to believe and live.[170] We commonly associate faith with the Creed, and appropriately so since the object of faith is what is true about God and God's relationship to humanity. But given who God is, and how God invites us to share in the divine life, it is also appropriate to associate faith with the way of life that we live in Christ, one described by Him and lived by Him, a way of life also reflective of the fullness of life (and pure act) that God is and in which He calls us to participate.

---

[169] For a perfect example of how the beatitudes present an account of happiness which in certain ways is accessible to unaided human reason (and thus helpfully explicated in classical philosophical terms), and yet ultimately transcends that capacity and thus invites a response of faith, see Thomas Aquinas, *Commentary on the Gospel of Matthew*, 404–408, 413, and 427–28.

[170] Above faith was aligned with the first beatitude in the context of an alignment of the seven virtues with the first seven beatitudes. The distinct claim of this conclusion is that parts of the Sermon may be aligned with the seven virtues, and faith particularly well corresponds to this opening section of the Sermon.

2

A VIRTUE ETHICS APPROACH TOWARD THE FULFILLMENT OF THE LAW IN MATTHEW 5:17–48

Do not think that I have come to abolish the law or the prophets. I have come not to abolish but to fulfill.

Amen, I say to you, until heaven and earth pass away, not the smallest letter or the smallest part of a letter will pass from the law, until all things have taken place.

Therefore, whoever breaks one of the least of these commandments and teaches others to do so will be called least in the kingdom of heaven. But whoever obeys and teaches these commandments will be called greatest in the kingdom of heaven.

I tell you, unless your righteousness surpasses that of the scribes and Pharisees, you will not enter into the kingdom of heaven.

You have heard that it was said to your ancestors, "You shall not kill; and whoever kills will be liable to judgment."

But I say to you, whoever is angry with his brother will be liable to judgment, and whoever says to his brother, "Raqa," will be answerable to the Sanhedrin, and whoever says, "You fool," will be liable to fiery Gehenna.

Therefore, if you bring your gift to the altar, and there recall that your brother has anything against you,

leave your gift there at the altar, go first and be reconciled with your brother, and then come and offer your gift.

Settle with your opponent quickly while on the way to court with him. Otherwise your opponent will hand you over to the judge, and the judge will hand you over to the guard, and you will be thrown into prison.

Amen, I say to you, you will not be released until you have paid the last penny.

You have heard that it was said, "You shall not commit adultery."

But I say to you, everyone who looks at a woman with lust has already committed adultery with her in his heart.

If your right eye causes you to sin, tear it out and throw it away. It is better for you to lose one of your members than to have your whole body thrown into Gehenna.

And if your right hand causes you to sin, cut it off and throw it away. It is better for you to lose one of your members than to have your whole body go into Gehenna.

It was also said, "Whoever divorces his wife must give her a bill of divorce."

But I say to you, whoever divorces his wife (unless the marriage is unlawful) causes her to commit adultery, and whoever marries a divorced woman commits adultery.

Again you have heard that it was said to your ancestors, "Do not take a false oath, but make good to the Lord all that you vow."

But I say to you, do not swear at all; not by heaven, for it is God's throne;

nor by the earth, for it is his footstool; nor by Jerusalem, for it is the city of the great King.

Do not swear by your head, for you cannot make a single hair white or black.

Let your "Yes" mean "Yes," and your "No" mean "No." Anything more is from the evil one.

You have heard that it was said, "An eye for an eye and a tooth for a tooth."

But I say to you, offer no resistance to one who is evil. When someone strikes you on (your) right cheek, turn the other one to him as well.

If anyone wants to go to law with you over your tunic, hand him your cloak as well.

Should anyone press you into service for one mile, go with him for two miles.

Give to the one who asks of you, and do not turn your back on one who wants to borrow.

You have heard that it was said, "You shall love your neighbor and hate your enemy."

But I say to you, love your enemies, and pray for those who persecute you,

that you may be children of your heavenly Father, for he makes his sun rise on the bad and the good, and causes rain to fall on the just and the unjust.

For if you love those who love you, what recompense will you have? Do not the tax collectors do the same?

And if you greet your brothers only, what is unusual about that? Do not the pagans do the same?

So be perfect, just as your heavenly Father is perfect.

The verses in Matthew 5:17–48 contain some of the most challenging passages in all of Scripture.[1] They are challenging in several ways. First, they are

---

[1] Ulrich Luz claims, "Our verses belong to the most difficult ones of the Gospel." See *Matthew 1–7: A Commentary* (Minneapolis: Augsburg Fortress, 1989), 259. Philip Ziegler cites Douglas Hare's claim that Mt 5:17–20 is the "most difficult passage to be found anywhere in the Gospel." See his "'Not to Abolish but to Fulfill:' The Person of the Preacher and the Claim of the Sermon on the Mount," *Studies in Christian Ethics* **22.**3 (2009): 275–89, at 276. See also Robert Guelich, *The Sermon on the Mount: A Foundation for Understanding* (Waco, TX: Word Books, 1982), 161, where he calls this "one of the most

challenging to simply understand. Enormous amounts of ink have been spilled in delineating the varying ways "fulfill" (Mt 5:17) can be understood, and which way it is intended here. The term "perfect" (Mt 5:48) in the closing words of Matthew 5 has also posed a stumbling block to ready interpretation. Throughout the thirty or so verses in between these words, there are a variety of phrases that are difficult to understand on varying levels. Scholars debate whether or not "until heaven and earth pass away" (Mt 5:18) references a temporal or even conceptual limit on the validity of the law, or just the opposite, an expression to indicate its unending validity. Such questions of ultimacy are addressed alongside very particular concrete matters, such as the true sense of "offer no resistance to one who is evil" (Mt 5:39).

In addition to the difficulty of determining the meaning of these various verses, there is also a challenge in determining how to live them out, given the specific and at times daunting ethical guidance that is offered. Scholars have always recognized that these verses offer extensive ethical guidance. Ulrich Luz calls these verses "concrete and extreme in their demands."[2] Due to the practical difficulty of observing the specific commands of these verses, an enormous literature exists that surveys the varying strategies for determining how to live out the seemingly unrealistic morality of the Sermon on the Mount, and the norms found in 5:17–48 are most often what scholars are trying to explain, or even explain away.[3]

---

perplexing passages in the first gospel." Hans Dieter Betz reports Adolf von Harnack's quip that patristic exegesis on Mt 5:17 could easily fill an entire book. Betz, *The Sermon on the Mount: A Commentary on the Sermon on the Mount, Including the Sermon on the Plain (Matthew 5:3–7:27 and Luke 6:20–49)* (Minneapolis: Fortress Press, 1995), 175.

[2] Ulrich Luz, *The Theology of the Gospel of Matthew* (New York: Cambridge University Press, 1995), 51.

[3] In Catholic moral theology, a particularly impactful analysis of varying ways to treat the moral guidance of the Sermon is found in Servais Pinckaers, *Sources of Christian Ethics* (Washington, DC: The Catholic University of America Press, 1995), 134–40. For other extensive typologies of how the moral guidance of the Sermon ought to be regarded, see Harvey MacArthur, *Understanding the Sermon on the Mount* (New York: Harper, 1960), 105–27 and Carl Henry, *Christian Personal Ethics* (Grand Rapids, MI: William B. Eerdmans, 1957), 278–326. Luz claims that while the challenging nature of his text has always been apparent, it is only with the Reformers that the "unfulfillability" of the Sermon is emphasized (*Matthew 1–7*, 221). Before then it was assumed to "lead all Christians on the way of Christian perfection" (220). Luz claims it is unsurprising that the Reformers' approach eventually leads to the (mere) internalization of the Sermon. Such a focus on intention rather than action is strikingly un-Matthean, Luz claims, since Matthew is always focused on deeds (222). Davies and Allison evidence a view of the Sermon's ethical demands as unrealistic when they say the strict formulation of Mt 5 may be impossible to live but their "radical formulation has in fact accomplished more than a balanced, casuist formulation ever could have." See *The Gospel According to Saint Matthew*, 507–508, n. 2. There is much that is problematic here. There is the assumption, as Luz notes, really only present after the Reformation, that Mt 5 is impossible to live out. More disturbing is the stereotypical morality of obligation approach that sees rules merely

Yet despite the fact that the verses addressed in this chapter contain the most obviously "moral" material in the Sermon, the purpose of this chapter is *not* to identify the "morality of the Sermon on the Mount" on matters such as anger, lust, divorce, oath-taking, non-violence, and loving your enemy. Excellent work exists on all of these questions.[4] And of course the matters addressed in this chapter will impact one's interpretation of these moral matters, and vice versa. But the purpose of this chapter, in line with the project that is this book, is to examine how a virtue ethics approach to moral theology can help our understanding of these verses that compose the Sermon on the Mount, and in turn how a virtue-centered approach to morality can be specified and further illuminated by this portion of the Sermon on the Mount. Therefore, the focus of the chapter on Mt 5:17–48 is on the fulfillment of the law. The chapter's main section is an analysis of the term fulfill in Mt 5:17. Thinkers from the very beginnings of Christianity until today have distinguished varying ways that the law is fulfilled. Given the focus of this book, and the obviously moral content of the six "antitheses" in Mt 5:21–48, the analysis here begins with reflection on how Christ fulfills the *moral* law. But again from the early Church though contemporary biblical scholarship, Christian thinkers have distinguished the moral from the ceremonial law and examined how these are fulfilled by Christ in distinct manners. Thus, attention is consistently paid to the ceremonial law in this chapter as well.

Section I on the fulfillment of the (especially moral) law delineates the meanings of "fulfill," and does so using the content of the six antitheses of 5:21–48 as the data for that analysis. Section II continues the analysis of the antitheses, in particular the question of "why these antitheses?" Reminiscent of the analysis of explanations for beatitudes as a set in Chapter 1, Section II examines possible rationales for the particular set of six antitheses that are found in this portion of the Sermon. This section offers hypotheses for the subgrouping of the six antitheses which are illuminative of how Jesus fulfills the law in both the moral and the ceremonial senses. By this point in the chapter, it is evident how central Jesus is for fulfillment of the law. Therefore, Section III returns to a topic addressed briefly in Chapter 1 and examines the central importance of Jesus Christ for this section of the Sermon, and indeed the Sermon as a whole. Finally, the conclusion continues the pattern of this book in suggesting a virtue or virtues in light of which each section of the Sermon might be fruitfully understood. For reasons that should be quite

as instrumental, prompting action closer to some unrealizable ideal rather than prescribing activity constitutive of happiness.

[4] One exemplary such book is Glen Stassen and David Gushee, *Kingdom Ethics: Following Jesus in Contemporary Context* (Downer's Grove, IL: Intervarsity Academic, 2003), which contains chapters on all of the specific issues mentioned in the antitheses as well as an excellent bibliography.

evident once the reader reaches the conclusion, I propose that the verses examined in this chapter are helpfully understood in connection with the virtues of temperance and fortitude.

I. "FULFILLING" THE LAW

This section of the Sermon on the Mount in Mt 5:17–48 is very clearly structured. It opens with four verses that are programmatic for the rest of the section.[5] Starting with "Do not think I have come to abolish the law or the prophets" (5:17a),[6] a seeming reference to an erroneous interpretation being made about the Christ and the law, Jesus goes on to claim that "I have come not to abolish but fulfill" (5:17b).[7] The following two lengthy verses further emphasize the continuing validity of the law. The end of these opening verses, "I tell you, unless your righteousness surpasses that of the scribes and Pharisees, you will not enter into the kingdom of heaven" (5:20) contains references to the crucial Sermon themes of "righteousness" and "kingdom of heaven," further indicating the importance of this passage. Though some attention will be given to the two "until" clauses of Mt 5:18, the focus of this section will be on explaining the meaning of "fulfill," since the fulfillment of the law is the "greater righteousness" that constitutes entrance into the "kingdom of heaven." My discussion in this section proceeds as follows. I first survey varying interpretations of the term fulfill. We find a consistent distinction in the tradition, echoed in recent scholarship, between the moral and ceremonial law. The discussion thus proceeds by examining how the law is fulfilled first in a moral sense and then in a ceremonial sense. Unsurprisingly, the conclusion here will be that a virtue-centered approach to moral theology can help us better understand how Jesus fulfills the law, in not only the moral but even the ceremonial sense.

---

[5] The contemporary biblical scholarship on these verses is enormous. For excellent distillations of that literature, see Betz, *The Sermon on the Mount*, 166–97; Guelich, *The Sermon on the Mount*, 134–74; Davies and Allison, *The Gospel According to Saint Matthew*, 481–503; and Luz, *Matthew 1–7*, 255–73. These works address a host of issues about these verses (e.g., linguistic analysis and origin) which are beyond the scope of this project.

[6] For a rival view of the significance of "or" rather than "and" to connect law and prophets, see Guelich, *The Sermon on the Mount*, 137–42 and Luz, *Matthew 1–7*, 264. Luz claims the two conjunctions are functionally equivalent here, while Guelich claims the "or" suggests a pre-Matthean saying concerning the law, with Matthew deliberately adding "the prophets" to emphasize that Jesus's coming fulfills not only the law but all of the scriptures: "the question of the Law's continuing validity now becomes a part of the larger context of Jesus' coming as the one who brings that new relationship between God and humankind promised in the Scriptures. The normative character of the law remains in the picture (5:18, 19), but set within the broader panorama of Jesus' coming as the Bringer of the age of salvation to fulfill the Scriptures" (142).

[7] For more on how this verse is a response to both "Christian antinomians and Jewish accusers," see Davies and Allison, *The Gospel According to Saint Matthew*, 501 n. 24.

A. *"FULFILLING" THE LAW: SURVEYS OF POSSIBLE*
INTERPRETATIONS

One obvious strategy to determine the meaning of the crucial term fulfill in
Mt 5:17 is to define it in terms of its opposite, the term "abolish," to which it is
contrasted in the very same verse. Although this functions to limit the
possible acceptable meanings of fulfill (that is, it cannot mean abolish), the
multiplicity of alternatives to abolish render this approach inadequate.[8]
Another obvious strategy would be to survey varying interpretations of this
term through history and/or in the writings of various contemporary interpreters. Yet any clear synthetic typology of meanings from various historical
authorities is made extraordinarily difficult by the variety of their interpretations. In his helpful historical survey, Luz claims that the one constant
in interpretation of this term is that each one speaks of a multiplicity of
meanings.[9] To offer but a few examples, Chrysostom saw four ways that Jesus
fulfills the law.[10] Augustine seems to have changed his views on the different
senses of fulfill across different writings, but each time he names two senses of
fulfill.[11] Thomas Aquinas consistently describes five ways that the new law
fulfills the old, though his lists of the five vary slightly in different places.[12]

---

[8] See Gerhard Delling, "πλήρης" in *Theological Dictionary of the New Testament* (vol. 6),
ed. Gerhard Friedrich and Geoffrey W. Bromiley (Grand Rapids, MI: William
B. Eerdmans., 1968), 293–94.

[9] See Luz, *Matthew 1–7*, 261–64 for a survey from Irenaeus through the Reformation. Luz
notes that as early as Irenaeus in the second century a distinction was made between the
ceremonial and moral law, an important point later in this chapter.

[10] See *Homilies on Matthew*, XVI.3–4 (71–73). Jesus confirmed all the prophets said of him
by his actions; he transgressed none of its precepts; he empowered people to observe the
law; and he added to the code of laws. Chrysostom's explicit attention to the distinction
between what Christ did and what he enabled us to do is reminiscent of Luz's two
groups below.

[11] In his *On the Lord's Sermon on the Mount* (New York: Newman Press, 1948), i.8.20,
Augustine claims there are two senses of fulfill: to supplement the law's deficiencies and
to carry out its content. In Augustine's *Answer to Faustus, A Manichean*, trans. Ronald
Teske (Hyde Park, NY: New City Press, 2007), XVII.6, he claims that Christ fulfills the law
in grace and truth (Jn 1:7), in grace when what is commanded is carried out in love, and in
truth when what is foretold in prophecies is shown to come to pass. Given the rhetorical
context of the latter text, Augustine is at pains to emphasize the continuity of old law and
new, and thus does not say the new law supplemented the old law's deficiencies. Part of the
apparent tension here is the use of the English term "deficiencies." See n. 41.

[12] See Thomas Aquinas, *Summa Theologiae* I–II 107, 2, where Thomas Aquinas says the
new law fulfills the old by justifying humanity through Christ's passion, something the
old law was unable to accomplish. Jesus also fulfilled the old law in his works by living by
its observances. He fulfilled the old law in his teaching in three ways: by explaining its
true sense, by offering the safest way to comply with it, and by adding some counsels of
perfection. The fivefold list in Thomas Aquinas's *Commentary on Matthew*, trans. Jeremy
Holmes and Beth Mortensen (Lander, WY: The Aquinas Institute for the Study of Sacred
Doctrine, 2013), differs. First, "those things that were prefigured in the law and prophets

Martin Luther recognizes one of Augustine's sets of two meanings and whittles it down to one.[13]

Contemporary biblical scholars are not more consistent. Robert Guelich offers three distinct interpretations before claiming that the term means "fill up," as in to "bring to its final conclusion all the Law stood for."[14] W. D. Davies and Dale Allison outline nine possible senses of the term fulfill before offering three conclusions which are quite helpful and affirmed here.[15] First, the passage makes Jesus the center of attention rather than primarily the law and/or prophets. Second, the law's truth is confirmed, as it is fulfilled and not set aside. Finally, Jesus's demands surpass the law's demands, but the two are not contradictory.[16]

Luz's six-fold typology of possible meanings for fulfill is presented here as particularly helpful since he distinguishes between Jesus's teachings on the one hand (group 1), and ministry on the other (group 2), with three ways of understanding each.[17] If fulfill refers to teachings, Jesus could be saying that his teachings "bring out the true meaning" of the teachings found in the law (1a). In this sense there would be nothing "added" to the law. This interpretation of fulfill is especially attractive where there is a concern not to emphasize the ethical requirements of the gospel. It is also deployed when some group (a contemporary equivalent to the scribes and Pharisees) is considered to be perverting the law. For both of these reasons this is clearly the approach of Luther.[18] It might be asked why the law needs to be fulfilled by Jesus's teaching if nothing is added. As evidenced in Luther, those who take this approach commonly refer to 5:20, "unless your righteousness exceeds that of

concerning Christ he fulfilled in his actions;" second, by observing the law's requirements; third, by offering the grace to live out the law; fourth, "by satisfying for the sins by which we were made transgressors of the law;" and fifth, "by applying certain perfections of the law" (469; see also 463).

[13] See *Sermon on the Mount* in *Luther's Works* 21 on 5:17 (69–70). Luther rejects Augustine's claim in *On the Lord's Sermon on the Mount*, I.8.20 that the new law supplements the law's deficiencies. It has none and Jesus simply restores its true meaning.

[14] See Guelich, *The Sermon on the Mount*, 139–40. He goes on to further explain this sense: "Jesus' ministry fulfills the Law by fulfilling the 'covenantal-promise' of the total realization of the right relationship between God and his people" (140). Guelich himself recognizes that his preferred interpretation has difficulty explaining in what sense the law remains valid as indicated in vv. 18–19, but nonetheless he claims this is the meaning in Matthew. This concession is an early hint of what becomes a consistent problem in Guelich's work, namely, claiming that Jesus "sets aside" the old law (258).

[15] Davies and Allison, *The Gospel According to Saint Matthew*, 485–86

[16] Davies and Allison, *The Gospel According to Saint Matthew*, 487.

[17] Luz, *Matthew 1–7*, 260–61. For a comparable recognition in contemporary biblical scholarship of how fulfill can refer to Jesus's life on the one hand, or activity (by Jesus and/or his followers) on the other hand, see Ian Boxall, *Discovering Matthew* (Grand Rapids, MI: William B. Eerdmans, 2014), 119–21.

[18] Luther, *The Sermon on the Mount*, 5:17 (69–70). Luther, of course, regarded the Catholic Church as his contemporary equivalent of the scribes and Pharisees.

the scribes and Pharisees...." Fulfillment is required not because Jesus's teaching about the law offers anything new, but because it was not being lived out in its true meaning.

Luz describes two further ways of understanding fulfill in reference to Jesus's teachings. A second way of understanding Jesus's teachings as fulfilling the law is that Jesus quantitatively "adds" or "supplies" new material content to the law (1b). According to this interpretation, Jesus does indeed add material content to the law.[19] The third way Jesus's teaching fulfills the law is more qualitative. Luz notes that as early as the Origen thinkers have asserted what is added to the law is the grace to live it (1c).[20]

In all three of these cases, there is something new about the law as presented by Jesus. Whether it be a return to its true meaning despite human perversions and/or the addition of new material content and/or the graced ability to live out the law, the law as presented by Christ is new. In all of these cases, we are describing how the *moral* law presented by Christ is new. In others words, if the old law prescribed human activity reflective of the Jewish people's covenantal relationship with God, Jesus also prescribes human activity reflective of the new covenant, which fulfills rather than abolishes the old.[21] The prescription of human activity with regard to temporal goods, done in a manner reflective of God's covenantal relationship with humanity (in the case of the new law culminating in Jesus Christ), is precisely what makes the fulfillment of the law by Jesus "moral."

It is crucial that Jesus's fulfillment includes the moral sense of the law. Indeed, the six antitheses that Jesus offers in Matthew 5:21–48 are all examples of human activity concerning temporal activities in accordance with the new law. Too often thinkers fail to clearly differentiate in a manner akin to Luz how fulfill refers both to the teachings of Jesus about human (moral) activity and to the life and ministry of Jesus as fulfilling the law. Sometimes this distinction is even explicitly rejected as a later addition in the Christian tradition. Yet the inaccuracy of this claim is evident not only by its developed use as early as Augustine if not before, but also by its use in certain contemporary biblical scholarship.[22] After briefly noting here Luz's three

---

[19] Whether the new law adds any prescriptions is precisely the point on which Augustine seems to have vacillated. I suggest a way to understand how one could affirm these two seemingly inconsistent claims later in this chapter.

[20] Luz, *Matthew 1–7*, 262, citing Origen's *Fragment 97*.

[21] Though the theme of covenant does not receive extended attention in this chapter, it is obviously foundational for any treatment of fulfillment of the law. The law, of course, only makes sense in the context of God's covenantal relationship with His people.

[22] The claim about the novelty of the moral/ceremonial distinction is evident in recent discussions about supersession prompted by Michael Wyschogrod's important article on Thomas Aquinas and the old law, in which he claims this distinction begins with Thomas Aquinas. See Wyschogrod, "A Jewish Reading of St. Thomas Aquinas on the Old Law," in *Understanding Scripture: Explorations of Jewish and Christian Traditions of*

senses of fulfill with regard to Jesus's ministry, we will first focus on the moral law as fulfilled by Christ, reflecting the focus of Mt 5:21–48. We then return to the way that the life *of* Christ fulfills the law, and thus how life *in* Christ continues to fulfill the law in this manner.

Luz distinguishes three ways that the "ministry of Jesus" fulfills the law. First, the "story of Jesus" fulfills the promises of the law and prophets (2a). It is Jesus to whom the law and prophets point and promise, and thus he fulfills that promise. Second, Jesus's life and ministry fulfills the law and prophets in the sense that He is obedient to the law (2b). Note that while all three senses of fulfill in each set of three are closely related to those in the other set – after all, how Jesus's life fulfills the law matters for how disciples should live in accordance with the law – this is especially true of this second one (2b). How Jesus lives in obedience to the law is governed by the sense in which the new law is related to the old. Finally, the third sense in which Jesus's ministry fulfills the old law according to Luz is by bringing it "to its goal and end" through His death and resurrection (2c).[23] To anticipate the conclusion of this chapter, this third most obviously teleological interpretation of fulfill is not only endorsed here, but its application is extended to how we understand Jesus's teachings fulfilling the old law, an interpretation supported by the similarly teleological meaning of "being perfect" as found in the culminating verse 5:48.

B. JESUS'S MORAL TEACHING AS FULFILLMENT OF THE LAW

We begin here with an analysis of how Jesus's teaching about how to live fulfills the law not only because it is the first of the two ways to understand fulfill as described by Luz, but also because the six antitheses are evident examples of how Jesus's moral teaching is the fulfillment of the old law. Once again, the purpose of this section is not to develop any extended treatment of Christ's teaching on retaliation or anger or the like, though of course some sense of that teaching is required for the task here. The task here is rather to look at the six antitheses as a set of data to use in order to better understand what Jesus meant when He said He has come not to abolish but to fulfill the law.

The phrasing of the six antitheses ("You have heard that it was said . . . but I say to you. . .") can lead to that unfortunate label "antithesis" implying the latter is antithetical to the former. It can be wrongly assumed that Jesus's

Interpretation, ed. Clemens Thoma and Michael Wyschogrod (New York: Paulist Press, 1987), 125–40. But the inaccuracy of this is evident from a rather developed use of the distinction in Augustine (*Answer to Faustus*, XIX) and according to Luz its use as early as Irenaeus (Luz, *Matthew 1–7*, 261).

[23] Luz, *Matthew 1–7*, 261. Given the context, "end" here obviously means *telos*, not termination.

teaching is over and against the old law.[24] Most contemporary scholars continue to use this label due to its prominence, but they simply note that it is in important ways an unfortunate term.[25] That practice is adopted here, and Mt 5:17 on Jesus fulfilling not abolishing the law is taken to govern the antitheses. But how does Jesus's teaching fulfill the old as evident in the antitheses? A likely reason for the multiplicity of interpretations of fulfill even as applying solely to the moral law is that the relationship between the old and new differs in different antitheses. As the first two are probably the easiest to interpret, they provide a good place to begin.

1. FIRST AND SECOND ANTITHESES: OVERVIEW OF FULFILL The opening antitheses in Mt 5:21–30 concern first killing and anger, and second adultery and lust.[26] In both cases, Jesus notes that not only certain exterior actions (murder and adultery), but also their corresponding interior dispositions (anger and lust), are prohibited as contrary to our covenantal relationship with God and others. These first two antitheses are in a sense easy to understand in terms of how the new law fulfills the old. As Thomas Aquinas says, Christ, like a good physician, does not just treat the symptom but also the root/cause of bad action.[27] And since lust and anger are commonly the origin of adultery and murder, the new law proscribes these as well.[28]

Before using these two antitheses to address Luz's three senses of how Jesus fulfills the moral law, it should be noted that these antitheses present a perfect occasion to explore a topic that can only be mentioned here, yet

---

[24] Guelich at times provides an example of using "antithesis" in an unfortunate sense, as when he refers to 5:21–28 as "set in clear antithesis to the Law" (*The Sermon on the Mount*, 161). For a more nuanced treatment of the antitheses see 177, though he still problematically claims there that the third, fifth, and sixth "antitheses live up to their name by clearly setting aside their corresponding premises" (177; see also 181).

[25] Betz is an example of clarifying how the term ought not be taken (even though it is the *prima facie* sense), yet still using the term. It is noteworthy that he traces the use of this term back to Marcion (*The Sermon on the Mount*, 200).

[26] For recent biblical scholarship on these two antitheses, see Luz, *Matthew 1–7*, 282–98.

[27] See Thomas Aquinas, *Explanation of the Ten Commandments* (http://dhspriory.org/thomas/TenCommandments.htm): "It is for all this that Christ taught us not only to beware of murder but also of anger. The good physician removes the external symptoms of a malady; and, furthermore, he even removes the very root of the illness, so that there will be no relapse. So also the Lord wishes us to avoid the beginnings of sins; and anger is thus to be avoided because it is the beginning of murder." Davies and Allison make a similar claim, saying that in the first antithesis "both the inner emotion of hatred [*sic*] and its outer workings are rejected" (*The Gospel According to Saint Matthew*, 513). Why they consistently say "hatred" rather than "anger" is not clear (e.g., 522).

[28] Biblical scholarship and traditional commentaries also focus on the significance of the three distinct prohibitions with regard to anger and their corresponding liabilities, as well as who exactly is implicated in the prohibition of lust (only men? only lust toward married women? and so forth.). See, for example, Augustine, *On the Lord's Sermon on the Mount*, i.9.22–24 and Guelich, *The Sermon on the Mount*, 239–43.

which is not only germane to a virtue approach to morality but also explicitly addressed and further illuminated by Jesus's words in the Sermon. That topic is the moral importance of the emotions. Jesus presents a crystal clear connection between interiority and ensuing action.[29] More precisely, since there are varying facets of interiority (e.g., intentionality, addressed in Chapter 3), Jesus addresses in these two antitheses the connection between the emotions and human action. There are several different ongoing scholarly debates about the morality of the emotions, and none can be addressed in any depth here.[30] Three observations regarding these verses are offered that could contribute to those debates. First, Jesus clearly indicates the emotions are morally significant because, though they are distinct from ensuing words or action (5:22), they are intimately connected to that ensuing action.[31] Second, Jesus clearly affirms that emotions themselves, and not simply ensuing actions, can be praiseworthy or (in these cases) blameworthy.[32] Third and finally, Jesus's words provide practical guidance on the

---

[29] Chapter 3 addresses an unfortunate dichotomy posited by some biblical scholars, with Mt 5 presented as concerning external action and Mt 6 presented as concerning interiority. These first two antitheses defy such a claim. Davies and Allison reject such a division, saying Mt 5 is about both action and intention (*The Gospel According to Saint Matthew*, 513 and 524).

[30] For an example of such debate on the morality of emotions in philosophy between neo-Aristotelians and neo-Kantians, see Martha C. Nussbaum *Love's Knowledge: Essays on Philosophy and Literature* (New York: Oxford University Press, 1996), 54–105; Martha C. Nussbaum, *Therapy of Desire* (Princeton, NJ: Princeton University Press, 1996), 78–101; and Nancy Sherman, *Making a Necessity of Virtue* (Cambridge: Cambridge University Press, 1997), 24–98, 248–54. In Thomistic scholarship there have been several excellent recent books on the topic, including: Nicholas Lombardo, *The Logic of Desire: Aquinas on Emotion* (Washington, DC: The Catholic University of America Press, 2011); Diana Fritz Cates, *Aquinas on the Emotions* (Washington, DC: Georgetown University Press, 2009); and Robert Miner, *Thomas Aquinas on the Passions: A Study of* Summa Theologiae *I–II 22–48* (Cambridge: Cambridge University Press, 2011). There is an even more precise Thomistic debate on the "spontaneity" of the passions. See Gieseppe Butera, "On Reason's Control of the Passions in Aquinas's Theory of Temperance" (PhD diss., The Catholic University of America, 2001); Nicholas Kahm, "Thomas Aquinas On the Sense Appetite as Participating in Reason" (PhD diss., The Catholic University of America, 2014); Craig Steven Titus, "Passions in Christ: Spontaneity, Development, and Virtue," *The Thomist* **73** (2009): 53–87; Paul Gondreau, "The Passions and the Moral Life: Appreciating the Originality of Aquinas," *The Thomist* 71 (2007): 419–50; and, Servais Pinckaers, "Reappropriating Aquinas's Account of the Passions (1990)," in *The Pinckaers Reader*, ed. John Berkman and Craig Steven Titus (Washington, DC: The Catholic University of America Press, 2005), 273–87.

[31] See, for example, Augustine, *On the Lord's Sermon on the Mount*, i.9.24, on the stages of human action starting with emotion alone and unfolding into action. He uses Mt 5:27–28 on lust to more precisely delineate stages of human action in general, in what today we would call action theory (i.12.34–35). Luz recognizes that this notion of progression in 5:22 is dominant in the tradition, even though he discards that interpretation (*Matthew 1–7*, 283).

[32] Two questions must be distinguished here. One concerns whether all occasions of an emotion, e.g., anger, are prohibited. Despite the apparent blanket condemnation of anger

habituation of the emotions. The drastic injunctions about cutting off one's right hand or plucking out one's right eye are variously interpreted, but in any case surely represent an effort to render vicious emotions impotent.[33] More nuanced are the injunctions of the first antitheses. Jesus offers practical advice on acts of reconciliation, which the context suggests not only enjoin good action but also quell vicious anger. Surely the stages of increasingly "complete" action in 5:22 offer a path to influence the very roots of such action. In summary, these verses provide a perfect occasion to address the morality of emotion.

Back to the primary task of this section, how are these first two antitheses amenable to Luz's three ways of understanding how the new moral law fulfills the old? Does Jesus simply restore the "true meaning" of the law (1a) or "quantitatively" add material content (1b)? In other words, were prohibitions of anger and lust already part of how the Jewish law was understood, and some people (presumably the "scribes and Pharisees") had contorted a true grasp of the law to live it only outwardly and not inwardly (like the "whitewashed tombs" of Mt 23:27)? Some biblical scholars claim this is indeed the case, in which case Jesus's fulfillment of the law does indeed "bring out the true meaning" of the old law, as in Luz' first sense of fulfill.[34]

in 5:22, the bulk of the Christian tradition regards Jesus as prohibiting only vicious anger. A variety of ways, often based on this text, have been offered to delineate what constitutes virtuous or vicious anger. See William C. Mattison III, "Interpretation of Jesus' Prohibition of Anger (Matt 5:22): The Rise and Fall of the Person/Sin Distinction from Augustine to Aquinas," *Theological Studies* 68.4 (2007): 839–64. Luz (reminiscent of Jerome) rejects such a distinction between just and unjust anger, such that Jesus's words are unqualified (*Matthew 1–7*, 287; see also Davies and Allison, *The Gospel According to Saint Matthew*, 521). A second question is whether the emotion itself is liable to judgment, or rather only decisions that lead to emotions. "Whoever looks at a woman with lust" can be interpreted not as a prohibition of inordinate sexual desire per se, but the purposeful look that engenders such a disordered emotional response. Luz notes there is a strain in the tradition that "weakens" this prohibition of disordered emotions in this way (*Matthew 1–7*, 293; he unsurprisingly mentions Jerome among such thinkers). Though there is insight here that there must in some sense be "purposefulness" (or as Thomas Aquinas would say, participation in reason) for an emotional response such as lust to be sinful, nonetheless thinkers such as Thoms would hold that the lust (or anger) itself, and not simply the purposeful action leading to it, can indeed be sinful.

[33] The interpretation of Mt 5:29–30 affirmed here is that the injunctions are hyperbolic, enjoining decisive though not literal action. See Guelich, who also calls it hyperbole (*The Sermon on the Mount*, 196). For examples of traditional commentators addressing the significance of the hand vs. eye, or left vs. right, see Thomas Aquinas, *Commentary on Matthew*, 509, and Augustine, *On the Lord's Sermon on the Mount*, I.13.37–38, respectively.

[34] Luz claims that "Jesus' demand is nothing new within contemporary Jewish *parenesis*" (*Matthew 1–7*, 284; see also 296). Guelich, *The Sermon on the Mount*, 194, references rabbinic teaching against lust as well as adultery. See Davies and Allison, *The Gospel According to Saint Matthew*, 511–12 and 522 for attention to not only Jewish but contemporary Roman thought on liability for interior movements. They cite B. S. Jackson

Others claim that Jesus's explicit proscription of interior states, such as anger and lust, can indeed be understood as something "new."[35]

This provides an occasion to state how fulfill is understood here with regard to the moral law, and in doing so, identify how looking at these verses through the lens of virtue ethics can aid our understanding of the Sermon. In some ways, the question of whether the first two antitheses add "material content" to the law (1b) or not (1a) reflects a non-virtue-centered approach to morality that Fr. Servais Pinckaers, O.P. has called a "morality of obligation."[36] The primary question of such an approach is, "am I permitted to be angry or lustful or not?" The concern is whether or not we have an additional moral rule, or obligation, in play. In such an approach, there is inadequate attention to how living in accordance with the rule or obligation is in service to, indeed constitutive of, the ultimate goal of happiness.

Pinckaers supports instead what he calls a "morality of happiness." In such an approach, attention to moral obligations is important, but not primary. The central question is how can I live a good and happy life. This of course entails living according to moral rules, rules which at times are experienced as obligations. Yet even when experienced as such, the rules are ideally understood not simply as obligations to be obeyed, but as prescribing activity actually constitutive of happiness.[37] We do not kill or commit adultery because these activities are antithetical to flourishing in relationship with God and others. Moral laws proscribe activities that corrode our (individual and communal) happiness. They prescribe activities that are constitutive of such flourishing. Understood in this manner, the goal or *telos* of the law is happiness or flourishing, which is life in covenantal relationship, friendship, with God and with others. The law identifies activities that either are constitutive of or impede that flourishing.

Given this approach to morality, does the new law understood in the moral sense add new material content? Yes and no. No, in the sense that the

---

"Liability for Mere Intention in Jewish Law," in *Essays in Jewish and Comparative Legal History*, Studies in Judaism in Late Antiquity 10 (Leiden, 1975), 202–34.

[35] Luz, *Matthew 1–7*, 285 claims it is the placement of anger under the purview of binding law rather than mere *parenesis* that is new. This is unfortunately evidence of a morality of obligation described below.

[36] For more on this notion, see Servais Pinckaers, O.P., *The Sources of Christian Ethics*, 17–22, 247–48, 266–72. See also his *Morality: The Catholic View*, trans. Michael Sherwin (South Bend, IN: St. Augustine's Press, 2001), 65–75. See also William C. Mattison III, *Introducing Moral Theology: True Happiness and the Virtues* (Grand Rapids, MI: Brazos Press, 2008). 19–37.

[37] Recall from Chapter 1 Herbert McCabe's quote on this defining feature of a virtue-centered approach to morality. See his *Good Life: Ethics and the Pursuit of Happiness* (New York: Continuum, 2005), 5–6.

old law and the new law share the same goal.[38] In fact Thomas Aquinas goes as far as saying the old law "contains" the new law.[39] Hence the new law could never abolish the old. And when new activities (such as anger and lust) are identified as violations of the goal of the law, or as in conformity with the goal of the law (as we will discuss, letting our yes mean yes and our no mean no), those activities will always be compatible with the old law. However, since the new (moral) law is indeed in greater conformity with the common *telos* of the old law and new law, it may prescribe or proscribe activities not named in the old law. Again as Thomas Aquinas says, the new law's dictates are made more explicit than the old, and in that sense can be said to be "greater."[40] So yes, the new law can be said to add material content. But this is most properly understood not primarily as an additional set of obligations, but rather as further depiction of activity that is conformity to the goal of both the old law and new law alike.[41] It is the greater righteousness referenced in 5:20. It is also how to best understand the "perfection" named in 5:48.

The culmination of these Matthew 5 verses on the relationship between the old law and new law is the 5:48 injunction to "be perfect, as your heavenly Father is perfect." The immediate context for this verse is the sixth antithesis, where the new law injunction to love of enemy is presented as reflective of our heavenly Father's lack of partiality in allowing the sun to shine and rain to fall on the just and unjust. However, this final verse is also a conclusion to

---

[38] See, for example, Thomas Aquinas, *Summa Theologiae* I–II 98, 1: "the end of the Divine law is to bring man to that end which is everlasting happiness." See also, *Summa Theologiae* I–II 99, 2 "the chief intention of the Divine law is to establish man in friendship with God."

[39] Thomas Aquinas, *Summa Theologiae* I–II 107, 3.

[40] Thomas Aquinas, *Summa Theologiae* I–II 107, 3. Note here he insists that nothing prevents something greater from being contained in the old, as a seed contains the tree virtually (ad. 3).

[41] This is how to explain the abovementioned apparent discrepancy in Augustine's works. In debate with Faustus he is understandably concerned to emphasize the commonality between old law and new, so he emphasizes that the new law fulfills the old "not so that what had been lacking might be added to the law" (XVII.6). In his *On the Lord's Sermon on the Mount*, the English translation uses the unfortunate "supplementing its deficiencies," but a look at the Latin indicates no such deficiencies but rather a bringing out what is "less held:" (i.8.20) "*In hac sententia duplex sensus est; secundum utrumque tractandum est. Nam qui dicit: Non veni solvere legem sed implere, aut addendo dicit quod minus habet aut faciendo quod habet. Illud ergo prius consideremus quod primo posui. Nam qui addit quod minus habet, non utique solvit quod invenit sed magis perficiendo confirmat. Et ideo sequitur et dicit: 'Amen dico vobis, donec transeat caelum et terra, iota unum vel unus apex non transiet a lege, donec omnia fiant'* (Mt 5:18). *Dum enim fiunt etiam illa quae adduntur ad perfectionem, multo magis fiunt illa quae praemissa sunt ad inchoationem. Quod autem ait: Iota unum vel unus apex non transiet a lege, nihil potest aliud intellegi nisi vehemens expressio perfectionis....*" (Latin text is taken from *De Sermone Domini in Monte*, in *Corpus Christianorum* (Series Latina 35), ed. Almut Mutzenbecher (Turnhout: Brepols, 1967). This point is aided by a proper understanding of "perfect," treated below due to its use in 5:48 but also evident in Augustine's text cited here.

the entire set of verses treated in this chapter.[42] How is life according to the new law a way to "be perfect," and how can this be better understood in light of a virtue approach to morality?

Though "perfection" is a legitimate translation of *teleioi*, equally apt is the term "complete."[43] We are more complete in living our covenantal friendship with God (who Himself is of course fully perfect, complete) when we live the new law which fulfills the old. The terms "surpassing" righteousness (5:20) and "perfection" (5:48) form an *inclusio* around the six antitheses (5:21–48). The antitheses depict how the new law constitutes a greater, more perfect, righteousness. Thus, the concluding injunction "be perfect" is a reference to the fulfillment that is the new law. Though English connotations of perfect can suggest an impossible standard that is thus relegated to a mere ideal, the term complete more helpfully suggests a continuum of activity, such that one can be more or less complete, all the while the *telos* functioning to prompt and specify activity.[44] Luz helpfully describes perfection as found in 5:48 as a "task which all Christians face and which motivates us all."[45] According to the virtue perspective of this book, that injunction is for activity that is in greater conformity to the covenantal friendship with God and others that is the goal of the law.[46] Thus, rather than some crushing and/or impossible obligation, the injunction to be perfect enjoins us to live in greater conformity to the common *telos* of the old law and new law alike.

Before continuing with the remaining antitheses, we turn to the third of Luz's meanings for fulfill in the moral sense, namely, the claim that the new law qualitatively "completes" and "makes perfect" the old law (1c).[47] Since humanity has consistently demonstrated an inability to live out even the

---

[42] See Davies and Allison, *The Gospel According to Saint Matthew*, 508 on how six antitheses culminate in this verse.

[43] See Gerhard Delling, "τέλος" in *Theological Dictionary of the New Testament* (vol. 8), ed. Gerhard Friedrich and Geoffrey W. Bromiley (Grand Rapids, MI: William B. Eerdmans, 1968), 49–87. This aptness is especially evident in the Latin *perficio*. See Davies and Allison who say it can be translated "complete in development" (*The Gospel According to Saint Matthew*, 561–63.) Guelich prefers to translate the term as "whole" (233–37).

[44] See Chapter 3 for more on how a more remote end nonetheless specifies activity.

[45] Luz, *Matthew 1–7*, 347.

[46] Despite Luz's helpful understanding of how "be perfect" motivates activity, he demonstrates an unfortunate distrust of classical virtue ethics when he claims that *telos* in 5:48 should not be understood in the context of Greek thought on virtue, but rather a Jewish context (*Matthew 1–7*, 346). That Jewish thought contextualizes the Sermon is of course affirmed here, though Luz unfortunately assumes that context defies the possibility of classical thought on virtue illuminating this text.

[47] Luz says least about this one of his six senses, unfortunately. Given the common claim in the tradition, one noted by Luz (*Matthew 1–7*, 262), that the new law entails grace to follow it, and Luz's own claim that this third sense is a "qualitative" rather than "quantitative" change (261), Luz's third sense is understood here to mean the availability of grace to live out this moral teaching.

activity of the old law, let alone the further depiction of life in covenantal relationship or friendship with God and others offered in the new law, the new (moral) law of Christ is properly understood not only as a fuller law in terms of the activity constitutive of that goal, but also the new ability to live it. Hence, thinkers from throughout the Christian tradition have understood the new law, often in connection with St. Paul's law of grace, to be the grace of the Holy Spirit.[48] For instance, Augustine cites Rom 5:5 ("the love of God has been poured out in our hearts by the Holy Spirit who has been given to us") and immediately goes on to say:

> The law, therefore, is fulfilled either when what is commanded in it is carried out or when what was foretold in it is shown to us. For the law was given to us through Moses, but it was made grace and truth through Jesus Christ [see Jn 1:7]. Grace pertains to the fullness of love, truth to the fulfillment of the prophecies. And because both come through Jesus Christ, he did not come to destroy the law and the prophets but to fulfill them.[49]

Here Augustine refers to grace and truth from John, a consistent reference in the tradition, to explain two ways that the law is fulfilled, two ways that parallel Luz's two (sets of three each) offered here. But more immediately relevant, he describes the fulfillment of what the law commands, (that is, the moral law) as made possible through the grace of Christ.[50]

Thomas Aquinas similarly connects the new law with God's grace. He claims that the new law in writing refers to the Sermon on the Mount.[51] But most properly the new law is not a written law, but rather the grace of the Holy Spirit through faith in Christ.[52] These thinkers consistently appealed to the *old law* itself for this characterization of the new. In Jeremiah 31:31–34, we read that the Lord will make a new covenant with his people, which will entail a law "written on their hearts" (31:33).[53] Clear differentiation is made between the old law and new law, and the new law is presented as more

---

[48] An examination of the commonalities and any differences between Matthew and Paul on topics such as the new law and grace is beyond the scope of this chapter. Paul's thought is clearly more extensive on this topic, and thus commonly referenced.

[49] Augustine, *Answer to Faustus*, XVII.6. See also XIX.30 where Augustine claims the commands of the law are fulfilled "by the newness of the Spirit, who gives help and sets free the confession of the humble through confession by the grace of salvation."

[50] See also Chrysostom, *Homilies on Matthew*, XVI.3 for this claim that fulfillment occurs through the bestowal of grace to fulfill the law's commands. Though this claim is present in Luz (even if only briefly referenced), it is less common in biblical scholarship today. At times it is even rejected explicitly as "eisegetical." See, for example, Davies & Allison, *The Gospel According to Saint Matthew*, 486, n. 14.

[51] Thomas Aquinas, *Summa Theologiae* I–II 108, 3.

[52] Thomas Aquinas, *Summa Theologiae* I–II 106, 1.

[53] That connection between Jer 31 and Mt 5 can be found in contemporary biblical scholarship. See, for example, Guelich, *The Sermon on the Mount*, 140. Ez 36:26–27 is also cited in this context.

perfect or complete than the old. The primary reason for that perfection is the fact that the law is written on the people's hearts, and this interior transformation is understood to be the grace of the Holy Spirit given through faith in Christ.[54]

This attention to the new law as the graced ability to live out the activity of the law enables us to address the question of the difficulty of living out the new law, particularly when its prohibitions are even more challenging, such as anger and lust in addition to murder and adultery. Thomas Aquinas's treatment of the "burdensomeness" of the law is helpful here. He recognizes the new law more "expressly" prohibits interior acts (e.g., lust and anger) and thus may seem to be heavier. But in one of his most direct connections between the new law and virtue, Thomas Aquinas claims even these prohibitions are easier to heed for the one with virtue. He even uses the standard virtue ethics phrase, echoing Aristotle, that virtue enables one to perform acts with "pleasure and promptness."[55] The possession of virtue entails an interior transformation that makes even more outwardly difficult acts easier. He goes on to claim that this is especially true for one with love, which in this context can surely be understood to refer to charity.[56] Given his previous definition of the new law as the grace of the Holy Spirit given through Christ, Thomas Aquinas is claiming here that the new law is the graced ability (what we will call later infused virtue[57]) to perform even interior acts reflective of covenantal

---

[54] This examination of the new law as the grace of the Holy Spirit through Christ is one of the many obvious places to examine the gifts of the Holy Spirit, a crucial topic for moral theology that is not addressed extensively in this project. For more on the new law as grace of the Holy Spirit, see Servais Pinckaers, "The Return of the New Law to Moral Theology," in *The Pinckaers Reader*, ed. John Berkman and Craig Steven Titus (Washington, DC: The Catholic University of America Press, 2005), 369–84. This essay is especially helpful if read in conjunction with the one that follows it in this collection, namely, "Morality and the Movement of the Holy Spirit: Thomas's Doctrine of *Instinctus*," 385–95. In this latter essay, Pinckaers explicitly connects the grace of the Holy Spirit that is the new law to the gifts of the Holy Spirit. For two excellent recent studies of the gifts of the Holy Spirit, see James W. Stroud, "Thomas Aquinas' Exposition of the Gifts of the Holy Spirit: Developments in His Thought and Rival Interpretations" (PhD diss., The Catholic University of America, 2012), as well as John M. Meinert, "*Donum Habituale*: Grace and the Gifts of the Holy Spirit in St. Thomas Aquinas" (PhD diss., The Catholic University of America, 2015).

[55] See Thomas Aquinas, *Summa Theologiae* I–II 107, 4.

[56] For the matter of differentiating the old and new law by associating them with fear and love, respectively, see Thomas Aquinas, *Summa Theologiae* I–II 107, 1, ad. 2. This answer actually corroborates the meaning of the new law as the grace to fulfill its precepts. This response also makes some fascinating claims about the possibility of people under the old law having charity and the grace of the Hoy Spirit, a point relevant later in this chapter.

[57] Note that not all graced ability is the habitual grace called infused virtue. For more on actual as distinct from habitual grace, and operative as distinct from cooperative grace, see Meinert, "*Donum Habituale*." The claim here is not that the new law of grace is identical to infused virtue, but rather the claim is that it includes infused virtue, as particularly evident in this passage in Thomas Aquinas.

friendship with God, and thus is actually less burdensome than the old, as Jesus indicates when he says "my yoke is easy and my burden light."[58]

All the principle elements of how the new moral law fulfills the old are now evident in this treatment of antitheses one and two. The new law shares a common *telos* with the old, and both prescribe activity constitutive of that *telos*. Thus the new law can be said to enjoin the true meaning of the old (1a). Yet the new law enjoins activity that is a more complete, more perfect, participation in that *telos* (1b). Finally, as signaled in the old law itself and particularly Jer 31, the new law is primarily a law written on hearts, which is the grace of Christ (1c). In summary, the moral sense of the new law is the grace of the Holy Spirit and the activity constitutive of covenantal friendship with God and others that it animates.

2. THIRD, FOURTH, FIFTH, AND SIXTH ANTITHESES — FULFILL-MENT DESPITE DIFFERENT MATERIAL CONTENT Now that the dynamic of how the new law fulfills the old as evidenced in these first two antitheses is established, we turn to the remaining antitheses, since at first glance Jesus's ensuing injunctions seem not only to add new material to the new law but to repudiate the old law.[59] The basic claim here, facilitated by a virtue ethics approach to morality and law, is that while the prescriptions of the new law may appear to repudiate the old in terms of their material content, attention to how both old law and new law are teleologically oriented toward a common goal reveals how the new law fulfills but does not abolish the old.[60]

The third antithesis (Mt 5:31–32) notes that while it was said "whoever divorces his wife must give her a bill of divorce," Jesus claims divorcing one's wife leads her to adultery, and divorcing and remarrying is committing adultery.

---

[58] Thomas Aquinas, *Summa Theologiae* I–II 107, 4.

[59] In a footnote on Mt 5:21–48 (p. 1343), the editors of the *Catholic Study Bible* (New York: Oxford University Press, 2011) make this striking (and disappointing) claim: "Six examples of the conduct demanded of the Christian disciple. . . . Three of them accept the Mosaic law but extend or deepen it (Mt 5:21–22; 27–28; 43–44); three reject it as a standard of conduct for the disciple (Mt 5:31–32; 33–37; 38–39)." It is unclear why the editors place the sixth antithesis with the first two as "extending" or "deepening" the old law when in some sense it seems most materially different as addressed below (hating vs. loving the enemy). Regardless, though their claim that the new law "rejects" the old is denied here (as it is by Jesus in Mt 5:17), this passage is further evidence of how the first two antitheses are more easily read in continuity with the old law than the last four. For further affirmation that the final four warrant distinct treatment due to the less obviously continuity of activity between old law and new law, see Davies and Allison, *The Gospel According to Saint Matthew*, 507. See also Boxall for how the first, second, and sixth are distinct from the third, fourth and fifth, and yet also how all six are best understood as Matthean "radicalization" rather than any abrogation (*Discovering Matthew*, 130–31).

[60] As will be evident in the next section, this interpretation is also key for understanding how the new law fulfills the old ceremonial law.

The fourth antithesis (Mt 5:33–37) claims that it was said do not swear falsely, but make good to the Lord on all that you vow, and Jesus says to his audience not to swear at all. In the fifth (Mt 5:38–42), while it has been said an eye for an eye and tooth for a tooth, Jesus enjoins his hearers to offer no resistance to one who is evil. Finally, in the sixth antithesis (Mt 5:43–47), Jesus notes it was said to love the neighbor and hate the enemy, but he says love the enemy and pray for those who persecute you. In these final four antitheses, we have seeming conflict between the material content of the old law and new: divorce, no divorce; oaths, no oaths; measured retaliation, no retaliation; hatred of enemy, love of enemy. How can the new law be said to fulfill the old in these instances? I examine the last four antitheses in different order so as to make a set of progressing points about the new law's fulfillment of the old even in these cases.

The set of points I make are the following. While treating the fifth antithesis, I describe how the old law "limits" the way certain activities are done so as to proscribe doing the activity in a manner antithetical to the goal of the old law and new law alike. Since it does not command the activity at hand be done in this "limited" way, the activity of the new law may be different in material content but shares the same goal and indeed is a more perfect instantiation of the goal of old and new law alike. While treating the fourth antithesis, I note how the new law may offer prudential guidance in best attaining the goal of the old law and new law alike. The third antithesis provides an occasion to note the importance of different eras in salvation history for how the law prescribes activity toward covenantal friendship with God. The sixth antithesis points back to Luz's first two senses of fulfill, namely the restoration of the true meaning of the old law and also an adding of material content or "scope" to the old law. This last antithesis also points toward a theme prominent in the next chapter of the Sermon, namely the importance of faith in our heavenly Father for living out the Sermon.

a. Fifth Antithesis – Prescribing Limits and Enjoining Greater Perfection

I begin with the fifth antithesis, since literature abounds on the seemingly stark difference between the *lex talonis* and the famous "turn the other cheek" *parenesis*. As is commonly noted with regard to this antithesis, the old law prescription is not a command but a manner of limiting or governing the activity at hand so that it be done more in accordance with its purported goal.[61] If resistance is purportedly oriented toward the restoration of justice after an injustice has occurred, a way to ensure that goal is better met is through measuring rectification of injustice in accord with the original offense, rather than allowing it to escalate into vendetta and

---

[61] For a thorough treatment of the *lex talonis* as well as an extensive bibliography, see Betz, *The Sermon on the Mount*, 275–83.

increasing violence. This is the way that the material action prescribed by the old law (an eye for an eye) is constitutive of the goal of restoration of justice.

If the old law injunction governs human activity in accordance with that goal, is Jesus's injunction a countermanding of the old law? It is argued here that it is not, though of course that depends on how one interprets "offer no resistance to one who is evil." Scholarship on how to interpret this verse is voluminous, and no attempt is made here to adjudicate it.[62] One position focuses on a proper translation and understanding of "resistance" in "offer no resistance to one who is evil" (5:39). Hans Dieter Betz differentiates retaliation from simple resistance and says the passage "clearly presents Jesus as unequivocally prohibiting retaliation," which he says means "to return evil with evil."[63] This position emphasizes the common goal and thus compatibility of the old and new law, yet it is unclear how the new law fulfills the old. Though this interpretation is affirmed here, more needs to be said on how the new law fulfills the old. The new law fulfills the old by affirming the non-centrality of a proportionally measured response. Measured "retribution," to use Betz's term for permissible rectification of injustice, is not the main purpose, and thus it is not required. Therefore, retribution can be abandoned if the rectification of injustice can be otherwise achieved. On this interpretation retribution can also be undertaken if necessary for reconciliation, and indeed such activity would be constitutive of justice.[64] But even then the forceful response would not be the ultimate point.[65]

---

[62] For a sample of such scholarship at the nexus of biblical interpretation and moral theology, see Stassen and Gushee, *Kingdom Ethics*, 149–74 and Richard B. Hayes, *The Moral Vision of the New Testament: A Contemporary Introduction to New Testament Ethics* (New York: Harper Collins, 1996), 317–46.

[63] Betz, *The Sermon on the Mount*, 281.

[64] For a helpful example of recent scholarship on the use of force as an expression of justice and politics oriented toward peace, rather than any abdication of these, see Joseph E. Capizzi, *Politics, Justice and War: Christian Governance and the Ethics of Warfare* (Oxford: Oxford University Press, 2015).

[65] This position assumes retribution can be licitly undertaken if needed, which is, of course, contrary to pacifist interpretations of this passage as prohibiting any forceful rectification of injustice. Though such a position is not affirmed here primarily out of concern to affirm continuity between the old law and new, pacifism has a long and distinguished history in Christianity. For an example of recognizing the potential validity of this position even while affirming the possibility of forceful rectification of injustice, see the U.S. Bishops' document *The Harvest of Justice is Sown in Peace: A Reflection of the National Conference of Catholic Bishops on the Tenth Anniversary of the Challenge of Peace* (Washington, DC: The U.S. Conference of Catholic Bishops, 1994), pt. I, sec. B. While the attempt to recognize both just war and pacifist traditions in Christianity is laudable, it seems some recognition that they are ultimately incompatible is necessary. If the pacifist position were to be true, note it would not defeat the argument offered here as to the way the new law fulfills the old, but rather simply shift correct interpretation of this antithesis to a dynamic described below with regard to the third antithesis on divorce.

This hopelessly brief treatment leaves scores of questions unaddressed, but it suffices to make the point relevant to this chapter. No matter what one's position in debates over the nature and permissibility of resistance, Jesus's words are understood as oriented toward more a perfect reinstantiation of justice, not as any disavowal of that endeavor.[66] The new law injunction shares the goal of the old, but more completely, more perfectly instantiates that goal, hence fulfilling not abolishing the law. What the old law prescribes is best understood as a "limit."[67] It cordons off what is always antithetical to the goal of the old law and new law alike by providing a measure that must be observed. What is said about this fifth antithesis holds true of the remaining ones (and indeed the two examined above).

Two things can be said about this sense in which the new law fulfills the old. First, the new law remains in accord with that limit even if it prescribes activity materially different than that which is named as guarding the limit. One who offers no resistance does not violate "an eye for an eye."[68] One who does not swear at all does not swear falsely, and so forth. Both Augustine and Thomas Aquinas observe that the limits set by the old law are not commands but permissions. They prohibit activities (such as marriage, rectification of injustice, and so forth) from being done in a manner that defies their goal, but in so naming those limits do not command them to be done in that "limited" way.[69] Note the assumption here is that the old law proscribes something that always violates covenantal friendship with God and others in God. In the parlance of Catholic moral theology, it names an absolute norm, a way of doing some activity that is always corrosive of the goal of that activity. Yet the new law enjoins a way of doing that activity that need not be an absolute norm but is a more perfect way of doing the activity, in terms of instantiating the goal of that activity. I will return to this point in my discussion of the fourth antithesis and prudence. Yet given this distinction between what is required and what is simply enjoined as a more perfect action, a second point is in order on the counsels of perfection, which are so commonly associated with the antitheses.

Second, this is the most fitting place to address an interpretation of the new law that became commonplace in the medieval period, namely, the

---

[66] Betz is exemplary here: "There can be no question that total nonresistance to evil constitutes an irrational and unjustifiable position incompatible with the rest of early Christian teaching and its numerous admonitions to combat, avoid, or escape from evil" (*The Sermon on the Mount*, 280).

[67] Thomas Aquinas, *Summa Theologiae* I–II 107, 2, ad. 2 "For the Law fixed a limit to revenge, by forbidding men to seek vengeance unreasonably."

[68] See Davies and Allison, *The Gospel According to Saint Matthew*, 507 on how obedience to the new law does not constitute disobedience to the old.

[69] Thomas Aquinas, *Summa Theologiae* I–II 107, 2, ad. 2. See Augustine, *On the Lord's Sermon on the Mount*, i.16.43.

notion of counsels of perfection. Though the concept of acting in greater conformity with the goal of the law than is specified by the commandment is clearly present before the Middle Ages, the naming and further development of the counsels occurs most famously in Thomas Aquinas.[70] In one of the more beautiful passages in the *Summa*, Thomas Aquinas first locates the scriptural basis for the counsels in Proverbs:

> The counsels of a wise friend are of great use, according to Prov. (27:9): "Ointment and perfumes rejoice the heart: and the good counsels of a friend rejoice the soul." But Christ is our wisest and greatest friend. Therefore His counsels are supremely useful and becoming.[71]

The notion is further connected by Thomas Aquinas to New Testament texts such as the antitheses, but especially the Mt 19 story of the rich young man, who claims to have observed the commandments since his youth, but is then invited by Christ into further perfection. Thomas Aquinas defines the counsels in distinction to commandments. Whereas the latter are always required since they concern matters *necessary* to gain eternal happiness,[72] the counsels enjoin us to activities that enable us to attain this end in a "better and more expedient" manner.[73] Thus, though the counsels enjoin more perfect activity, they are not obligatory as the commandments are.

The counsels have fallen on hard times in post-conciliar Catholic moral theology, mainly because they have been understood in a manualist perspective as part of a two-tiered morality. In such an approach, the primary concern is what is obligatory: commandments are; counsels are not. If morality is primarily about what is obligatory, the counsels are optional. As noted above, recent Catholic moral theologians such as Fr. Servais Pinckaers, O.P. have decried a morality focused on obligation. A morality of obligation focuses primarily on what is obligatory or not, with morality concerned solely about the former, and with the latter understood as matters of spirituality

---

[70] See Thomas Aquinas, *Summa Theologiae* I–II 108, 4. For a brief and helpful overview in contemporary biblical scholarship of the notion of counsel as related to the Sermon, see Luz, *Matthew 1–7*, 219–20. Luz claims the term counsel is first employed in relation to the Sermon with Rupert of Deutz c. 1100. While this attribution to Rupert of Deutz with regard to the Sermon may be accurate, the concept precedes the Middle Ages. For instance, Thomas Aquinas, *Summa Theologiae* I–II 108, 2, ad. 3 cites Augustine's *On the Harmony of the Gospels*. See Augustine, *Harmony of the Gospels*, in *Nicene and Post-Nicene Fathers of the Christian Church* (vol. 6), trans. S. D. F. Salmond and ed. Philip Schaff (New York: Charles Scribner's Sons, 1908), ii.30.71–74, esp. 73 (pp. 136–38) for treatment of the difference between Christ's commands and those actions that are not required.

[71] Thomas Aquinas, *Summa Theologiae* I–II 108, 4 s.c.

[72] Though commonly translated as "bliss," the Latin term is "*beatitudinem aeternum*," I–II 108, 4.

[73] See Thomas Aquinas, *Summa Theologiae* I–II 108, 4 (translation mine): "*Consilia vero oportet esse de illis per quae melius et expeditius potest homo consequi finem praedictum.*"

or asceticism. In a morality of happiness approach there is a recognition that both obligatory actions (which indeed there are) and more perfect actions are oriented toward a common goal (eternal happiness).

The counsels have also fallen upon hard times recently since from a manualist perspective these two tiers are then commonly associated with different states of life: the commandments are for the laity; the counsels are for the religious and/or ordained. And since Vatican II's Constitution on the Church *Lumen Gentium* made evident that the evangelical counsels of poverty, chastity, and obedience apply to all believers even as lived differently, anything associated with a rigid two-tiered morality has been dismissed in more recent Catholic moral theology.[74]

This is not the place to offer any rehabilitation of the counsels of perfection. But two points here might contribute to that endeavor before returning to the immediate topic of this chapter. First, though commonly associated with a morality of obligation, the counsels need not be presented in that way. If Pinckaers is correct that St. Thomas's virtue-based moral theology was exemplary of a morality of happiness, then they cannot be understood in that manner within his thought. In other words, their defining characteristic should not be "not obligatory," but rather "more perfectly participating in that toward which obligations also orient us." Second, the counsels similarly need not be grafted onto a problematic two-tiered morality rightly decried by *Lumen Gentium*. Indeed, that Vatican II Constitution is accurately read not as a dismissal of the counsels but as an invitation to all of the faithful (not just religious and/or ordained) to live them.

What does this chapter's argument about the fulfillment of the moral law contribute to any such treatment of the counsels? As should be evident now, the argument of this chapter is that the new law is a more complete, more perfect participation in the goal of covenantal friendship with God and neighbor, a goal shared with the old law. The new law depicts activity more fully constitutive of that goal, and it is even primarily understood as the grace to enable such activity to occur. To the extent that the counsels name (graced) activity that is more perfectly constitutive of eternal happiness, this chapter contributes to a more accurate understanding of the counsels, one not rooted in a morality of obligation perspective.

b. Fourth Antithesis – The New Law and Prudence

Turning to the fourth antithesis, is Jesus's injunction against oaths a repudiation of the old law commandment not to swear falsely? This question can be largely addressed by the previous part's analysis of the fifth antithesis. With regard to swearing, both the old law commandment and new law injunction

---

[74] See William Mattison III and David Cloutier, "Method in Catholic Moral Theology after *Veritatis Splendor*: A Review Essay," *Journal of Catholic Moral Theology* 1.1 (2012): 170–92.

share the goal of honest and honorable communication. The old law is not a command to offer oaths but a commandment against swearing falsely. It sets a limit, proscribing a way (swearing falsely) of doing an activity (communication) that is always corrosive of the goal of that activity. As to the new law injunction, one who takes no oaths does not abolish the old law but observes it by not swearing falsely. But by not swearing and instead letting one's "no mean no and yes mean yes," one is acting in a materially different manner than the one swearing truthfully, yet more perfectly instantiating the same goal as that person.

This is not to say discussion over the proper place of oaths in the Christian life is unwarranted. But reminiscent of debates over the use of force, whatever one's position on that question, to be in accordance with the new law (and old law) one's communication must be honest. Also reminiscent of the fifth antithesis is the question of whether the new law injunction here posits what moralists call an "absolute norm," such that swearing is never permissible because it is an activity that can never be constitutive of virtue (in this case justice). Recall with regard to force that this is commonly addressed by defining resistance not as the use of force per se, but as unjust "retaliation." That way of disavowing the presence of an absolute norm is not available here since there is less ambiguity in the term swearing. This is troubling since it would mean the new law repudiates the old by forbidding activity that could be in accordance with the old. How are we so sure the new law injunctions are not absolute norms? I offer three initial observations and then a further reflection on prudence.

The first observation is admittedly tautological (that is, the new law is not abolishing the old because then it would be abolishing the old). If the new law did enjoin an absolute, it would indeed seem to repudiate activity in accordance with the old law. And since Jesus Himself starts this section of the Sermon claiming he will not abolish but fulfill, it does not seem reasonable to assume he is abolishing the old law here.

Second, the vast majority of authoritative thinkers in the Christian tradition have not interpreted this verse to prohibit all swearing.[75] There are of course exceptions.[76] And particularly with the argument offered in the next part on the difference that era in salvation history makes, perhaps the rarer interpretation is accurate. Perhaps in this era of grace in Christ, oaths and forceful resistance – which, according to this position, have always been

---

[75] Luz claims "the history of influence is characterized by attempts to remove the sting of the text and to make its demand easier or to evade it" (*Matthew 1–7*, 318). "The entire tradition of the Great Church since the early Middle Ages almost unanimously set Matt 5:33–37 aside and accepted oaths..." (320). He surveys various strategies to do so, including the stereotypically Catholic "two tier" approach as well as the Lutheran "two kingdoms" approach.

[76] One noteworthy exception is Chrysostom, *Homilies on Matthew* XVII.5 (105–10).

antithetical to covenantal friendship with God and others in God – are now able to be foresworn completely by humanity. But reminiscent of the antithesis on offering no resistance, the injunction not to swear at all has been interpreted in the bulk of the Christian tradition as not prohibiting all swearing.

Third and finally, the ensuing verses that describe the swearing prohibited by Jesus do not focus on swearing per se, but rather suggest that the swearing proscribed by Jesus entails at least an implicit assumption of providential control over reality that is illegitimate for human persons. It is God, not humanity, who is provident over heaven, earth, Jerusalem, and even our own bodies. In this context, Jesus's injunction not to swear but rather let one's no mean no and yes mean yes is an injunction to communicate in a manner that reverently recognizes our creatureliness rather than pridefully assumes the truth (which is the point of human communication) is malleable to our manipulation or management.[77]

In sum, what is most important for this chapter is establishing how the new law fulfills the old. Regardless of one's position on the morality of oaths in the Christian life, the current chapter's virtue-centric perspective enables us to understand better how the new law fulfills the old by enjoining activity more perfectly constitutive of the goal of the old law and new law alike.

Assuming that Jesus's words in Mt 5:34 do not offer an absolute prohibition, why does he say do not swear "at all?" This question helps introduce the relevance of prudence for the antitheses. One of the more common claims about passages such as this, in Christian thinkers but also in Jewish interpreters on related matters, is that the law offers prudential guidance. The well-known Jewish expression for this is "putting a fence around the law."[78] In other words, setting a more stringent standard of action than absolutely necessary by law can be a more prudent, or "better and more expedient," way to observe the law. This claim is echoed in the tradition of commentary on this antithesis. Augustine claims "the warning against swearing is a guard against the sin of perjury."[79] Thomas Aquinas, in naming the ways the new law fulfills the old, says the second way is that the Lord prescribes the "safest way of complying with the statutes of the Old Law. Thus the Old Law forbade

---

[77] Luz comes close to this rationale for Jesus's repudiation of oaths when he says that Jesus is most "concerned about the sanctification of God's name and God's majesty" (*Matthew 1–7*, 316). See also Chrysostom, *Homilies on Matthew*, XVII.5 (106) who says Jesus has "withdrawn him from swearing by his head ... and signifying that thou art not master even of thyself." For more on a managerial approach to temporal activities that defies our Heavenly Father's provident gratuity, see Chapter 4.

[78] See Luz, *Matthew 1–7*, 318–19 (noting that Calvin is a prominent Christian promoter of this view).

[79] Augustine, *Answer to Faustus*, XIX.25.

perjury: and this is more safely avoided, by abstaining altogether from swearing, except in a necessary situation."[80]

A task of prudence is to set and choose the means to the common end of old law and new law alike. Christ the teacher instructs his audience on how to do so more prudently with regard to an activity like communication. Whether or not one is persuaded by Augustine's and Thomas Aquinas's claims that swearing does not violate an absolute norm (hence it is permissible in "case of necessity"), one can clearly hold this view and still affirm that what the new law enjoins is a more perfect (even if not the only) way to live out the goal of the old.[81] From a morality of obligation perspective, this type of new law fulfillment can be understood as not obligatory but safer in increasing the chances one avoids violating a commandment. Yet from the virtue perspective offered here, the new law injunction can be understood as enjoining prudent activity that constitutes a more perfect participation of the person in the ultimate end sought.

c. Third Antithesis – Morality in a New Era

Turning further back to the third antithesis, we find one of the most heavily analyzed passages in Matthew's gospel.[82] These verses are crucial for any discussion of divorce as well as divorce and remarriage. There is a seeming absolute prohibition of divorce and remarriage, and yet also the famous "exception clause" (Mt 5:32: "unless the marriage is unlawful"), the meaning of which has spawned extensive debate. None of that literature can be engaged here in any significant fashion. The immediate question for our purposes is what is the relationship between Jesus's teaching on divorce and the old law teaching on divorce? More specifically, given that divorce is evidently permissible in the old law and at the very least only very rarely permissible in Jesus's teachings, do Jesus's teachings repudiate or countermand the old law?[83] Again, the answer is no, for the reasons mentioned above.

---

[80] Thomas Aquinas, *Summa Theologiae* I–II 107, 2 (translation partially mine): "*Adimplevit dominus praecepta legis, ordinando quomodo tutius observaretur quod lex vetus. Sicut lex vetus statuerat ut homo non peiuraret, et hoc tutius observatur si omnino a iuramento abstineat, nisi in casu necessitates.*"

[81] On swearing being at times necessary, see Thomas Aquinas, *Summa Theologiae* I–II 107, 2 and also Augustine *On the Lord's Sermon on the Mount*, i.17.51. On the common goal of old and new law alike, Thomas Aquinas, *Summa Theologiae* I–II 107, 3 as well as Augustine, *Answer to Faustus*, XIX.25: "What the law wanted to accomplish, namely that no one would sin by committing perjury, would be more easily preserved if one did not swear."

[82] Luz notes in his treatment of this antithesis that roughly sixty books were produced on this passage in the two decades prior to his writing (*Matthew 1–7*, 301), with the majority attempting the reconcile the text with Catholic teaching on divorce.

[83] I say at the very least rarely rather than wholly prohibited given the presence of the exception clause here and Mt 19. Of course many scholars interpret that clause in a manner more akin to contemporary Catholic teaching on indissolubility, such that the

Reminiscent of both the fifth and fourth antitheses, in this one both old law and new law prescriptions share a common goal, namely the preservation of marriage. Much as "an eye for an eye" is best understood as a way to limit retaliation with an eye toward the goal of justice, the old law procedures for divorce are consistently interpreted as a limit on divorce.[84] From more of a morality of obligation perspective, we can observe that one who does not divorce does not violate the requirement that anyone who divorces must give the wife a bill of divorce; after all, there is no divorce. But from a virtue-oriented morality of happiness perspective that regards rules more teleologically, we can describe more robustly how Jesus's teaching both shares a common goal with the old law and more completely instantiates that goal through the prohibition of divorce.

I assume here that Jesus's new law prohibition of divorce as well as divorce and remarriage does indeed posit an absolute norm, unlike his prohibitions of resistance or swearing. The new law injunction is not understood simply as a non-obligatory counsel or a prudential way to avoid violating an absolute norm (though *a fortiori* it is these too). This obviously reflects an interpretation of this passage in line with the Catholic practice of prohibiting divorce. On what basis is this interpretation made? As noted at the start of this chapter and this very part, adjudicating the extraordinarily complex issues addressed in Mt 5:21–48 is beyond the scope of this chapter. But what is within the scope of this chapter is what such a challenging interpretation must assume about the new law, which is true of all the antitheses and would have to be true of this one for the Catholic interpretation to hold. It returns us to the new law understood as the grace of the Holy Spirit.

Interpretation of this passage is commonly conducted with the parallel passage in Mt 19:3–12 on divorce. Again we find extensive scholarship on Jesus's position on divorce as well as topics such as the exception clause (19:9). But most relevant here is Jesus's recognition of the reason for the difference in his teaching and the old law. Acknowledging the old law teaching on divorce, Jesus says it was due to the people's hardness of heart that Moses permitted (that is, did not command) divorce.[85] Jesus references Genesis 2 to explain how from the beginning it was not so, culminating in

---

"divorce" permitted by Jesus in Matthew is more a declaration of nullity given an unlawful marriage. Adjudicating that debate is not the task here. Yet it should be noted lest one think this latter interpretation is simply reading a Catholic theology of marriage into Mt 5 & 19 that this is a position affirmed in even certain non-Catholic contemporary biblical scholarship (e.g., Luz, *Matthew 1–7*, 308).

[84] See, for example, Betz, *The Sermon on the Mount*, 246 and 258 and Guelich, *The Sermon on the Mount*, 198–99.

[85] See Betz, *The Sermon on the Mount*, 256 on the importance of the old law permitting yet not commanding divorce. Betz claims further on that "the supposition that Jesus' prohibition against divorce contradicted the Torah is explicitly denied in Mark and Matthew" (258).

the famous verse "what God has joined together, no human being must separate" (19:6).[86] Thus the old and new law both prescribe activity directed toward a common goal, with the old law "tolerating" divorce due to human weakness.[87]

This raises the obvious question, if Moses permitted divorce due to hardness of heart, what has changed such that Jesus can now teach against divorce? Presumably there is some newfound ability to live out the teaching on marriage that had not existed. That sense of fulfill as applied to the new law is of course the one that corresponds to Luz' third sense, namely, the new law's qualitative difference as a law of grace making possible what was otherwise not possible before. Therefore, this antithesis is a fitting occasion to note another way that the new law fulfills the old law. As with all antitheses but perhaps most evidently here, the new law provides the grace of Christ to make possible what was not possible (at least for all) and thus could not have been commanded in the era of the old law. Once again, this does not explain why the new law injunction can be read as an absolute norm in some cases (third antithesis) and not others (fourth and fifth antitheses). But it does address another important way the new law fulfills the old. Having mentioned the importance of stages in salvation history for the fulfillment of the new law, and a new law sacrament (that is, marriage), we have a ready transition to the next part of this chapter on the new law as fulfillment of the ceremonial law. But we first conclude this review of the antitheses with a brief examination of the sixth and final antithesis.

d. Sixth Antithesis – Restoring the True Meaning

As to the sixth antithesis, we have here perhaps the most challenging case of where the material content of Jesus's injunction seems to repudiate or abolish the old law. Jesus says "you have heard it was said to love the neighbor and hate the enemy, but I say to you love your enemy and pray for those who persecute you." While in the previous three antitheses, it can be said that one avoids violating the old law in observing the new (e.g., one who does not swear does not swear falsely), in this case the positive injunction to hate the enemy appears countermanded by the positive injunction to love the enemy.

---

[86] See Luz, *Matthew 1–7*, 302 on how "Moses' permission ... is coordinated with and subordinated to Jesus' proclamation of the original will of God." See also Betz, *The Sermon on the Mount*, 255–57. Guelich also connects this passage to Mt 19:6, yet unfortunately concludes "Jesus does not merely 'radicalize' or extend the Law's demand; he actually *sets aside* the letter of the Law..." (202, emphasis added; see also 210–11).

[87] For this language of God "tolerating" divorce, see Matthew Levering, *Christ's Fulfillment of Torah and Temple: Salvation According to Thomas Aquinas* (Notre Dame, IN: University of Notre Dame Press, 2002), 26 (and n. 47).

Biblical scholars commonly note that there is no explicit injunction to hate the enemy in the old law.[88] Though this solution may remove the new law's abolishing of the old, it renders Jesus ignorant of the old law!

It is this antithesis that is most amenable to interpretation in Luz's first sense of the new law fulfilling the old, namely, getting at the true meaning of the old law. "You have heard it said" refers to the divine law as found in scripture in most antitheses. But it need not in every case. And here it evidently does not. It seems to refer to a common interpretation of the old law in the rabbinic tradition.[89] Therefore, here Jesus would indeed be fulfilling by restoring the true meaning of the old law.[90] Lest this seem inaccurate since it is not in line with how other antitheses present the new law as fulfilling the old, it should be noted that this interpretation of the sixth antithesis is not novel. Thomas Aquinas explicitly offers it, noting that Jesus's statement of the old law refers to a false interpretation of the old law by the Pharisees, since we are commanded to hate sin, not a person.[91] Contemporary Biblical scholars affirm this position as well.[92]

Two more observations are warranted on how the new law fulfills the old in this sixth antithesis. First, even if Jesus corrects a popular assumption or rabbinic interpretation of the old law as prescribing only love of neighbor to the exclusion of enemy, it is also the case that the expansive scope of the love command to include even the enemy is emphasized in this presentation of the new law. Luz claims that love of enemy is so central to Christian discipleship that it was assumed in the early church to constitute the "basic law" of faith.[93] He claims it is the climax of Jesus's presentation of the greater righteousness as presented in the antitheses.[94] These claims may seem to suggest not only newness of the new law but discontinuity with the old.

---

[88] Guelich, *The Sermon on the Mount*, 225–26; Luz, *Matthew 1–7*, 343; Betz, *The Sermon on the Mount*, 30; and Davies and Allison, *The Gospel According to Saint Matthew*, 549.

[89] For this claim that "hate your enemy" represents rabbinic interpretation, as well as speculation as to whose interpretation (including possibly an Essene target), see Guelich, *The Sermon on the Mount*, 226 and Betz, *The Sermon on the Mount*, 303–4. Betz (304) supports Luz (345) that "hate your enemy" is a rhetorical counter formulation to "love your neighbor."

[90] Augustine (*On the Lord's Sermon on the Mount*, i.21.71–72) considers the related question of whether Jesus's injunction to love the enemy contradicts passages in scripture that seem to enjoin evil on the enemy, and he concludes these passages prophetically predict rather than enjoin. "Otherwise ... divine Scripture would appear self-contradictory, a thing that cannot be" (i.22.76).

[91] Thomas Aquinas, *Summa Theologiae* I–II 107, 2, ad. 2.

[92] Luz says of this sixth antithesis "With none of the other antitheses does the 'Protestant' thesis that the Antitheses are not directed against the Old Testament but against Jewish interpretation have as much support" (*Matthew 1–7*, 344).

[93] Luz, *Matthew 1–7*, 347. Here he references Tertullian.

[94] Luz, *Matthew 1–7*, 340. See also 345 where he claims love of enemies is the fulfillment which belongs to the greater righteousness.

Yet Betz best captures the simultaneous continuity between old law and new and yet innovation of the new law in the Sermon:

> The passage is a classic example of Jesus' exegesis of the Torah: far from breaking with the Torah, he interpreted it in terms of Jewish hermeneutics of the time in order to propose a startlingly innovative interpretation that is nonetheless compatible with common sense.[95]

In restoring the true meaning of the law, showing "innovation" in explicitly expanding the old law's scope, and presumably assuming reliance on the grace of the Holy Spirit to live out this challenging activity, the love of enemy as found in the sixth antithesis is a perfect example of the new law's moral fulfillment of the old.

Second, this sixth and final antithesis most explicitly ties the new law's prescribed activity to imitation of our heavenly Father. This theme of articulating who God is to govern human activity that is faithful to this God is discussed most explicitly in Chapter 4. Yet it is also addressed in the next section on grouping the antitheses, where I point out that this antithesis mimics the fourth antithesis in ascribing a rationale for new law activity to an accurate understanding of who God is and who we are in relation to God. As Guelich notes, it enjoins the audience to the limitless love that characterizes God.[96] Guelich also notes that it references the reward of the seventh beatitude, the peacemakers who become children of God. Guelich claims that "sonship" is properly understood eschatologically as not only a present reality but also a future promise.[97] In imitating our heavenly Father's indiscriminate love, we become more perfect, or complete, as our heavenly Father is perfect.

In summary, having reviewed the six antithesis, how does the new law fulfill the old with regard or the moral sense of the law? It is argued here, with great similarity to the work of Luz[98] and sharing much in common with classical figures such as Augustine and Thomas Aquinas, that the old law and new law share the same *telos* of covenantal friendship with God and others in God. Both prescribe activity by which believers participate in that goal. The new law fulfills the old law by prescribing activity in more perfect conformity to that goal. Luz's three ways that the new law fulfills the old, described here as how human activity can be in greater conformity to that goal, are evident in the antitheses.

---

[95] Betz, *The Sermon on the Mount*, 309. For a contrary view, see Guelich, *The Sermon on the Mount*, 229, who claims that love of enemy is set by Matthew "over and against" the Old Testament's love command.

[96] Guelich, *The Sermon on the Mount*, 254.

[97] Guelich, *The Sermon on the Mount*, 231.

[98] Note the three characteristics that follow do not line up with Luz's three distinct ways fulfill can be used with reference to Jesus's teaching. The third here aligns with the third for Luz. But the first two describe different ways that activity is more perfectly in conformity with the goal, whether or not that "quantitatively" entails new material content.

First, the new law may restore the true meaning of the law. This is especially evident in the sixth antithesis where a problematic interpretation of love of neighbor is countermanded. But it is also evident wherever Jesus offers prudential guidance (e.g., "do not swear at all") on how to achieve the common goal of old law and new law alike. It is even evident where Jesus enjoins the fullest scope of the old law's goal, as when wholehearted (aggressive and desirous) activity is proscribed, or when the love command's fullest implications toward even the enemy are stated.

These lead to Luz's second sense, where Jesus seemingly quantitatively adds material content to the law, as with anger and lust, or forsaking divorce, swearing, and retribution. But as is hopefully evident from the above analysis, though Jesus prescribes or proscribes activity that may differ in material content, it is but a more complete participation in the goal of old law and new law alike. Third and finally, as best evidenced by the third antithesis on divorce but surely true of all six, the new law fulfills the old since it is the grace of the Holy Spirit that enables one to live in conformity with that goal of eternal happiness, which though challenging and a sacrifice in this life is ultimately most life-giving.

C. FULFILLMENT OF THE CEREMONIAL LAW

All of this mention of a newfound ability to live the moral law raises the question of who Jesus Christ is, a topic taken up at the end of the chapter. But it also directs us to the ceremonial law, since that newfound ability has everything to do with who Christ is as the fulfillment of the law. Examining the fulfillment of the ceremonial law is the task for this brief part. It correlates with Luz's second group of three interpretations of the term fulfill, in reference to Jesus's ministry as distinct from his teachings.

That correlation actually requires some explanation since it may initially seem unwarranted. After all, the old ceremonial law prescribes acts by believers in worship, whereas Luz's second group of three understandings of fulfill concerns how Christ's own life and ministry fulfills the law and prophets. It is true that Luz there refers to the way that the life (and death and resurrection) of Christ fulfills the law, a task for the final section of this chapter. So why connect Luz's second group with the ceremonial law?

There are two reasons. First, despite the obvious attention in the antitheses to the moral law, when Christ says he has come to fulfill not abolish the law and prophets in Mt 5:17, he speaks of the law in general, and not simply the moral law. So Christians from the very beginning of Christianity have recognized the need to explain how Christ fulfills the law in the ceremonial as well as moral sense. The easiest way to explain why Christians do not continue to observe the old ceremonial law would be to interpret Mt 5:17 to mean that Jesus only refers to the moral law.[99] Yet they have not done this.[100] Any treatment of the fulfillment of the law must address the ceremonial law.

Second, it is legitimate to correlate the fulfillment of the ceremonial law with Luz's second set of understandings of fulfill since Christians believe through the observances of the new law, and especially the sacraments, they participate in the life, death, and resurrection of Christ. The next section engages in more speculative connections between Mt 5:21–48 and the sacraments of the new law. The focus of this part, continuing to be guided by Luz's overview of the meanings of fulfill, is how Jesus fulfills the old ceremonial as well as moral law.

The previous section presented a case, supported through the commitments of a virtue approach to morality, that both the old law and new law share a common *telos* and prescribe activity that orients the person toward – and indeed is in important ways constitutive of – that *telos*. And yet the new law constitutes a greater participation in that *telos*, meaning it can be said to fulfill and not abolish that law even while at times enjoining materially different activity. In a very real sense, we can say the old moral law is observed by the person who is observing the new law. The thesis of this part is that the new law can truly be said to fulfill and not abolish the old ceremonial law by a similar dynamic, even when the material activities are not the same. To establish this thesis, I first turn to a very brief overview of a recent debate on supersessionism that helps to identify the potential problems in Christians claiming that Jesus fulfills rather than abolishes the old law. Next, I delineate several related lines of inquiry prompted by this debate, and I note which one is the focus of this inquiry (and which others are not). Finally, I explain how the above conclusions regarding Jesus's fulfillment of the moral law can indeed illuminate how Christian new law practices which participate in the life and death and resurrection of Christ fulfill rather than abolish the old ceremonial law.

1. RECENT DEBATES OVER CHRISTIAN "SUPERSESSIONISM" Post-Holocaust twentieth-century theology has paid a great deal of attention to

---

[99] Indeed, this is one path taken by Augustine's Manichean interlocutor, Faustus. See *Answer to Faustus*, XIX.2–4.

[100] In the groundbreaking essay, "A Jewish Reading of St. Thomas Aquinas on the Old Law," Michael Wyschogrod claims that the very reason for Thomas Aquinas's distinction between types of old law is to explain why the ceremonial law can be abandoned while the moral law is not. There are two problems with this. First, the distinction is found well before Thomas Aquinas, not only in Augustine as mentioned here but as far back as Irenaeus. (See Luz, *Matthew 1–7*, 261 on this point.) But as to the function of the distinction, it is *not* used to explain why Jesus abolishes rather than fulfills part of the law. It is used to note the different ways Jesus fulfills all of the old law, including the ceremonial. Of course, one may remain unsatisfied by the argument for how the old ceremonial law is fulfilled, but the problem then is not the positing of the distinction.

contemporary and historical relationships between Christianity and Judaism. That attention has turned not only to varying time periods, but also to various facets of that relationship, including anti-Semitism, the role of Christianity in the Holocaust, and so forth. That literature is far too broad to be examined here.[101] Instead. the focus here is on one far narrower topic as examined in a recent scholarly debate. The topic is how Christianity regards the ongoing practice of the Jewish law.

This scholarly debate has waves of historical precedents. Indeed, it was the central issue at what is commonly called the first "council" of the church recounted in Acts 15, the so-called Council of Jerusalem.[102] We read in Augustine's work attention to this issue in his debates with the Manichees, and we see that he and Jerome address the question in importantly distinct ways. Thomas Aquinas gave a great deal of attention to this question, and recent scholarship continues to uncover the breadth of that attention in his *corpus.*[103] The most recent wave of debate over this question was prompted by Michael Wyschogrod's 1987 essay entitled, "A Jewish Reading of St. Thomas Aquinas on the Old Law," followed by his 1995 "Letter to a Friend."[104]

In the first essay, Wyschogrod examines Thomas Aquinas's *Summa Theologiae* treatment of the old law and draws two main conclusions. First, he contests the moral/ceremonial distinction as simply a way to justify the impermanency of the old law, since the time will come when "the Old Law, or at least a portion of it, will have been *abolished.*"[105] Wyschogrod questions the legitimacy of this distinction as not biblical.[106] But his argument about the

---

[101] For a helpful delineation of the varying issues in Jewish-Christian relations, and the varying epochs in which they were addressed, see Matthew Anthony Tapie, *Aquinas on Israel and the Church: The Question of Supersessionism in the Theology of Thomas Aquinas* (Eugene, OR: Pickwick Publications, 2014), 9–24.

[102] For more on Acts in the context of supersessionism, see John Perry, "Are Christians the 'Aliens Who Lived in our Midst?': Torah and the Origins of Christian Ethics in Acts 10–15" *Journal of the Society of Christian Ethics* 29.2 (2009): 157–74.

[103] A fine example of recent scholarship on this topic in Thomas Aquinas is Tapie's *Aquinas on Israel and the Church.* Tapie's main contribution to Thomistic scholarship is presenting the complexities of Thomas Aquinas's thought on this question throughout the Pauline commentaries, where his position is not nearly as straightforward as "the standard read" of his view based solely on the *Summa Theologiae.* Tapie also makes contributions to contemporary debates over supersessionism as noted previously.

[104] Wyschogrod, "A Jewish Reading of St. Thomas Aquinas on the Old Law," 125–40 and Wyschogrod, "Letter to a Friend," *Modern Theology* 11.2 (April 1995): 165–71. Other pieces covered this topic in that same 1995 volume of *Modern Theology*, though they do not address the immediate topic here.

[105] Wyschogrod, "A Jewish Reading of St. Thomas Aquinas on the Old Law," 126, emphasis added. See also, 127: "In light of the need to distinguish the permanent from the transient in the Old Law, making the proper distinctions within the Old Law becomes a matter of crucial importance."

[106] Wyschogrod, "A Jewish Reading of St. Thomas Aquinas on the Old Law," 137. See also Wyschogrod, "Christianity and Mosaic Law," *Pro Ecclesia* 20 (1993): 451–59, at 453. But

biblical origin of the distinction is less developed and less important than the role it plays in the second claim he ascribes to Thomas Aquinas and rejects. His second conclusion is that Thomas Aquinas errs (in a way that later authors charge is supersessionist) in his *Summa Theologiae* argument that the practice of the old ceremonial law by Christians is not only "dead" as in ineffective, but also "deadly" as in mortally sinful. Thomas Aquinas claims that the practice of the old ceremonial law amounts to a denial of Christ. Since these observances prefigure Christ, the practice of them after Christ's passion is a denial of the salvific efficacy of the passion, since they celebrate as to come what has in fact already come. Wyschogrod states:

> The argument that the Mosaic commandments predict Christ and that to adhere to them after Christ is a mortal sin because one is denying that he has come by so doing is a rather thin reed on which to hang the case for the ceremonial commandments turning into mortal sin after Christ.[107]

Years later in his "Letter to a Friend," Wyschogrod exhorts his (hypothetical Jewish-born and recently converted to Christianity) friend to continue to observe the ceremonial law.

In the decades after Wyschogrod's essays, scholarship has blossomed on this topic of "supersession." This is not only a response to the Holocaust, but a fitting further exploration of *Nostra Aetate's* claim that "God ... does not repent of the gifts He makes or of the calls He issues [to the Jews] – such is the witness of the Apostle. . . . [T]he Jews should not be presented as rejected or accursed by God."[108] Concern for the status of Old Testament law after Christ is not simply a "politically correct" attitude toward Christians' "older brothers in the faith."[109] The theological issue at hand is God's faithfulness to His promises, which by all accounts He offered to His Chosen People, the Jews. How can the practice of God's prescribed ceremonial law ever be mortally sinful without impugning the faithfulness of God? Jews involved in this scholarship of course recognize that Christians think that the old law is fulfilled in Christ, and that will have ramifications for their view of and

---

that is the extent of his argument against it. It is not clear he would target the distinction itself if it did not play the role he purports in abolishing part of the Old law and not others. Wyschogrod also shifts later in this essay from the moral/ceremonial law which is Thomas Aquinas's to the natural law/ceremonial law distinction. The natural law is indeed related to, but not to be equated with, the old (presumably moral) law. In fact, it is Augustine's antagonist Faustus who claims it is only the natural law, not law of the Hebrews, that is fulfilled by Christ. See his *Answer to Faustus*, xix.

[107] Wyschogrod, "A Jewish Reading of St. Thomas Aquinas on the Old Law," 136

[108] Vatican Council II, *Nostra Aetate*, www.vatican.va/archive/hist_councils/ii_vatican_council/documents/vat-ii_decl_19651028_nostra-aetate_en.html, 4.

[109] John Paul II so referred to the Jews in his 1989 discourse during his visit to the Rome Synagogue on April 13, 1986. See www.vatican.va/jubilee_2000/magazine/documents/ju_mag_01111997_p-42x_en.html.

practice of the old law, even as they disagree with that view and practice.[110] Yet they claim any such Christian view of and practices regarding the old law that fails to explain how God's promises to the Jews hold even in the era of the church is "supersessionist."

As evident in this vaguely worded definition, one of the main problems in this debate is what exactly is meant by "supersessionism" other than "a bad view of the church's relationship to Judaism." Matthew Tapie sorts through the varying usages of supersession in order to clarify its most precise meaning. He claims "Supersession is the Christian claim that with the advent of Christ, Jewish law is fulfilled and *obsolete*, with the result that God *replaces* Israel with the Church."[111] The common terms used that evidence a supersessionist view of Jewish law according to Tapie are "cancel," "render obsolete," and "replace."[112] It should now be very clear why this debate appears in the present chapter. All these terms indicate a law abolished rather than fulfilled. Thus, in a sense the recent scholarship on supersessionism is about determining what constitutes fulfillment rather than abolishing. And at the heart of that debate since Wyschogrod is how Christians regard the ongoing practice of Jewish ceremonial law.

2. REFINING THE QUESTION This recent debate actually contains several related but importantly distinct lines of inquiry, and it is necessary here to carefully delineate them in order to focus on the one most germane to this chapter. Tapie claims that at the heart of debates over supersessionism is whether or not there is any "positive theological significance [of the practice of the old ceremonial law] after the passion of Christ."[113] This is an enormously important question. Note that it actually contains two distinct subquestions. One concerns the permissibility of Jewish Christians practicing the old ceremonial law. Another is whether or not (non-Christian) Jewish practice of the ceremonial law is inherently alienating from God. As I argue

---

[110] See Wyschogrod, "A Jewish Reading of St. Thomas Aquinas on the Old Law"; David Novak, *Talking with Christians: Musings of a Jewish Theologian* (Grand Rapids: William B. Eerdmans, 2005); Bruce Marshall, "*Quasi in Figura*: A Brief Reflection on Jewish Election, after Thomas Aquinas," *Nova et Vetera* 7.2 (2009): 523–28; and R. Kendall Soulen, *The God of Israel and Christian Theology* (Minneapolis: Fortress, 1996).

[111] Tapie, *Aquinas on Israel and the Church*, 23–4l, emphasis added. Tapie relies most heavily on the work of R. Kendall Soulen who distinguishes punitive supersessionism (the claim that God revoked His promises to the Jews due to their lack of recognition of Christ) from economic supersessionism (Soulen, *The God of Israel and Christian Theology*, 1). See also Bruce Marshall's definition of supersessionism, which "involves, more precisely, the thought that the gifts God gave and the promises God made to the Jews now apply to us, the Church, *instead* of to the Jews. They have been *taken away* from the Jews and given to us" ("*Quasi in Figura*," 477).

[112] Tapie, *Aquinas on Israel and the Church*, 23, 24, 38.

[113] Tapie, *Aquinas on Israel and the Church*, 25.

below, neither of these important questions is most directly germane to the task of this chapter. But as they are closely related to that task, a brief word on each is in order.

First, can Christians practice the old ceremonial law in a manner compatible with their Christian faith?[114] Wyschogrod claims that failing to recognize this as a legitimate possibility for Christians is supersessionist. This is why he targets Thomas Aquinas's claim that the practice of the old law after the passion is mortally sinful. Tapie's work shows that though there are clear supersessionist strains in Thomas Aquinas's thought,[115] there are far more resources for understanding the "positive theological significance" of the old ceremonial law than commonly thought, particularly in the Pauline commentaries.[116] It should also be noted that there are resources to consider the possibility of Christians observing the old ceremonial law right in the very *Summa* question where Thomas Aquinas claims its practice is mortally sinful. Thomas Aquinas follows Augustine and Jerome in claiming that the practice of the old ceremonial law was not mortally sinful (though it was ineffective) in the period just after Christ's passion. He draws the line for the close of that intermediate era with the "publication of the gospel."[117] Yet even before that closure, the disciples, who were the ones proclaiming the gospel, continued old law practices. Thomas Aquinas notes how Paul circumcised Timothy![118] Why was this permissible? How would this not amount to a denial of Christ's coming? Thomas Aquinas says:

[114] For more on this important question, see Mark S. Kinzer, *Postmissionary Messianic Judaism: Redefining Christian Engagement with the Jewish People* (Grand Rapids: Brazos, 2005); as well as the subsequent response to Kinzer by Matthew Levering (and David Novak in the forward) in *Jewish-Christian Dialogue and the Life of Wisdom: Engagements with the Theology of David Novak* (New York: Continuum, 2010).

[115] See Tapie, *Aquinas on Israel and the Church*. In my own research, I have noted the variety of terms Thomas Aquinas uses when describing the old law. He never says "supercede," and at times his terms are translated into English with greater supersessionist overtones than they possess in Latin. For instance, the English Dominicans translation of *Summa Theologiae* I–II 107, 2, ad. 4 says the ceremonial law is "abolished by their fulfillment." But the Latin reads: "*dicendum quod caeremonialia praecepta legis non commemorantur Matth. V, quia eorum observantia totaliter excluditur per impletionem.*" The ceremonial laws are not quoted in Mt 5 because their observance is excluded by their fulfillment. There is no mention of abolishing, which would be most problematic given the explicit mention of Mt 5. Likewise in, I–II 107, 2, ad. 1 the Latin is rendered by the English verb "void," which would also be problematic. The Latin term is "evacuate." Nonetheless, Thomas Aquinas does uses terms like "*tolleantur.*" See Marshall, "*Quasi in Figura,*" 481 for a review of problematic terms in Thoms.

[116] Tapie bases the heart of his case on Thomas Aquinas's *Commentary on Romans*, especially 3:1–2. See Thomas Aquinas, *Commentary on the Letter of Saint Paul to the Romans*, trans. F. R. Larcher, O.P (Lander, WY: The Aquinas Institute for the Study of Sacred Doctrine, 2012).

[117] See Thomas Aquinas, *Summa Theologiae* I–II, 103, 4. He notes their differences and sides with Augustine over Jerome.

[118] Note it is important to Thomas Aquinas that Paul did *not* circumcise Titus, who was not born a Jew. See *Summa Theologiae* I–II 103, 4, ad. 1.

It was lawful for the Jewish converts to Christianity to observe them, provided they did not put their trust in them so as to hold them to be necessary unto salvation, as though faith in Christ could not justify without the legal observances.[119]

With what intention could Christians practice old law observances and not place such trust in them? Of course Thomas Aquinas recognizes that certain acts materially similar to old ceremonial law observances could be practiced outside of a religious context and not be mortally sinful, the most obvious being circumcision.[120] But this was clearly not the case with Paul circumcising Timothy. As to that reason Thomas Aquinas mentions in this period of early promulgation of the gospel, it could be permitted for the sake of unity between Christian and Jews. In short, there are resources even in Thomas Aquinas's thought for understanding how old ceremonial law practices can be observed by Christians *qua* religious practices in a manner that does not constitute a denial of Christ.[121]

Second, can there be "positive theological significance" in the practice of the old ceremonial law today by Jews who are not Christian? This is another common concern of participants in the supersessionism debates, since the failure to recognize any "positive theological significance" of the old ceremonial law even after Christ's passion appears to be a reneging of God on His promises. Again this issue is not the focus of the present treatment, but a word on it is in order. Need the practice of the ceremonial law be alienating for its practitioners after Christ's passion?[122] Thomas Aquinas claims it need not be before the "publication of the gospel." This requirement is an important recognition of the public and communal unfolding of salvation history. It guards against making the permissibility of participating in old ceremonial law practices dependent solely on the intention of the practitioner. That said, there may be resources in Thomas Aquinas's own thought here and his writing on unbelief to suggest whether or not a practicing Jew necessarily commits the sin of unbelief, particularly if one facet of the promulgation of the gospel is the person's ability to receive that promulgation.[123] Once again,

---

[119] Thomas Aquinas, *Summa Theologiae* I–II 103, 4, ad. 1.

[120] Interestingly for today given the frequency of circumcision, Thomas Aquinas mentions circumcision as permissible when for the sake of health. *Summa Theologiae* I–II, 103, 4, ad. 1.

[121] Though such resources do exist, any proposal akin to Jewish Christian practice of ceremonial law today would clearly fall outside Thomas Aquinas's permitted era for such acts, and thus any such proposal – which is not being developed here – would have to extend his thought.

[122] I say alienating from God to avoid the theological question of the possibility of mortal sin for such people.

[123] See Thomas Aquinas, *Summa Theologiae* II–II 10, 1 for his claim that those "who have heard nothing about the faith" are not guilty of the sin of unbelief. This is obviously a delicate topic and thus too little has been written on it recently, but such work is sorely needed.

though there may be resources in Thomas Aquinas for what Tapie calls the "positive theological significance" of Jewish practice of the old ceremonial law after the passion of Christ, any robust account of such would surely have to extend Thomas Aquinas's thought.

These two sub-questions, both of which concern the possibility of the "positive theological significance" of practicing the old ceremonial law after the passion though in different populations of people (Jewish Christians and non-Christian Jews, respectively), are enormously important theological questions in their own right and crucial for Jewish-Christian relations. Yet they are not the focus of this chapter's inquiry into the fulfillment of the old law. For this latter topic, we approach the supersessionist debate from the "other side," if you will. The question here is, can Christians who *do not* observe the old ceremonial law be said to fulfill it, or do they abolish it? It should be clear why this topic can be informed by the above treatment of the new moral law's fulfillment of the old, even where there is material difference in activity.

The thesis presented here is that the explanation of how the old moral law is fulfilled by the new law presented in the previous section makes a contribution to this discussion on the ceremonial law. Indeed, the previous sections' conclusions regarding the fulfillment of the old moral law by the new law can help us to understand why Christian practice of new law observances, even while materially different from old law observances, can rightly be said to fulfill rather than abolish the old ceremonial law.

3. THE NEW LAW AS FULFILLMENT OF THE OLD CEREMONIAL LAW Once again we have an occasion of how the lack of material observance of the old law can actually not be an abolition of that law, depending on how and why the material prescriptions are not followed. The first step in this case, as with the moral law, is to recognize that the ceremonial old law has a *telos*, namely, living in a manner reflective of covenantal friendship with God and others in God.[124] Activity in accordance with the ceremonial law is oriented toward, and indeed constitutive of, that friendship.

A helpful way to explore the crucial role that the ceremonial law plays in that *telos* is to inquire as to the permanency of the old ceremonial law. In the old law, we find affirmations of it enduring forever,[125] and even in the verses that are the topic of this chapter, Jesus claims not only that the law will last "until heaven and earth pass away" and "until all things have taken place," but also that until then "not a single letter, not a single part of a letter will

---

[124] See Thomas Aquinas, *Summa Theologiae* I–II 101, 1 and 2; I–II, 103, 3 for the *telos* of the old ceremonial law; and I–II, 107, 1 on the common *telos* of old and new laws.

[125] See, for example, Deut 5:29 and 29:29.

pass from the law" (5:18).[126] This would seem to suggest that the practice of the old law is an end in itself. Yet then again it seems even on the terms of the old law itself that it is not. The old law points toward a time of fulfillment, commonly labeled the kingdom of God or heaven, and vividly depicted in Old Testament passages, such as Isaiah 2 and 11 among others.[127] When the lion lies with the lamb, when swords are beaten into plowshares, would a moral law like the *lex talonis* remain in force? Yes and no. It would govern the restoration of justice, but since that justice would be restored it would not be lived materially even as it could be said to be observed. Would the ceremonial law continue to be observed? Yes and no. Surely the end to which it orients people would be lived. But presumably the practices constituting life in accordance with that end would look different (e.g., no sin offerings). Still the very point of any human activity in such a situation would be the point of the old law's dictates. In fact, we could say that the old ceremonial law, like the old moral law, will be lived out in the kingdom of heaven by its fulfillment. Nonetheless the material differences of activity in living out that covenantal friendship reveal that the ceremonial law is not that end in itself.

Perhaps this very claim seems supersessionist. If it is supersessionist simply to say that the material observance of the old ceremonial law is not an end in itself, then that charge does apply here. But that is not an apt definition given that the old law itself recognizes the difference between life under its statutes and a future time to come. Indeed, the same may be said of the "non-ultimate finality" of new law observances.[128] As more explicitly examined below, the sacraments of the church are the heart of the new law observances.[129]

Sacramental theology is well developed on the extent to which the sacraments both point toward, and indeed participate in, the end of covenantal

---

[126] Guelich claims the two temporal clauses in 5:18 express "a deliberate tension between Jesus' coming and the continuing validity of the Law" (*The Sermon on the Mount*, 148). He claims this verse indicates "the Law's validity extends only to the end of this age" (144), whereas Luz interprets these temporal clauses to mean "never" (*Matthew 1–7*, 265–66). See also Betz, *The Sermon on the Mount*, 184 and Davies and Allison, *The Gospel According to Saint Matthew*, 492.

[127] The passages referenced here are Is 2:2–5 and Is 11:1–12. Note these are distinct from the set of passages that reference a new law that God instills on human hearts, such as Jer 31:31–34, Ez 11:19, and Ez 36:26.

[128] For the anticipatory status of even the new law observances, see Robert Barron, "The Eucharist as the *Telos* of the Law in the Writings of Thomas Aquinas," in *Exploring Catholic Theology: Essays on God, Liturgy and Evangelization* (Grand Rapids, MI: Baker, 2015), 131–43. 135: "Even those sacraments of the new law, deriving their power from the Incarnation, are themselves anticipatory of something more perfect, namely the bliss of the heavenly worship."

[129] See Thomas Aquinas, *Summa Theologiae* I-II 107 and 108 for Thomas Aquinas's identification of sacraments with new law observances.

friendship with God and others in God. They reflect, instantiate, and augment that friendship. Yet are the sacraments "ends in themselves?" When the fullness of communion with God and others – to which the sacraments point, instantiate, and increase – is actually attained, would the church continue to live out the sacraments? Yes and no. Yes, in that the end toward which they point and in which they participate would be fully achieved. So that which gives formality to the sacraments would be achieved. Yet the material practices of the church's sacraments would not continue.[130] Consider two examples. The people of God would continue to be Eucharistic, indeed in a manner far beyond this life. And yet bread and wine would not be consecrated and consumed. We will be spousal in ways beyond what is possible in this life due to Christ's spousal union with his church (Eph 5:31–32), but as the Lord himself says we will be neither married nor given to marriage (Mt 22:23–33; Lk 20:27–40; Mk 12:18–27). Christians believe that the sacraments are instantiated by Christ, himself the very union of God and humanity, and that they orient us toward and are constitutive of that covenantal union with God made possible by Christ in the Incarnation and his death and resurrection. They do so in a manner that is beyond – or "fulfills" – what God's own prescriptions in the old ceremonial law accomplish. But they are not ends in themselves. They are, as Augustine says, signs.

Thus far, the old and new laws' common *telos*, and common participation in that *telos*, has been established. Yet while both the old and new are both rightly understood as oriented toward the kingdom of heaven, no attention has yet been given to how the new law fulfills the old. How is the old law not abolished by living the new, seemingly "instead" of the old? Worse yet, my consistent use of the term "material" could (wrongly) be taken to imply that the material content of the old law ceremonial observances is unimportant so long as the proper end is in sight.[131] If it could be shown that the material content of old law and/or new law observances were unimportant, this objection would indeed hold true. And if there were no continuity of activity between the old law and new law, then the new would indeed abolish rather

---

[130] For more on these three clear stages, with both the old law and new law pointing toward and thus subordinate to eternal happiness, yet the new law instantiating it more perfectly, see Thomas Aquinas, *Summa Theologiae* I–II 101, 2; 103, 3. See also Chrysostom, *Homilies on Matthew* XVI.6 (77) for this claim about both the old law and new law as imperfect when compared with what is to come. For the claim that even the new law sacraments are figurative, see Matthew Levering, *Christ's Fulfillment of Torah and Temple*, 160 n. 59, as well as Robert Barron, "The Eucharist as the *Telos* of the Law."

[131] For a review of (despite obvious differences) the "common thread among Marcion, the Manicheans, the spiritualists of the Reformation period, and the Anabaptists" whereby the "devaluation of the Old Testament" occurs hand in hand with "flight from the world" resulting in a "devaluation of Christian praxis," see Luz, *Matthew 1–7*, 272–73.

than fulfill the old. But this is not at all the case in the Christian tradition. A look not only at Thomas Aquinas but also Augustine suffices to make this point.[132]

The consistent claim by these two authors is not that the new law replaces the old but that the old law "prefigured" the new, and thus when the new arrived it fulfilled and "succeeded" the old. In his great debate with Faustus the Manichean who rejected the old law, Augustine was faced with the challenge of defending the legitimacy of the old law, and yet explaining why Christians do not find themselves bound to observe its ceremonial precepts. Augustine insists that the only precepts not observed from the old law are those (ceremonial) ones that "prefigure" Christ. Since those observances point toward Christ, the arrival of Christ has enormous implications on how one lives out the sacraments (a term Augustine applies to both old and new law observances). Yet he insists that rather than render the specific material content, if you will, of the old sacraments unimportant, this indicates the crucial importance of the old law practices because it is in their material content that they prefigure Christ. He exclaims at one point, "And if you mention more explicitly any other kind of sacrifice, I shall show you in it too that Christ was prophesied."[133] Thus the material content of old sacraments is not at all unimportant. They point to Christ in that very material content, and thus with the coming of Christ they are done differently though with the same *telos* and with continuity of activity.

It is Thomas Aquinas who spills an enormous amount of ink explaining in great detail how different old ceremonial laws prefigure Christ and correlate to new law observances. Question 102 of the *Prima Secundae* on the causes of the ceremonial precepts is one of the longest questions in the *Summa*. In it, he reviews in incredible detail the gamut of old law sacrifices, holy things, sacrifices, and observances, each time explaining why the exact material detail of each is important in prefiguring Christ. In doing so, he reveals just how important the material content of the old law is. It is in that material content that the old ceremonial law prefigures Christ and indeed the practice of the new law. In a similar way that scriptural interpretation, while legitimately theological and transcending the literal sense can never defy or be unconnected to that literal sense, the importance of each "letter" (or "the smallest part of a letter") of the law is indeed seen by how carefully Augustine and especially Thomas Aquinas interpret the "letter" of the old law as prefiguring Christ. The old law practices prefigure Christ and new law practices. There is a common *telos* and continuity of activity in the old and new law, and thus the new can be said to fulfill and not abolish the old.

---

[132] The claim that the law prefigures Christ is made before Augustine. See Richard Patrick Crosland Hanson, *Origen's Doctrine of Tradition* (London: SPCK, 1954), 293, for Origen's view of the old law prefiguring Christ.

[133] Augustine, *Answer to Faustus*, XVIII.6.

The participant in recent debates over supersessionism who most directly addresses that topic in light of the question of this section about fulfillment is Mathew Levering. After reviewing mainly the work of Thomas Aquinas in more detail than offered here, he reaches this direct conclusion: "the Mosaic law, in a real sense, *is still observed by Christians.*"[134] This claim is only possible in any "real sense" by attending to the common *telos* and continuity of activity in the old ceremonial law and the new law practices. Levering goes on to say:

> Christians, by sharing in Christ's passion, will forever observe the ceremonial and judicial precepts – although now in a way proper to a universal "body" that enjoys Trinitarian communion through Christ the "Head." In Th's view, Jewish Christians, sharing in Christ's fulfillment of Mosaic law, do not lose their identity. Rather, they enter into the (supernatural) fullness of their identity.[135]

Levering further says the ceremonial and judicial precepts "come to an end in the positive (teleological) sense of attaining their ultimate end, in which they rest or last forever."[136]

We seem to have strayed far from the antitheses of Mt 5 at this point in the chapter, so it is worth recalling what prompted the above discussion before returning to the antitheses in the following section. This first section of the chapter explains the varying ways that the new law fulfills the old. Its first part presents various meanings of "fulfill," and its second part offers an argument of how the new moral law can indeed fulfill the old even when the old is not being materially observed. In this third part that virtue-centric argument is applied to recent debates over supersessionism, and particularly whether a Christian can be said to fulfill rather than abolish the old ceremonial law even while not materially observing its precepts. The answer posited here is yes. By sharing in the same *telos* and engaging in new law practices instituted by and directly reflective of what (or whom) the old ceremonial law prefigured, the new law (especially the sacraments) fulfills the old. It does not abolish it. Nor does this mean material observances are unimportant as long as different activities share in the same *telos*. Instead, the new law fulfills

---

[134] Levering, *Christ's Fulfillment of Torah and Temple*, 28.

[135] Levering, *Christ's Fulfillment of Torah and Temple*, 30. It is unfortunate that he uses the term "supernatural" since it could wrongly imply the old law does not orient us toward the supernatural end of eternal happiness, which it does. Levering of course also attends to Christ's fulfillment of the moral precepts. He notes that for Thomas Aquinas, Christ's suffering fulfilled all three types of old law precepts. See *Summa Theologiae* III 47, 2, ad. 1

[136] Levering, *Christ's Fulfillment of Torah and Temple*, 30. Elsewhere, he recognizes three stages of old law, new law, and eternal happiness, and thus this quote should not be taken to mean the last two are conflated. See also Thomas Aquinas, *Summa Theologiae* I–II 103, 3, ad. 1: "The Old Law is said to be 'forever' simply and absolutely, as regards its moral precepts; but as regards the ceremonial precepts it lasts forever in respect of the reality which those ceremonies foreshadowed."

rather than abolishes the old to the extent that the material observances of the old law prefigure Christ and life in Christ according to the new law.

This section, however, does not merely articulate an interpretation of fulfillment of the moral law in Mt 5:21–48 and apply it to a debate that is not directly relevant to those verses. Though the antitheses are most obviously moral, Jesus's own claim in Mt 5:17 that he fulfills not abolishes the law requires attention to the ceremonial law since the law includes the ceremonial law. Indeed, as we see in the next section's reflection on why Jesus offers the group of antitheses he does, it is also possible to interpret the set of six antitheses more theologically to reference not only the moral law but also the ceremonial law through an alignment with the sacraments of the church.

II. GROUPING THE ANTITHESES

Though part of the argument of this section flows directly from the previous one on the ceremonial law, this section has a broader and freestanding purpose. The basic question for this section is, given that there are six clear antitheses, why are there six? Whenever scripture presents a clear grouping, it is legitimate to inquire as to the rationale of the grouping. For instance, do the different parts of the group all represent some common thing, and each part accentuates some constitutive part of the whole? Or might the members of the group be sub-grouped so as to illuminate the topic of the group as a whole? Finally, might the members of the group be fruitfully aligned with some other group, enabling the two groups to mutually illuminate one another? We saw this with regard to the beatitudes where the seven main beatitudes of Mt 5:3–9 were posited as depicting eternal happiness, and in a manner that accentuated the different facets of the whole toward which they point. They were also presented as able to be divided into subgroups depicting a progression into eternal happiness. Finally, they were aligned with the virtues in a manner whereby the groups were mutually illuminative.

This section poses the same questions with regard to the six antitheses. As mentioned in the Introduction and Chapter 1, in some ways I find this to be a particularly exciting part of this research project, reflective of how the truth, which is one, can be manifest in varying manners. In this I submit myself to the tutelage of Christian greats who saw significance to such groupings, perhaps most notably Augustine. Though I endorse the more speculative project of this section (and elsewhere in this book) to provide theologically informed rationales for groups or sets found in the Sermon, I recognize that some may find this effort forced, perhaps even compulsive. And thus I want to clearly state that the above arguments as to how the new law fulfills the old, informed by a virtue-centric approach to moral theology, are not dependent on the argument or reflections of this ensuing section. In other words, the above arguments can stand even if one is unconvinced by the following. In this section, I argue that the very content of the six antitheses of Mt 5:21–48 considered as a group further reinforces how the new law fulfills the old in both the moral and ceremonial senses, albeit in distinct ways.

A. GROUPING THE ANTITHESES: THE MORAL SIGNIFICANCE

Groupings of the six Matthean antitheses are far from uncommon, and this includes contemporary biblical scholars. What differs significantly are the bases on which those groupings occur. So for instance, contemporary biblical scholars commonly recognize that the antitheses seem to be organized into two sets of three, for reasons driven by sources and literary form. There is a clear parallelism between the first three antitheses and the second three, due both to which Old Testament book is referenced in the old law (Exodus for the first three and Leviticus for the second three) and the corresponding and diminishing in length introductory phrases in the first, second, and third members of each group.[137] Even though this division into groups is noted, no theological significance is made of it. As another example of grouping the antitheses, one rooted in source criticism, scholars commonly debate the origin of the six antitheses and posit one group of antitheses from earlier in the tradition since they have parallels in Luke (3, 5, and 6 are paradigmatic) and another group of antitheses originating in Matthew (1 and 2 are paradigmatic).[138] However, these groupings reflect the importance of the origin and composition of the inspired text, and I have seen no other claims as to the moral significance as to either set of the two groupings.[139]

---

[137] See Luz, *Matthew 1–7*, 274–75 for a literary analysis of the six, as well as attention to the question of source and groupings based on source origin. Guelich, *The Sermon on the Mount*, 17–18, also surveys source critical theories before offering his own grouping based on distinctively Matthean tradition (1, 2, 4) and which are found in Luke as well but redacted by Matthew (3, 5, 6) 268–71. Davies and Allison confirm this grouping on the basis of source criticism (*The Gospel According to Saint Matthew*, 505). Guelich divides the first three from last three not by old law reference, but by the respective third and second person voice of the commands. He then, for reasons unclear and unsubstantiated, claims the first set "are in the form of legal ordinances that are definable and enforceable," while the last three "simply set forth absolute commandments and prohibitions" (177; also 179). Davies and Allison say there are two clear groups of three (1–3, 4–6) based both on the introductory formulae and the location of the reference Old Testament texts (504).

[138] The fourth antithesis proves most difficult to explain in these debates. For an overview of positions in groupings of the antitheses, as well as evidence of the difficulty posed by the fourth antithesis, see Luz, *Matthew 1–7*, 274–76.

[139] Though it may be a bit overstated, Betz claims that not only has little attention been given to the significance of the arrangement of the antitheses, but that the topic is little discussed: "What is the reason for the arrangement of the six antitheses? There clearly appears to be a rationale behind the six antitheses and their arrangement in the SM, but the rationale behind it has so far eluded scholarship; few scholars even discuss the

Though generally not presented as explicit subgroupings, claims about the varying ways that the new law fulfills the old law in a moral sense can be said to reflect such groupings. So when Augustine claims that the two ways the new law fulfills the old are by "supplementing its deficiencies or by carrying out its content," we can speculate as to a group of antitheses for each sense of fulfill.[140] The same may be said for others, noted in Section I, who posit distinct meanings of fulfill in interpreting 5:17. However, while one may speculate as to groupings in these cases, no claim is made by any of these thinkers as to the broader significance of those groups.

The current argument of this part of the section is that the six antitheses can be seen as reflecting and further illuminating the two cardinal virtues of temperance and fortitude. In the anthropology of the virtue ethics tradition, these two virtues have always been understood to govern two root human dynamisms, which will be labeled here desire and aggression.[141] It is certainly acknowledged here that the anthropological differences in different virtue-centric traditions are quite significant.[142] However, in all cases the virtuous life entails the reasonable governance of what are called here desire and aggression.[143] Thus, it should not be surprising that Christ's own Sermon on

question" (*The Sermon on the Mount*, 201). He then proceeds to offer perhaps the closest thing in biblical scholarship to a "moral" explanation of the set, namely, that all delineate ruptures in love (205).

[140] Augustine, *On the Lord's Sermon on the Mount*, i.8.20.

[141] There are no problem-less English equivalents for the *concupiscible* and *irascible* in the Latin tradition, or each of the two horses (*thumos* and *epithumia*) in the Platonic tradition.

[142] The most obvious example is the Platonic anthropological model of the two horses of desire and spiritedness being reined in by the charioteer of reason, as distinct from the Thomistic anthropology of the appetitive on the one hand being subdivided into intellectual, e.g., will (governed by justice) and sensitive or passions (itself further subdivided into two, with the concupiscible passions governed by temperance and the irascible governed by fortitude) and the apprehensive on the other hand with practical reason being governed by prudence or *phronesis*. But there is even starker difference in the Stoic anthropology which is monolithic (rather than Plato's tripartite, e.g.); even in the case of the Stoics, however, the main virtue of *phroensis* or prudence is seen as regulating the passions. While the differences are quite important, and beyond the scope of this essay, in all cases the virtuous life concerns the regulation (to use a purposely vague term) by reason of what is called here desire and aggression. For more on the ramifications of these anthropological differences on the topic of virtue, see Julia Annas, *The Morality of Happiness* (New York: Oxford University Press, 1995) and Richard Sorabji, *Emotions and Peace of Mind: From Stoic Agitation to Christian Temptation* (New York: Oxford University Press, 2003).

[143] Again, there are differences over how this is understood to occur, and they are significant. The possibility of desire and aggression being "seats" or "subjects" of virtue was debated in antiquity and the Patristic period. For excellent treatments on the differences in these eras see Sorabji, *Emotions and Peace of Mind* and Simo Knuuttila, *Emotions in Ancient and Medieval Philosophy* (New York: Clarendon Press, 2004). For a helpful snapshot of a medieval version of this debate see Bonnie Kent, *Emotions of the Will: The Transformation of Ethics in the Late Thirteenth Century* (Washington, DC:

the Mount, which as Augustine said is a "charter of the good life," should attend to the virtuous habituation of these dynamisms. My claim here is that antitheses 1, 5, and 6 concern aggression and the virtue of fortitude, while 2, 3, and 4 concern desire and the virtue of temperance.[144]

The strongest and most obvious support for this claim is the content of the opening two antitheses. In these two antitheses, we see all dynamics that I claim are found in each of the two groups of three antitheses: root interior dynamisms; further developing exterior action; social institutionalization of the dynamisms; and practical guidance as to the proper habituation of these dynamisms.[145] Turning to the first antithesis on anger, Jesus addresses one of the most frequently examined passions in the Western tradition, one that is seen as the paradigmatic passion for the spirited or irascible part of the person, called here aggression. In doing so, Jesus reveals that even this deeply interior, and on all accounts passive and responsive, human phenomenon is within the purview of the transformation and perfection of Christian discipleship. It is not only murder that is prohibited. And it is not only vicious words spoken in anger ("You fool!") or inchoate utterances ("Raca!") that are prohibited but even anger itself distinct from any ensuing action. Of course that deeply interior movement can progress to increasingly exterior action, possibly even to murder, and Jesus's punishments with each make it clear that increasingly active anger is even more condemnatory.[146]

Thus, Jesus begins the antitheses with anger, that important yet often distorted guardian of justice, and is willing to address our most interior movements. Yet he is also attentive not only to increasingly exterior acts of anger, but even to the way that rectification of injustice is handled on a more social and institutionalized level, as he references reconciliation in the content of court (5:25–26). Finally, he offers practical guidance on reconciliation and ultimately on transforming one's anger with his words about leaving the

---

The Catholic University of America Press) and Marie-Dominique Chenu, "Body and Body Politic in the Creation Spirituality of Thomas Aquinas," *Listening: Journal of Religion and Culture* **13**.3 (1978): 214–32. Today this debate continues, as in the venues noted above concerning the morality of the emotions.

[144] I have not seen a direct claim such as this in the tradition of commentary on the Sermon. The closest to it I found is in John Chrysostom, who claims that the two most basic human passions are anger and lust, so it makes sense that Jesus begins with antitheses one and two. Yet he does not group all six, or align them with virtues. *Homilies on Matthew*, XVII.2 (97).

[145] For a similar claim that the antitheses entail directives to action that help form the disciple, which they call "transforming initiatives," see Stassen and Gushee, *Kingdom Ethics*, 125ff.

[146] That the punishments increase with more complete expressions of anger is a standard interpretation in the tradition. See Augustine, *On the Lord's Sermon on the Mount*, I.9.24 and Aquinas, *Commentary on Matthew*, 488–89. For a contemporary example, see Betz, *The Sermon on the Mount*, 220. As Betz notes there, not all biblical scholars affirm this view (e.g., see Luz, *Matthew 1–7*, 283).

gift at the altar (5:23–24).[147] These increasingly institutional and practically helpful tendencies are evident in the ensuing antitheses as well.

The second antithesis concerns lust. It may sound typically Catholic to place sexual desire at the heart of human desire more generally. Yet it should be noted that the delicate interplay of desire in general and sexual desire in particular is one that is evident throughout the Western tradition. Thus in addressing lust, Jesus can be said to address the proper expression of the concupiscible appetite in general, in both interior movement and external action.[148] Again we have in the second antithesis a reference not only to an act (adultery) but also to the more passive and responsive interior movement that is sexual desire, in this case distorted into lust.[149] In this second antithesis, Jesus does not attend to any of the ways that human desires are socially institutionalized, but that comes in later antitheses (third and fourth). We do see here, however, practical guidance for not acting out of lust, and even reforming the emotional response itself (5:29–30).[150]

Much as we saw in the above section on the fulfillment of the moral law, we have in these first two antitheses a sort of synopsis of dynamics that follow in the ensuing antitheses. Jesus addresses the two most basic root human dynamisms of anger and desire. Though no explicit mention is made of fortitude and temperance, the traditional association of those two cardinal virtues with those human dynamisms makes naming those two virtues in this context an easy step. The antitheses, as we see here, address not only those two dynamisms at their root, but also their increasing exteriorization into action, even to the level of social institutions. Jesus also

---

[147] For an example of biblical scholarship claiming that here Jesus offers practical guidance oriented toward reconciliation, see Davies and Allison, *The Gospel According to Saint Matthew*, 516–20.

[148] Luz notes the common application of this passage to desire in general: "It ultimately prohibits any 'inordinate' desire," citing Augustine's *On the Lord's Sermon on the Mount*, i.12 (*Matthew 1–7*, 236). See also Luz, 295, on Hellenistic Judaism's association of lust and sin in general. For an historically contextualized overview of different approaches toward understanding desire in general and sexual desire more specifically as related to one another, see William Mattison III, "Movements of Love; A Thomistic Perspective on *Eros* and *Agape*," *Journal of Moral Theology* 1.2 (2012): 31–60.

[149] There is some debate over whether this antithesis prohibits simply the experience of lust, or a more deliberate act since it says "whoever *looks at a woman* with lust." It would be more difficult (though not impossible) to hold that Jesus is addressing the moral importance of the emotions were this the only antithesis referencing an emotion. But coupled with the previous one on anger, where Jesus prohibits simply anger, this interpretation is persuasive.

[150] For a review of scholarship on whether or not these stark injunctions are literal or hyperbolic, as well as the significance of the "right" eye or hand, see Luz, *Matthew 1–7*, 297 and Betz, *The Sermon on the Mount*, 236–39. As will be examined in more detail in Chapter 3, the work of Robert C. Tannehill (*The Sword of His Mouth* (Eugene, OR: Wipf & Stock Publishers, 2003), 86–88) is instructive here, as he speaks of such injunctions describing "focal instances" to prompt actual if not literal response.

offers practical guidance as to the habituation of these dynamisms, a topic addressed in more detail in Chapter 3.

How are the ensuing four antitheses understood in light of aggression and desire, and thus fortitude and temperance? The grouping offered here is that antitheses 1, 5, and 6 concern anger and fortitude, while 2, 3 and 4 concern desire and temperance. Furthermore, there is a sense of progression and development in each group of three antitheses. Here I continue treating the antitheses, more briefly with the last four, in textual order as I turn to the third and fourth antitheses.

The third antithesis continues the focus in the second on desire and more particularly sexual desire by discussing marriage. Here again we see Jesus focusing on the proper expression of desire, and in this case sexual desire. Yet in this case, he addresses a more complex social institutionalization of that desire (5:31–32). As mentioned above, the scope of this project precludes any examination of Jesus's teaching on divorce, marriage, the exception clauses, and so forth. There are two basic points relevant for this section of the chapter. First, the third antithesis continues the focus of the second on desire, and sexual desire in particular. Second, Jesus addresses not only the root of human emotion but the far more complex institution of marriage, which indicates how life in Christ is transformative of basic human dynamisms as well as their complex social institutionalization.

As noted above, some may lament the use of antitheses on sexual desire and marriage to address broader dynamics of desire and temperance. This is understandable, though once again it is hard to deny how fundamental sexual desire is in humanity, and how important marriage is for the social order. Yet for those with this concern the fourth antithesis on truthfulness may be particularly attractive. As noted above, this antithesis is commonly the one that commentators struggle most to "place" in relation to the other five, no matter on which basis they group the antitheses. And indeed in my own interpretation of the antitheses as a group, this seems to fit the desire/aggression model least neatly. But upon further reflection it is evident that truth-telling and honest communication are indeed at the heart of well-ordered desire and thus temperance.

Our desires, be they deeply interior and/or socially institutionalized, are reflective of and originate in some apprehension of the truth. Good desire requires truthful apprehension. Bad desires reflect inaccurate apprehension, and conversely it is commonly our disordered desires that lead us to misapprehend the truth or to twist the truth. Hence Jesus's insistence on truthfulness here is an enormously important corrective to distorted desires. Once again we find a practical injunction ("let your no mean no and your yes mean yes" [5:37]) on how to have well-habituated desires. We also find proscriptions of swearing by heaven, earth, Jerusalem and even one's own head (5:34–36), activities that seem to reflect a disordered desire for providential control over reality that far exceeds our status as creatures. The passage reminds us that it is God who reigns. As noted above and below with the sixth antithesis, the final antithesis of this group culminates in a claim about who God is, one that has moral import. Here we are reminded that God – not us despite our prideful desires to the contrary – is the "great king" (5:35), and thus as creatures we apprehend the truth, not dictate it to conform to our desires. For all of these reasons, this antithesis on truthfulness is crucial for well-ordered desire and thus the virtue of temperance.

We now turn to the last two antitheses, those that complete the group including the first on anger. The thesis here is that these three antitheses enjoin the well-ordered activities of the dynamism of aggression that is well habituated by the cardinal virtue fortitude. They do so in a way that extends from the deeply interior to the socially institutionalized. Finally, they include practical guidance to aid the virtuous habituation of the human dynamism of aggression.

As noted in Section I, the fifth antithesis is one of the most extensively studied and hotly debated passages in scripture. The question for this analysis is the following, and thankfully much simpler: how can this antithesis be understood as part of a set of three where Jesus addresses how to have the well-ordered aggression known as fortitude? In this passage, the old law's limit on rectification of injustice is fulfilled by a willingness to forego (just) retribution for the sake of restoration of right relationship. Both old and new law injunctions clearly concern restoration of relationship that occurs with injustice. The human dynamism of aggression, which empowers a person to rise up against difficulties of all sorts, is paradigmatically about responses to injustice.[151] These verses clearly instruct Jesus's audience about how to act in such situations in accordance with the new law. They even offer practical guidance, such as giving to those who seek to borrow, returning an unjust aggressor's acts with generosity, and giving equally to those who deserve it and do not (5:39–42). All of this practical guidance aids in the development of well-ordered aggression, and thus the virtue of fortitude.

One more observation is worth making before turning to the sixth antithesis. The first antithesis clearly addresses ruptures in right relations with those close to us. Twice Jesus references one's "brother." The fifth antithesis extends the scope of Jesus's teaching beyond those who are our brothers. Though one who slaps you or who seeks to borrow could of course be a "brother," the fact that Jesus refers to a broader circle of people is evident in

---

[151] Anger is treated throughout the Western tradition as paradigmatic of this human dynamism. This is most obviously seen in the very etymology in Latin of the *irascible* appetite, which is named after anger (*ira*).

the reference to soldiers pressing one into service. It is even more explicit in the sixth antithesis on love of enemy.[152]

In the sixth antithesis, we again find matter relevant to aggression and the restoration of right relationship, since Jesus addresses the enemy and those who persecute. In an even more obvious manner than the previous antithesis, the scope of love and prayerful concern are expanded to the enemy. Much as the fourth antithesis, the culmination of the set on desire, concludes with reference to who God is in a manner with moral importance, this sixth one does the same. Jesus enjoins the audience to love impartially, much as our heavenly Father sends sunshine and rain on the good and bad, unjust and just alike (5:45). Jesus enjoins relentless action toward restoration of right relationship (justice) with all, and in doing so demonstrates that the height of fortitude, which is the truly good habituation of our aggressive capacities, occurs when the difficulty at hand is a commitment to right relationship even with those who oppose it.

With the emphasis on justice in these antitheses that address aggression, and the attention to truthfulness in those treating desire, it should be clear that the claim here that the antitheses are fruitfully understood in connection to fortitude and temperance should not be taken to exclude any important role for justice or prudence.[153] It should be equally clear that a grasp of the human dynamisms of aggression and desire so central to virtue ethics aids our understanding of the Sermon. And Jesus in turn, through all the ways mentioned above, teaches how the new law as presented in written form in the Sermon is a more "complete" (5:48) habituation of these dynamisms.

B. GROUPING THE ANTITHESES: THE CEREMONIAL SIGNIFICANCE

I claimed in Section I that though the six antitheses most obviously describe the moral law, it is appropriate in this chapter on Mt 5:17–48 to address the fulfillment of the ceremonial law since Christ claims he fulfills not abolishes the law (Mt 5:17–20), and this surely includes the ceremonial law.[154]

---

[152] See Luz, *Matthew 1–7*, 288, who recognizes that both the primary referent for the first antithesis is the immediate community, *and* that it even there has a trajectory beyond the immediate community.

[153] The importance of prudence and especially justice for the antitheses is once again a reminder of the connectivity of the virtues, an axiomatic thesis in classic accounts of virtue. For an outstanding recent account of the connectivity of the virtues, including various Christian and pagan formulations of it as well as a defense of it in response to contemporary challenges esp. from the social sciences, see Andrew Kim, "Thomas Aquinas On the Connection of the Virtues" (PhD diss., The Catholic University of America, 2013).

[154] Since this chapter repeatedly distinguishes the moral and ceremonial law, it is necessary to note that Thomas Aquinas's full categorization of Old Testament law includes also

The question for this brief section is, do the ensuing antitheses of Mt 5:21–48 in any way address the fulfillment of the ceremonial law? More particularly, is the specific set of six antitheses found in the Sermon at all reflective of the new law's fulfillment of the old ceremonial law? The answer offered here to both questions is yes. The importance of who Christ is as fulfillment of the ceremonial law constitutes part of the answer to the first question, and that is addressed in the following section. This present part addresses how the antitheses as a set reflect the new law as fulfillment of the old ceremonial law.

I argued above that participation in the life of Christ constitutes fulfillment of the ceremonial law, which prefigures Christ, even as the material observances differ. Thinkers such as Augustine and Thomas Aquinas have painstakingly delineated how the observances of the old law prefigure Christ. The paradigmatic observances of the new law life in Christ are the sacraments.[155] Therefore, if we were to look for evidence of the fulfillment of the old law in the antitheses, it is reasonable to look for echoes of the sacraments in these verses. The claim of this part is that the antitheses can be fruitfully understood in conjunction with the seven sacraments to further indicate the new law as fulfillment of the old.

This argument may appear a bit of a "stretch." After all, people do not read the antitheses and think, "This is reminiscent of the seven sacraments!" Indeed, I have found no treatment of the antitheses that makes such a claim. Additionally, the very number of the antitheses defies easy alignment. There are six antitheses and seven sacraments so some creative alignment is required. As will be seen below, what is suggested here is not a one-to-one alignment or even doubling two sacraments with one antithesis. Furthermore, the case made here that the antitheses converge with the sacraments "runs through," or is

judicial precepts. See Thomas Aquinas, *Summa Theologiae* I–II 99, 2–4; III 47, 2. An extensive analysis of how what Thomas Aquinas calls judicial precepts are fulfilled is beyond the scope of this chapter, but that bracketing is only justified if there is a case for including the judicial into one of these two types of law. Though how to do so is not argued here, that it can be done is evident in Augustine who long before Thomas Aquinas speaks of the fulfillment of the old law with reference to Jn 1;17, "in grace and truth." Christ gives us the grace to fulfill the old law's commands (moral) and fulfills the Old Testament's prophecies in truth (ceremonial). See *Answer to Faustus*, XIX.8. See also XVIII.4 and XIX.18. Wyschogrod, "A Jewish Reading of St. Thomas Aquinas on the Old Law" also focuses on these two types of law in his treatment of Thomas Aquinas (126–27; 130; 136–37). Thomas Aquinas himself at times mentions just moral and sacramental (see *Summa Theologiae* I–II 103, 3, ad. 1; I–II 107, 1, ad. 3). At other times, he seems to group the three type into two categories (e.g., *Summa Theologiae* I–II 101, 1). (For more on the fulfillment of the law with attention to the judicial see Levering, *Christ's Fulfillment of Torah and Temple*, 25–27). A complete treatment of the relationship between the judicial precepts and the moral and/or ceremonial is beyond the scope of this work, but it is indeed legitimate to focus on the moral and ceremonial for the reasons noted here.

[155] For an association of the new law with the sacraments, see Thomas Aquinas, *Summa Theologiae* I–II 108.

dependent on, the virtue-centric claim above that the six antitheses may be divided into two groups, one correlating with the governing of human desire and the other correlating with the governing of human aggression. So the correlation of antitheses and sacraments is only successful to the extent that one grants that the antitheses address desire and aggression.

Yet despite all of these caveats, and even despite my concern that this more tenuous connection between antitheses and sacraments might foment dismissal of other more solid connections between groups suggested elsewhere in this book, I present the claim nonetheless. I do think that the antitheses are aptly read as addressing desire and aggression,[156] and if that is the case then using that connection to further connect the antitheses to the sacraments is legitimate. Second and most importantly, as with other alignments in this book, the claim here is certainly not that one only understands the material at hand, in this case the antitheses, if one sees the proposed alignment. The far more modest claim is that when scripture presents some sort of set it is legitimate to reflect on why the set is presented as such. And if the set has some sort of coherent intelligibility as parts of a whole, it is not at all surprising that it relates in some manner to another set that is comprehensive or holistic. As explained in the Introduction, such convergences point to a deep wisdom about the beauty of scripture, and how it draws us into contemplation of and relationship with the Author of scripture who is Author of all.

What connection is suggested here? The sacraments of whole life commitment (e.g., marriage and Holy Orders) may be fruitfully aligned with the antitheses governing human desire. The restorative sacraments (reconciliation and anointing of the sick) may be fruitfully aligned with the antitheses governing aggression. The sacraments of initiation (baptism, Eucharist, and confirmation) establish discipleship in the church and make living the new law morally and sacramentally even possible. Finally, though the Eucharist as sacrament of initiation is placed with the other two such sacraments, unsurprisingly as the source and summit of the Christian life it can be fruitfully understood with the other two groupings as well.

We begin with initiation. Biblical scholars commonly address the question, "to whom is the Sermon addressed?" More particularly, is it for the "inner circle" of Jesus's disciples, or for everyone.[157] This question is often addressed in the context of reflection on the feasibility of living out the high standard presented in the Sermon (especially in the antitheses). There is

---

[156] Recall that John Chrysostom claims the antitheses address anger and lust in *Homilies on Matthew*, XVII.2 (97).

[157] For the audience of the Sermon in the context of the disciples (5:1–2) and the crowds (7:28–29) see Davies and Allison, *The Gospel According to Saint Matthew*, 419; Luz, *Matthew 1–7*, 224; Betz, *The Sermon on the Mount*, 80–82; and Guelich, *The Sermon on the Mount*, 59–60.

textual support for both answers. After all, the Sermon begins with these verses: "When he saw the crowds, he went up the mountain, and after he had sat down, his disciples came to him. He began to teach them, saying . . ." (Mt 5:1–2). These words indicate the Sermon is given to the disciples as set off from others. Yet at the end of the Sermon we read, "When Jesus finished these words, the crowd was astonished at his teaching, for he taught them as one having authority, and not as their scribes" (7:28–29). Apparently the crowd was indeed present. Which was it? Eschewing the strictly historical question of who is present at different parts of the Sermon, Frank Matera masterfully addresses this issue in a manner attentive to an underlying question applicable to today, namely, to whom is this teaching directed, Christians or everyone? He claims the answer is both. Of course it is offered to and heard by everyone as indicated by the crowd in Mt 7:28. All are welcome to life in Christ. However, it can also be said to be directed to the disciples in that only those who follow Christ and are given the grace to do so are interested in and able to live out this new law.[158]

Why is this relevant for the connection between sacraments and antitheses? The sacraments of initiation are of course how a disciple is incorporated into the body of Christ that is the church. The sacraments make the person part of God's story, or more accurately since all persons are part of God's story, an active participant or collaborator in the full coming of the kingdom. Thus the three sacraments of initiation serve as the foundation for living the new law. Much as circumcision did for the old law, they mark out the believer, and set them on a path of discipleship to Christ. They are the sacraments of the new law that fulfill the ceremonial law and make possible the moral law as presented in the antitheses.

The sacraments of restoration or healing can be understood in connection to the three antitheses of aggression. This may seem odd, and again we face a limitation by the English term aggression. Aggression, or spiritedness (the irascible) is a rising up against a threat to one's individual and communal flourishing. Though we commonly experience our own and other people's

---

[158] See Frank J. Matera, *The Sermon on the Mount: The Perfect Measure of the Christian Life* (Collegeville, MN: Liturgical Press, 2013), 3–4: "Jesus' disciples, although characterized by 'little faith,' have taken the initial step. They have responded to his call. They have seen the in-breaking of the kingdom of heaven in his words and deeds, and they now belong to the community of disciples that will be the church of the risen Lord. The sermon is not an impossible ideal because they belong to a community of like-minded disciples. The practicality of the sermon is a question only for those who are not his disciples. Apart from a community of like-minded disciples, the sermon will always be impractical and idealistic. For those who do not live in the sphere of the in-breaking kingdom of God, the realm of God's grace, the sermon will always be impractical and idealistic since the sermon is intended for disciples . . . What he proclaims, then, presupposes faith in his proclamation of the in-breaking kingdom of God." See also Luz, *Matthew 1–7*, 224. He takes this occasion to reject a "two tier" approach to the audience question.

aggression as self-centered and self-assertive, when it is well-governed, aggression (including anger and the rectification of injustice that is virtuous retaliation) is actually oriented toward the restoration, or healing, of threats and attacks to interpersonal relations. This is of course the heart of reconciliation, be it between God and people or among people. Furthermore, we commonly think of the restoration of the corporate whole (common good) being primarily about moral evil, which of course it commonly is. This is what is governed in the three relevant antitheses, and this is what occurs with the sacrament of reconciliation. But the designation of anointing as a sacrament of healing is a reminder, just as Jesus's healing miracles are a reminder, that the inauguration of the kingdom of heaven means dispelling not only moral evil but also natural evil.[159] Hence the sacraments of healing converge with the antitheses of aggression.

The sacraments of whole life commitment are fruitfully understood in connection to the three antitheses of desire. The most obvious basis of connection here is between the sacrament of marriage on the one hand, with the treatment of sexual desire, marriage, and even truthfulness (since marriage is a public promise or vow) and the antitheses of desire on the other hand. Given this more obvious connection in the case of marriage, the sacrament of Holy Orders could be included with recognition that Holy Orders is an incorporation of a man into the priesthood of Christ, who himself is spouse to his bride the church. But even more fundamentally, the antitheses of desire run the gamut from basic human emotion to socially instituted and interpersonal ways we channel our energies. Jesus's new law enables that to occur honorably, truthfully, and faithfully. The whole life vocations that are priesthood and married life are also channelings of a person's energies into a communal, interpersonal path of life in service to the people of God. Thus, the antitheses of desire converge with the sacraments of whole life commitment.

Finally, it is worth saying an additional word about the Eucharist, which *Lumen Gentium* calls the "source and summit of the Christian life."[160] Since the Christian life in the new covenant is thoroughly sacramental, it is fitting that the Eucharist can easily be connected to the antitheses not only through the foundational sacraments of initiation but also with the antitheses of desire and aggression. After all, the Eucharist is the very incorporation into

---

[159] For this twofold emphasis of Jesus's ministry, see the verses immediately preceding the Sermon, Mt 4:23–25. For more on this, see Luz, *Matthew 1–7*, 204–8, and Davies and Allison (who link these verses with Mt 5:1–2), *The Gospel According to Saint Matthew*, 410–19. Guelich also links these verses to 5:1–2 (*The Sermon on the Mount*, 50).

[160] *Lumen Gentium* 11: "The sacred character and organic structure if the priestly community are brought into being through the sacraments and virtues ... Taking part in the Eucharistic sacrifice the source and summit if the Christian life, they offer the divine victim to God and themselves along with him."

Christ, the participation in the divine nature, that is the vocation and goal of any Christian life, be it ordained, married, or otherwise. Furthermore, the Eucharist is at its root a reenactment of the paschal sacrifice, the ultimate healing sacrament and restoration of right relations between God and all humanity. Hence, the Eucharist is fittingly understood with both groups of antitheses, of desire and aggression. It is the sacrament most at the heart of the new law, and thus appropriately understood with all of the antitheses.[161]

In summary, Jesus's claim to fulfill the old law directs us not only to the fulfillment of the moral law, but also that of the ceremonial law. The former is particularly obvious in the antitheses. It is a significant contribution of doing this inquiry through the lens of virtue ethics that the prominence of the two root human dynamisms is evident in these verses. The fulfillment of the ceremonial law is less so. But if (as Christian thinkers have consistently maintained) there is correspondence between the old observances and Christ, including the observances of new life in Christ best typified in the sacraments, then it is appropriate to note the convergence between the sacraments of the new law and the antitheses where Christ describes the new law's fulfillment of the old.

Again, if one remains unpersuaded by the alignments offered in this section, then still the argument of the chapter can hold. Even without the antitheses corresponding to the virtues of temperance and fortitude, the new law fulfills the old in the manner depicted in the previous section. Furthermore, even without the antitheses corresponding to the sacraments, the ceremonial law is still fulfilled in Christ, in the manner depicted above and again in this final section on the centrality of Jesus Christ for Mt 5:17–48 and indeed the entire Sermon.

III. JESUS CHRIST AND THE NEW LAW

There really is no one perfect chapter in this book to examine the centrality of Christ for the Sermon, not because Christ is unimportant to any section of the Sermon, but because he is absolutely crucial to all parts of it. It can be therefore misleading to address the person and authority of Christ in this chapter if it is taken to imply that only the verses addressed in this chapter require attention to the centrality of Christ. That is not true. For instance, as briefly referenced in Chapter 1, the beatitudes are basically a self-portrait offered by Jesus. This opening invitation into the life of true happiness is an invitation into life in Christ.[162] Furthermore, the previous chapter presented

---

[161] For more on the Eucharist as the *telos* of the law, old and new alike, see Robert Barron, "The Eucharist as the *Telos* of the Law," 131–43.

[162] According to Guelich, *The Sermon on the Mount*, "The Christological focus at the outset [beatitudes and 5:17] becomes the basis for all that follows in the Sermon" (173).

the salt and light verses as not only thoroughly ecclesiological, but also rooted in the church's Christo-centric identity. The centrality of Jesus Christ for the Sermon can indeed be addressed in any chapter of this book. Nevertheless, the person of Christ is addressed here for two reasons. First, this section of the Sermon most obviously establishes Jesus's authority as interpreter of the law. Second, and even more importantly, the basis of that authority is Jesus's identity, as he himself is the fulfillment of everything to which the law and prophets point.

First, if anything is evident about Jesus in these verses, especially to Jewish hearers of the Sermon, it is Jesus's extraordinary authority. The closing lines of the Sermon itself state this: "When Jesus finished these words, the crowd was astonished at his teaching, for he taught them as one having authority, and not as their scribes" (7:28–29). But even more extraordinary are Jesus's own statements about the law. He has come not to abolish it but to fulfill it. Given the detail of the above analysis it can be forgotten what an astounding claim this is, that Jesus himself fulfills the law. And perhaps even starker to Jewish hearers yesterday and today are the very formulations of the six antitheses, where in each case Jesus offers some variation of "you have heard it was said . . . , but I say to you. . . ."[163] Let alone surpassing the authority of the scribes (7:29), Jesus surpasses the authority of Moses! He is not merely *the* authoritative interpreter of the old law; he is the genesis of a new covenant that fulfills the old.[164]

It is common in scholarship on Mathew's gospel to recognize the parallels between Jesus and Moses. They are so numerous and obvious that there can be no doubt that in some important sense Jesus is being presented by Matthew as a new Moses.[165] Some scholars bristle at naming Jesus the "new Moses," which may initially seem odd given the obvious parallels. But upon closer examination their point is accurate. We must be wary in calling Jesus a

---

[163] According to Guelich, the passive voice in the antitheses ("you have heard it was said") is an example of the "divine passive," such that it could as easily be translated "God said." This translation makes the authority of Jesus even more astounding to all hearers ("God said . . . but I say to you. . . ."). See *The Sermon on the Mount*, 180 and 185.

[164] Guelich inquires as to the literary form of antithesis in Judaism and claims "one never finds a parallel in Judaism for authoritatively setting a demand against the immutable Law" (*The Sermon on the Mount*, 185). Once again Guelich speaks too strongly in saying Jesus's words are "against the immutable law," but his point about the speaker's authority in relation to the law certainly stands. See also Davies and Allison, *The Gospel According to Saint Matthew*, 726.

[165] To name but a few: the extensive parallels between Jesus's birth and early life and that of Moses; the very deliverance of a definitive Sermon on a Mount evocative of Sinai; the very organization of Matthew's gospel with seemingly five "books" evocative of the Pentateuch; and Jesus's establishment of a new covenant celebrated by a meal. For more on parallels between Matthew's Gospel and Moses, see Davies and Allison's overview of positions and an explanation for their hesitancy about the new Moses designation (*The Gospel According to Saint Matthew*, 427); also see Luz, *Matthew 1–7*, 224.

new Moses not because his authority does not match that of Moses, but because his authority exceeds that of Moses, and the role that Jesus plays in humanity's covenantal friendship with God is well beyond that of Moses. So if Jesus is called a new Moses to demonstrate the commonality in *telos* of the old and new laws, this is indeed appropriate. But if Jesus is called a "new Moses" so as to suggest that Jesus's role in salvation history is the same as Moses' (and not more), then scholars are indeed wise to be wary of using this moniker.

With this in mind, we can turn to Pope Benedict's reflection on this part of Matthew's gospel, a poignant presentation of a claim that is also prevalent in more academic biblical scholarship on these verses. Referencing the antitheses, Pope Benedict says "Jesus' 'I' is accorded a status that no teacher of the Law can legitimately allow himself. . . . [H]e himself is on the same level as the Lawgiver – as God."[166] Furthermore, the identity of Jesus and his extraordinary authority is not simply a matter of the source of his teaching on the law, though it is that too. It is also at the heart of what is new about the new law. As Pope Benedict powerfully depicts in recounting Rabbi Neusner's dialogue from *A Rabbi Talks with Jesus*, the Rabbi is asked "What did he [Jesus] leave out [of the law]?" to which Neusner replies, "Nothing." When asked "Then what did he add?" Neusner replies "Himself."[167] Jesus is what is new about the new law. Jesus is the authoritative interpreter of the material content of the new law, in a manner whereby it fulfills the old. He makes possible the living of the law in a way not possible without him. And He Himself is the *telos* of the law, the very union of God and humanity toward which the old law orients humanity.

And so the second reason why it is most fitting to reflect on Jesus Christ in this chapter is because he is in his person the fulfillment of the law. This does not simply mean Jesus lives in accordance with the law. Through his life, death, and resurrection Jesus Christ does indeed bring the law (and prophets) to fulfillment. Jesus Christ, as the Son Incarnate, is the covenantal unity of God and humans toward which the law points, and toward which it guides humanity like a pedagogue. The verses offer no explicit reflection on Christology, but they are deeply Christological.[168] Rabbi Neusner accurately apprehends the magnitude of what these verses mean about the centrality of Jesus Christ, that the man Jesus Christ is God. The Incarnate Word is the very divinization of humanity in friendship with God, the *telos* of the law.

---

[166] Benedict XVI, *Jesus of Nazareth, From the Baptism in the Jordan to the Transfiguration*, trans. Adrian D. Walker (New York: Doubleday, 2007), 102.

[167] Benedict XVI, *Jesus of Nazareth*, 105, quoting Jacob Neusner, *A Rabbi Talks with Jesus* (Montreal: McGill-Queen's University Press, 2000), 107–8.

[168] As Davies and Allison note with regard to the antitheses, "the implicit Christology is remarkable" (*The Gospel According to Saint Matthew*, 512).

CONCLUSION

Thus we come full circle to Luz's two sets of meanings of fulfill. One set concerns what Jesus taught, and this is easily connected to the moral law. But the other set concerns who Jesus is as fulfillment of the law in his life, death, and resurrection. Reminiscent of the last chapter's connection between ethics and eschatology, we have here a connection between who Jesus is as fulfillment of the law and how to live accordingly. Last chapter it was noted that people commonly ask whether the beatitudes are best understood eschatologically, as descriptions of what is promised by God for us in the future, *or* ethically, as how to live in order to attain that promise. There I argued against such a dichotomy, maintaining that the continuity of activity in this life and the next provides an explanation for how the beatitudes are both ethical and eschatological. There is a similar dynamic at work in these verses.

Is Jesus's claim to fulfill primarily about conduct and moral teaching, or is it about his coming? Contemporary biblical scholars recognize this question and are better at avoiding the dichotomy than they were with the beatitudes. Guelich claims the most important sense of fulfill concerns the coming of Jesus, but there is an ethical dimension of his coming as it pertains to us: "Discipleship implies a new relationship with God through Jesus's ministry, as well as the concomitant conduct in keeping God's will."[169] In a statement that would apply well to the beatitudes as well as these verses, he goes on to say, "[T]he Kingdom future is but consummation of Kingdom present."[170] Betz notes that the coming of Christ is not simply gift, but also entails human action.[171]

Therefore, it is evident in these verses that the life, death, and resurrection of Christ are the decisive fulfillment of the law and the prophets. Yet life in Christ is not something that simply happens to us (although it is that too), but also something in which we participate. This is most obvious in these verses by the new law understood in the moral sense. The new law fulfills the old, both in the activity specified and in the ability through grace to live it out. That grace of the Holy Spirit through faith in Christ is only possible because of Christ's identity as the Word become flesh. Furthermore, those who live life in Christ are invited to participate in that life not only morally but also through worship that fulfills the old ceremonial law, most notably the sacraments. These practices reflect, instantiate, and further nourish the life made possible by the life, death, and resurrection of Jesus Christ.

The second section offered extensive speculative attention to how the six antitheses address the human dynamisms of desire and aggression, and thus depict the fulfillment of the moral law through the virtues of temperance and

---

[169] Guelich, *The Sermon on the Mount*, 160.
[170] Guelich, *The Sermon on the Mount*, 172.　　　[171] Betz, *The Sermon on the Mount*, 190.

fortitude, and depict the fulfillment of the ceremonial law through the sacraments of the Church. Thus, there is less need in this conclusion for a reflection on how the two cardinal virtues of temperance and fortitude converge with this portion of the Sermon. Instead this conclusion closes with a reminder of that crucial closing verse of this section of the Sermon, 5:48: "Be perfect as your heavenly Father is perfect."

As noted above, these words fall at the end of the sixth antithesis and can be seen as the conclusion of that single antithesis. That is true in a sense. The sixth antithesis, like the fourth one which also concludes one of the two sets of three proposed here, contains teaching about who God is. That teaching has implications for human action. Since God alone is provident as seen in 5:34–36, we are to resist our desire to dictate reality and instead be governed by the truth. Since God loves both the just and unjust, we are to resist our inclination to mete out justice on our terms and instead love and pray for the good and evil alike. In both these ways we are perfect as our heavenly Father is perfect, and indeed the same may be said for all of the antitheses, for which the fourth and sixth serve as culminations. So 5:48 is therefore rightly understood as a conclusion to this entire section of the Sermon that begins with a claim that Christ fulfills the law (5:17). In these verses, Jesus enjoins us toward perfection, or complete conformity with the *telos* of the law which is friendship with God. He enjoins us toward fulfillment of, or more perfect conformity with, the law in its moral and ceremonial senses. And in a manner echoed in Mt 19:21, he invites his audience toward the perfection that is himself, lived out by us in discipleship to him.

3

INTENTIONALITY, GROWTH IN VIRTUE, AND CHARITY IN MATTHEW 6:1–6, 16–18

[But] take care not to perform righteous deeds in order that people may see them;
  otherwise, you will have no recompense from your heavenly Father.
When you give alms, do not blow a trumpet before you, as the hypocrites do in the
  synagogues and in the streets to win the praise of others. Amen, I say to you,
  they have received their reward.
But when you give alms, do not let your left hand know what your right is doing,
so that your almsgiving may be secret. And your Father who sees in secret will
  repay you.
When you pray, do not be like the hypocrites, who love to stand and pray in the
  synagogues and on street corners so that others may see them. Amen, I say to
  you, they have received their reward.
But when you pray, go to your inner room, close the door, and pray to your Father
  in secret. And your Father who sees in secret will repay you. . . .
When you fast, do not look gloomy like the hypocrites. They neglect their
  appearance, so that they may appear to others to be fasting. Amen, I say to you,
  they have received their reward.
But when you fast, anoint your head and wash your face,
so that you may not appear to be fasting, except to others your Father who is
  hidden. And your Father who sees what is hidden will repay you.

In this chapter, we turn to a passage that lies at the spatial heart of the
Sermon on the Mount and addresses themes that are central to the Sermon
as read through the lens of virtue ethics. This passage addresses one of the
most important topics in a virtue-centered action theory, namely, intentionality. Thus the first section of this chapter addresses the topic of intentionality as evident in Mt 6:1–6, 16–18 and as connected to a Thomistic action
analysis. Two consistent terms in these verses are "reward" and "hypocrite,"
and these concepts offer important scriptural contributions to a virtue ethics
analysis of intentionality. The second section addresses the verses' rather
specific and practical guidance on the formation of virtue. I argue that these

verses' attention to interiority should in no way be thought to exclude the importance of exterior actions, and that indeed these verses offer specific, action-based guidance as to the development of virtues. The conclusion examines these verses in light of the theological virtue of charity.

It may help at the outset to situate the claims of this chapter in relation to contemporary biblical and moral scholarship on these verses and themes. Three stand out (though note they do not strictly correlate with this chapter's sections). First, the literature on Thomistic action theory, particularly on the relationship between the object and end of an act, is literally voluminous.[1] Though the analysis offered here will draw on that literature, no attempt is made here to advance that scholarship, except in one way. Thomistic action scholarship is regarded as less attentive to Scripture. It is hoped that this chapter can help ground those scholarly debates more firmly in Christ's own words in Scripture, not only as "warrant" for those debates but as a potential source of guidance within the debates.

Second, the revival in virtue ethics in the past decades has led to increased attention to moral formation through the development of virtue, with varying emphases on the thought of Thomas Aquinas, historical developments after Thomas Aquinas, and even connections to the sciences.[2] This chapter hopes to more explicitly relate those discussions to Scripture as well, again not only to provide scriptural warrant for such discussion but also to glean substantive guidance from the Sermon on this topic.

Finally, contemporary biblical scholarship most frequently addresses these verses and their context in the Sermon in one of two ways. They are commonly seen as a treatment of interiority (as distinct from exterior acts as treated in Mt 5:21–48), and/or a treatment of our "vertical" relationship with

---

[1] For a seminal article on the origins of the use of "object" in moral theology, see Lawrence Dewan, "'*Objectum*': notes on the invention of a word" in *Wisdom Law and Virtue: Essays in Thomistic Ethics* (New York: Fordham University Press, 2008). For helpful examples of the recent scholarship in Thomistic circles on the moral object, see Steven Long, *Teleological Grammar of the Human Act: Introductions to Catholic Doctrine* (Naples, FL: Sapientia Press, 2007); Martin Rhonheimer and William F. Murphy, *The Perspective of the Acting Person: Essays in the Renewal of Thomistic Moral Philosophy* (Washington, DC: Catholic University of America Press, 2008), and Martin Rhonheimer, *The Perspective of Morality: Philosophical Foundations of Thomistic Virtue Ethics* (Washington, DC: Catholic University of America Press, 2011); Steven J. Jensen, *Good and Evil Actions: A Journey through Saint Thomas Aquinas* (Washington, DC: Catholic University of America Press, 2010). These and other works on the object of action are cited below, along with attention to distinct "waves" of scholarship on the moral object over the past few decades.

[2] Servais Pinckaers, *The Sources of Christian Ethics* (Washington, DC: Catholic University of America Press, 1995); Jennifer A. Herdt, *Putting on Virtue: The Legacy of the Splendid Vices* (Chicago: University of Chicago Press, 2008); Craig Steven Titus, *Resilience and the Virtue of Fortitude* (Washington, DC: Catholic University of America Press, 2006). For an overview of scholarship in the revival of virtue ethics over the past few decades, see David Cloutier and William C. Mattison III, "Review Essay: The Resurgence of Virtue in Moral Theology," *Journal of Moral Theology* 3.1, *Virtue* (2014): 228–59.

God (as distinct from "horizontal" relationships with others as treated in 5:21–48). Biblical scholarship has provided rich contributions to understanding the content of these verses. Nonetheless, this chapter complements those contributions by calling into question too sharp a distinction between interior and exterior acts, as well as the "vertical" and "horizontal" in the Sermon.

One more prolegomenous point is warranted here on the structure of these verses. The verses addressed in this chapter are perhaps the most obviously structured in the Sermon, and that structure is therefore relatively uncontested in the literature.[3] The passage consists of what one contemporary biblical scholar calls a "finely balanced" structure containing instruction on three "characteristically Jewish forms of piety," namely, almsgiving (6:2–4), prayer (6:5–6), and fasting (6:16–18). In each case there is an injunction not to perform actions in a certain way, with vivid descriptions of hypocrites who do just that. There is also an exhortation to practice piety in a secret or hidden manner, so that our "heavenly Father who sees in secret will repay you." This triadic structure is introduced by a characteristically Matthean "summarizing heading" (6:1).[4] Finally, there is an expansion of the middle element of the triad on prayer, constituted mainly by the words of the Lord's Prayer (6:7–15).[5] Since the components of the triad are so similar, this chapter focuses mainly on those similarities, with consideration also of the opening summary statement. Thus all three sections of this chapter focus on what these verses have in common, though the third and final section does attend to why these three acts are chosen and what distinct contributions they offer to the unified messages of these verses.

I. "TO BE SEEN BY OTHERS": INTENTIONALITY AND HUMAN ACTION

Commentators from the Patristic period until today have recognized the central role played by intention in these verses. The passage identifies certain actions: "performing righteous deeds," "giving alms," "praying," and "fasting"

---

[3] There are rare exceptions. For instance, see Jonathan T. Pennington, *Heaven and Earth in the Gospel of Matthew* (Leiden: Brill, 2007), 242–47, who claims this section properly ends with 6:21. The main questions still debated by biblical scholars concern not the structure of these verses but authorship. Various Matthean and pre-Matthean permutations are considered for the authorship of: 6:1; 6:2–6, 16–18, and 6:7–15. See Luz, *Matthew 1–7: A Commentary*, 354–55, 362; Betz, *The Sermon on the Mount*, 349–51; Guelich, *The Sermon on the Mount*, 273–74; Davies and Allison, *The Gospel According to Saint Matthew*, 572–75.

[4] Walter T. Wilson, "Seen in Secret: Inconspicuous Piety and Alternative Subjectivity in Matthew 6:1–6, 16–18." *The Catholic Biblical Quarterly* 72.3 (2010): 475–97, at 475. See also Guelich, *The Sermon on the Mount*, 273; Davies and Allison, *The Gospel According to Saint Matthew*, 575–78; Betz, *The Sermon on the Mount*, 351–53.

[5] Note that 6:7–15 consisting mainly of the Lord's Prayer/Our Father is not treated in this chapter but rather addressed in Chapter 6.

(vv. 1, 2, 5, 16, respectively). But in each case the performance of these deeds is qualified by some variation of the phrase "in order to be seen by others."[6] Thus we have a certain action which is done for a further goal, namely, to be seen by others. The passage of course goes on to enjoin the audience not to perform such acts to be seen by others, but rather in secret, so that our heavenly Father who sees in secret will reward them. The juxtaposition of the hypocrites and those who perform such acts for heavenly recompense invites some explanation of the difference between the two groups. This is where commentators have relied on intentionality. Chrysostom claims it is "not just the thing, but the intent, that he [God] punishes and rewards," an insight affirmed by Augustine as well.[7] With specific reference to almsgiving Chrysostom goes on to say, "It is not just the giving alms which is required, but the giving as one ought, the giving for such and such an end."[8] On that same sort of action, Guelich claims, "The issue here is not the difference between public and private giving. The issue is the *ultimate motivation* for our giving."[9] Betz affirms this interpretation saying, "The point here is . . . whether the intention of the performer is to be seen by [others] or by God."[10] Intentionality is at the heart of interpretation of these verses.[11]

---

[6] See Betz, *The Sermon on the Mount*, 329 for a most literal translation. He translates the qualifier as "for the purpose of" in v. 1 to represent the Greek *pros* [+ aorist passive infinitive], while he uses "in order that" in vv. 2, 5, 16 to translate *hopos*. Note that the difference in causal phrasing between v. 1, on the one hand, and vv. 2, 5, 16, on the other, is part of the argument for the Matthean addition of verse 1, a question not explored here. No claim is made here about the significance of the use of different terms. On *pros*, see Bo Reicke, "πρός," *Theological Dictionary of the New Testament* [vol. 6]: 720–25, at 724.

[7] John Chrysostom, *Homilies on Matthew* XIX.2 (131). References to John Chrysostom's *Homilies on Matthew* given here are from Jaroslav Pelikan, ed., *The Preaching of John Chrysostom*. The reference includes homily, section, and in parentheses the page number from this edition. See Augustine, *The Lord's Sermon on the Mount*, no. 5, 117. See also Thomas Aquinas, *Commentary on the Gospel of Matthew, Chapters 1–12*, trans. Jeremy Holmes and Beth Mortensen, 560; Martin Luther, *The Sermon on the Mount*, trans. Jaroslav Pelikan, 1–294 in *Luther's Works 21, 131*; John Wesley and Kenneth C. Kinghorn, *John Wesley on The Sermon on the Mount Volume 2: The Standard Sermons in Modern English Volume 2, 21–33* (Abingdon Press, 2002), 152.

[8] John Chrysostom, *Homilies on Matthew* XIX.2 (132).

[9] Guelich, *The Sermon on the Mount*, 303, emphasis mine (see also 305).

[10] Betz, *The Sermon on the Mount*, 353. See also W. D. Davies and Dale Allison, *Matthew: A Shorter Commentary* (Bloomsbury: T & T Clark, 2005), 88: "The Problem is not whether but how, not the thing but the intent." See Georg Strecker, *The Sermon on the Mount: An Exegetical Commentary* (Nashville: Abingdon Press, 1988), 100: "the decisive difference between the right and the wrong behavior is the aim, which should be directed not toward people but toward God."

[11] Walter Wilson claims that the two most common topics of interpretation for these verses are intentionality and the status of the three acts as Jewish cultic acts. See Wilson, "Seen in Secret," 476. He rejects an interpretation whereby the text is a refutation of Jewish external practices in preference for household cultic acts. Yet reflection on the status of these three acts as important Jewish cultic acts is not limited to this interpretation, as his article goes on to show. Indeed, the two topics can be immediately related, as when Betz interprets these

Intentionality is also a central topic for a virtue ethics approach to moral theology.[12] An intention is the goal or purpose of an action which renders that action intelligible or meaningful. Though intentionality may be spoken of in the broader sense of simply goal-directed behavior, for human persons intentional action is a reflection of human rationality.[13] With the intellect a human person apprehends or grasps a goal and with the will or rational appetite the person responds accordingly to that goal (e.g., pursues it). As Thomas Aquinas famously argues, genuinely human acts (that is to say, moral acts) are those that proceed from the intellect and will. A person is said to have dominion over such acts.[14] These acts are voluntary and thus evaluable as praiseworthy or blameworthy. Therefore intentionality is crucial to ethics.[15] Furthermore, as explained below, intentionality not only enables us to understand and evaluate particular actions, but it is also the lynchpin in the formation of habits such as virtues.

verses as "cultic didache" on how to properly approach the divine, which includes proper dispositions and attitudes. See *The Sermon on the Mount*, 332. See also his article "A Jewish Christian Cultic *Didache* in Matthew 6:1–18," in Betz, ed., *Essays on the Sermon on the Mount*, trans. Lawrence Welborne (Philadelphia: Fortress Press, 1985), 55–69 .

[12] It is noteworthy that one of the thinkers who prompted the revival of virtue ethics today Elizabeth Anscombe (particularly her seminal article "Modern Moral Philosophy") wrote a book called simply *Intention* (Ithaca, N.Y: Cornell University Press, 1957). For the importance of a first-person perspective as characteristic of virtue ethics, see Julia Annas, *The Morality of Happiness*, 440 and 443. See also David Cloutier and William C. Mattison III, "Review Essay: The Resurgence of Virtue in Recent Moral Theology" *Journal of Moral Theology* 3.1 (2014): 228–59. Note that John Paul II's encyclical uses the phrase the "perspective of the acting person" (§78) to name this first person perspective. Years before *Veritatis Splendor*'s emphasis on the perspective of the acting person, Servais Pinckaers, O.P. examined the differences between what he called "reflective moral" (first-person) knowledge and "positivist scientific" (third-person or observer perspective) knowledge. See his *The Sources of Christian Ethics*, 58–74.

[13] For the continuities and yet distinctiveness of human goal-directed action and say, that of non-human animals, see Thomas Aquinas, *Summa Theologiae* I–II 1, 2. See also Herbert McCabe and Brian Davies, *The Good Life: Ethics and the Pursuit of Happiness*, 58–73. For more on this topic, with recognition of differences among non-human animals, see Alasdair MacIntyre, *Dependent Rational Animals: Why Human Beings Need the Virtues*, (London: Duckworth, 2009), esp. 43–51.

[14] Thomas Aquinas, *Summa Theologiae* I–II 1, 1. See I–II 1, 3 for the claim that human acts are moral acts.

[15] Of course while intentionality is crucial to ethics, the Thomistic-based account of intentionality employed here is not the only one available. For an outstanding (and brief) Thomistic account of practical reasoning "situated" in relation to various contemporary accounts of intentionality and practical reasoning more broadly understood, see Jean Porter's *Nature as Reason: A Thomistic Theory of the Natural Law* (Grand Rapids, MI: Eerdman, 2005), 234–48. There she not only overviews distinct Thomistic approaches to intentionality (234) but also goes on to survey recent broadly Kantian (235–39) and broadly Humean (or "sentimentalist") (239–45) approaches to practical reasoning.

Intentionality is thus at the heart of both a virtue ethics approach to moral theology and the verses under consideration this chapter. At the very least, then, these verses provide an opportunity to explore the topic of intentionality. Scholars participating in the, say, Thomistic action scholarship that is influential on this chapter, can point to these verses as authorizing their more technical debates. But do these verses simply warrant, or do they actually contribute to, reflection on the importance of intentionality for human action? It is suggested here that the Scripture contributes to these discussions, primarily through two terms that will structure the ensuing two parts of this section. The first part examines the importance of a goal or end (*finis*) on human activity. It will rely on Thomistic action analysis to explain how the end is so formative for the meaning of more proximate acts. It also provides an analysis of the Matthean term "reward" as a contribution to action theory scholarship. The second part of this section focuses on those more proximate acts, traditionally called "objects" in Catholic moral theology. Given the first part's emphasis on the importance of the further end for the meaning of immediate acts, this section examines the extent to which the proximate acts have any meaning "on their own," as it were. It argues that despite the enormous importance of the end for human action, the object remains a crucial facet of the human act. The use of the term "hypocrite" in these verses helps to substantiate this claim.

A. THE IMPORTANCE OF THE END IN HUMAN ACTION – "THEY HAVE RECEIVED THEIR REWARD"

The verses under consideration here make it quite evident that the end or further goal prompting our immediate action matters. Before examining this in more detail with particular emphasis on the concept of reward, a word on terminology is in order. In the above quotations, authors use the term "intention" to refer to the further goal (to be seen by others) of the immediate acts (prayer, fasting, giving alms). As we will see below, this is also done in the Catholic moral theological tradition when distinguishing "object" and "intention" as parts of the act.[16] But there is something misleading about this use of intention. It can wrongly suggest that the object is not chosen with its own immediate goal, or intention. This has engendered confusion in action theory debates, a confusion addressed in the next part. For now, it suffices to note that in the broad sense, intentionality refers to goal-directed activity, or activity toward an end (*finis*, or purpose, or point). Since an act can have an

---

[16] Thomas Aquinas actually refers to object (*objectum*) and end (*finis*). See Thomas Aquinas, *Summa Theologiae* I–II 18, for example, art 2, 6. But the trio of object, intention, and circumstance has become so entrenched in moral theology that it seems unalterable, despite the problematic connotation possible by distinguishing object from intention, as noted below.

immediate goal (e.g., giving money to the poor) and a further goal (e.g., to be seen by others), there is a sense in which both the object and intention are "intentional." Hence the confusion. In this chapter, I will use the terms "further goal" and "immediate goal" instead of intention and object, respectively. I will only use intention in a manner limited to the further goal when it is juxtaposed with object, so as to try and avoid the mistaken impression that there is no intentionality or purposefulness in immediate acts/objects.

The verses at hand clearly indicate that the further goal matters for the meaning and evaluation of the act. The verses describe two sets of people who perform "righteous deeds." What distinguishes them is not, as indicated above by Guelich, the presence or absence of other people.[17] It is the further goal of their actions. Indeed, the passage makes it clear that the further goal is not merely an internal mental event in the agent that changes the meaning of an otherwise same act. The difference in further goal not only changes the meaning of the act but is evident in how that immediate goal is pursued. If one's further goal is to be seen by others, almsgiving is accompanied by fanfare. Prayer is performed in prominent public places. And fasting is purposely manifested as such. Yet if the "audience"[18] is God, each of these activities is performed in a manner bereft of public display, revealing a "doctrine of God" as present even in the hidden that engenders an "inconspicuous piety."[19]

With these two varying further goals, it **is** *and* **is not** the case that we have two groups of people doing the "same thing" but for different reasons. It is the case that both groups choose an activity (e.g., giving alms) with an immediate finality or purpose that makes it recognizable as such, even when the further goal differs. That topic is addressed in the second part of this section. But it is also the case that the change in further goal changes the way the immediate activity is performed, as well as its meaning. Thus, in a real sense the two groups are performing different acts. The importance of the further end of human action is the topic of this part of the section,

---

[17] There is a long tradition of explaining how the verses under consideration in this chapter are compatible with the Mt 5:16 injunction to let one's light shine "before others." The consistent position in the tradition and in contemporary biblical scholarship is that they are compatible since the issue is not whether one's act is indeed seen by others, but whether or not one chooses acts "that they may see your righteous deeds and glorify your heavenly Father" (5:16). In 5:16 the further goal of being seen is God's glory, whereas in these verses being seen by others is an end in itself. See Augustine, *The Lord's Sermon on the Mount*, II.1.2; Aquinas, *Commentary on the Gospel of Matthew*, 561; Davies and Allison, *The Gospel According to Saint Matthew*, 576.

[18] See Betz, *The Sermon on the Mount*, 352–53 for the concept of audience. See also Wilson, "Seen in Secret," 482–91.

[19] For more on the Matthean "doctrine of God" and ensuing "inconspicuous piety" from the perspective of biblical scholarship, see Betz, *The Sermon on the Mount*, 339–46.

proceeding in two subparts. The first relies on Thomistic action theory to examine why the further end is so important. The second mines the resources of these verses, particularly through the notion of reward, to corroborate and advance that claim.

1. THOMISTIC ACTION THEORY AND THE FURTHER END OF HUMAN ACTION The enormous impact of the further goal in the meaning of the immediate activity is explored here through Thomas Aquinas's analysis of the human act. Thomas Aquinas examines whether an act derives its goodness or badness from the object or the end. At times, Thomas Aquinas speaks as if there are various separable components of an act, and all must be good for an act to be good.[20] In the case of Matthew 6:1–6, 16–18, we might imagine him saying that if an act that is good in genus and species (e.g., almsgiving) is being done toward an evil end with corresponding circumstances, it is thus vitiated. This analysis would be correct. However, taken on its own it can make the components of an act seem extrinsically connected to one another. Put differently, it can make it seem that the almsgiving of the hypocrite and the almsgiving of the one seeking heavenly required are the same.

But at other times, Thomas Aquinas emphasizes just how important the end is for transforming a human action. In explaining how a human act can be good or evil not only due to its object, but also on account of its end, he describes a human action as a hylomorphic (or we might say "organic") unity of object (akin to matter) and end (akin to form).[21] From this perspective, an activity like almsgiving done for different ends may be materially the same in both cases, but is formally different due to the difference in end. Its form is what most properly makes something what it is, and the importance of this claim should be recognized. Thomas Aquinas uses an (admittedly odd) example from Aristotle to illustrate this claim. If someone were to steal money in order to commit adultery (presumably with a prostitute), Thomas Aquinas follows Aristotle in claiming that the person would be more adulterer than a thief (although he is both).[22] The further end of action defines the action even more than its immediate finality. This explains the next few articles where Thomas Aquinas elaborates on this claim.

In the very next article, Thomas Aquinas asks, "whether the species of an act derived from its end is contained under the species of an act as derived from its object as under a genus, or vice versa?"[23] This confusingly worded question might be rephrased for our purposes as follows: Is there a broad

---

[20] He lists four: genus (akin to natural species); species (derived from object); circumstances; and end. See Thomas Aquinas, *Summa Theologiae* I–II 18, 4.

[21] Thomas Aquinas, *Summa Theologiae* I–II 18, 6: "the species of a human act is considered formally with regard to the end, but materially with regard to the object of the external action."

[22] Thomas Aquinas, *Summa Theologiae* I–II 18, 6 citing Aristotle's *Nicomachean Ethics* 2.

[23] Thomas Aquinas, *Summa Theologiae* I–II 18, 7.

class of almsgivers, subdivided into those who do it to be seen by others and those who do it for God? If this were true than the object would provide the genus and the end would supply the species. But Thomas Aquinas claims the opposite is the case. The end provides the genus and the object the species. So those who do things to be seen by others include those who give alms for that purpose (as well as presumably those who do other things, including prayer and fasting). And those who do things for our heavenly Father include those who give alms for that end (as well as others, including presumably those who fast and pray for that end). This is of course basically the same claim as Aristotle's about adultery and theft. But the image of end rather than object providing genus is even more stark. It suggests that among those who give alms, those who do it to be seen by others and those who do it for our heavenly Father are entirely different genus of people.

Why is this? How can people who from an observer's perspective are doing the same thing be wholly different sorts of people? After all, that they are different sorts of people is not simply a Thomistic claim relying on Aristotelian philosophical categories; it is also the message of Mt 6:1–6 and 16–18. Three types of acts are described there, but really only two sorts of people: hypocrites and those who perform for God. Indeed, it is reasonable to suppose the hypocrites will do all three acts (for the one end of being seen by others) and those who wish to be seen by our heavenly Father will do all three acts for that end. So why does this passage corroborate the (Aristotelian and) Thomistic claim that end provides genus and not object? The answer is that both the Sermon and Thomas Aquinas are describing action "from the perspective of the acting person."[24] Human persons choose immediate activities for further goals, and those immediate activities are taken up and transformed by further ends.[25] Yet why is this so? Why is the end so important for action from the perspective of the acting person that it not only differentiates what further goals we seek but even "in-forms" the acts we do in search of those goals? Our verses offer some guidance with the crucial concept of "reward."

2. REWARD IN MATTHEW 6:1–6, 16–18 How do these verses indicate the importance of the further goal pursued for the meaning of human

---

[24] This important phrase in contemporary Catholic moral theology is taken from *Veritatis Splendor* 78 and is examined in more detail below with regard to object.

[25] Hence the next two articles in Thomas Aquinas's *Summa Theologia* following those treated here concern the question of indifferent actions. While Thomas Aquinas recognizes that certain types of actions can be called indifferent (he lists picking up straw from the ground or walking in a field), he claims that an individual action, or better any action chosen by an individual agent, cannot be indifferent. Any human act from deliberate reason must be good or evil when full account is given of its object, end, and circumstances. So from the perspective of the acting person, assuming the act is truly human in that it engages one's reason and will (unlike, say, stroking one's beard), every individual act is good or evil. See Thomas Aquinas, *Summa Theologiae* I–II 18, 8–9.

actions? One striking way they do so is through the concept of reward. There is an obvious sense in which the actions of both the hypocrites and those who wish to be seen by the heavenly Father are related to the further ends they pursue. In both cases, their actions lead to corresponding rewards. Turning first to the hypocrites, we read that those who pray, fast, and give alms "to be seen" by others "have received their reward." The text makes it clear that the actions they perform are compensated. What reward is received? The hypocrites receive the recognition of others that is the further end of their actions. In contrast to the hypocrites, those who do such deeds for the kingdom of heaven are repaid by their heavenly Father.[26] What exactly is this reward received? A variety of interpretations have been offered.[27] Given the context in the Sermon, it seems most appropriate to label the reward the kingdom of heaven, or alternatively God Himself.[28] In both cases, the agents receive their rewards, whether that is being seen by others or receiving our heavenly Father's reward. The fact that these verses describe in two different manners the ways that hypocrites and those acting for our heavenly Father receive their rewards suggests that they may offer some contribution to the question of how a further end informs immediate action. This subpart mines biblical scholarship on these verses for contributions on this question.

What can we thus learn about the relationship between immediate acts and further goals by the way these verses depict the rewards of the two groups of people? The first point to be made is that biblical scholars' commonly recognize the different Greek words used in these passages to express the notion of reward. The fact that the same word (the noun *misthros*) is used to describe the reward received by the hypocrites in all three cases, along with the fact that the same word (the verb *apodidomi*) is used to describe how people are repaid by our heavenly Father, invites some analysis of the contrast. Some biblical scholars find significance in this difference. Guelich claims the term used for the hypocrites is a technical commercial term meaning "to pay in full."[29] Davies and Allison make a similar observation and translate the term literally as "drawing up a

---

[26] For the functional equivalence of heavenly Father with Father who sees in secret/sees what is hidden, see Pennington, *Heaven and Earth in the Gospel of Matthew*, 236–37. See also Betz, *The Sermon on the Mount*, 339.

[27] See Wilson, "Seen in Secret," 456n51 for an overview of varying answers to the question of what constitutes the reward of Mt 6:4, 6, 18. His own noteworthy interpretation is that it is divine forgiveness. Davies and Allison speculate it is divine praise (*The Gospel According to Saint Matthew*, 584).

[28] Thomas Aquinas says of the term "reward" in 5:12 that it is the "enjoyment of God" (*Commentary on the Gospel of Matthew*, 449). Augustine says it is happiness at II.1.4, II.3.14, II.12, and esp. II.12.40. Betz claims it refers to the last judgment and heaven (*The Sermon on the Mount*, 360–61). Guelich also says reward "points to the final judgment," *The Sermon on the Mount*, 280.

[29] Guelich, *The Sermon on the Mount*, 279.

receipt."[30] Both commentators claim this connotation is a depiction of the inferior quality of the hypocrites' reward. Guelich notes it can be paid in full now as a "calculable wage," in contrast to the heavenly reward which cannot and is thus reserved for the future.[31] Davies and Allison also note the transactional sense of the hypocrites' reward and claim they are owed nothing further.[32] In these authors there is at least an implied contrast with the verb *apodidomi* used to describe how our heavenly Father repays, since none of the authors listed above describe this verb in any commercial or transactional sense.[33] One aspect of that commercial term that prompts commentators to separate it from the reward offered by God is the *quid pro quo* aspect of it, implying there is equivalence between what is done to earn the reward and the reward earned. This concern warrants a brief *excursus* on theological concerns about "reward" that are pertinent to but extend beyond these verses in Matthew 6.

§

Excursus: Uneasiness with Reward in Biblical Scholarship

Discussion of reward from our heavenly Father raises a concern about reward that requires some brief treatment here.[34] In his *The Theme of Recompense in Matthew's Gospel*, Blaine Charette castigates contemporary biblical scholarship for its consistent dismissal of the importance of the theme of recompense/reward in Matthew's gospel. He charts the frequency with which reward terminology is found in Matthew.[35] Yet he also documents the (at best) unease with and (at worst) rejection of that theme in Matthew.[36] That dismissal of reward leads some to question whether the

---

[30] Davies and Allison, *The Gospel According to Saint Matthew*, 582.

[31] Guelich, *The Sermon on the Mount*, 303.

[32] Davies and Allison, *The Gospel According to Saint Matthew*, 582. See also Blaine Charette, *The Theme of Recompense in Matthew's Gospel* (Sheffield, England: JSOT Press, 1992), 98, where he describes the hypocrites as "purchasing social prestige."

[33] Yet interestingly Betz (*The Sermon on the Mount*, 360) describes *apodidomi* as a commercial transactional term and makes no such claim about *misthros*. Betz is the only scholar in the literature who reverses this observation, so perhaps it is an error. Despite the allure of assigning significance to the different terms used, caution is in order for that argument. Even if Betz is wrong, *misthros* is the term used in 6:1 to warn the audience they will receive no reward from their heavenly Father if they perform righteous deeds to be seen by others.

[34] For an overview of the best twentieth-century scholarship on reward leading up to his own fine article, see Bo Reicke's "The New Testament Conception of Reward," in *Aux Sources de la Tradition Chrétienne. Mélanges offerts à Maurice Goguel*, ed. J. J. von Aïlmen (Paris, 1950), 195–206.

[35] Charette, *The Theme of Recompense in Matthew's Gospel*, 12.

[36] For the former, he cites R. T. France, *Matthew: Evangelist and Teacher* (Munnich: Kaiser, 1989), 268: "At the level of terminology it must be recognized that Matthew does not

Matthean language is an accurate portrayal of the historical Jesus.[37] Though his book does not attempt any extended explanation of this phenomenon, he does note two possible reasons for this reaction. The first is to offer a contrast between Jesus's teaching and a crude view of Judaism: "it is affirmed . . . that whereas the teaching of early Judaism is characterized by *quid pro quo* reckoning based on the equating of recompense with achievement, in the teaching of Jesus any thought of reward as payment has been removed."[38] Second, there is a presumed understanding of the relationship between grace and merit in which "The disciple has no right to reward; whatever reward is given for the efforts of the disciple is undeserved and indeed cannot be deserved."[39] As a result of this common stance in biblical scholarship:

> It is one of the ironies of modern research on the theme of recompense in the Gospels that the reconstituted teaching of Jesus is so dissimilar to the teaching of Jesus as reported in Matthew, especially when one considers that Matthew is the most important source of what can be known about Jesus' teaching on this theme.[40]

seem to share the coyness of many modern Christians with respect to rewards." See 13n.2. As to the latter, he cites J. Jeremias, *New Testament Theology* (New York: Charles Scribner's Sons, 1971), 216: "Here it is clear that while Jesus takes up the word 'reward,' he in fact presupposes that the disciples have completely detached themselves from striving for a reward." See 99n3. See also James I. H. MacDonald, "The Concept of Reward in the Teaching of Jesus," *The Expository Times* (June 1978) 269 and 271. Charette finds this disdain in Luther (as cited in Paul Ramsey's *Basic Christian Ethics*, 134), whose text (from *Bondage of the Will*) he quotes when he says: "Christian commentators have been moved to describe the concept of reward in general as 'primitive,' as 'ugly prudential teaching,' or as '*quid pro quo* morality' designed to appeal only to those who, in Luther's words, 'with an evil and mercenary evil, seek the things of self even in God'" (269).

[37] See Charette, *The Theme of Recompense in Matthew's Gospel*, 14; Strecker, *The Sermon on the Mount*, 102.

[38] Charette, *The Theme of Recompense in Matthew's Gospel*, 13. This is a useful place to note the common discussion in the biblical literature over whether what is targeted in Mt 6 is Jewish piety *per se*, or a degraded form of it (in which case it could equally apply to Christian piety to be seen by others). Though the former interpretation is well-attested through the history of interpretation (Betz, *The Sermon on the Mount*, 360), the latter is by far the consensus today. The assumption that Jewish piety is "*quid pro quo* reckoning" is rejected here for similar reasons. For a clear example of the derision toward Jewish piety as inherently *quid pro quo*, see Reicke, "The New Testament Conception of Reward," 202. This is a most obvious recent case of setting Mt 6 "in clear opposition to Jewish practice" which he describes as "Jewish moralism" with reward on the basis of "strictly personal merits" (202). (He even goes on to align the "treasure on earth" from 6:19 with "Jewish ideas.") For the opposite view, see Betz, "A Jewish Christian Cultic *Didache*," 62 where he says that the guidance offered by Jesus in Mt 6 is "completely in keeping with the religious thought and practice of Judaism." The consensus today is well represented by Luz: "The hypocrites are not identified with a certain group but remain a general negative type. However, the evangelist Matthew most likely is thinking of the scribes and Pharisees" (*Matthew 1–7*, 357, cf. 360).

[39] Charette, *The Theme of Recompense in Matthew's Gospel*, 14.

[40] Charette, *The Theme of Recompense in Matthew's Gospel*, 13.

Charette's study is in large part an attempt to identify an accurate understanding of reward as presented in Matthew's gospel.

What should be said here about this uneasiness with reward and merit? First, there are indeed legitimate concerns that underlie such uneasiness. Most importantly, any description of reward or merit that assumes that a person can earn eternal reward without God's grace, or that a person can place some sort of obligation on God such that God owes a person, is clearly incompatible with Christian faith. Yet, an emphasis on reward or merit need not assume these things. For instance, as Thomas Aquinas makes clear in his treatment of merit, claiming a person can merit eternal life does not mean it is possible without God's grace.[41] Eternal life is still the fitting or appropriate reward for such activity on the part of a person, even if the activity is not possible without God's grace. For the activity is nonetheless truly one's own even if not possible on one's own.

Despite its use of terminology that is not endorsed here, the well-reputed *Theological Dictionary of the New Testament* article on reward (*misthros*) is an effective example of what is and is not true about heavenly reward.[42] Preisker claims God does not give reward "as a judge who judges justly, but as a father who gives generously."[43] He recognizes the presence of the theme of reward in Matthew, but says (revealing his uneasiness) "it is taken out of the sphere of law and calculation, and consequently purified."[44] These lines make it evident he dismisses any conception of humanity having a "calculating" claim on God.[45] He relies on a distinction

---

[41] See Thomas Aquinas, *Summa Theologiae* I–II 114, 1–3. See also Joseph Wawrykow, *God's Grace and Human Action: "Merit" in the Theology of Thomas Aquinas* (Notre Dame, IN: University of Notre Dame Press, 1995). Wawrykow offers a nuanced explanation of how merit does indeed imply an obligation, but yet how it is actually an obligation of God *to* God (181, emphasis in original; citing I–II 114, 1 ad. 3).

[42] Ernest Würthwein and Herbert Preisker, "μισθός," *Theological Dictionary of the New Testament* (1939–1940) 4: 699–736. Preisker's entry is featured in Reicke's list of the best scholarship on reward in the first half of the twentieth century.

[43] Würthwein and Preisker, "μισθός," 716. See also Charette, *The Theme of Recompense in Matthew's Gospel*, 100: "The language of reward merely indicates that God takes his children seriously and responds to their actions. He has prepared a reward for them but its attainment depends on their faithfulness."

[44] Würthwein and Preisker, "μισθός," 717. This quotation seems to assume that reward is normally placed in such a sphere, requiring its "purification." Betz also struggles to delineate the proper understanding of our heavenly Father's repayment, claiming: "Employing this term does not mean, however, that God owes the secret donor a debt, but that the donor has a credit due to his righteousness which God will uphold" (*The Sermon on the Mount*, 360).

[45] Charette echoes this legitimate concern, claiming Matthean reward "is removed from the realm of legal obligation and rights," and "is not a simple quid pro quo" (*The Theme of Recompense in Matthew's Gospel*, 99). Charette comes closer than many to understanding the relationship between activity and reward more intrinsically, as discussed below and in Chapter 1. Yet certain aspects of his work read as if the faithful activity attains

(not endorsed here)[46] between "reward" (acceptable, properly understood) and "merit" (completely repudiated) to make this point:

> This does not mean there is no reward. The one point that is made is that reward is not according to achievement. Achievement and reward stand in a mutual relation which is incomprehensible to those who think in terms of a correct schema of merit and reward, and who thus regard God's relation to men as that of a precisely calculating employer to his employees.[47]

His use of "achievement" is unclear. If it means human activity is not connected to reward than his claim is rejected here. But given the affirmation of reward, presumably it means "human activity on its own" or without God's grace.[48]

In sum, contemporary biblical scholars are wary of using the term reward with regard to God. They generally do so, but distinguish it from a problematic view of reward as earned on one's own with God's help, and thus obligating God. This latter problematic sense is commonly ascribed to the term "merit," though once again the term merit (at least as employed by theologians such as Thomas Aquinas) need not have the problematic connotations ascribed to it.

§

This uneasiness with the notion of reward is granted here. But the term is used here in a manner that requires God's grace and is not some binding obligation imposed on God. With this in mind, what else can be said about the notion of reward in Mt 6:1–6, 16–18 that might inform this part's reflection on the importance of the further end on immediate action?

---

delayed reward, rather than being constitutive of that reward. "[B]y marking the goal of faithful service, it [reward] provides the inducement to faithful service. Far from denying or condemning the human need for reward the present passage assumes such a need and utilizes it. According to the ethic of the passage, God does not demand that the disciple relinquish recognition and reward, merely that such recognition and reward be deferred until they can be received directly from God" (*The Theme of Recompense in Matthew's Gospel*, 100).

[46] Though appeal is made here to Thomas Aquinas, the term "merit" has a history far preceding his work. See J. N. Bakhuizen van den Brink, "Mereo(r) and meritum in Some Latin Fathers," *Studia Patristica* 3 (1961): 333–40.

[47] Würthwein and Preisker, "μισθός," 717. See also "The concept of merit is completely repudiated. That of reward remains" (718) and "Jesus speaks, then, of reward, but all thought of merit is unconditionally excluded" (719). Guelich claims God rewards but the "basis is not one's merits" (*The Sermon on the Mount*, 277). Presumably he must think merit to mean without God's help, since elsewhere he clearly affirms a correlation between human acts and God's reward, as when he claims God rewards and punishes "commensurate with the conduct of his own" (302).

[48] See Würthwein and Preisker, "μισθός," 718: "This reward cannot be earned by any achievement. It cannot be merited."

Commentators consistently attend to the difference in verb tense in the two rewards. The hypocrites "have received their reward," the present perfect indicating that the attainment of the further goal is complete. Yet we are told that our heavenly Father "will repay" the second group. For these people the reception of the reward is complete in the future. In both cases the immediate acts lead to the reward. But there is a difference in the time in which that attainment occurs. What does this tell us about how immediate acts and further goals are related?

There is a sense in which this is a basic claim about effectiveness. If you act in manner governed by the ultimate goal to be seen by others, others will indeed see you and you will have received what you sought. If you act in a manner governed by the ultimate goal to be seen by our heavenly Father, you will be repaid by our heavenly Father. Yet commentators also commonly observe that the difference in tense here is a reflection of the different quality of reward sought in either case. The past tense of the hypocrites' reward is best read as an affirmation of the limited nature of that reward.[49] What is ultimately sought by the hypocrites is something that can be obtained fully in this life. As noted above, Guelich refers to the reward of the hypocrites as a "calculable wage," and Charette claims they are "purchasing social prestige."[50] There is something of some value here, but its value is so limited that it can be (seemingly immediately) achieved in this life by our actions. Yet the further goal of those seen by our heavenly Father, namely, the kingdom of heaven, is a reward that transcends what is earthly and thus can only come fully in the future.[51] Therefore, the difference in further goal sought by these two groups entails a difference in time of attainment due to the different quality of the further goal sought. Put simply, both activities lead to reward, but the difference in rewards sought results in instant or delayed gratification.

This interpretation of the difference in reward and corresponding difference in verb tense in Mt 6:1–6, 16–18 is affirmed here. However, it is complemented by an interpretation of the relationship between activity and reward that sheds additional light on how further goals are intimately related to immediate activities. It recalls the claims made in Chapter 1 about how

---

[49] As Guelich says, the hypocrites' "efforts do not extend beyond the limits of their audience" (*The Sermon on the Mount*, 279). The praise they receive is the "full extent" of their reward, not any token of future additional praise (303).

[50] Guelich, *The Sermon on the Mount*, 303; Charette, *The Theme of Recompense in Matthew's Gospel*, 98; see also Davies and Allison, *The Gospel According to Saint Matthew*, 582.

[51] Although his demarcation of parts of the Sermon is not adopted here, for this point Pennington's claim that Mt 6:1–18 actually ends with Mt 6:19–21 is illustrative, as those verses describe starkly the difference in quality between earthly and heavenly reward. See *Heaven and Earth in the Gospel of Matthew*, 242–47. This is taken up again in the following chapter. See also Strecker, *The Sermon on the Mount*, 101.

activity is constitutive of and intrinsically connected to the further goal sought. The claim here is that in both groups their activity is constitutive of the reward, or further goal, sought. The Scripture does not say that people saw the hypocrites and so they received their reward, although given how they perform that is likely also true. Their doing deeds in a manner shaped by that further end is a participation in that further end. The reward is not arbitrarily or extrinsically connected to (in other words, merely the "result of") the action performed; rather, the activity performed for such a further goal is so shaped by that goal as to constitute a participation in the goal.[52] Acting in such a manner not only attains that goal in terms of securing results (presumably other people do in fact see the hypocrites), but it also participates in or is constitutive of that reward such that the activity is informed (literally) by the further end. Indeed, agents who perform immediate activities for such a further goal are intransitively shaped by that further goal by apprehending it and acting on it. When Jesus says they have received their reward, it is not simply a claim about results. It is a claim about performing activities so shaped by a further goal that they can rightly be said to instantiate that reward, both in the meaning of the agent's activity from the perspective of the acting person, and in how that activity reflects and further ingrains the character of the agent.[53]

Yet if it is true that immediate activity is constitutive of the further goal so as to (at least partially) instantiate the reward now, why do we read in Mt 6:1, 4, 6, 18 that our heavenly Father "will" repay such people? As was seen in Chapter 1 on the beatitudes, the kingdom of heaven is only fully attainable in the eschatological future. Those who perform for God receive a reward that is not limited like the reward that of the hypocrites and thus can only be fully received when the kingdom of heaven arrives in its fullness.

This of course raises the question of whether or not those who do righteous deeds for their heavenly Father receive any reward now. Above it was argued that the reception of reward by the hypocrites now is not only a function of their more limited further goal which is able to be received now, but also a function of how their activity is constitutive of, a participation in, that further goal and thus the further goal is attained now as partially

---

[52] Recall the succinct description of this feature of virtue ethics by McCabe and Davies: "happiness is not just the *result* of praiseworthy action; it is *constituted* by praiseworthy action" (*The Good Life*, 6).

[53] For language of intentional action having transitive and intransitive effects, see Paul Wadell, *The Primacy of Love: An Introduction to the Ethics of Thomas Aquinas* (New York: Paulist Press, 1992), 34, where he cites John Finnis's *Fundamentals of Ethics*. Wadell uses these terms to indicate, respectively, the impact our activity has on the world around us and on our own characters. This claim about the intransitive impact of action on an agent's character relies on, yet goes one step further than, this section's claims on intentional action. Section 2 of this chapter addresses how intentional actions serve to inculcate character through the formation of habits.

constituted by their activity. Is the same true of those who do such deeds for their heavenly Father? There is no explicit statement of this in the verses under consideration here. But two things can be said that make such an interpretation credible.

First, while these verses do not explicitly describe present reward by our heavenly Father, nor is there any explicit rejection of reception of present reward. The use of the future tense is an explicit claim that the Father's repayment is not complete on earth. However, it is unwarranted to conclude from this that there is no continuity between future reward and the present. Indeed, the majority of biblical scholars who address the question of whether those acting for heavenly reward receive any such reward in the present consistently respond that they do. This is all the more noteworthy given the context of attempting to temporally differentiate the reward of the hypocrites from the reward of those who act to be seen by our heavenly Father. For instance, Guelich claims, "The future reward, in contrast to the present reward of the hypocrites, points to the final judgment."[54] Betz says it is a theme of the Sermon that "one must avoid *all* reward in this world so as to insure reward by God in the world to come."[55] Yet both of these authors go on to then affirm reward from our heavenly Father in the present as well. Guelich explicitly says future reward should not be understood in contrast to present reward, while Betz claims: "The future tense of the verb may refer not only to the last judgment but also, in accordance with 6:33, [to] this-worldly rewards."[56] Thus the different verb tense for reward in these verses is indeed rightly seen as revelatory of the different quality and temporal fruition of the distinct rewards. But the affirmation of future reward for those who are seen by our heavenly Father should not be understood as a repudiation of any present reward, including continuity of activity in the present state and future reward.

Therefore, while it is surely the case that the Sermon consistently (e.g., 6:19–21, 6:24) enjoins seeking heavenly reward over earthly treasure, and

---

[54] Guelich, *The Sermon on the Mount*, 280.

[55] Betz, *The Sermon on the Mount*, 346. While discussing 5:12, Betz oddly claims that "reward can be claimed only once" and thus must be future, but he provides no explanation or substantiation of this claim (*The Sermon on the Mount*, 152). The limited transactional reward of the hypocrites is also affirmed by Guelich (*The Sermon on the Mount*, 277). Such a claim would make reward only extrinsically related to activity, and so is challenged here. See Strecker, *The Sermon on the Mount*, 100–102 and 208.

[56] Guelich, *The Sermon on the Mount*, 282; Betz, *The Sermon on the Mount*, 360–61. Betz cites Guelich, 280, and thus assumes Guelich affirms only future rewards. Betz says the same about Luz (Betz, *The Sermon on the Mount*, 361n242), but the text he cites in Luz, *Matthew 1–7*, (358) affirms only that God rewards in the last judgment – which is contested by no one – without any exclusion of present reward. See also Davies and Allison, *The Gospel According to Saint Matthew*, 587 for an affirmation of reward in the present in the case of prayer.

while it is true that the full attainment of heavenly reward is a future reality, it is saying too much to assert that one must avoid all reward "in this world." That is to conflate earthly and heavenly reward with present and future, respectively. Though these are indeed correlated, it is a further claim to assume that heavenly reward is in no way continuous with activity in the life, just as it would be a further claim to assume the hypocrites receive no "reward" continuous with their present activity in the next life.[57] These assumptions may be the case, but the text does not at all demand that interpretation.

Second, given that this topic, namely the relationship between human activity in this life and the reward that is the kingdom of heaven, is treated most explicitly in the Sermon on the Mount in the verses on the beatitudes, it seems quite reasonable to assume the kingdom of heaven attained is already present as well as not yet fully present in the life of discipleship constituted by single-minded devotion to our heavenly Father. After all we read of the poor in spirit and even those who suffer persecution for righteousness' sake that "theirs *is* the Kingdom of heaven" (Mt 5:3, 10, emphasis added). And as documented in Chapter 1, the consistent history of Christian interpretation of the beatitudes has affirmed a present as well as future reward. It is possible to interpret this presence as merely the anticipation of what is not yet present.[58] And surely that is one way the further goal sought by these people is already present. Yet the kingdom is not simply a state of affairs where one finds one's self, but is also (partially) constituted by human participation through grace-enabled activity. Thus in the single-minded devotion of prayer, fasting, and giving alms for one's heavenly Father the further goal of the kingdom of heaven is indeed in a true but incomplete sense present.[59] Perhaps it is no surprise that the closest affirmation in contemporary biblical scholarship of one crucial thesis of this book – namely, that there is continuity between the grace-enabled virtuous activity of the disciple in this life and the reward that is the kingdom of heaven – is found in a treatment of reward. According to Bo Reicke in his chapter on reward:

> It will turn out that there is a constant feature in all these aspects of reward: What the servant receives in reward is nothing but communion with God –

---

[57] Mt 7:21–23 tells us otherwise, as examined in Chapter 5.

[58] For a sense in which one possesses what is sought, see Thomas Aquinas, *Summa Theologiae* I–II 5, 3 ad. 1.

[59] As noted in the previous paragraph. The converse can also be said of the hypocrites. Their "reward" attained in the *eschaton* will indeed be anticipated by and continuous with their activity as hypocrites. For as examined in more detail below, their instrumentalization of God – which is really a rejection of the God who cannot be instrumentalized – is a separation from God that is begun in this life and complete in the next (7:21–23, 7:13–14, and 7:26–27). See Charette, *The Theme of Recompense in Matthew's Gospel*, 98 and Betz, *The Sermon on the Mount*, 358.

but as the service of God is just a form of communion with God, there is an intimate relation, if not identity, between this service and this reward.[60]

In sum, this first part of Section 1 has attempted to examine what Mt 6:1–6 and 16–18 teaches us about the relationship between immediate activities and further rends, with Thomistic action analysis and scriptural commentary illuminating one another. These verses not only reveal how seemingly the "same" activities are done differently depending on the further goal, but also how that further goal impacts the meanings of those immediate activities. It is the further goal more than anything that defines whom a person is, whether a hypocrite or one seeking our heavenly Father. The Scripture even offers resources, through the notion of reward, for explaining how deliberate human action – while not equal to the reward sought – is constitutive of the reward attained, and thus in an important sense a beginning of, a participation in, the reward.

B. THE IMPORTANCE OF THE OBJECT IN HUMAN ACTION – "DO NOT BE LIKE THE HYPOCRITES"

This section's first part makes an argument about the importance of the end, or further goal, of human action, with particular attention to the term "reward." Having made that argument, it may seem that the further goal is wholly determinative of human action since it is so crucial for evaluating more immediate actions and for examining what sorts of persons we become in so acting. However, it would be inaccurate to claim that the further goal of an action alone is important in understanding what we do. Put in the terminology referenced above, it is not the case that only the intention (further goal) matters; the object (immediate action) is also important. This may seem strange given both the above analyses and the verses under consideration in this chapter. After all, the previous part went to great length to explain not only how important the further goal is, but how it even impacts the meaning of the immediate activity, such that the action can be said to be constitutive of that further goal. Yet while true, it is not the case that the further goal is wholly determinative of an immediate act's meaning. A return to Thomistic action theory will help us explain why. And once again, we will find that the Scripture text at hand not only authorizes such inquiry, but actually contributes to it, mainly through the use of the term "hypocrite."

Despite the importance Thomas Aquinas accords to the end of an action as described above, it is always the object he names as the primary locus for

---

[60] Reicke, "The New Testament Conception of Reward," 196. What he calls constant feature, I call continuity. What he calls intimate relation, I call intrinsic relation. What he calls service of God, I call grace-enabled virtuous activity.

evaluating an act. This may seem unintelligible if one has an inadequate understanding of the object. For instance, one could wrongly assume that the object is simply the physical description of a piece of behavior that is bereft of intentionality until supplied by the end (in other words, by the intention or further goal). If this is one's assumption, then affirming the primary importance of the object to assess an action makes no sense, for the object in this attenuated sense would not truly be a "human" or moral act. But this is not Thomas Aquinas's understanding of the object. For Thomas Aquinas, the object of an act is a chosen piece of behavior, "from the perspective of the acting person."[61]

[61] See Rhonheimer in *The Perspective of the Acting Person* (contra McCormick), 68ff. As referenced in an earlier note, there are actually two distinct recent "waves" of scholarship on the moral object in Catholic moral scholarship. This quotation from Rhonheimer targets Richard McCormick and other proportionalists who thought that attention to the object alone is insufficient to identify intrinsically evil actions. Those debates largely ceased with the promulgation of *Veritatis Splendor*, with its affirmation of the importance of the object and, at least as importantly, its articulation of the object as something "from the perspective of the acting person" (78). A second wave of debate has since ensued, among people who were against the proportionalists, as to the extent to which natural species or natural teleology is to be included in descriptions of object. All of these participants recognize *Veritatis Splendor* and its affirmation of the importance of "the perspective of the acting person." Yet given the heavy reliance on that phrase by one "side" in this second wave of debate (e.g., Rhonheimer), emphasis on this quality of human action is commonly taken to indicate an affinity with that side's view of the object. (For an example of trying to wrestle that phrase from that side, see David Crawford, "Moral Experience: Interpreting Veritatis Splendor's 'Perspective of the Acting Person,'" *Communio* 37 (2010): 266–83.) This very technical debate cannot be engaged here in any significant degree. For examples of important contributions to it, see the following books: Steven Long, *Teleological Grammar of the Human Act: Introductions to Catholic Doctrine*, (Naples, FL: Sapientia Press), 2007; Stephen Brock, *Action and Conduct: Thomas Aquinas and the Theory of Action* (Edinburgh: T&T Clark, 1998); Kevin Flannery, *Acts Amid Precepts: The Aristotelian Logical Structure of Thomas Aquinas's Moral Theory* (Washington, DC: Catholic University of America Press, 2001); Steven Jensen, *Good and Evil Actions*; Joseph Pilsner, *The Specification of Human Actions in St. Thomas Aquinas* (Oxford; New York: Oxford University Press, 2006). For articles, see the volume *Nova Et Vetera (English Edition)* 6.1 (Winter 2008) for the following: Stephen L. Brock, "Veritatis Splendor §78, St. Thomas, and (Not Merely) Physical Objects of Moral Acts": 1–62; Lawrence Dewan, O.P. "St. Thomas, Rhonheimer, and the Object of the Human Act," 63–112; Steven Long. "*Veritatis Splendor* §78 and the Teleological Grammar of the Moral Act," 139–56. See also Kevin Flannery, "The Multifarious Moral Object of Thomas Aquinas," *The Thomist* 67 (2003): 95–118 and Kevin Flannery, "The Field of Moral Action According to Thomas Aquinas," *The Thomist* 69 (2005): 1–30; Steven Long, "A Brief Disquisition regarding the Nature of the Object of the Moral Act according to St. Thomas Aquinas," *The Thomist* 67 (2003): 45–71; Steven Jensen, "A Long Discussion regarding Steven A. Long's Interpretation of the Moral Species," *The Thomist* 67 (2003): 623–43; Steven A. Long. "Response to Jensen on the Moral Object," *Nova Et Vetera*, 3 (1), Winter 2005: 101–108. Note that the key essay in Rhonheimer's *The Perspective of Morality* is "The Perspective of the Acting Person and the Nature of Practical Reason: The 'Object of the Human Act' in Thomistic Anthropology of Action," *Nova Et Vetera* 2.2 (Fall 2004): 461–516. That book also has Rhonheimer's "Intentional Actions And The Meaning Of Object: A Reply To Richard McCormick," *The Thomist* 69 (2005): 279–311. For some historical context on object and end in Thomas Aquinas, see Tobias Hoffmann,

It possesses intentionality, or finality, or purpose, even if that immediate finality is distinguished from further finality (end or further goal).[62] At times Thomas Aquinas does refer to what we might call the physical description of an action (what he at times calls the natural species).[63] This is not the first locus of evaluation; the object is. Indeed, Thomas Aquinas says the object as a chosen from the perspective of the acting person serves as form to the matter of the (physical) activity, a claim reminiscent of how the end provides a formality to the object.[64] Perhaps the best way to understand the object in relation to a physical description of behavior would be that the object is the most basic level of description of an act that is still nonetheless choiceworthy. For instance, pulling one's finger is a physical description of an act but not choiceworthy. Even shooting a gun is a description of an act but not choiceworthy since there is no evident "point" of such an act. But stopping an aggressor or eliminating my rival are indeed choiceworthy pieces of behavior. These are objects of actions.[65]

Turning to Scripture, whence comes that "point" of the immediately chosen activity? Is the point, or object, simply a function of the description of the behavior in a manner accessible to any external observer? Or is the object a description of what is chosen "in the perspective of the acting person?" The Scripture's use of the term hypocrite indicates the latter is the case. The object is something "performed" (6:1), something chosen. There is a "natural species" of the act, namely something given on the basis of physical characteristics of the act mediated through socially developed supports for such a meaning. But the activity is chosen by the hypocrite. It is thus formative on the agent in a manner that a differently chosen activity, say, refusing to pray (or harming a poor person), is not. The agent in the

---

"Moral Action as Human Action: End and Object in Aquinas in Comparison with Abelard, Lombard, Albert, and Duns Scotus," *The Thomist* 67 (2003): 73–94 and Dewan, "*Objectum*."

[62] Were this a more thorough engagement with contemporary scholarship on Thomas Aquinas's action theory, more discussion would be required here on *Summa Theologiae* I–II 18, 7 where he distinguishes simple from complex acts. Simple acts are where the immediate action's finality is simply oriented toward the further end, as fighting well in battle is ordained to victory. In complex actions, the immediate act is not simply ordained to the further end, as when one steals to give alms (or we might say here, gives alms to be seen by others). When acts are simple, they take their species from the end due to its consonance with the object. Yet where the object is not ordained to the end the object also specifies the act. Matthew 6:1–6, 16–18 clearly deal with complex acts, and thus attention to both object and end is necessary.

[63] See, for example, Thomas Aquinas, *Summa Theologiae* I–II 1, 3 ad. 3; 20, 6; 18, 5, ad. 3.

[64] Thomas Aquinas, *Summa Theologiae* I–II 18, 2, ad. 2. See Long, *Teleological Grammar of the Human Act*, 83–84 on the formal aspect of a moral acting including natural species. See Jensen, *Good and Evil Actions*, 275–78 for a helpful account of the relationship between teleology in natural species and object.

[65] The issue of act (or object) description is a notoriously difficult one in Catholic moral theology. For a particularly helpful approach, see Charles Pinches, *Theology and Action: After Theory in Christian Ethics* (Grand Rapids, MI: Eerdman, 2002).

passage "performs righteous deeds" (6:1). Though the meaning of the acts (praying, fasting, giving alms) is not wholly dictated by the choosing of them as such, they are indeed chosen as such. Hence the further point to which they are directed is not the only source of evaluation of the act. The chosen activity itself has a meaning, or object, that is formative on the agent for reasons beyond its further end (and not limited to but inclusive of its natural species).

This is particularly evident in cases where a different deed is chosen for the same further end. People who choose to flaunt prayer to be seen by others are not hypocrites; they are not disjointed in the way the hypocrites of this passage are. They are still people who do things to be seen by others, so that the further goal is indeed formative for them. But they are not disjointed since their immediate activity is actually ordered to their further goal. This is not so with hypocrites who perform an immediate activity with a finality that is ordered away from their own further goal. Both groups of persons choose immediate activities that have finality (communication with God or avoiding such communication), and in being chosen by the agents each finality is formative. However, only in the case of the hypocrite is there disjoint between the immediate activity and further goal. Being a hypocrite is only possible if the immediate act has a chosen finality.

What do these verses therefore teach us about the status of the object? It seems clear that the acts performed have some recognizable status distinct from the further end toward which they are directed. As biblical scholars consistently maintain, the etymology of "hypocrite" is from the theater. It refers to an actor, where there is a persona presented that is distinct from the person "behind the mask," if you will.[66] Yet there is an important dis-analogy with the mask. Hypocrites do not simply "put on" something exterior to themselves. They perform deeds, in other words, make choices that have a finality that is inconsonant with their own further finality. They are performing righteous deeds. Yet there is self-contradiction. They are simultaneously choosing in opposite directions. Thus, there is disjointedness and dis-integrity in the hypocrite; it is not simply a lack of full consistency or integrity.

Even without the technical action theory language of end and object, biblical scholars present precisely this disjointedness in their explanations of hypocrisy in the context of Matthew 6:1-18.[67] It is not simply an

---

[66] Guelich, *The Sermon on the Mount*, 278; Betz, *The Sermon on the Mount*, 356; Luz, *Matthew 1-7*, 357; Dan Otto Via, "The Gospel of Matthew: Hypocrisy as Self-Deception," *Society of Biblical Literature Seminar Papers* 27.1 (1988): 508–516, at 512. Davies and Allison also make this point with regard to the etymology of hypocrite in relation to actor (*The Gospel According to Saint Matthew*, 580–81), and even claim the term's use by Jesus could be supported due to archeological evidence of a theater at time of his life near Nazareth. For this they cite R. A. Batey, "Jesus and the Theater," *New Testament Studies* 30 (1984): 563–74.

inconsistency external to the hypocrite, such as a disjoint between what the hypocrite does and how it is perceived. That disjoint also exists, but it results from a deeper disjoint, one internal to the hypocrite. As Georg Strecker describes:

> The Pharisees and scribes live in a contradiction; the proper outward appearance does not jibe with the egoist direction of their will [sic]; they are like whitewashed tombs that on the outside are beautiful to look at but on the inside are full of dead bones (23:27–28). They adorn themselves with broad phylacteries and long fringes, they claim the most prominent seats in the synagogues, and such behavior is aimed entirely at outward effect (23:5–6 also 23:25–26). Their hypocrisy is an attempt to appear to be, rather than to be, to establish an image that hides their real intentions. Thus they are proto-types of the self-alienated, divided and thus imperfect person.[68]

The hypocrites are not only divided but self-divided and self-contradictory. Rather than choosing righteous deeds in service to God, they choose righteous deeds (oriented ultimately to service to God) to instead serve themselves, thus dis-integrating themselves and instrumentalizing God.[69] It is this disjointedness, this tension between the finality of the righteous deeds as chosen by the hypocrite and the further finality of the hypocrite, that both reveals the status of the object as chosen and evaluable, and engenders the disjoint and self-contradiction that is at the heart of hypocrisy.[70]

Two further comments are warranted on hypocrisy. First, there is some debate among contemporary biblical scholars as to whether the hypocrisy of those mentioned in Matthew 6:1–18 is what one author calls "objective" or "subjective." In other words, do those targeted by Mt 6:2, 5, 16 know that there is a disjoint between their righteous deeds and further goals, or not? If they do not, there remains discontinuity (objective hypocrisy) but not

---

[67] Via, "The Gospel of Matthew," 512

[68] Strecker, The Sermon on the Mount, 99. Note the equation of the hypocrites with scribes and Pharisees. The commonality between the hypocrites of Mt 6 and the scribes and Pharisees of Mt 23 makes it clear that scribes and Pharisees can indeed be hypocrites. But equating them with the hypocrites in Mt 6 suggests that only they are the targets of Mt 6. For more on whether the targets of Mt 6:1–6, 16–18 are simply the scribes and Pharisees, or a broader target which may include scribes and Pharisees, see Betz, The Sermon on the Mount, 347 & 357; Davies and Allison, The Gospel According to Saint Matthew, 581.

[69] For this notion of instrumentalization, see Charette who says the hypocrite "is not giving service to God or others but merely purchasing social prestige by means of religious activity" (The Theme of Recompense in Matthew's Gospel, 98).

[70] Biblical scholars point to further evidence of such self-contradiction in 6:16, where we read the hypocrites "look gloomy" to be seen by others. Scholars note that this is actually a "masterful" pun (Luz, Matthew 1–7, 354). The Greek here literally means to "look unseemly" (Strecker, The Sermon on the Mount, 128). Or as Guelich paraphrases, "they make themselves unnoticeable in order to be noticed" (The Sermon on the Mount, 305).

intentional deception or duplicity (subjective hypocrisy).[71] Scholars on both sides note that the term hypocrite as used in the first century did not necessarily (though could) possess a negative connotation of duplicity or being "two-faced." For instance, Guelich claims, "Attaching such a conscious lack of integrity to the term [hypocrite] belongs neither here in 6:1–18 nor in the other occurrences of the term in the Gospel."[72] Other scholars share this view that the hypocrites of Mt 6 are not duplicitous.[73] Davies and Allison seem more balanced in simultaneously recognizing that a negative sense of the term is not necessitated, and also claiming that it indeed seems warranted in the context of Matthew 6.[74] Other scholars affirm this view as well.[75] Perhaps most vociferous of the latter is Georg Strecker: hypocrisy is not the "unconscious sinful existence of sinful humanity as such" but rather "a conscious dissembling, just as its antithesis, righteousness, is a conscious human attitude."[76] Note that each side recognizes the discontinuity between chosen acts and further end, so neither outcome of that debate undermines the claim of this part of the chapter, namely, that immediately chosen acts retain their own finality distinct from their further end. Nonetheless, the

[71] For these terms see Strecker, *The Sermon on the Mount*, 99. See David M. Rhoads, "The Gospel of Matthew: The Two Ways: Hypocrisy Or Righteousness," *Currents In Theology and Mission* 19.6 (1992), 456 who calls "objective hypocrisy" "blind" hypocrisy.

[72] Guelich, *The Sermon on the Mount*, 278.

[73] See Paul Minear, "False Prophecy and Hypocrisy in the Gospel of Matthew," in *Neues Testament Und Kirche: Festschrift for Rudolf Schnackenburg*, ed. Joachim Gnilka (Freiburg: Herder, 1974), as cited in Charette, *The Theme of Recompense in Matthew's Gospel*, 97n5; see also Otto Via, who claims: "Hypocrisy *is not* pretending consciously to be more righteous than one is but *really* believing *erroneously* that one is righteous, that one has met the divine requirements" ("The Gospel of Matthew," 514). Yet he interestingly finds this occasion of erroneous conscience culpable. See also his *Self-Deception and Wholeness in Paul and Matthew* (Minneapolis, MN: Fortress Press, 1990), 92–98. For a popular presentation of this view, along with four types of hypocrisy in Matthew, see Rhoads "The Gospel of Matthew: The Two Ways, Hypocrisy or Righteousness," 456. This piece is a fine example of how those who affirm the hypocrisy as objective tend to expand the notion of hypocrisy to refer to the broader "human condition" of sinfulness (Via, "The Gospel of Matthew," 513; *Self-Deception and Wholeness in Paul and Matthew*, 96) and/or to read Matthew 6 through the lens of 23:25–28 and 7:3–5 where it seems those criticized are not aware of their limitations (e.g., Via, *Self-Deception and Wholeness in Paul and Matthew*, 95). See Rhodes for an example of how the meaning of hypocrisy can be stretched to include even people who observe the first half but not second half of the antitheses in Matthew 5:21–48.

[74] See Davies and Allison, *The Gospel According to Saint Matthew*, 580–81. See also 499 where they affirm that the hypocrisy is not blind.

[75] Luz, *Matthew 1–7*, 357n31; Charette, *The Theme of Recompense in Matthew's Gospel*, 97.

[76] Strecker, *The Sermon on the Mount*, 99. Despite the problematic language of "attitude," Charette is right to recognize not only the duplicity in the hypocrisy of Mt 6 but also that righteousness is a "conscious human attitude," or as stated in this book, an intentional activity.

position adopted here is that the hypocrisy derided in Matthew 6 is indeed subjective, or duplicitous and two-faced, rather than blind.[77]

Second, one biblical scholar makes an interesting observation regarding the ambiguity inherent in hypocrisy. On the one hand, there is in the hypocrite misrepresentation of their "true nature." On the other hand, being a hypocrite *is* their inner nature.[78] Can one "become" a hypocrite? It seems the two parts of this section enable one to address this question, and thus it provides a fitting conclusion to this section and even an entry into the next. One can indeed become a hypocrite, but what it means to be a hypocrite is to misrepresent one's inner nature. As the first part of the section affirmed, the further goal of wanting to be seen by others is what most properly characterizes the hypocrite's nature. That is who they are, and they become habituated as such persons by performing intentional actions toward that further goal. But unlike those who perform patently self-glorifying actions to secure acclaim, the hypocrites choose immediate activities that are representative of allegiance and obedience to God. As commentators commonly note, the hypocrites are "insiders," unlike the "pagans" of Mt 6:7–8 and 6:32.[79] They know enough about allegiance to God to act accordingly in their immediate acts, and thus God does play some role in their lives. Yet since God is instrumentalized in service to their own glory, "on a much deeper level they live as if God played no role in their lives."[80] Their disjointedness reflects the contradiction between their immediate acts and further goal. Since both levels of action express intentionality and are formative on these

---

[77] Guelich recognizes "their actions betray their desire to be seen and recognized by others" and "they are indeed actors concerned with appearance," and yet says "their appearance contradicts their relations with God and others *even if unconsciously*" (*The Sermon on the Mount*, 278–79, my emphasis). Given their "desire" and "concern," it is not clear how their hypocrisy can be "unconscious." Even if it is in some sense true that they desire to be righteous before God, it would seem that desire is at the very least subordinate to a desire to be seen as righteous by others. It should be noted that Thomas Aquinas considered hypocrisy intentionally deceptive and thus a sin. See Aquinas, *Commentary on the Gospel of Matthew*, 564 and 572. According to him, it is a type of "dissimulation": "just as it is contrary to truth to signify by words something different from that which is in one's mind, so also is it contrary to truth to employ signs of deeds or things to signify the contrary of what is in oneself, and this is what is properly denoted by dissimulation. Consequently dissimulation is properly a lie told by the signs of outward deeds" (Thomas Aquinas, *Summa Theologiae* II–II 111, 1). He then claims, with reference to Matthew 6, "hypocrisy is dissimulation, not, however, any form of dissimulation, but only when one person simulates another, as when a sinner simulates the person of a just man" (Thomas Aquinas, *Summa Theologiae* II–II 111, 2).

[78] See Charette, *The Theme of Recompense in Matthew's Gospel*, 96.

[79] See, for example, Betz, *The Sermon on the Mount*, 347. The change in focus from hypocrites to pagans from Mt 6:1–6 at 7–8, and back again at 16–18 is further corroboration of the claim that Mt 6:7–8 and 6:9–15 comes from a different source than Mt 6:1–6, 16–18. See also Luz, *Matthew 1–7*, 364–66.

[80] Charette, *The Theme of Recompense in Matthew's Gospel*, 98.

agents, there is indeed formation that occurs. Yet it is a formation that ingrains dis-integrity, that disintegrates. The following section explores the relationship between intentional action and habit formation in more detail mining these verses for guidance for growth in virtue.

II. GUIDANCE ON GROWTH IN VIRTUE

There is a common assumption in contemporary biblical scholarship that Mt 5:21–48 and Mt 6:1–18 are differentiated by a distinction that may be roughly labeled exterior action (Mt 5) and interiority (Mt 6). Luz claims that Mt 6 shifts to address the "inwardness of the same righteousness of which he spoke in the Antitheses."[81] Davies and Allison put it this way:

> 5:21–48 has to do primarily with *actions*, 6:1–18 primarily with *intentions* (cf. Luz). One might even argue that 6:1–18 is a sort of commentary on what precedes it. If 5:21–48 tells the disciple *what* to do, the little 'cult-didache' tells him *how* to do it.[82]

This section of the chapter examines the topic of growth in virtue. This quotation on intentions instead of actions is a helpful foil for that analysis, since the quotation's claim about the separation of action and intention and the assignment of each to different parts of the Sermon is at worst wrong, and at best misleading.

The thesis of this section is that Mt 6:1–6, 16–18 offers specific, action-oriented guidance for developing virtues. These verses are indeed about interiority. But they demonstrate the vital connection between actions and intentionality, instead of focusing on intentionality after treatment of actions in Matthew 5 as the scholars noted above aver.[83] In fact, these verses not only

---

[81] Luz, *Matthew 1–7*, 363.

[82] Davies and Allison, *The Gospel According to Saint Matthew*, 621. See also Davies and Allison, *Matthew: A Shorter Commentary*, 88. Davies and Allison cite Luz, *Matthew 1–7*, 363 in edition cited here: "in chap. 6 he [Matthew] does not move on to another theme, such as piety or religious exercises; instead he speaks of the inner dimension of the same righteousness of which he spoke in the antitheses." See also Charette, *The Theme of Recompense in Matthew's Gospel*, 95 on ethical demands to inner integrity. For a contrary view, see Thomas Aquinas, *Summa Theologiae* I–II 108, 3 where he claims that the entire Sermon (after the depiction of happiness in 5:3–12 and the establishment of the authority of the apostles in 5:13–16) is about interiority (*actus interiores*).

[83] Mt 5:21–48 (or really 5:17–48) and Mt 6:1–18 both begin with introductory references to "righteousness" (5:20, 6:1) that govern the ensuing tightly structured verses (5:21–48 and 6:2–18). Thus some explanation of how they are distinct yet properly understood in relationship to one another is indeed appropriate (and witnessed in the chapter break-down of this book). But the one cited here is problematic. Indeed, as seen in the previous chapter on the antitheses, one of the ways the law is perfected is through further attention to interiority, as with the first two antitheses' attention to affectivity corresponding to action.

illuminate the connection between act and intention with regard to particular actions, but they also offer guidance on how intentional actions are crucial for the formation of habits (including virtues but also vices) as well as the formation of that ensemble of habits we call a person's character. This section will once again use the concerns and resources of virtue ethics to aid the understanding of Scripture. But then it will rely on Scripture to illuminate and specify the standard concerns of virtue ethics. The first part examines the relationship between intentional actions and the habits which constitute a person's character. Intentional actions reflect a person's habits. Yet they are also formative of habits, ingraining weaker habits, further strengthening stable ones, or even reversing habits through contrary actions. The second part uses the work of two recent biblical scholars, in particular, to explain how the metaphors used in these verses invite concrete action and how the attention to audience in these verses addresses the role of community in character formation.

A. INTENTIONAL ACTION, DEVELOPMENT OF HABITS, AND CHARACTER FORMATION

This brief foray into virtue ethics action theory explains the connection between intentional action and habit formation in preparation for the following part's examination of the contribution of Mt 6:1–6, 16–18 to this topic. As described above, intentional action is goal-directed. When human persons act intentionally, they apprehend with their intellectual capacities (reason) and respond willfully/deliberately on the basis of how they apprehend things, namely, as worthy of seeking, or fleeing, and so on[84] How we apprehend (understand) or "see" things is crucial for influencing how we act, a central theme in this book.[85] Therefore, our intentional action reflects how we see things, and what we deem important. This crucial importance of assessing, deliberating, and choosing well in the moral life is the reason for the emphasis on prudence in virtue ethics.[86] If practical reasoning

---

The most common approach to distinguishing these two sections of the Sermon is to claim 5:21–48 is about the law and 6:1–18 about the cult. (See, e.g., Davies and Allison, *The Gospel According to Saint Matthew*, 578; Betz, *The Sermon on the Mount*, 330ff.) This interpretation is addressed more in the following section, but it should be noted that it is not the same as the exterior/interior distinction.

[84] In Thomistic terminology, the apprehensive and appetitive powers work in concert.

[85] Recall the portrayal of the kingdom of heaven in the beatitudes, with its constitutive activities. The next chapter addresses Mt 6:22–23 on the importance of the eye, or how we see things, for activity concerning temporal matters.

[86] See Tjp, as Aquinas, *Summa Theologiae* I–II 58, 4. For helpful overviews of prudence, see Annas, *The Morality of Happiness*; Josef Pieper, *The Four Cardinal Virtues: Prudence, Justice, Fortitude, Temperance* (New York: Harcourt, Brace & World, 1965); James Keenan S.J., "The Virtue of Prudence," 259–71 in Stephen J. Pope, ed., *Ethics of Aquinas* (Washington, DC: Georgetown University Press, 2002).

(or practical decision-making) is how people assess situations and make and execute decisions, then prudence (or practical wisdom or "common sense"[87]) is the habit or stable disposition to do that well, in a manner that reflects an accurate assessment of the way things are.

By acting intentionally in a manner reflective of how we understand things, we develop habits, which are stable dispositions to do a certain type of activity (e.g., decision-making, relating to others, facing difficulties, and engaging pleasurable activities) in a certain way that is reflective of that way of seeing things. Much can be said about the nature of habits (good ones of which are called virtues and bad ones vices), but two points suffice for this context. First, habits are stable characteristics, or qualities, of *persons.* They qualify persons, and though they are intimately related to particular actions (arising from actions and inclining to future such actions), they are not to be equated with particular actions.[88] In fact on occasion a particular action might be in tension with a person's habit for that activity.

Second, habits "carry" intentionality. As evident in the verses under consideration in this chapter, people who give alms to be seen by others do not possess the same habit as those who give alms for their heavenly Father. Both consistently do acts that look the same from an observer's perspective, and even have the same immediate finality. But habits reside in persons not acts, and persons can consistently choose immediate acts for different further ends. Hence, the difference in further goal not only in-forms the meaning of the immediate acts but also the habits that are developed by the persons performing such acts. Some people giving alms become generous. Others become hypocrites. Just as the last section explained how acts that are seemingly the same can actually have different meanings, so, too, can differ-ent people possess habits to perform seemingly similar acts and actually have different habits. Intentionality is not only crucial for acts but also for the habits that characterize individual people. For this reason, it is most appro-priate in a chapter treating verses on intentional action to address the formation of habits.

The discussion thus far can make it seem as if how we see things is simply the root of our intentional actions, and ultimately our habits. From this view, how we see things is a cause of, but not influenced by, our actions and habits.

---

[87] McCabe uses the latter term as an alternative to the English prudence, given the latter's connotation of wariness, which is not always *à propos* of prudence. Herbert McCabe, O.P., *God Still Matters* (London: Continuum, 2002), 152.

[88] See Aquinas, *Summa Theologiae*, I–II 49, 3. Habits are a sort of middle ground between a person and their acts. They are possessed by persons (and more precisely qualify a certain capacity of that person), even though they may change and thus cannot be equated with the person. Further, they order the person toward certain sorts of acts, though they are not the same as an act.

This is incomplete. How we see things not only drives how we act and the habits we develop, but it is also shaped by how we act and the habits we develop.[89] To the coward, a threatening situation appears more fearful. To the glutton, food or drink appear nearly irresistibly attractive. To the hypocrite, occasions of piety are apprehended as occasions to impress others. This cyclical relationship between the sorts of persons we are and how we see things is the basis for the ancient claim that the virtues are connected, or unified. While prudence is needed for the exercise of the moral virtues, the moral virtues are needed in order to see things and make decisions prudently.[90]

This raises a perennial quandary in virtue ethics. If I need to see well in order to pursue good goals, but I also need to pursue good goals in order to see things well, how can I ever start to do either? Put differently, if prudence is needed to obtain the moral virtues, but the moral virtues are needed to obtain prudence, how can I ever become virtuous? As Thomas Aquinas explains following Aristotle, and as any parent will say, the way to become virtuous is to start acting that way even before becoming that sort of person.[91] Go worship, serve the poor, do homework, try different sports, eat new foods. When a child, for instance, first attends Mass or does homework or eats vegetables, they are not yet attuned to such activities as fitting to them (in other words, connaturalized to them through the second nature dispositions that are habits). They may even resist them. And of course there is a delicate balance for a parent or educator between on the one hand introducing children to something life-giving to which they are not yet accustomed, and on the other hand forcing them to do something and in doing so

---

[89] Aquinas, *Summa Theologiae* I–II 58, 5.

[90] The connectivity of the virtues is a complicated question. While perhaps universally affirmed by the ancients, it is nearly universally denied today. See Jean Porter, "Virtue and Sin: The Connection of the Virtues and the Case of the Flawed Saint," *The Journal of Religion*, 75.4, October 1995, 521–39. Even among those who affirm the connectivity of the virtues, there is significant variation in how that connection is understood. It suffices here simply to note two basic approaches. The virtues could be connected because they all essentially reduce to one virtue which is expressed in varying situations. Such a position was held by the Stoics (and arguably Plato) with regard to prudence, and by Augustine with regard to love. Alternatively, the virtues could be connected by a sort of reciprocity between those governing the apprehensive powers (primarily prudence) and those governing the appetitive powers (the moral virtues). This latter view affirmed here, was held by Aristotle and Thomas Aquinas. For an excellent analysis of the issue of the connectivity of the virtues in ancient, medieval and contemporary ethics, see Andrew Kim, "Thomas Aquinas on the Connection of the Virtues," PhD diss., The Catholic University of America, 2013.

[91] See Thomas Aquinas, *Disputed Questions on the Virtues* (Cambridge and New York: Cambridge University Press, 2005) a. 9 ad. 13 of the disputed question on virtue in general. See also Kim, "Thomas Aquinas on the Connection of the Virtues,"145. Kim cites Daniel McInerny, *The Difficult Good: A Thomistic Approach to Moral Conflict and Human Happiness* (New York: Fordham University Press, 2006), 76–80.

preclude their appreciation of it.[92] For if one does not possess a habit inclining toward activities in such a way, doing them in such a way will not seem (or be seen as) fitting to the person. And so to do them the person must trust that doing the activities in such a way is indeed fitting for them, even if they do not "see" it.[93] But most importantly for this part of the chapter, doing activities in such a way is what enables one to start to "see" the point or purpose of those activities as good, and possibly develop a corresponding habit to act in that way. This is the process of habit formation.

This brief primer in some central claims of virtue ethics prepares us to examine how Matthew 6:1–6, 161–18 corroborates and illuminates this process of growth in virtue. But before doing so, another word is in order on hypocrisy. Any injunction to act in a manner not representative of "who we are" as represented by our habits (with their corresponding intentionalities) smacks of hypocrisy.[94] Is acting in such a way hypocritical? It depends on why one is acting so. If we perform acts that have a finality that is in tension with our finality in performing these acts, the answer is surely yes. As described above, in this case there is a disjoint between the further goal and the immediate goal of the actions hypocrites perform. There is self-contradiction. That is hypocrisy. As also mentioned above, note that hypocrisy can actually become habitual, such that for habitual hypocrites performing righteous deeds to be seen by others is indeed representative of who they are. In such a case the disjointedness or dis-integrity is between the immediate goal of the action and the person's further goal, even if such disjointedness is ingrained habitually.

Yet if a person acts in a manner not reflective of their habits, but for a further goal that is not opposed to such acts, it need not be hypocrisy. For instance, one could act in hopes of obtaining the habit that will incline them to see and act in this manner in the future. This would not at all be hypocrisy, but simply good *ascesis*, or disciplining of one's desires. One might even be so unable to see the immediate goal of certain activities that one does them only

---

[92] This topic is addressed in the next chapter in the context of the challenging Mt 7:6. This is also an occasion to describe the importance of properly exercised authority (church, parents, mentors, and so on) in the formation of character, a task beyond the scope of this chapter. For an excellent recent treatment of authority, see Victor Lee Austin, *Up with Authority: Why We Need Authority to Flourish as Human Beings* (New York; London: T & T Clark, 2010).

[93] The term "trust" here is the opening for the influence of authority. The authority "sees" it that way and the person trusts in the authority. Of course this can sadly work in a deforming manner, as with destructive cases of peer pressure, child abuse or scandalous religious figures.

[94] There is helpful recent literature on precisely this topic, most notably Jennifer Herdt's *Putting on Virtue: The Legacy of the Splendid Vices* (Chicago: University of Chicago Press, 2008).

out of trusting deference to some guide.[95] This, too, would not be hypocrisy since that further goal is not opposed to the immediate goal of the activity (even if in this case the two are more extrinsically related from the perspective of the acting person). We now turn to the Scripture verses that are the focus for this chapter to ascertain what contribution they offer, not only to the question of the relationship between immediate act and further goal, but also on the relationship between intentional action and habit formation.

B. METAPHORS AND AUDIENCE

Informed by the resources of virtue ethics in understanding the relationship between intentionality and habits as well as the dynamics of habit formation (habituation), we return to the Scripture text. How do these verses further illuminate these topics in virtue ethics? The central claim of this section is that Mt 6:1–6, 16–18 offers not only descriptions of how two different groups of people may perform righteous deeds but also an exhortation to – along with practical guidance on how to – become people who are rewarded by our heavenly Father. These verses not only describe but also help us develop into certain sorts of people. It is here we will see that any attempt to make 6:1–18 about intentionality in a manner exclusive of exterior actions is off base.

These verses clearly manifest the close connection between intentional action and character formation. Reminiscent of the beatitudes, in these verses the audience is not only enjoined to perform certain types of actions, but also to become certain sorts of people. More precisely, they are enjoined not to be like certain sorts of people, the hypocrites. "Do not be like them" (6:8; cf. 6:5).[96] They are then told how hypocrites become like that and how they ought to act instead.[97] The intimate connection between who we are and what we do, as well as the importance of intentionality in what we do, could not be more evident.

Clearly the verses commend piety performed for our heavenly Father over pious actions performed to be seen by others; hence the command mood in the verbs enjoining secret or hidden piety (6:3, 6:6, and 6:17). Yet what is easily missed is that the verses do not just portray how the two groups act differently and commend one over the other. We have here concrete guidance on how to become people who are rewarded by our heavenly

---

[95] The language here is purposely mild. But despite the acknowledged potential for abuse, by deference I mean obedience, and by guide I mean authority. Thus, *properly understood*, this sentence could read "one does it only out of obedience to authority."

[96] In 6:2 and 6:16, the audience is enjoined simply not to act like the hypocrites. But combined with 6:6 and especially 6:8, the connection between such action and who one becomes is clear.

[97] That doing the latter will make them children of their heavenly Father is unstated but certainly the case (5:9; 5:16; 5:45; 5:48; 6:4; 6:6; 6:8; 6:9; 6:15; 6:18; 6:26; 6:32; 7:11; cf. 7:21 where Jesus says "my Father in heaven").

Father, even before we are such people. These verses describe in detail how to become people who practice what Betz calls "inconspicuous piety."[98] This is why any significant distinction between exterior acts and interiority in interpreting these verses is at best misleading. Rather than a focus on interiority "primarily" instead of exterior actions, we have an exhortation to, and guidance in developing, a certain type of interiority *through* exterior actions. Though contemporary biblical scholarship does not adequately recognize this connection, there are resources in that scholarship to buttress this claim. Two are treated here.

One commonly treated topic in biblical commentaries concerns how to interpret the specific actions described in the verses, namely: not letting the left hand know what the right hand does; praying in one's inner room with the door closed; and washing and anointing oneself in times of fasting. How ought we to understand these actions as described in their specificity? These actions are generally not interpreted literally by commentators.[99] There are two common strategies for understanding the meaning of these vivid actions. First, commentators have spilled much ink on inquiries such as the figurative meaning of the left and right hands,[100] first century architecture and the "inner room,"[101] and whether or not the washing and fasting prescribed in 6:18 is normal hygiene or some celebratory activity.[102] Whether these analyses are historical-critical or figurative, they are united in seeking significance in the exact manner in which the actions are performed. There is much to commend in these analyses, and some that even contribute to this project. For instance, commentators from Augustine to Strecker have noted the significance of anointing for times of rejoicing, and have thus taken from the reference to anointing in 6:18 an injunction not only to avoid looking dejected while fasting, but to rejoice in the occasion to practice piety for our heavenly Father.[103] Though no such interpretation is offered here, nor is the analysis here a rejection of such approaches.

---

[98] Betz, *The Sermon on the Mount*, 343–46.

[99] I mean here literal in the sense of exactly. This is not a statement about the importance of the literal sense of a Scripture passage, which in Thomistic analysis is always primary. See Thomas Aquinas, *Summa Theologiae* I 1, 10, ad. 1.

[100] See Augustine's detailed analysis of varying ways to interpret left and right (*The Lord's Sermon on the Mount*, II.2.6–8) and Aquinas, *Commentary on the Gospel of Matthew*, 565–67.

[101] See Carolyn Osiek, "'When You Pray, Go into Your ταμεῖον' (Matthew 6:6): But Why?" *Catholic Biblical Quarterly*, 71(4, 2009) 723–40.

[102] See Betz, *The Sermon on the Mount*, 422, esp. n. 650.

[103] See Augustine, *The Lord's Sermon on the Mount*, II.12.42 and Strecker, *The Sermon on the Mount*, 129. Thomas Aquinas indicates that fasting must always be accompanied by sadness however (*Commentary on the Gospel of Matthew*, 605). The question of whether fasting is ideally done with the pleasure and promptness that normally accompanies full possession of virtue is a challenging one that cannot be addressed here.

A second strategy is to regard the images as hyperbole.[104] In other words, they do not offer specific guidance for action. Rather, they are exaggerated metaphors to describe hidden or secret piety that are not to be literally imitated. This is certainly true in that no commentators I have encountered enjoin a literal imitation of these acts. Some of the acts are arguably impossible[105] and some are contradicted by Jesus and his disciples' own practice in the gospels.[106] So the actions enjoined in Mt 6:1–6, 16–18 are indeed drastic and not to be imitated precisely. Yet it is important in describing these actions as hyperbolic that we not dismiss their enjoining concrete action just because we are not to imitate these acts literally.[107] The work of Tannehill is instructive here. He refers to actions such as these as "focal instances." Such actions do indeed provide an imaginative "shock" "on the basis of deliberate tension with ordinary human behavior." Yet rather than dissuading imitation, such actions are best understood as having an "openness" that "invites the hearer 'to extend ... this pattern to new situations.'"[108] Regardless of the exact shape that takes, the command mood of these verses makes it clear that some such action is indeed required. By enjoining such action, these verses not only depict what children rewarded by their heaven Father look like, but also provide vivid instruction to the audience on how to become just such people.

Another topic in biblical scholarship on Mt 6:1–6, 16–18 and "practical guidance in development of virtue" concerns the importance of community in such development. Since Alasdair MacIntyre's argument for a return to virtue, combined with his well-known claim that every morality assumes a sociology, virtue ethicists have been attentive to the important role of society (at varying levels) for specifying and inculcating virtues.[109] A virtue ethic

---

[104] Guelich, *The Sermon on the Mount*, 280; Davies and Allison, *The Gospel According to Saint Matthew*, 583; Wilson, "Seen in Secret," 477; Luz, *Matthew 1–7*, 357.

[105] Most references to hyperbole in the previous note concern Mt 6:3 on not letting the left hand know what the right is doing.

[106] Though Jesus frequently prays alone, Matthew commonly reports Jesus praying in public (See Wilson, "Seen in Secret," 478n16 for citations to Mt: 11:25; 14:19; 19:13; cf. 21:13).

[107] For instance, Luz claims that whether the proper understanding of washing and anointing in 6:18 is "exaggerated and hyperbolic" or "basic hygiene" is "unimportant"; either way "the issue is not so much a concrete instruction as the basic attitude of hiddenness and inconspicuousness in acts of piety" (303). This claim can be understood as dismissing the importance of concrete action for a focus on some "attitude" that is ambiguously connected to action. That would be inaccurate. Luz does, however, go on to say that hearers are to discover for themselves what constitutes washing and anointing in their situation, which seems exactly right.

[108] Luz, *Matthew 1–7*, 328n34, citing Tannehill, *The Sword of His Mouth*, 1975, 382 (86–88). Though Luz cites Tannehill with regard to Mt 5:39–42, he also mentions Tannehill with regard to Mt 6:16–18 on 361n69.

[109] See Alasdair MacIntyre, *After Virtue*, 2nd ed. (Notre Dame, IN: University of Notre Dame Press, 1984), 23. The exact quotation is "Every moral philosophy – and emotivism

cannot be solely an ethic for individuals but must attend to social ethics. Yet it might seem that the verses under examination in this chapter do not address the importance of community. In addition to the injunction to hidden performance, the emphasis on intentionality – which is rightly ascribed to an individual agent – can lead one to think that these verses focus solely on "personal piety."[110] But this need not be the case. The recent work of Walter Wilson is instructive on this topic.

Wilson's research on these verses reveals that the two most common emphases in contemporary interpretation of them are an analysis of them as Jewish cultic acts[111] and a focus on intentionality. Despite his preference for the latter and recognition of some limitations of certain interpretations along the lines of the former, Wilson argues that the interpretation focusing on intentionality is rightly seen as related to communal practices, such as Jewish cultic acts. He deploys recent scholarship on asceticism to argue that practices such as prayer, fasting, and almsgiving are crucial for enculturation, or formation in the context of community.

Though not writing with any explicit attention to virtue, Wilson's use of scholarship on asceticism is quite illuminative as to how intentional action is formative of a person's character and identity.[112] Wilson follows mainstream scholarship on these verses in recognizing that the acts described here are "conventional acts of piety" for Jews of the time.[113] Yet he also recognizes that the "meaning of these practices is not fixed or self-evident, but is subject to reinterpretation depending on the intentionality that informs them."[114] This is of course simply to return to the opening section of this chapter on the importance of the further end for the meaning of acts. But Wilson's main

---

is no exception – characteristically presupposes and sociology." For attention to this dynamic in post-conciliar Catholic moral theology, see Cloutier and Mattison, "Review Essay," 231.

[110] Unfortunately, Betz claims this is indeed the "concentration of this passage." He goes on to claim that "The individual occupies center of attention." See "A Jewish Christian Cultic *Didache* in Matthew 6:1–18," 68.

[111] This is often accompanied by a claim that the verses subvert Jewish cultic practices and/ or favor domestic cultic activities over public Jewish ones. While recognizing these verses surely reflect Matthean community self-identification as distinct from rival Jewish practices (479), Wilson rightly claims that any interpretation of them as a rejection of public cultic practices is unfounded. See Wilson, "Seen in Secret," 478n16.

[112] See Wilson, "Seen in Secret," 482–83. Wilson relies heavily on the work of Richard Valantasis, whose aptly named "Constructions of Power in Asceticism," *Journal of the American Academy of Religion* 63 (1995): 775–821 focuses on how the ascetic resists a dominant culture through an "elicited" alternate audience (483). Though it is not clear whether or not Valantasis's work considers the possibility of audience and communities that are not mainly expressions of power, he helpfully describes the nexus between intentional action, audience, and enculturation.

[113] Wilson, "Seen in Secret," 484. See also Guelich, *The Sermon on the Mount*, 301 and Betz, "A Jewish Christian Cultic *Didache* in Matthew 6:1–18."

[114] Wilson, "Seen in Secret," 484.

contribution here is explicit attention to the formative impact of these acts in the context of community. The acts are of course communal in that they arise out of conventional Jewish practices at the time. Yet they are also communal in that all intentional action has an "audience."[115] This observation is particularly obvious in the verses under consideration here, where people perform righteous deeds to be seen, either by others or by our heavenly Father. But Wilson argues that Matthew's audience is being invited to resist the "dominant culture's" performance of these acts in a manner to be seen by others:

> [R]ejecting prevailing modes of socialization, the readers can now conceive of these performances as moments in the development of a resistant self, an alternate subjectivity that is "rehearsed" in an alternative performance space.... [T]hrough the modality of such secrecy, these acts become conscious acts of withdrawal and resistance.[116]

By naming the process whereby Mathew's audience is invited to resist enculturation into the dominant culture, Wilson appropriately reminds us how intentional acts such as those in Mt 6:1–6, 16–18 are not individualistic but thoroughly communal, both in their origin and in their capacity for enculturation. After all, it is the dynamic of generating habits and that ensemble of habits called character that makes intentional action so crucial for enculturation.

Despite claiming to describe in his article "the processes of social formation in Matthew's community," Wilson unfortunately focuses solely on resistance to being enculturated by the dominant culture.[117] He even goes so far as to say that Matthew's audience can "orient their intentionality so as to eschew the enculturating function of these practices"[118] and "these acts are not to be performed as acts of enculturation."[119] Given his argument, he must of course mean that these acts are not forming people to be members of the dominant community, which is presumably characterized predominantly by self-exaltation. True enough. But these acts are indeed quite formative, and do indeed "enculturate" people; they simply do so into an alternate community, one where members are invited and enabled to live as children of their heavenly Father.[120] It would help if Wilson recognized his "resistant subjectivities"[121] were as communally situated as those of the dominant culture.

---

[115] Wilson, "Seen in Secret," 482–83.   [116] Wilson, "Seen in Secret," 485.

[117] Wilson, "Seen in Secret," 476.   [118] Wilson, "Seen in Secret," 485.

[119] Wilson, "Seen in Secret," 484.

[120] Bridget Burke Ravizza uses the term "diacritical community" to describe such witness. See her "Selling Ourselves on the Marriage Market," *America* 191.7 (Sept. 2004): 21–23 at 22. She cites Robert Webber and Rodney Clapp *People of the Truth: A Christian Challenge to Contemporary Culture* (New York: Morehouse Publishing, 1993).

[121] Wilson, "Seen in Secret," 485.

Even if the primary audience in Matthew 6:1–6, 16–18 is our heavenly Father, those living as children of our heavenly Father are also a community. This counter-cultural community can of course be called simply the Church.[122]

In sum, there are evident resources in contemporary biblical scholarship to support the central thesis of this section, namely, that Mt 6:1–6, 16–18 offers specific, action-oriented guidance for developing virtues. Though not to be literally imitated, the various instructions on praying, fasting, and giving alms are indeed "focal instances" of those activities that invite some sort of concrete action. Such concrete intentional action not only reflects the agent's habits, but they can also inculcate habits with their corresponding intentionality. Legitimate attention to agent intentionality prompted by these verses should not eclipse the importance of community for these verses. Indeed, the community both helps specify the actions performed and in turn is formed by individuals performing these actions. This dynamic rests in no small part on the fact that all such action has an audience, and the enjoined audience here is our heavenly Father and His people.

CONCLUSION

This more robust conclusion recapitulates the claims of previous sections, but it does so for the purpose of establishing why the verses under examination in this chapter are fruitfully examined in conjunction with the virtue of charity. Section 1 focuses on a crucial topic for both these verses and virtue ethics in general, namely, intentionality. It explains how immediate acts maintain a formative finality but focuses especially on how important the further end of human action is for grasping the meaning of that action and assessing its formative impact on the person. Consonant with Chapter 1's claims about how human activity in this life can be constitutive of the eternal happiness that is the kingdom of heaven, Section 1 explains how actions performed for a further end are so shaped (or "in-formed") by that goal so as to constitute a participation in it. Section 2's focus on growth in virtue explains how, through specified actions, habits can be developed in a person, habits that also "carry" intentionality and thus constitute a participation in the further goal of the habitual activity. These verses therefore enjoin activity for the sake of our heavenly Father who sees in secret. They also provide concrete guidance on how to become the sorts of people (in other words, habituated people) who live toward, and in a real way already participate in, the kingdom of heaven.

---

[122] Note that this argument about the importance of these practices for community formation augments the long-standing affirmation in commentators that Mt 6:1–6, 16–18 is not in tension with Mt 5:16.

What has any of this to do with charity? These verses address action done for the sake of God. To live for the sake of God, to "love the Lord your God with all your heart, with all your soul, and with all your mind" (Mt 22:37–40), is at the heart of the Christian life. This love of God is called charity, and thus the tradition of theological reflection on charity is clearly related to, prompted by, and illuminative of these verses. Though any extended treatment of charity is beyond the scope of this book (let alone this conclusion), I turn briefly here to the thought of Augustine and then Thomas Aquinas to substantiate how reflection on charity is fitting in the context of these verses in the Sermon.

Despite the term "virtue" never appearing in the foundational Book 1 of *Teaching Christianity* (*De Doctrina Christiana*), this treatise by Augustine, though recognized for its enormous impact more broadly on later theologians, is also a crucial text for a virtue-centered approach to morality, despite its import on that level being nearly universally neglected.[123] Through terminology that can be challenging today given the impact of Kant's thought on how we hear the term "use," Augustine distinguishes what is to be "enjoyed" from things that are "used."

> Enjoyment after all, consists in clinging to something lovingly for its own sake, while use consists in referring what has come your way to what your love aims at obtaining. [124]

What Augustine is describing here is intentional action, goal-directed activity from the perspective of an acting person. He is describing in part how some things are pursued for the sake of further ends. Unsurprisingly, he names God as the proper "object" of enjoyment, and thus "love of God" encapsulates the Christian life.[125] All other activities are done for the further sake of God. As one translator lucidly offers, "whatever else occurs to you as fit to be loved must be *whisked along* toward that point to which the whole impetus of your love is hastening."[126] Charity is therefore love of God above all else, and doing all activities for the further sake of love of God. Hence the relevance of Augustine's thought on charity for the verses under consideration here.

---

[123] See Augustine, *Teaching Christianity* (New York: New City Press, 1996). For a helpful overview of the impact of this text on later theologians, see a pair of volumes on this work and its impact on the Middle Ages, both of which grew out of a 1991 conference at Notre Dame: Duane W. H. Arnold and Pamela Bright, eds., "*De Doctrinia Christiana*": *A Classic of Western Culture*, Christianity and Judaism in Antiquity 9 (Notre Dame, IN: University of Notre Dame Press, 1995) and Edward D. English, ed., *Reading and Wisdom: The· "De Doctrina Christiana" of Augustine in the Middle Ages*, Notre Dame Conferences in Medieval Studies 6 (Notre Dame, IN: University of Notre Dame Press, 1995).

[124] Augustine, *Teaching Christianity*, 1.4.4.

[125] To anticipate a topic for next chapter, Augustine is very clear that there is "one single end" (*Teaching Christianity*, i.29.30; see also i.22.20–21).

[126] Augustine, *Teaching Christianity*, i.22.21, emphasis added.

Augustine goes on to examine in some detail those "other activities." He examines how we are to love others (including the enemy) out of charity, as well as the proper place of love of ourselves (including our bodies). Asserting the existence of an "order of love," Augustine claims "living a just and holy life requires one to be capable of an objective and impartial evaluation of things; to love things, that is to say, in the right order."[127] Not coincidentally to the verses treated in this chapter, Augustine claims the right order of love may be summarized as loving God above all else, then our neighbor, and then ourselves.[128] In Mt 6:1–6, 16–18, we find a set of activities all done for the sake of our heavenly Father, activities that in a sense "cover it all": our relationship with God (prayer); our relationships with the neighbors (almsgiving); and ourselves (fasting). In short, while Augustine does not explicitly use the language of virtue here, he does indeed address further goals and immediate activities, and how love of God above all else informs all other activities in the Christian life. He does so through a treatment of charity, and thus examination of these verses in Mt 6 converges with reflection on charity in the Christian tradition.

What we find in Augustine is that reflection on the love of God that is charity immediately turns to the relationship between love of God and all other loves, especially love of neighbor. Before turning to the thought of Thomas Aquinas for further substantiation of the relevance of charity for Mt 6:1–6, 16–18, it is worth pausing to identify a frequent assertion in contemporary biblical scholarship on these verses as to the relationship between love of God and love of neighbor. As was the case in Section 2, a common assumption in biblical scholarship serves as a foil for the analysis offered here.

A common strategy in commentaries on these verses is to "place" them in the Sermon as serving a role distinct from the preceding clearly defined set of verses, Mt 5:21–48. As Walter Wilson states baldly with regard to these two passages, "the first [textually, meaning Mt 5:21–48] addresses the topic [righteousness] in terms of right relationships with others, the second [Mt 6] in terms of a right relationship with God."[129] Indeed this description of Mt 6:1–6, 16–18 as about relationship with God *as distinct from* relationship with others is present in much of the most respected scholarship on the

---

[127] Augustine, *Teaching Christianity*, i.27.28.

[128] Augustine, *Teaching Christianity*, i.27.28. For a similar claim in Thomas Aquinas, see *Commentary on the Gospel of Matthew*, 563. A more technical Thomistic virtue analysis would have to attend to the fact that while Thomas Aquinas himself claims the activities of Mt 6 cover God, others, and self (Thomas Aquinas, *Commentary on the Gospel of Matthew*, 563) he "places" almsgiving as an act of charity (Tjp, as Aquinas, *Summa Theologiae* II–II 32, 1) and prayer as an act of religion under justice (Tjp, as Aquinas, *Summa Theologiae* II–II 83, 3). Though that analysis is beyond the scope of this chapter, it is quite feasible in a way that does not contradict Thomas Aquinas's argument about the importance of the infused moral virtues.

[129] Wilson, "Seen in Secret," 475–76.

Sermon.[130] There is something true to this reading of Mt 6. In each case, the acts are enjoined to be seen by our heavenly Father who will repay us. It is thus true that they are all properly understood "in terms of a right relationship with God." To use the language of Section 1, the activities enjoined there have (or should have) the same further end.

Yet as also explained in Section 1, recognition of the enormous importance of an activity's further end need not exclude recognition of the importance of the immediate act in its finality. To regard these verses as focusing on our ("vertical") relationship with God *as distinct from* our ("horizontal") relationship with others, or for that matter as distinct from the whole myriad of our activities not directly toward God, is not only theologically inadequate but, more pertinent here, not justified by the text of Mt 6. This question of the relationship between love of God and other activities is crucial for this passage since in each of the three acts described the act is done for (and rewarded by) our heavenly Father. Yet the acts differ as to whom they concern most immediately: others (giving alms); God (prayer); and ourselves (fasting). How can reflection on this passage in light of charity help address an inadequate assumption in biblical scholarship on the place of these verses in the Sermon as to the relationship between love of God and neighbor? We have already seen in Augustine the impact of love of God above all else on our other loves. We now turn to Thomas Aquinas, whose work on charity as the form of the virtues and the relationship between charity and the infused moral virtues addresses precisely this topic.

Note at the outset that the turn from Augustine to Thomas Aquinas in this conclusion is reflective of the sections in the chapter. Section 1 examines actions and the importance of intentionality (at varying levels) for comprehending human actions from the perspective of the acting person. Augustine's thought in *Teaching Christianity* is certainly foundational for a virtue-centered approach to morality, but it does not explicitly employ the language of virtue. Section 2 focuses on growth in virtue. Thomas Aquinas defined charity more explicitly than Augustine as a virtue, and he explained its relationship to various activities using the language of virtue. Two of Thomas Aquinas's arguments are briefly presented here as augmenting the case that the verses treated in this chapter are fruitfully read in light of charity.

---

[130] Guelich uses the terms "horizontal" and "vertical" (*The Sermon on the Mount*, 300). He also says the "greater righteousness" of 5:20 "reflects itself in conduct toward others (5:21–48) as well as toward God (6:1–18)" (170; cf. 255). See also Betz, *The Sermon on the Mount*, 332. It is worth recalling here that Chapter 2's analysis of the antitheses indicated the importance of claims about who God is (particularly in the fourth and sixth antitheses) for the activities delineated there. Though the ensuing paragraphs lament the inadequacy of treating Mt 6 as concerning our relationship with God to the neglect of our other loves, it should also be lamented that Mt 5 be read as treating our relations with others to the neglect of our relationship with God.

First, Thomas Aquinas follows Lombard in claiming that charity is the "form" of the virtues.[131] It is the grace-enabled theological virtue of charity that directs us to love of God, and also to do the activities of other virtues for the sake of our supernatural destiny of friendship with God. As Thomas Aquinas words it, "charity ... directs the acts of all other virtues to the last end."[132] This is precisely the dynamic which occurs in Mt 6.[133] In his account of the infused moral virtues Thomas Aquinas provides further detail on how that "direction toward the last end" impacts the other virtues.

The second resource in Thomas Aquinas's thought that establishes the connection between these verses and charity is his work on the infused moral virtues. Thomas Aquinas grants that charity suffices to orient us toward friendship with God directly. Yet what habits or virtues govern other activities done in further relation to God? He implicitly asks, does charity suffice to orient the acts of the moral virtues acquired on our own by unaided reason toward our supernatural end?[134] His answer is no. He grants that "moral and intellectual virtues can indeed be caused in us by our actions, but such are not proportionate to the theological virtues" and the supernatural end toward which they orient us.[135] He goes on to say the "power of those naturally instilled principles does not extend beyond the capacity of nature. Consequently, people need in addition to be perfected by other principles in relation to their supernatural end."[136] Thus, "the soul needs further to be perfected by infused virtues in regard to other things, yet in relation to God."[137] These grace-enabled (or "infused") virtues that guide us in "other things yet in relation to God" as our supernatural law end are the infused moral virtues.

Thus when charity as form of the virtues commands acts of moral virtues to be ultimately oriented toward the supernatural end, those moral virtues are trans-formed, literally. Thomas Aquinas continues in the following article to explain why the acts of the infused moral virtues differ in species from those of the acquired moral virtues. Using his stock example of fasting, he claims

---

[131] Thomas Aquinas, *Summa Theologiae* II–II 23, 8. See also Thomas Aquinas, *Disputed Questions on the Virtues*, q. 2 ("On Charity"), art. 3. In this latter text, Thomas Aquinas also calls charity "mother" and "root" of the virtues.

[132] Thomas Aquinas, *Summa Theologiae* II–II 23, 8. For an excellent treatment of how charity commands the acts of the other virtues, see Michael Sherwin, O.P., *By Knowledge and By Love: Charity and Knowledge in the Moral Theology of St. Thomas Aquinas* (Washington, DC: Catholic University of America Press, 2004).

[133] In his *Disputed Questions on the Virtues*, q. 2 ("On Charity"), art. 3, Thomas Aquinas uses not only his stock Aristotelian example of stealing to commit adultery to describe activities done for the sake of further ends but also "the example of one who gives alms either for the sake of God or for the sake of vainglory."

[134] Thomas Aquinas *Summa Theologiae* I–II 63, 3. See also his *Disputed Questions on the Virtues*, q. 1 ("On the Virtues in General"), art. 10.

[135] Thomas Aquinas, *Summa Theologiae* I–II 63, 3 ad. 1.

[136] Thomas Aquinas, *Summa Theologiae* I–II 63, 3 ad. 3.

[137] Thomas Aquinas, *Summa Theologiae* I–II 63, 3 ad. 2.

that when eating is done virtuously for the natural end (e.g., not hindering health, not hindering reason) that can be different from when it is done virtuously for the supernatural end (e.g., chastising the body). Hence the formal object of an act of infused virtue differs from that of an acquired virtue.[138] Even when an act of, say, acquired temperance may appear from an observer's perspective to be the same as an act of infused temperance, they have different ends from the perspective of the acting person and thus different "rules" or measures. So they differ as to the meaning (and quite often the observable description) of the act. This seemingly straightforward claim that those who act for our heavenly Father do the "same" things differently actually raises enormous questions about the relationship between the natural and supernatural ends and about the relationship between (and possibility of coexistence of) the acquired and infused moral virtues, but these issues cannot be addressed here.[139] But for the purposes of this conclusion it should be clear that an analysis of these verses in light of charity, buttressed with Thomas Aquinas's reflection on the relationship between charity and the other virtues, precludes any sharp separation between love of neighbor and love of God as too commonly found in recent biblical scholarship. We have also come full circle to the start of this chapter. Thomas Aquinas's account of how charity transforms the moral virtues, such that different sorts of acts are performed and different sorts of people are habituated when the activity is for the sake our eternal home, is directly relevant to these verses is Matthew 6.[140] Hence,

---

[138] Thomas Aquinas, *Summa Theologiae*, I–II 63, 4. See also *Disputed Questions on the Virtues*, q. 1 ("On the Virtues in General"), art. 10 ad. 8.

[139] For a review of the literature and the standard claim that both the acquired and infused virtues can "coexist" in the same person, see William C. Mattison III, "Can Christian Possess the Acquired Cardinal Virtues?" *Theological Studies*, 72 (2011) 558–85. There I argue these two sorts of virtue cannot coexist in one person. See also Angela McKay Knobel, "Can the Infused and Acquired Virtues Coexist in the Christian Life?" *Studies in Christian Ethics* 23:4 (2009) 381–96. See also her "Two Theories of Christian Virtue," *American Catholic Philosophical Quarterly*, 84 (2010) 599–618.

[140] Though perhaps obvious, it must be stated that there is an important disjoint between the difference between acquired and infused moral virtues, on the one hand, and the difference between acting well to be seen by others or by our heavenly Father, on the other hand. In the latter as found in Mt 6, those hypocrites who act to be seen by others develop vice, not acquired virtue. Whether there can be some category of "true but imperfect" virtue, whereby people can, say, fast or give alms for some true but (only) natural good rather than for our heavenly Father, is not directly addressed by these verses. Though they do not therefore provide resources for examining that issue, they do indeed occasion discussion of what is commonly called the possibility of "pagan virtue." For helpful treatments of that issue in the context of Augustine and Thomas Aquinas, see the following: Bonnie Kent, "Moral Provincialism," *Religious Studies* 30 (1994): 269–85; Brian J. Shanley, "Aquinas on Pagan Virtue," *The Thomist* 63 (1999): 553–77; Thomas M. Osborne, "The Augustinianism of Thomas Aquinas's Moral Theory," *The Thomist* 67 (2003): 279–305; Angela McKay "Prudence and Acquired Moral Virtue," *The Thomist* 69 (2005): 535–55; Thomas M. Osborne, "Perfect and Imperfect Virtues in Aquinas," *The Thomist* 71 (2007): 39–64; Angela McKay Knobel, "Aquinas and the

examining these verses in conjunction with the tradition of theological reflection on charity is not only warranted but bears great fruit.

Not for the last time in this book do we see how the Sermon on the Mount evokes reflection on the infused moral virtues. We return to this topic in the following chapter. For now, it suffices to note the fittingness of examining these verses in light of charity. There is an additional structural basis for that fittingness. Charity is surely the heart of the Christian life of discipleship. And the verses treated in this chapter are found at the spatial heart, the center, of the Sermon on the Mount.[141] But more substantively, these verses address topics that are absolutely crucial for any (but especially a virtue-centered) morality, namely intentionality and the meaning of human actions; the formation of character through the development of habits (hopefully virtues); and, the impact on love of God above all else (in other words, charity) on, well, all else. The impact of that further end is not the exclusion of all else, nor simply the de-prioritization of all else (though this latter is true at times), but the transformation of all else when done for the sake of our heavenly Father who sees in secret.[142] We turn in the next chapter to more detailed analysis of that transformation on our engagement with temporal goods and our relations with others.

Pagan Virtues," *International Philosophical Quarterly* 51.3 (2011): 339–54; David Decosimo, *Ethics as a Work of Charity: Thomas Aquinas and Pagan Virtue* (Stanford, CA: Stanford University Press, 2014).

[141] Though true, most precisely the verses omitted in this chapter, 6:7–15, are the spatial center of the Sermon. That spatial centrality is part of the basis for privileging the Lord's Prayer with its own distinct and climactic treatment in the final chapter.

[142] As an aside, this Thomistic teaching on the infused moral virtues is enormously helpful in explaining how Christians can both allow the love of God to direct all of their activities, and yet still collaborate fruitfully with non-believers on activities such as serving the poor, teaching children, and providing health care. Those latter activities retain their proximate finalities whether or not they are animated by charity.

4

SEEKING FIRST THE KINGDOM

Temporal Goods and Relations with Others in Matthew 6:19–7:12

Do not store up for yourselves treasures on earth, where moth and decay destroy, and thieves break in and steal.

But store up treasures in heaven, where neither moth nor decay destroys, nor thieves break in and steal.

For where your treasure is, there also will your heart be.

The lamp of the body is the eye. If your eye is sound, your whole body will be filled with light;

but if your eye is bad, your whole body will be in darkness. And if the light in you is darkness, how great will the darkness be.

No one can serve two masters. He will either hate one and love the other, or be devoted to one and despise the other. You cannot serve God and mammon.

Therefore I tell you, do not worry about your life, what you will eat [or drink], or about your body, what you will wear. Is not life more than food and the body more than clothing?

Look at the birds in the sky; they do not sow or reap, they gather nothing into barns, yet your heavenly Father feeds them. Are not you more important than they?

Can any of you by worrying add a single moment to your life-span?

Why are you anxious about clothes? Learn from the way the wild flowers grow. They do not work or spin.

But I tell you that not even Solomon in all his splendor was clothed like one of them.

If God so clothes the grass of the field, which grows today and is thrown into the oven tomorrow, will he not much more provide for you, O you of little faith?

So do not worry and say, "What are we to eat?" or "What are we to drink?" or "What are we to wear?"

All these things the pagans seek. Your heavenly Father knows that you need them all.

But seek first the kingdom (of God) and his righteousness, and all these things will be given you besides.

Do not worry about tomorrow; tomorrow will take care of itself. Sufficient for a
day is its own evil.

Stop judging, that you may not be judged.

For as you judge, so will you be judged, and the measure with which you measure
will be measured out to you.

Why do you notice the splinter in your brother's eye, but do not perceive the
wooden beam in your own eye?

How can you say to your brother, "Let me remove that splinter from your eye,"
while the wooden beam is in your eye?

You hypocrite, remove the wooden beam from your eye first; then you will see
clearly to remove the splinter from your brother's eye.

Do not give what is holy to dogs, or throw your pearls before swine, lest they
trample them underfoot, and turn and tear you to pieces.

Ask and it will be given to you; seek and you will find; knock and the door will be
opened to you.

For everyone who asks, receives; and the one who seeks, finds; and to the one who
knocks, the door will be opened.

Which one of you would hand his son a stone when he asks for a loaf of bread,
or a snake when he asks for a fish?

If you then, who are wicked, know how to give good gifts to your children, how
much more will your heavenly Father give good things to those who ask him.

Do to others whatever you would have them do to you. This is the law and
the prophets

Given how clearly structured different sections of the Sermon on the Mount
are leading up to 6:19, by comparison the verses addressed in this chapter
appear to be a far more loosely organized collection of sayings. In fact, in the
tradition of commentary on the Sermon as well as recent biblical scholarship
they are often referred to as just that.[1] Even so, Mt 6:19–7:12 (or at times

---

[1] John Meier, in his *The Vision of Matthew: Christ Church and Morality in the First Gospel*
(New York: Paulist Press, 1978), claims with regard to Mt 6 that "After verse 18, Matthew's
concern for architectonic structure lessens" (65). Calvin claims we have in this section
"detached sentences, not a continuous discourse" (*Harmony of the Evangelists*, 335). Luz
labels 6:19–34 as Jesus's "critique of possessions," without suggesting any such structure
for 7:1–12 (*Matthew 1–7*, 391). Davies labels 5:17–48 "teaching *vis-à-vis*" Torah," 6:1–18 as
"commandments concerning almsgiving, prayer, and fasting," and 6:19–7:12 as Jesus
addressing "social issues" (98). Guelich describes these "apparently disjointed sayings"
in 6:19–7:12 by saying they seem not to "exhibit any visible interrelationship with each
other" (322). He then goes on, however, by relying on Bornkamm, to correlate these
sayings to petitions in the Lord's Prayer (324–25; cf. 363). For an overview of approaches to
organizing these seemingly unorganized sayings, see Betz 423–28. Betz devotes consider-
able ink to disputing the Bornkamm reading endorsed by Guelich. Betz's extensive
overview concludes with his claim that "since no one has been able to figure out the
rationale for the arrangement of the sayings in 6:19–7:12, all one can do is to propose some
'informed guesses.' They are largely speculative" (427).

6:19–34 and 7:1–12) are treated as a distinct section (or two) mainly because of the obvious unit at Mt 6:1–18 and the clearly concluding verse at 7:12 which precedes the most evidently eschatological material of 7:13–27. Yet despite this common assumption that Mt 6:19–7:12 is a unified section only by default, it is argued here that there is actually an evident internal structure to these verses, and that the various parts of that structure are unified around the theme of single-mindedness. Chapter 3 addressed single-mindedness in contrast to hypocrisy, and through examinations of the relationship between immediate acts and further goals. The argument of this chapter is that 6:19–7:12 is unified by the climactic verse 6:33: "seek first the kingdom of God and his righteousness and all these will be provided as well."[2] In fact, examining these verses with a virtue-centered approach to morality not only aids the gleaning of moral guidance from this section, but it also helps to reveal the structural coherence of these verses. The thesis proposed here is that the verses examined in this chapter are unified by the theme of seeking first the kingdom and its righteousness, with the ensuing impact of such prioritization on all other activities of the disciple.

How is this coherence evident in the structure of these verses?[3] The climatic verse 6:33 appears as part of an extended pericope, involving the metaphors of the birds of the air and flowers of the field, as well as injunctions not to worry and affirmations of divine providence. It is the centerpiece of this section of the Sermon.[4] Though each one in the two sets of three could stand on its own, each of the three is closely related to the two others. And both sets of three are related as groups to the centerpiece 6:25–34 and especially the unifying verse 6:33 on seeking first the kingdom and its righteousness.[5]

Section 1 examines the first three sayings in 6:19–24 to make a case that they are unified by the theme of the singularity of one's last end, and the resulting impact that one's last end has all of one's actions. As examined in more detail below, the first and third sayings make it quite clear that a person can have only one master, one ultimate end. Further, we have in these sayings some indication of what ought to characterize one's last end. Finally, there is the quixotic 6:22–23 on the eye as lamp of the body. Certain claims of a virtue-centered approach to moral theology, especially on the last end and its impact on practical decision-making, help to buttress contemporary biblical scholarship in the interpretation of these verses.

---

[2] The importance of this verse is signified by the appearance of two crucial terms for the Sermon: the kingdom and righteousness.

[3] I am grateful to Fr. Frank Matera for pointing out the parallelism of 6:19–24 and 7:1–11.

[4] For an affirmation of there being eight distinct sayings, see Betz, *The Sermon on the Mount*, 423. That includes three sayings before, centerpiece, three afterwards, and the concluding 7:12.

[5] See Davies and Allison, *Matthew: A Shorter Commentary*, 107 for a rival structure.

Section 2 examines the centerpiece of the verses treated in this chapter, namely, 6:25–34. The argument of Section 2 is that these verses continue the themes of 6:19–24, but extend them with a portrait of a generously providing God, or as the title says, a "God of provident gratuity." Biblical scholarship on "worry" as well as the lilies and birds, augmented by the resources of a virtue-centered approach to morality addressed in Section 1, combine to reveal how these verses explain how faith in a God of provident gratuity transforms how we see temporal goods, and thus enables us to better engage in practical decision-making.

Section 3 examines the three sayings in 7:1–11. As in Mt 6:19–24, we find in Mt 7:1–11 three distinct sayings also unified by a common theme as well as a connection to 6:33. While 6:19–24 and the ensuing verses 6:25–34 depict the impact of seeking first the kingdom and its righteousness on all of our activities with regard to temporal goods, 7:1–11 focuses on how seeking first the kingdom and its righteousness transforms our relations with others: our "brothers," those on the outside, and even God. Though each of the sayings can stand on its own (as with those in 6:19–24), the three are unified to one another by their concern for relations with other persons. They also share with all verses treated in this chapter a focus on how seeking first the kingdom impacts all of our actions.

The conclusion of this chapter briefly examines the summation verse 7:12. It then presents a case that the verses examined in this chapter are helpfully read with the virtues of prudence (6:19–34) and justice (7:1–12) in mind. Reminiscent of Chapter 3 and as will be clear after the preceding sections, I argue that these verses not only suggest the virtues of prudence and justice, but even more specifically suggest the faith-informed and charity-animated virtues of infused prudence and infused justice.

I. THE NATURE AND FUNCTION OF THE LAST END IN MT 6:19–24

As evident already throughout this book, the convergences between the Sermon on the Mount and virtue ethics are many and obvious. But perhaps in no other passage in the Sermon is there more obvious convergence with virtue ethics than 6:19–24, a group of three straightforwardly ethical passages.[6] The last chapter noted the importance of intentionality in a virtue-centered approach to morality. An equally important feature of a

---

[6] This claim about convergence between biblical text and ancient philosophy is not simply the speculation of a moral theologian. While exegeting these verses, Hans Dieter Betz explores the possibility that 6:19–21 contains proverbial material from the time of Plato (*The Sermon on the Mount*, 437), and that 6:22–23 has its origin in Greek philosophy as well (450).

virtue-centered approach to ethics is attention to the "last end" and its impact on all activities in a person's life.[7] The six verses under consideration in this section address the nature and function of the last end in a person's life. Though there is less "further illumination" of virtue ethics by the Sermon in these six verses, they introduce Mt 6:25–34 which do indeed provide such further illumination.

It is worth pausing at the outset of this section to describe the last end in virtue ethics so that this convergence is especially evident. I rely here primarily on the work of Thomas Aquinas, with obvious reliance on Aristotle. In the very opening articles of the first question in the *Prima Secunda* on the moral life, Thomas Aquinas addresses how distinctively human action, in other words, free action, is intentional, or goal-directed. This leads him almost immediately to ask "whether there be any last end of a human life," and "whether it be possible to have many last ends."[8] In line with the consistent position in classical virtue ethics, Thomas Aquinas claims that there must be a last end, or ultimate point, of human life, lest a human life be ultimately pointless. Thomas Aquinas relies on Aristotle's argument from *Physics* to claim that since human actions are done for the sake of an end or goal, if there were no ultimate goal of those actions, there would be neither any start to human action, nor any rest as it would proceed to infinity. Furthermore, since it is a property of the last end to fully satisfy human desire such that nothing be lacking, one could not tend toward more than one thing to fully satisfy as both would by definition be incomplete.[9] This last end that fully satisfies human desire is called happiness. Thomas Aquinas claims that though all seek such fulfillment as the last end, people of course differ in what they think constitutes such happiness.[10] Yet regardless of one's answer to that question, there is one last end of all human action.

In her explication of this concept relying on Aristotle, Julia Annas describes it more accessibly by claiming the final end is simply "making sense of my life as a whole," "the idea that in a given individual his ends might form a hierarchy. . . . [M]y life is not just a series of, so to say, one damned end after another."[11] There is some overall coherence to a person's life, a coherence that, while surely not complete, does indeed evince a basic orientation or overall direction. Annas grants that "modern thinkers have found the notion of a single final end uncompelling," but notes that is because of their commitment at the outset to not take "thoughts about one's

---

[7] The classical treatments of this concept are Aristotle's *Nicomachean Ethics* I.7 and Thomas Aquinas's *Summa Theologiae* I–II 1, 4–8. See also Julia Annas' *Morality of Happiness*, 27–46.

[8] Thomas Aquinas, *Summa Theologiae* I–II 1, 4, and 5, respectively.

[9] Thomas Aquinas, *Summa Theologiae* I–II 1, 5. Here Thomas Aquinas cites Augustine, *City of God* XIX.1.

[10] Thomas Aquinas, *Summa Theologiae* I–II 1, 7.

[11] Annas, *Morality of Happiness*, 31.

life as a whole to be the starting point for ethical reflection," presumably instead preferring to focus on punctuated actions.[12] Classical virtue ethics assumes it as foundational that there is something one's life is "all about."[13]

Though affirmation of a single last end is an affirmation of a coherence or unity to an individual human life, a virtue-centered approach to morality of course recognizes that an individual person does not simply do one thing. How does the notion of a final end function so as to provide coherence to the variety of activities in any human life? Two ways are suggested here. First, there is the matter of prioritization. What comes first when different priorities conflict? Though a person may pursue a variety of endeavors, when they conflict some overall account is needed to enable one to pursue them in relation to one another.[14] However, the final end is not merely one's highest priority that one pursues either most frequently, or at particularly important moments in one's life. It is not simply one end among many, even if the most important one. This leads to the second function of the final end. Thomas Aquinas claims one ordains all that one does for the sake of the final end.[15] Given the importance of the end in specifying human action as discussed in the previous chapter, the significance of this claim should be clear.[16] The last end functions not only as one's highest priority, but also and perhaps even more significantly as shaping or "in-forming" all of one's more proximate actions. Even though a person engages in manifold activities in life, what one is "all about" shapes how those activities are done. Thus the identity of one's last end impacts all one's everyday activities. This point was first addressed in Chapter 3 on 6:1–6,16–18. It is also a crucial point of the second half of Matthew 6 and points us back to the biblical text.

In Mt 6:19–24, there is ready convergence between the biblical text and classical ethical reflection on the last end. The argument of this section is that these verses make three significant claims that converge with virtue ethics: a) the last end of the person is one; b) the true and enduring last end of humanity is God; and c) a proper orientation toward the last end is vital for guiding our everyday actions.

---

[12] Annas, *Morality of Happiness*, 33. Annas rightly identifies the last end as a common feature of classical virtue ethics, despite the variety of classical virtue ethics. Though a comparable understanding of the last end continues to characterize certain contemporary virtue-centered approaches to morality such as the Thomistic one offered here, she rightly notes that such a robust notion of the last end does not characterize all contemporary accounts of virtue ethics.

[13] For a helpful recent articulation of this concept, see David Decosimo's *Ethics as a Work of Charity* where he describes this notion using the term "final end conception."

[14] For treatment of this, see Julia Annas, *Morality of Happiness*, 32.

[15] Thomas Aquinas, *Summa Theologiae* I–II 1, 6.

[16] Though explaining it most precisely in *Summa Theologiae* I–II 18, it is noteworthy that Thomas Aquinas must also address the importance of the end in specifying human activity in these opening articles in the *Prima Secundae*. See I–II 1 and 3.

All three of these points are evident in the first of the three sayings in this section of the Sermon. First, by demanding the hearer decide whether to store up *either* treasures on earth *or* treasures in heaven, the text makes it quite evident that a person is oriented toward one or the other.[17] "For where your treasure is, there also will your heart be." As Luz comments, "the 'treasure' makes clear where the person's 'center' is located and what is most important to him or her."[18] Guelich also claims that these verses concern "where one's personal priorities lie."[19] More follows below on the term heart, but for now it is noteworthy that Guelich claims the term heart suggests "total allegiance," with "total" indicating there can be only one.[20] This point is affirmed even more bluntly in the third saying about two masters: "no one can serve two masters" and "you cannot serve God and mammon" (6:24).[21] There can be only one last end in one's life.

Second, the saying at 6:19–21 also immediately suggests why one ought to store up treasures in heaven by contrasting the quality of that treasure and earthly treasure. Classical ethical reflection on the last end requires it be both the greatest good (a condition of which is imperishability), and that it not be capable of being lost.[22] These are exactly the reasons Jesus offers in the Sermon for why one ought to store up treasures in heaven. Such treasure is not destroyed (as by moths). Further, it cannot be taken away (as by thieves).[23] By contrast, treasures

---

[17] The term "store up" suggests human activity as a participation in one's account of happiness, whatever the latter may be. In discussing how to store up treasures in heaven, Davies and Allison say it is achieved by all of the activities depicted in the Sermon, including the beatitudes, inconspicuous piety, and love of neighbor (*The Gospel According to Saint Matthew*, 632).

[18] Luz, *Matthew 1–7*, 396.   [19] Guelich, *The Sermon on the Mount*, 365.

[20] Guelich, *The Sermon on the Mount*, 328

[21] Augustine also connects 6:19–21 and 6:24 as well (*The Lord's Sermon on the Mount*, II.14.47). In language that clearly echoes I–II 1, 5, Thomas Aquinas comments on 6:24 by saying "it is impossible that one be directed to two things as last ends" (*Commentary on the Gospel of Matthew*, 620). Reminiscent of the concluding verses in the beatitudes, Jesus concludes these three sayings by using the second person "you." Having spoken more generally about the final end, this closing statement directly addresses the disciples, as if to ask: "will *you* choose God or mammon?"

[22] For a particularly clear example of this see Augustine, *Way of Life of the Catholic Church* II.13.44–46. See also Aristotle's *Nicomachean Ethics* where, after articulating the characteristics of the greatest good (I.7) he goes on to explain how it must be incapable of being lost, or mark a "complete life" (I.9–10).

[23] See Thomas Aquinas's *Commentary on the Gospel of Matthew*, 612–13 on how these verses explain both the enduring nature of heavenly reward, and instability of earthly reward. Guelich recognizes the contrast between perishable (earthly) and imperishable (heavenly) treasure here (*The Sermon on the Mount*, 327). See also Betz (*The Sermon on the Mount*, 433) and Davies and Allison (*The Gospel According to Saint Matthew*, 629) on the contrast between perishable and imperishable. As to the significance of moths and decay on the one hand and thieves on the other, Guelich claims that treasures in heaven are susceptible to loss neither by natural forces (moths and decay) nor (im)moral action (thieves and stealing). (*The Sermon on the Mount*, 326–27; affirmed by Davies and Allison

on earth can be destroyed and can be taken away. These disqualify such treasures as candidates for the last end. Again, the final verse of this section serves to reiterate this point: "you cannot serve God and mammon." In addition to implicating the hearers personally, these words make evident the striking contrast between the substantive content of the last end, God or mammon. Though scholars consistently note that "mammon" refers broadly to all material possessions, juxtaposed with God its inferiority is clear.[24]

Third and finally, Jesus concludes the first of the three sayings in this section by claiming that "where your treasure is, there also will your heart be."[25] Biblical scholars claim the "heart" is both an indication of one's whole person, and the source of all one's deeds. Guelich claims that "heart expresses the familiar biblical understanding of one's total person."[26] Davies and Allison explain the heart as the "source of one's deeds."[27] Thus in 6:21 we see why it is so important which treasures we seek, those of earth or heaven: "for where your treasure is, there also will your heart be."[28] Whatever one's

---

at *The Gospel According to Saint Matthew*, 630). This passage provides an opportunity for discussion not only of the characteristics of the last end but also the problem of evil in both natural and moral senses.

[24] For more on mammon, see Guelich, *The Sermon on the Mount*, 334; Luz, *Matthew 1–7*, 398; Betz, *The Sermon on the Mount*, 458; Davies and Allison, *The Gospel According to Saint Matthew*, 643. See Guelich's *The Sermon on the Mount* (334) and Betz's *The Sermon on the Mount* (458) for contrasting views on whether mammon refers to a more personalized demonic force. This is an obvious place to discuss the proper role of material wealth in the life of discipleship, a task beyond the scope of this chapter. Luz claims the entire section 6:19–34 is essentially a "critique of possessions" and occupies a central place in the Sermon (*Matthew 1–7*, 393). See also Aquinas, *Commentary on the Gospel of Matthew*, 620; Stassen and Gushee, *Kingdom Ethics*, 409–26; Davies and Allison, *The Gospel According to Saint Matthew*, 630; Betz, *The Sermon on the Mount*, 458–59.

[25] This is not the first time the term "heart" is employed in the Sermon, but the third. The first is in the beatitude of the pure of heart (5:8), which as noted above has been traditionally interpreted as a state of single-minded devotion toward God. The second preceding use of heart in the Sermon is also illuminative: "everyone who looks at a woman with lust has already committed adultery with her in his heart" (5:28). As explained in Chapter 2, the heart here is a reference to the source of human action. Though it is distinguished from exterior action (here adultery), it is also connected to, indeed the source of, such exterior action.

[26] Guelich, *The Sermon on the Mount*, 328. He says this is a depiction of "total allegiance," including presumably directing all of one's activities. Guelich notes 6:21 is the focal point of 6:19–21, shifting the emphasis from not only the nature of the treasure but also to one's person and the claim that treasure has upon one (328; see also 364). Another way to put this is not simply an emphasis on the final end, but the impact of one's final end on "where one's personal priorities lie" (Guelich, *The Sermon on the Mount*, 365). Luz affirms Guelich's claims on the function of 6:21 (*Matthew 1–7*, 396). He claims that the heart "is the center of the human being: the 'treasure' makes clear where the person's 'center' is located and what is most important to him or her" (*The Sermon on the Mount*, 396).

[27] Davies and Allison, *The Gospel According to Saint Matthew*, 632.

[28] Davies and Allison take the occasion of the verse to address the topic of reward in Matthew in a manner quite amenable to the analysis offered above in Chapter 3. They affirm its context in the "human hope for happiness" but also insist that "reward is in no

ultimate end is will be the source and goal of all of one's actions. Yet exactly how does the last end impact all of one's other activities? One way is evident from 6:24. That saying explains why one cannot serve two masters: "he will either hate one and love the other, or be devoted to one and despise the other."[29] Here we have one of the classic characteristics of the last end in virtue ethics, namely, its prioritization over all other activities.[30] Yet that is not the only way. Recall that the last end in-forms how all other activities are done. This is exactly what is indicated by the enigmatic second saying about the eye as lamp of the body (6:22–23).

In one sense the meaning of these two verses is evident. Since "the eye is the lamp of the body," it is important that the eye is "sound" such that the body be filled with light; otherwise if the eye is "bad" the whole body will be filled with darkness. Yet since the entire passage relies on a metaphor, namely, the eye as lamp of the body, the passage is only as comprehensible as that metaphor. A substantial body of scholarship has explained the meaning of this passage in light of ancient theories of vision.[31] There is also a significant disagreement in the literature as to whether the terms "sound" and "bad" with reference to the eye should be understood in a mainly physiological sense or in a more moral sense.[32] For the purposes of this section, those bodies of scholarship can be mined for the following conclusions.

way calculable, and it leaves no room either for religious egoism or for a claim on God" (*The Gospel According to Saint Matthew*, 634).

[29] There is often reflection on the different wording of the stances toward the two possible masters in the tradition, since these words serve as an occasion to discern how the stances differ in one who is oriented toward God or money, as well as their stance toward the other. See, for example, Augustine, *The Lord's Sermon on the Mount*, II.14.48 as well as Aquinas, *Commentary on the Gospel of Matthew*, 620–21. At issue is whether or not one can hate God. In Augustine's earlier work *The Lord's Sermon on the Mount*, he claims one cannot hate God and thus changes the order of the second part of 6:24. Yet in his *Retractions* (Washington, DC: The Catholic University of America Press, 1968) he claims it is not the case that one cannot hate God (I.18.8). Thomas Aquinas distinguishes hating God in Himself as and hating Him in His effects (*Commentary on the Gospel of Matthew*, 621).

[30] Biblical scholars less commonly soften this language of hatred with regard to mammon than they do with the Lucan injunction to hate one's family (Lk 14:26; cf. Mt 10:37). Yet that softening is somewhat evident in the consistent claim that this verse entails not a rejection of all material possessions, but a radical subordination of them to our devotion to God.

[31] The seminal article is Hans Diter Betz, "Mt 6:22f. and Ancient Greek Theories of Vision," pp. 43–56 of E. Best and R. Wilson (eds.) *Text and Interpretation: Studies of the New Testament in Presentation to Matthew Black* (Cambridge: Cambridge University Press, 1979). For an argument against this essay, see Kari Syreeni, "A Single Eye: Aspects of the Symbolic World of Matt 6:22–23" *Studia Theologica* 53 (1999): 97–118. See also Mark Whitters "The Eye Is the Lamp of the Body: Its Meaning in the Sermon on the Mount" *Irish Theological Quarterly* 71 (2006):77–88 and Dale Allison, "'The Eye is the Lamp of the Body (Matthew 6: 22–3 = Luke 11: 34–6) *New Testament Studies* 33 (1987):61–83.

[32] Guelich narrates different possible interpretations of "sound" as either a physiological term meaning "healthy," or more of a "moral" or "ethical" term such as "upright" or "guileless" (*The Sermon on the Mount*, 329–30). Guelich prefers the physiological

According to ancient theories of sight, the eye was understood less as a passive transparent entity and more as an active illuminating capacity.[33] As Betz indicates, the eye is not the source of illumination (which comes rather from within), but it is crucial to the process of illumination.[34] To speak more vernacularly, the function of the eye concerns "how we see things," both physiologically and ethically.[35] And how we see things impacts how we act. In describing this active function of the eye, Guelich claims this passage "compares the function of the eye for the body with one's life-controlling perspective."[36] It is life-controlling as evident precisely in how one acts. Here we see the impact of a sound eye on all of one's activities.

Yet what does it mean to say that one's "whole body" will be filled with light if the eye functions well (or conversely with darkness if it does not)? Once it is clear that the eye is not directing light into the body as a cavernous receptacle, we can see that the "whole body" refers not to one's corporeality which is illuminated on the inside, but rather to one's "person," to the "total existence of the person."[37] A bad eye leaves the whole person in darkness,

interpretation of both "sound" and "unsound" (*The Sermon on the Mount*, 331). See also Luz, *Matthew 1-7*, 396–98 and Grant Macaskill, "Mt 6:19–34: The Kingdom, the World, and the Ethics of Anxiety," *The Scottish Bulletin of Evangelical Theology* 23 (2005): 18–29, at 20. Macaskill takes the contrary position from Guelich.

[33] Guelich notes that the verse indicates that the eye functions in a more active sense (*The Sermon on the Mount*, 329). Nonetheless, he thinks the light/darkness motif is evocative of Mt 5:14 and 16, and suggests not simply the state of a "specific organ" but rather to "one's participation in the realm of light resulting from Jesus's coming" or "the total commitment of one's person in discipleship" (*The Sermon on the Mount*, 332). He even claims the "common denominator" of this three unit set of sayings in 6:19–24 is "the call for total allegiance" (*The Sermon on the Mount*, 332). It is this "total commitment" suggested by the verb "serve" (6:24) that requires the unicity of the last end (*The Sermon on the Mount*, 333).

[34] Betz claims, "the eye functions not by receiving its light from the outside by intromission. Instead the source of light is within" (*The Sermon on the Mount*, 452).

[35] Betz addresses the physiological/moral question at 450–51, and concludes "the terms seem to vacillate between physiological and ethical meanings, ambiguities that in such a thoughtful and tightly composed text can hardly be accidental. Rather, they must be intended and part of the argument" (*The Sermon on the Mount*, 450). He later says we ought to "begin with the physiological and then move to the ethical level of discourse' (*The Sermon on the Mount*, 451). This interpretation is affirmed here.

[36] Guelich, *The Sermon on the Mount*, 365.

[37] See Guelich's *The Sermon on the Mount* (367) and Luz's *Matthew 1-7* (398), respectively. For a classical connection of "whole body" with one's actions, see Augustine, *On the Lord's Sermon on the Mount*, II.13.45. The term "body" appears seven times in Matthew's Sermon, with three occurrences in the two verses under consideration here. In the two of the three instances in 6:22–23, as well as the two instances that precede these verses in the Sermon, body is used in conjunction with whole, as in the "whole body." Those previous two concern the "whole body" being thrown into Gehenna (5:29 and 30). The last two are found in the verses concerning worry about the body and clothing, addressed below. Contrary to a dualist understanding of the "body" as peripheral to the person, these verses indicate the contrary.

and a good eye leaves a person in light. What does it mean to be "filled with light" (or conversely, "in darkness")? Though not specified in 6:22–23, that passage's context wedged between 6:19–21 and 24 makes the answer obvious. As Guelich says, it is "a life lived with God at the center ('treasure in heaven')" such that "light in you refers to participation in the light manifested by Jesus's ministry."[38]

The preceding analysis of 6:22–23 has relied principally on recent biblical scholarship, mainly because it might seem that interpretation of these verses as corroborating a classical claim in virtue ethics about the connection between how we see things and how we act would be less likely to be found in that literature than classical theological commentaries. But as seen above, the interpretation offered here is indeed corroborated by recent biblical scholarship. What does the tradition of commentary have to say about this passage? Two points are relevant for this study.

First, the tradition of commentary corroborates Betz's claim that this passage intends both the physiological and moral meanings of "sound" in reference to eye, precisely to make an analogy. As Thomas Aquinas says, "for by the light of the eye, light is caught for directing all the members to their acts."[39] Without a biologically sound eye, the activities of the rest of the body's members will operate "as though in the dark."[40] On a "spiritual" level, the same is true. Thomas Aquinas says the passage is a warning lest the "heart which is the eye of the soul becomes darkened by training itself upon earthly things."[41] This interpretation not only makes sense given the context between 6:19–21 and 6:24, but it also reveals that there is purposeful interplay between the biological and moral senses of "eye." This interplay is also affirmed by Chrysostom, Luther, and Calvin.[42]

Second, what is referenced on the spiritual level by the "eye is the lamp of the body?" Thomas Aquinas notes that there are a variety of interpretations

---

[38] Guelich, *The Sermon on the Mount*, 367. Luz says of these verses "it is a question of light and darkness, wholeness and perfection" (*Matthew 1–7*, 398). Despite his extremely helpful work on the eye, Betz does not interpret the light and darkness with reference to 6:19–21 or 24. Seeking the "parenetical edge" of the passage he says "it gives no direct answer" and that "leaving him or her in that situation ["uncertainty"] seems to be the parenetic intent of the passage." Yet he does say one has to "find the answer elsewhere, probably by considering other passages" (*The Sermon on the Mount*, 453).

[39] This reference to light being "caught" evidences the shift that was occurring in the thirteenth century regarding how visual perception operates. For more on this shift, dated to approximately 1225 with Grosseteste and especially Bacon, see David Lindberg, *The Beginnings of Western Science* (Chicago: University of Chicago Press, 1992), 313–20.

[40] Thomas Aquinas, *Commentary on Matthew*, 614

[41] Thomas Aquinas, *Commentary on Matthew*, 615.

[42] See John Chrysostom, *Homilies on Matthew*, XX.3 (160); Luther, *The Sermon on the Mount*, 179; John Calvin, *Harmony of the Evangelists*, 335.

of "the eye is the lamp of the body" in the tradition.[43] A consistent interpretation in the tradition, and one emphasized here in the context of virtue ethics, is the eye as reason, or better, practical reason. Thomas Aquinas claims "as a lamp illuminates for seeing, so reason illuminates for acting."[44] Calvin claims, "God has given reason to guide them [our actions]."[45] And Chrysostom, while saying the lamp refers to the mind, describes its directive role by asking, "When the pilot is drowned, and the candle is put out, and the general is taken prisoner, what sort of hope will there be, after that, for those that are under command?"[46] In all these cases, the eye of the body is applied metaphorically to the role of practical reason in directing our actions. Particularly of interest is the language of command employed by Chrysostom, a term used in the Thomistic moral tradition to describe a crucial act of reason in decision-making.[47] It is also noteworthy that in his interpretation of 6:22–23, Thomas Aquinas references the Psalmist: "the light of your face is stamped upon me."[48] Thomas Aquinas consistently cites

---

[43] In his *Commentary on Matthew* (616–18), Thomas Aquinas lists four. The one focused upon here is the first. The third listed by Thomas Aquinas is the eye of faith, which also has relevance of this chapter as seen in the following section and conclusion. The second is Augustine's that the eye is understood as a reference to intention, continuing Augustine's interpretation of 6:1–7:12 as focusing on the clean of heart.

There is a disjointedness in Augustine reflection on this passage. He begins by stating that the "eye" of 6:22 refers to intention. Reminiscent of the preceding verses in 6:1–18, the injunction here is to a "single heart," where the intention is "love" and one's acts are done accordingly. "The 'eye' therefore we ought to take as meaning in this place the intention by which we do whatever we do. If it is clean and upright and keeping in view what it ought to keep in view, all our works which we perform in accordance with it are necessarily good" (*On the Lord's Sermon on the Mount*, II.13.45). This sense of "all our works" according with a proper ultimate goal is the interpretation endorsed here. Augustine then goes on to distinguish what we intend by our acts and what actually results (e.g., will a poor person benefit from our alms or use them for ill?), claiming that this verse teaches that acting with a good intention even despite a bad outcome constitutes "light" (*On the Lord's Sermon on the Mount*, II.13.46). Though right intention as characterizing a "good eye" is common in both interpretations, they differ as to what constitutes a bad eye (a self-serving motive or unintended negative effects, respectively).

[44] Aquinas, *Commentary on Matthew*, 615.

[45] Calvin, *Harmony of the Evangelists*, 335. Calvin of course goes on to say that this reason is tremendously diminished by sin. Here is a good place to see differences in moral theology in the context of interpretation of Sermon passages. All the more reason why commonalities such as interpreting 6:22–23 as regarding reason's guidance of human action are so noteworthy.

[46] Chrysostom, *Homilies on Matthew* XX.3 (161). Chrysostom goes on to say, "For God, he [Jesus] saith, gave us understanding that we might chase away all ignorance, and have right judgment of things." In the ensuing paragraphs, Chrysostom contrasts the seeming "virtues" that enable people to pursue worldly goods from true virtues which enable them to seek God. He compares the former to the courage of a circus performer, which is impressive on the tightrope but without bearing on real endeavors outside the show (XX.4, 163).

[47] See, for example, Thomas Aquinas, *Summa Theologiae* I–II 17, 1.

[48] Aquinas, *Commentary on Matthew*, 615, citing Ps 4:6.

this passage throughout his work when addressing the natural law, which for him is at least in part a "work of reason," or put differently, the accurate functioning of human practical reasoning. Since the virtue of practical reasoning functioning well is prudence, this corroborates the claim offered in the conclusion of this chapter that this part of the Sermon is helpfully understood in the context of the virtue prudence. In the context of these verses, Thomas Aquinas claims the eye is sound, or practical reasoning is functioning well, when "your reason is directed to one thing, namely, God," rather than to earthly treasures or mammon is referenced in 6:19–21 and 6:24.[49]

This returns us to the third of three conclusions about these verses' convergence with a virtue-centered approach to morality. An accurate apprehension of the last end is not only crucial in affording us proper priorities. It also enables us to see things accurately and respond accordingly in all of our practical decision-making. Seeing well and acting accordingly depends on an accurate apprehension of the last end. Making money (or power, or pleasure, and so on) the point of one's life not only idolatrously prioritizes these over God, but it also deforms how we engage in all of our activities given how the last end in-forms (in this case de-forms) those activities. Though a person who is "all about" money may take care of his family, attend to religious duties, care for the poor, and so on, all of that is done in a manner shaped by the last end of money. It renders all of one's activities darkness rather than light. "And if the light of the body is darkness, how great will the darkness be."

We are now able to understand in these three sayings of Jesus several points that are central to moral theology done from the perspective of virtue. First, there can be only one ultimate end in one's life, one that has priority over all others. Second, the true ultimate end is God, not earthly treasures (including money) that can be lost or fail to endure. Third and finally, one's ultimate end (or master, or treasure) in one's life is important beyond determining what comes before all else; that ultimate end also informs how all else is done. To transition to the following section, recall the earlier claim that with the exception of the explicit identification of the last end as God in 6:24, there is little in Mt 6:19–24 to further illuminate these three classic components of a virtue-centered approach to morality. But that further illumination does indeed occur in the ensuing verses.

II. A GOD OF PROVIDENT GRATUITY: MT 6:25–34

Though the previous three sayings are spoken by Jesus and enjoin the disciples to serve God and not mammon, they are nonetheless rather formal

---

[49] Aquinas, *Commentary on Matthew*, 616.

or abstract on their own. More specifically, they are not distinctive to the Christian life of discipleship. Perhaps more than any verses in the Sermon, they can read like part of a treatise on happiness in ancient ethical thought, delineating the formal characteristics of one's ultimate end and indicating its importance in shaping all other activities in life. The next ten verses continue the theme of the first three sayings, yet also extend it in two ways. First, we learn more about not what but Who our last end is, and His relationship to the rest of creation. Second, we learn not only that, but how this "last end" transforms our practical decision-making. In these verses we find continuity with the themes of 6:19–24, yet we also see how the Sermon illuminates and extends a classical ethics of virtue.

A. THE LAST END: OUR HEAVENLY FATHER

First, as to the further illumination of our last end, these verses are a clear continuation of the previous three sayings.[50] The claims that God is humanity's last end and that all of our actions should be governed accordingly are both central to these ten verses, which culminate in 6:33: "seek first the kingdom (of God) and his righteousness, and all these things will be given you besides."[51] Jesus repeatedly enjoins his hearers "do not worry" about food and drink and clothes. These are presented as inadequate candidates for our last end. Why so? One obvious reason is that they are not as important as other things. "Is not life more than food and the body more than clothing?" (6:25). It is not these but the kingdom and his righteousness that one ought to "seek first." Another reason is the ultimate inefficacy of worry: "Can any of you by worrying add a single moment to your life span?" (6:27). Note that these injunctions on how we act regarding practical matters are still rather abstract and formal. Having an accurate assessment of what is important in life, "putting first things first," and avoiding needless worry are standard bits of ancient wisdom.[52]

---

[50] This continuity is especially evident in the use of the term "therefore" to start 6:25. Davies and Allison claim that for Matthew the "therefore" references continuity with 6:19–24 (Davies and Allison, *The Gospel According to Saint Matthew*, 646). For Betz that word has been simply incorporated from Q (Betz, *The Sermon on the Mount*, 468). Luz also notes the "I tell you" (here in 6:25 and in 6:29) is reminiscent of the antitheses and reinforces Jesus's authority (*Matthew 1–7*, 403). Macaskill ("The Kingdom, the World, and the Ethics of Anxiety," 18–19) claims that 6:25–34 is further elaboration of 6:19–21.

[51] For more on how 6:33 is summation of all 6:25–34 (and connected to 6:24), see Davies and Allison, *The Gospel According to Saint Matthew*, 659. This passage is commonly cited as one of the most obvious passages borrowed from Q given its parallel at Luke 12:22–31. See Betz, *The Sermon on the Mount*, 466 and 469; Davies and Allison *The Gospel According to Saint Matthew*, 645; see also Richard Dillon, "Ravens, Lilies, and the Kingdom of God (Mt 6:25–33/Lk 11: 22–31)" *The Catholic Biblical Quarterly* **53** (1991): 605–27, at 608, discussed in detail below.

[52] For example, see Davies and Allison on how Jesus's comments about worry relate to Stoic *apathia* (*The Gospel According to Saint Matthew*, 647).

But the main emphasis of this passage is clearly God's generous providence (or as said in the title of this part, God's "provident gratuity") and the place of all creatures in that providence. The two metaphors of this passage make exactly these points. Jesus points out to his audience that the birds "do not sow or reap, they gather nothing into barns, and yet your heavenly Father feeds them." No longer do we have the unnamed "master," or the impersonal "treasures in heaven." Here we learn it is "your heavenly Father" who provides, the same Father in heaven whom Jesus taught his disciples to address just verses earlier in the Lord's Prayer. We are also reminded, when Jesus recounts how our heavenly Father feeds the birds of the air, that we are "more important than they" (6:26).

These same affirmations are made in the second metaphor. Having explained how the Father provides food for the birds, Jesus continues the parallelism of food and clothes in describing the lilies of the field, which "do not sow or spin." Yet "not even Solomon in all his splendor was clothed as one of them" (6:29).[53] Once again we are assured with the solemn words "I tell you" that our heavenly Father will provide for our daily needs. Furthermore, the relative importance of the lilies to God's human children is even more vividly emphasized when Jesus says, "If God so clothes the grass of the field, which grows today and is thrown into the oven tomorrow, will he not much more provide for you, O you of little faith?" (6:30). God's generous providence extends far more broadly than to human persons alone; but for a second time in three verses we have here an affirmation in the words of Jesus of the special place of the human person in God's creation.

At this point it should be clear not only how a virtue-centered approach to morality helps us better understand these verses, but also how these verses extend and specify virtue ethics. The affirmation of a personal God who cherishes humanity and providentially provides certainly extends beyond any abstract and impersonal notion of a final end. It is instead an affirmation of faith. Our Father is a provident and generous provider to all creation, and particularly to humanity. Failure to recognize this is a misapprehension – an inaccurate grasp – of the realities of who God is, and humanity's cherished role in God's creation.

Before turning to how this knowledge, in faith, of our heavenly Father as our final end transforms our practical decision-making, it is worth pausing to identify two ways in which the reality of our heavenly Father may be misapprehended, as identified in these verses. First, pagans by definition do not have this faith in a God of provident gratuity. They thus act accordingly

---

[53] For a presentation of a minority view in biblical scholarship, namely, that Jesus is positing Solomon as a negative example of concern for temporal goods, see Warren Carter, "Solomon in All of His Glory: Intertextuality and Matthew 6:29" *Journal for the Study of the New Testament* **65** (1997):3–25.

with regard to food, drink, and clothing, presumably seeking these things first (6:32: "all these things the pagans seek").[54] But even more prevalent is a second way this passage reveals how this reality of a God of provident gratuity can be misapprehended. Continuing the primary emphasis of Mt 6:1–18 on those within the community of faith (those "on the "inside"), we also hear Jesus admonish those of "little faith" (6:30). These people *do* know of God, and should know better than to be anxious over temporal goods, but nonetheless their faith is weak.[55] These verses are presumably aimed to augment that little faith.[56] This passage, therefore, while affirming faith in a God or provident gratuity in contrast to pagan absence of faith, focuses primarily on augmenting the faith of those who know God but need continual reminders of His gratuitous providence lest they "worry" over temporal goods.

B. FAITH IN OUR HEAVENLY FATHER AND TEMPORAL GOODS: AVOIDING WORRY

This reference to "worry" provides a transition to the abovementioned second way that these verses in the Sermon affirm yet extend classical ethical wisdom on the impact of the last end on practical decision-making. Their portrayal of God as a heavenly Father of provident gratuity is not simply a claim "added on" to the natural wisdom of virtue ethics, but rather is a claim that transforms the activity of practical decision-making. To anticipate the conclusion, Mt 6:25–34, with 6:19–24, concerns practical decision-making in light of a final end, an activity which when done habitually well has classically been called prudence. Given the faith-dependent vision here of the final end as our heavenly Father, as the kingdom of God and his righteousness, these verses present a vision of prudential practical reasoning that is transformed in light of faith, a type of prudence labeled in the Thomistic tradition as infused prudence.

---

[54] For the "striving for self-sustenance" as characteristic of the "Gentile" world in contrast to the kingdom, see Dillon, "Ravens, Lilies, and the Kingdom of God," 619–20. For a classic survey of standard candidates for happiness, with arguments why they all fail as last end except God, see Thomas Aquinas, *Summa Theologiae* I–II 2.

[55] The tone and content of these verses suggest the audience indeed already does recognize our heavenly Father, even if inadequately. After all, they do not inform the audience of our heavenly Father, but assume He is known with references to "your father in heaven" (6:26, 32), and rhetorical questions posed more as reminders of God's providence rather than informing the audience about that providence (6:26, 30)

[56] We are reminded here of the poignant gospel passage just chapters later (9:24): "I believe! Help my unbelief!" This topic of "little faith" presents an occasion for discussion of growth in the theological virtues. For more on how these verses serve as "prophetic admonition," see Dillon, "Ravens, Lilies, and the Kingdom of God," 617.

But the immediate task here is describing how these verses are better understood in light of a virtue-centered approach to morality, and in turn further illuminate such an approach. More specifically, what do these verses say about the impact of faith in a God of provident gratuity on practical decision-making with regard to everyday temporal goods?[57] Much as the previous chapter examined how love of God above all else (charity) impacts our other "loves," here we examine how faith in our heavenly Father transforms our assessment of – and thus how we seek – temporal goods. In short, these verses address how to engage in practical decision-making in light of faith in our heavenly Father. What do they enjoin?

The short answer, as evident by the five-fold appearance of the term in these mere ten verses, is "do not worry." It is precisely due to God's personal and generous providence that Jesus enjoins the disciples "*so* do not worry" about food, drink or clothing.[58] In other words, an accurate apprehension of God and His creation enables us to more accurately regard the proper place of temporal goods (such as food and drink and clothing) in our lives. How does this occur? Obviously the kingdom is to be sought first before "all these things." But how are "all these things" to be sought, or are they not at all? Without careful attention to this question, it can seem we are left with two undesirable reads of this passage with regard to seeking temporal goods. Luz claims that one common historical interpretation (which he says is typically Catholic) is to understand these verses as counseling radical renunciation of the pursuit of temporal goods, something possible only for the religious elite.[59] Another common interpretation throughout history applies the text to all Christians, and does so by focusing on the myriad of ways that seeking temporal goods does *not* constitute worry. But Luz laments that in doing so the text's "teeth become increasingly blunt" as "it is emphasized what the text does *not* say."[60] Once again, reminiscent of Chapter 2 on perfection, we have a challenging text in the Sermon that is regarded either as unrealistic or

---

[57] Practical decision making concerns contingent goods, matters which are accessible to unaided reason (such as what to eat, drink or wear). These are commonly called "temporal" goods or practical, daily activities, not because the acts of faith, hope and love occur only outside time or do not occur each day, or because speculative knowledge occurs only outside time or only rarely, but because the "object" or realm of activity for (hopefully prudential) practical decision-making is such obviously time-bound contingent matters. For more from a Thomistic perspective on how the virtue of prudence which governs practical decision-making is distinct from both faith and from speculative knowledge, see Thomas Aquinas, *Summa Theologiae* I–II 62, 2 and I–II 57, 3–5, respectively.

[58] Emphasis added. For the function of this transitional word see Betz, *The Sermon on the Mount*, 480 and Davies and Allison, *The Gospel According to Saint Matthew*, 657

[59] See Luz, *Matthew 1–7*, 410. Unsurprisingly he mentions the counsels of perfection here, which were also treated in Chapter 2.

[60] Luz, *Matthew 1–7*, 411. He includes among such "mitigations" distinctions between: today versus tomorrow; possession versus use; and, concern versus worry.

completely evacuated. Fortunately, looking at these verses through the lens of virtue ethics, augmented by recent biblical scholarship, can help to avoid both of these interpretations.

Turning to biblical scholarship, what can we learn from meaning of the term "worry?" Although the term *merimnao* translated here as "worry" occurs five times in our ten verses under consideration here (vv. 25, 27, 28, 31, and 34), the term is actually quite rare in the New Testament and in texts beyond the Scriptures.[61] Rudolf Bultmann notes that in each usage in this text and in the rest of the New Testament, its meaning is clearly negative. In other words, the term *merimnao* always names something to be avoided.[62] In this passage "worry" always concerns temporal goods, so one possibility is that we should not have any concern for such goods since it would always constitute "worry." Yet biblical commentators consistently note that this makes no sense given the rest of the New Testament, including Matthew's own gospel. Augustine cites dozens of Scripture citations when Jesus or Paul seem to have concerned themselves about temporal goods.[63] Contemporary biblical scholarship corroborates this, often by taking note of the "purse" that Jesus and his followers kept.[64] Thus while being "worried" about temporal goods is always problematic according to the Scripture text, this ought not to be equated with an injunction to have no concern about temporal goods. What distinguishes concern for temporal good that becomes "worry?"

Guelich's work is particularly helpful here. He claims we ought *not* to understand "worry" as a reference *solely* to either activity, or some anxious interior attitude. In other words, it is *not* the case that one is rightly said to "worry" if one acts on that worry, but not if one does not so act. Conversely it is *not* the case that "worry" is solely an interior disposition that accompanies activity, whatsoever the activity. It is rather some combination of activity and attitude. He defines "worry" as "undue concern or crippling anxiety (an attitude) that drives one to seek security by one's own *efforts* apart from God (an activity)."[65]

This interpretation of what is problematic about worry is corroborated in the work of Thomas Aquinas. Though he treats solicitude several places in his *corpus*, the most extensive treatments are found in his examination of this passage as

---

[61] The NAB inexplicably uses two different terms (worry, 25, 27, 31, and 34; be anxious about, 28) to translate this one Greek term. See R. Bultmann's essay on this term, "*merimnao*" in vol. 4 of *Theological Dictionary of the New Testament*, ed. by Gerhard Kittel and Gerhard Friedrich, trans. Geoffrey W. Bromiley (Grand Rapids: Eerdmans, 1964–1976), 589–93.

[62] For the differences between the terms for worry and seek, see Bultmann, "*merimnao*," 591–92 and Dillon, "Ravens, Lilies, and the Kingdom of God," 623.

[63] Augustine, *The Lord's Sermon on the Mount*, II.17.57.   [64] See Jn 12:6 and 13:29.

[65] Guelich, *The Sermon on the Mount*, 336, emphasis in original. This position on attitude and activity is corroborated by both Luz (*Matthew 1–7*, 404) and Davies and Allison (*The Gospel According to Saint Matthew*, 647).

well as his treatment of false similitudes of prudence.[66] There are several ways that solicitude can be contrary to virtue: when temporal goods are made one's last end; when they are sought excessively; when the soul is excessively occupied by thoughts of them; or when fear and desperation accompanies the seeking of them.[67] These possible ways that engagement with temporal goods can be deformed into vicious solicitude indicate that Thomas Aquinas also identifies occasions when one's activity (first and second of his four) and/or one's interior attitude (third and fourth of his four) render one's engagement with temporal goods as negatively "solicitous" in the manner decried in Mt 6.

Thus the two extreme interpretations Luz names are indeed the least complicated ways to define worry, but they are not the only possibilities. Both Guelich and Thomas Aquinas offer more nuanced descriptions of when engagement with temporal goods "crosses over" to constitute worry. In their descriptions of worry there seems to be an erroneous estimation of the importance of temporal goods, leading to disordered activity and/or interior attitude (such as fear or anxiety) about such goods. This inaccurate estimation resulting in a disordered response reinforces that these verses are helpfully read in conjunction with the virtue of prudence.

So too is that claim reinforced by the prominent presence of what Tannehill calls "strong words referring to perception" in these verses. He means vv. 26 and 28, where the text enjoins the audience to "Look" (at the birds of the sky) and "Learn from" (the wild flowers). Though the NAB used here translates v. 28 as "Learn from," other translations include "see," "observe," and "consider." These latter terms make the role of perception in learning more obvious. As Tannehill says, "we are not to look casually but observe carefully." The point is that in these verses, the audience is not simply being enjoined to act differently with regard to temporal goods, or

---

[66] Thomas Aquinas, *Commentary on the Gospel of Matthew*, 623–30 and Thomas Aquinas *Summa Theologiae* II–II 55, 6 and 7, respectively. Yet see also *Summa Contra Gentiles* III.135; *Summa Theologiae* II–II 188, 7; *Commentary on Philippians* c. 4 lect 1. It should be noted that while Thomas Aquinas's work is helpful in delineating what is problematic about "worry," Thomas Aquinas does not view "solicitude" (the Vulgate Latin is *solicitudo*) as inherently wrong. Foresight is a part of the virtue prudence. And solicitude is a type of foresight, foresight with "diligence" (*studio*), with "the vehement application of the soul" (*vehemens applicatio animi*). Not all such diligence or vehement application is contrary to virtue. Yet Thomas Aquinas does very clearly explain when it is, which is why his analysis is of service here. *Commentary on the Gospel of Matthew*, 623. Thomistic scholarship awaits a thorough study of *solicitudo*. For a helpful article on solicitude in the context of mindfulness, see Thomas Bushlack, "Mindfulness and the Discernment of Passions: Insights from Thomas Aquinas," *Spiritus: A Journal of Christian Spirituality* 14.2 (2014): 141–65.

[67] Thomas Aquinas, *Commentary on the Gospel of Matthew*, 623. In Thomas Aquinas *Summa Theologiae* II–II 55, 6, he lists three ways that solicitude is unlawful, seemingly combining the second and third listed here. For more on solicitude as part of prudence and more specifically foresight, see John Bowlin, *Contingency and Fortune in Aquinas's Ethics* (Cambridge: Cambridge University Press, 1999), 82.

change one's attitude. At root the passage is inviting the hearers to "see" such goods differently, to assess their importance properly. Such a seeing truthfully in practical matters so as to respond accurately is precisely the meaning of prudence.

How are the hearers invited to see things differently? As noted above, there is some assertion in these verses about the relative value of temporal goods, as well our ultimate (in)efficacy in securing them: "Is not life worth more than food"(25) and "can any of you by worrying . . . ?" (27). Yet most prominent in these verses is the assurance of God's provident gratuity with regard to these goods. In vv. 26 and 30, we find the allusions to the lilies and flowers, with the assurances that God provides for them and the ensuing "Are you not more important than they?" and "Will he not much more care for you?" The concluding verses in this pericope say with regard to temporal goods: "Your heavenly Father knows you need them all"; and then, after "seek first the Kingdom (of God) and his righteousness," the ensuing "and all these things will be given you besides." The thrust of these verses' guidance with regard to activities concerning temporal goods does not actually concern temporal goods directly, but rather concerns faith in God directly. Though less direct, this injunction to a more accurate apprehension of who God is has transformative impact on practical decision-making. Once again we turn to recent biblical scholarship, augmented by a more constructive interpretation, for guidance on engaging temporal goods without "worry."

As noted above, Richard Dillon labels these verses "prophetic admonition." He sees in these verses a "clash of different worlds." They are intended to disrupt our worldview and point toward another worldview that is truly "natural, the due order of things."[68] Dillon argues that the root of worry (or what he translates "anxiety") is actually our distorted worldview, which fails to recognize God's provident gratuity and thus relies solely on human activity for security.

> Anxiety, bred by the human "managerial complex" toward the future, is shown to be not just a feeling but a structure of our existence in the world. The whole agenda of people's labors to secure their future, with all the assumptions and illusions undergirding it, constitutes an enveloping sphere.[69]

We see in this quotation an alternative to faith in a God of provident gratuity, namely, the "managerial complex," which Dillon goes on to describe as a "compulsion to design and control the future, for oneself and others."[70] This misapprehension of reality, this failure to recognize our heavenly Father, both unduly elevates the importance of temporal goods,

---

[68] Dillon, "Ravens, Lilies, and the Kingdom of God," 618.

[69] Dillon, "Ravens, Lilies, and the Kingdom of God," 618.

[70] Dillon, "Ravens, Lilies, and the Kingdom of God," 621.

and leads to our worry in our labors to secure these goods which of course we are never fully able to secure.

Faith in our heavenly Father precludes any such managerial complex. Yet Dillon also shows how it precludes a quietistic inactivity.[71] Dillon notes how these verses present an "alternating current" presenting the "two sides of the coin of human creaturehood: *grandeur* and *limits*."[72] The audience is repeatedly reminded of their inefficacy ("can any of you by worrying") and of God's generous provision. Hence the limits of human activity. But the audience is also repeatedly reminded of their privileged place in creation in comparison with the birds and the lilies.[73] Why is humanity's privileged place in creation important with regard to the pursuit of temporal goods? It not only assures us God will provide, but it also indicates our role in that provision.

Faith in our heavenly Father precludes not only the managerial complex but also human inactivity that is unreflective of the grandeur of humanity as *imago Dei*. Reminiscent of 6:22–23 on the eye and the light of the body, God's providential care for humanity does not happen without humanity's active involvement through our practical reasoning. Dillon illustrates the balance between respect for providence and active participation in that providence in his analysis of the final verses of this section.[74] He reiterates the claim that "'Seeking the kingdom' is the way of life in which the compulsion to 'manage' the future for one's self and other has been replaced by a self-sacrificial trust in the saving plan of God." Yet he continues that very sentence noting "of which we can know only that it [God's saving plan] is advanced by any and all following of Christ. Matthew's 'righteousness' is his name for that faithful following (Mt 5:6,10,20; 6:1)."[75] Analyzing the term "seek" in 6:33, Dillon claims its present imperative denotes a "lifelong commitment to the *gift* of

---

[71] Dillon's extremes of the managerial complex on the one hand, and quietistic trust in God's providence on the other hand, are related to but not the same as Luz's extremes. Luz's extremes are on the one hand toothless interpretations of 6:25–34 that inoculate concern for temporal goods from transformation by faith in God, and on the other hand a (Catholic) disengagement from concern for temporal goods out of complete trust in God's providence.

[72] Dillon, "Ravens, Lilies, and the Kingdom of God," 621, emphasis in original.

[73] Here Dillon engages the common observation in biblical scholarship that this passage offers analogies "from lesser to greater" (*a minori ad maius*) and "from greater to lesser" (*a maiori ad minus*). Dillon associates these two with his claims about the passage suggesting human *grandeur* and limits, respectively. See "Ravens, Lilies, and the Kingdom of God," 620–22.

[74] Participation in God's providence is of course another way to describe participation in the eternal law, the traditional definition of natural law. Unsurprisingly given the focus of these verses on temporal goods, they provide a ready way to further explore the natural law in the context of the Sermon. The amenability of these verses to interpretation in light of natural law and prudence offers a helpful occasion to treat together topics (natural law and prudence) that are too often examined separately from one another.

[75] Dillon, "Ravens, Lilies, and the Kingdom of God," 625–26.

God's new world. There can be no passivity in accepting such a gift, for though it never leaves the Giver's hand, it beckons to a wholehearted participation in its advent."[76] Seeking first "is not merely first on an agenda that puts mundane worries in a subordinate position," but is rather a "quest for God's kingdom," "a 'lifelong commitment' (present infinitive) whose priority is all-encompassing."[77] Despite the obvious emphasis in Dillon's interpretation on God's providence over and against the managerial complex, there is similarly no space in Dillon's interpretation for human listlessness. Jesus did not "invite his follower to a carefree existence as goal unto itself. . . . His point was that trust in God as fatherly provider of life's basic needs *frees* the disciple for that larger vision *and commitment* which his ministry heralded: God's coming rule over all."[78]

Equipped with Dillon's analysis, we turn briefly back to interpretation of the birds and lilies. Clearly Jesus enjoins his listeners to be more like the birds and lilies who are recipients of God's provident gratuity. But what activity of these creatures ought the audience emulate? The common assumption in the tradition of commentary is their inactivity. After all, the birds "do not sow or reap, they gather nothing into barns." The lilies "do not work or spin." It is too quickly assumed that this means they do nothing, and perhaps human persons also ought to do nothing. But that is not what the text says. It is argued here that the birds and lilies are not offered as paragons of inactivity (something obviously not true, and often noted in biblical scholarship, with regard to the birds); rather, they are adduced as not engaging in *human* activity that would be beyond their particular creatureliness. Nowhere in the text is it said that these creatures do not participate in their own flourishing. It simply notes they do not do so in ways that are evidently beyond their capacities. Thus Jesus is not enjoining his audience to inactivity, but rather to avoid activity that is beyond human creatureliness. The managerial complex, the "compulsion to design and control the future, for oneself and others," reflects at worst a human temptation to usurp God's providence, and at best a lack of faith in God's providence and recognition of human creatureliness.

---

[76] Dillon, "Ravens, Lilies, and the Kingdom of God," 624.

[77] Dillon, "Ravens, Lilies, and the Kingdom of God," 623, citing here H. Giessen, *Christliches Handeln: Ein Redaktionskritische Untersuchung zum dikaiosyne-Begriffe im Matthäusevangelium* (EHS 23/181; Frankfurt/Bern: Lang, 1982), 178.

[78] Dillon, "Ravens, Lilies, and the Kingdom of God," 626, emphasis in original. This evident link of ethics and eschatology recalls Chapter's argument on the interconnection between the two, an argument with which Dillon would evidently concur: "the coherence of eschatology and ethics in Jesus's teaching thus imposes itself with special clarity in the anxieties instruction" ("Ravens, Lilies, and the Kingdom of God," 626). See also 624–25 on "seeking" as a "gift," and thus Jesus's moral teaching as "essentially an 'enabling of right conduct'" ("Ravens, Lilies, and the Kingdom of God," 625). Here he cites Helmut Merklein, *Die Gottesherrschaft als Handlungsprinzip: Untersuchung zur Ethik Jesu* (FB 34, 2nd ed.; Würzburg: Echter V., 1981) 139.

Much as birds and lilies should not act as persons, human creatures should not assume control of providence. To do so would reveal a fundamental misapprehension of the way things are, and result in vitiation of practical decision-making with regard to temporal goods.

We have come full circle toward a richer understanding of what constitutes worry, while at the same time explaining how these verses can also be read as enjoining that the opposite of worry be avoided as well. Worry with regard to temporal goods is an activity and/or attitude that reflects a poor estimation of the value of temporal goods immediately, but more fundamentally a misapprehension of God's provident gratuity and the creaturely human role for us in that provision. Thus these verses continue the theme of 6:19–24 in painting an accurate portrait of humanity's last end and depicting the resulting impact on practical decision-making. They counsel against worry in that decision-making, and thus offer guidance as to the virtue of prudence. Yet these verses do so primarily through a portrayal of who God is and who we are in relation to God (our grandeur yet limits). From a Thomistic virtue perspective, we might pose the question, are these verses about faith or prudence? The clear answer is both. They concern an accurate grasp of God in faith, which in turn informs how we regard practical matters.[79] In the language of Thomistic virtue ethics, this passage is about the virtue of infused prudence. It concerns accurate knowledge of temporal goods (so as to act well) in a manner enabled by God's grace, and oriented toward one's supernatural happiness of union with our heavenly Father (the kingdom and his righteousness) as apprehended in faith. We therefore see how these verses continue the classical virtue ethics themes in 6:19–24 on the identity of the last end and its impact on practical decision-making, but do so in a manner that further illuminates that dynamic through faith in our heavenly Father.

III. RELATIONS WITH OTHERS IN MT 7:1–11

The third and final section of this chapter examines Mt 7:1–11.[80] These verses are variously grouped as concluding the larger section beginning with 6:19, or as standing on their own.[81] The chapter structure of this book obviously affirms the first rationale, although it will also be clear by the end of this chapter how 6:19–34 and 7:1–11 are also distinct units in that larger section of the Sermon. I argue above that this larger section (6:19–7:12) contains a

---

[79] See Betz on how the sayings in this section "describe the activities of daily life" (Betz, *The Sermon on the Mount*, 427).

[80] Mt 7:12 is included in the verses treated in this chapter but it is addressed in the conclusion for reasons noted below.

[81] Betz treats 6:19–7:12 together, as do Guelich and Luz. Davies and Allison have separate chapters on 6:19–34 and 7:1–12.

central passage (6:25–34) encapsulated by the (centrally placed) verse "seek first the kingdom of God and his righteousness" (6:33). Furthermore, this central passage is flanked on both sides by a set of three sayings. The first three concern the nature and function of the last end, including its impact on our engagement with temporal goods. I noted in the previous section how that engagement is transformed in light of faith in a God of provident gratuity. The three sayings in 7:1–11 evidence a similar dynamic. Attention is turned from engagement with temporal goods to relations with other persons.[82] Yet there, too, we see how relations with others are transformed in light of faith in who God is. The thesis of this section is that the verses 7:1–11 contain a triplet of sayings all unified by the theme of how seeking first the kingdom transforms our relations with other persons. Whereas the set of three sayings at 6:19–24 were examined together above in common to make three points, the claim of this section is that the three sayings of 7:1–11 illuminate the impact of seeking first the kingdom on three distinct groups of persons with whom we relate, namely those in close relation to us; those "on the outside"; and God Himself. Hence this section proceeds in three parts corresponding to those distinct relations, in each case noting how they are transformed by who God is as our final end.

A. RELATIONS WITH OUR BROTHERS IN MT 7:1–5

The five verses that constitute Mt 7:1–5 concern judgment. The first two verses concern judging in general and are distinct from even while related to the ensuing three verses on the dynamics of identifying and removing the splinter in one's brother's eye. Nonetheless commentators consistently see these five verses as comprising a coherent unit.[83] The common theme is of course judging. Yet commentators also note that the term "brother" found in vv. 3, 4, and 5 applies to the whole dynamic of judgment treated here. There is some debate over who exactly is meant by "brother," but in any case some sort of relation to those whom we judge is presupposed, leading some commentators to treat these verses in the context of "fraternal correction."[84]

---

[82] Davies and Allison label 6:19–34 "God and Mammon" and 7:1–12 "The Treatment of One's Neighbor" (Davies and Allison, *The Gospel According to Saint Matthew*, 625 and 667, respectively).

[83] See, for example, Augustine, *The Lord's Sermon on the Mount*, II.19.63; Betz, *The Sermon on the Mount*, 492; Davies and Allison, *The Gospel According to Saint Matthew*, 630.

[84] See Betz, *The Sermon on the Mount*, 488 & 492. As Betz notes, the term "brother" functions differently in the Matthean and Lucan sermons. In the latter the term indicates a fellow disciple, while in the former it refers to a fellow Jew who is nonetheless not a follower of Jesus. In either case there is some basis of relationship between the people. See also Davies and Allison, *The Gospel According to Saint Matthew*, 674. Luther also places these verses in the context of fraternal correction. See *Sermon on the Mount*,

The most important question these verses raise, however, concerns not the target toward whom judgment is directed but rather the nature of the judgment that is prohibited by Jesus. Though not univocal, the tradition of commentary is remarkably consistent in distinguishing two senses of judgment. Judgment on the one hand can refer to "simple ethical judgments," or discerning the moral quality of an act.[85] On the other hand, it can mean to "condemn" or issue "censorious condemnation of another."[86] This assumes the term in general refers to a broader sort of activity that can be right or wrong, requiring some distinction as to what constitutes good versus bad judging.[87] With this standard approach, Jesus's prohibition in Mt 7:1–2 refers not to the activity in general but rather to the degraded form of judgment.[88]

Thomas Aquinas is representative of the tradition of commentary in his view that judgment is the act of justice, and while clearly capable of being done wrongly is not in itself forbidden.[89] This view is echoed in contemporary biblical scholars who see the act of judging as a natural human act. Betz claims "human conduct inevitably involves taking measure of each other."[90] As will be seen below, this is not a lament. Davies and Allison similarly claim that "it would in any case be futile to forbid people to exercise their faculties of discernment," and proceed to note a variety of occasions when Jesus

---

215–16. Though not specifying why he does so, Bonhoeffer treats vv. 1–5, and indeed 6–11, under the title of "the Disciple and Unbelievers" (*Cost of Discipleship*, 202).

[85] See Dale and Allison, *Matthew: A Shorter Commentary*, 105.

[86] See, respectively, Davies and Allison, *The Gospel According to Saint Matthew*, 669 and Guelich, *The Sermon on the Mount*, 350.

[87] There is thus a parallel between judging and concern for temporal goods. Both are "natural" activities that can be done well or poorly, and thus require specification as to what constitutes doing them virtuously. I am grateful to David Cloutier for this observation. Note it also buttresses the claim in the Conclusion that the verses in this chapter correspond to the virtues of prudence (6:19–34) and justice (7:1–12), since practical decision-making and judging are paradigmatic acts of those virtues, respectively.

[88] There are some who claim that no such distinction is necessary, since Jesus enjoins "completely judgment-free fellowship" (Luz, *Matthew 1–7*, 415–16). In other words, whatever judging is, it is always wrong. But this is a clear minority view. In fairness to Luz he seems more concerned to counter an interpretation whereby people limit application of this passage to the private sphere. See also Strecker, *The Sermon on the Mount: An Exegetical Commentary*, 143. Both Luz and Strecker acknowledge that 7:2 seems to assume we do indeed judge though that of course does not mean that any such judgment is permissible.

[89] Thomas Aquinas, *Summa Theologiae* II–II 60, 1–2. See also Chrysostom, *Homilies on Matthew* XXIII.1 (192) and Calvin, *Harmony of the Evangelists*, 346. For a different approach that nonetheless does leave occasion for judging, see Martin Luther (*Sermon on the Mount* 210–11) on judging for a fine example of his "two kingdoms" approach. Rather than differentiating types of judging as is most common in the tradition, he claims judging is forbidden in Christ's speaking to his disciples, but it is not forbidden (to them) in "the world."

[90] Betz, *The Sermon on the Mount*, 490.

Himself exercises these faculties.[91] Thus the consistent claim of biblical commentators is that Jesus here prohibits not "simple ethical judgments" but rather something more pernicious.

This raises the question of what distinguishes the sort of judging that is prohibited by Jesus in this passage from legitimate types of judgment. The tradition of commentary offers a variety of insights on this question. But perhaps the most important is the consistent claim is that permissible judgment must be oriented toward the amendment of the brother. Chrysostom describes this sort of judgment as medicinal.[92] Augustine says it must be for the person's amendment, and should not be done out of a divided heart, or as we might say, with ulterior motives.[93] Thomas Aquinas claims it must be oriented toward justice and cannot be out of bitterness.[94] This claim is prevalent also in recent biblical scholarship. Davies and Allison claim it is indeed permissible to see fault in the brother "in order to help," and when done in such a manner it is with "mercy, humility, and tolerance."[95] Luz claims "the measure for judging is love," and goes on to quote Augustine approvingly.[96] Thus the primary characteristic of permissible judging is that it be done for the good of the other.

Of course it is commonly recognized that the human tendency to judge is frequently vicious and self-serving rather than toward the good of the other. So the tradition of commentary is also full of prudential guidance on judging. This advice is called prudential since, rather than identifying the defining characteristic of permissible (as in the previous paragraph) or impermissible judging, guidance is offered as to how to avoid the sort of judgment prohibited by Jesus. Augustine advises that we always try to see others' actions in the best light when their motivation is in any doubt, guidance reiterated by Luz.[97] Augustine also gives extensive advice on reflecting on one's own

---

[91] Davies and Allison, *The Gospel According to Saint Matthew*, 668.

[92] Chrysostom, *Homilies on Matthew*, XXIII.1 (192). He later describes is at an act to "correct with tenderness" (XXIII.2, 193).

[93] Augustine, *The Lord's Sermon on the Mount*, II.19.63–66. In a fascinating interpretation of the mote and the beam, Augustine claims the former represents anger and the latter hatred. He claims anger is permissible (unlike hatred) since it is compatible with wishing for the other's amendment (Augustine, *The Lord's Sermon on the Mount*, II.19.63). For more on Augustine's interpretation of this passage and its impact into the Middle Ages, see William C. Mattison III, "Jesus's Prohibition of Anger (Mt 5:22): The Person/Sin Distinction from Augustine to Aquinas," *Theological Studies* **68** (2007): 839–64.

[94] Respectively, Thomas Aquinas, *Summa Theologiae* I–II 60, 1 and 2 and *Commentary on the Gospel of Matthew*, 632.

[95] Davies and Allison, *The Gospel According to Saint Matthew*, 673 and 668, respectively.

[96] Luz, *Matthew 1–7*, 414.

[97] Augustine, *The Lord's Sermon on the Mount*, II.18.59; Luz, *Matthew 1–7*, 414. Making a similar but slightly distinct point, Thomas Aquinas counsels against judgment with regard to interior things that we cannot assess accurately. Aquinas, *Commentary on the Gospel of Matthew*, 632.

sinfulness in the area being addressed in the brother,[98] and Chrysostom and Thomas Aquinas both advise not even making judgments in areas where one is a sinner one's self.[99] John Calvin advises that one not be too eager to judge.[100] In all of these cases, commentators offer prudential guidance on judging to help their audiences avoid the sort of judgment prohibited by Jesus.

This brief survey of biblical commentary reveals a rather consistent interpretation of these verses with regard to judging. Judging is prohibited if not directed toward the amendment of the brother. The tradition also offers extensive practical advice to help prevent such prohibited judgment from being chosen. What contribution if any does a virtue-centered approach to morality offer for interpretation of these passages? That perspective helps accentuate a claim which, while present in the tradition of commentary, is particularly evident from a virtue perspective. Reminiscent of 6:19–34, we have in these verses explicit recognition of the importance of seeing well for the activity at hand, and some specification of what characterizes such "seeing well." In the terminology of virtue ethics, this passage on relations with other concerns justice, yet requisite for true justice is the accurate grasp of the practical matter at hand afforded by prudence.

In the previous section's analysis of 6:25–34, Dillon's research was mined to explain the frequent use of perception terms. There the birds and lilies were presented so that the audience would see more accurately with regard to temporal goods and God's provident gratuity. Those verses enjoin the audience to "look at" or "see" God's gratuitous providence in non-human creatures in order to then make better choices with regard to the prioritization of temporal goods. The assumption is that if we see things more accurately, we will act accordingly. In 7:3–5 a similar dynamic is in play. The audience is enjoined to "notice" the beam in one's own eye rather than solely "perceiving" the mote in the brother's eye. The verses aim to identify a lack of accurate apprehension with an eye toward correcting it, resulting

---

[98] See Augustine, *The Lord's Sermon on the Mount*, II.19.64. There Augustine not only makes this basic point, but also provides further detail about how one should approach one's brother regarding an activity where one is still a sinner, where one used to be a sinner, or where one has not been a (presumably habituated) sinner.

[99] Chrysostom *Homilies on Matthew* XXIII.2 (196). Thomas Aquinas, *Summa Theologiae* II–II 60, 2 ad. 3. There Thomas Aquinas cites Chrysostom, but the discrepancy in citation is due to his citing the (mistakenly attributed to Chrysostom) *Opus Imperfectum*. See also *Commentary on the Gospel of Matthew*, 632. In *Commentary on the Gospel of Matthew*, (627), Thomas Aquinas claims one can indeed judge another regarding some activity where one sins if the sin is private, since this indicates "it displeases him that he sins, and thus he can reproach another." But if the sin is public Thomas Aquinas assumes it is out of malice and thus he should never reproach the other.

[100] Calvin, *Harmony of the Gospels*, 346.

in better activity. Indeed, the audience is told not only to see the beam in one's own eye, but to remove it, thus enabling one to "see clearly to remove the mote from your brother's eye."[101] For the third time in as many sections in this chapter, we find in the Sermon an injunction to good vision for the sake of good action. Noticing the beam in one's own eye not only enables its removal, but also enables one to "see clearly" the faults of the brother in order to exercise judgment that is truly aimed at the amendment of the brother. Thus, in line with a persistent theme in 6:19–7:12 and a fundamental facet of virtue ethics, we have in these verses a continued emphasis on the importance of seeing accurately, with particular application to relations with others.

The importance of prudence, seeing rightly, for the action at hand, in this case judgment, is an affirmation of the central role that prudence plays in a virtue-centered approach to morality. Even when there is no explicit use of the language of virtue ethics, this point is found throughout the tradition of commentary on these verses. In his treatment of judgment, Thomas Aquinas's very first question concerns whether or not judgment is an act of justice, rather than an act of prudence. After all, it is the case that a judgment relies on an accurate act of practical reasoning, which is the realm of prudence. As he explains why judgment is rightly understood as an act of justice, he concedes that most properly speaking judgment is an act of reason: "judgment is an act of justice in so far as justice inclines one to judge aright, and of prudence in so far as prudence pronounces judgment."[102] In his *Commentary on Matthew*, he explains it similarly. There he claims "two things are necessary in judging: knowledge of the case and judgment."[103] This close connection between prudence and justice in the act of judging is found throughout the tradition of commentary including contemporary biblical scholarship.[104] These claims invite further inquiry as to the nature of judgment and its connection to the various facets of practical reasoning. Yet the point here is that the seeing rightly that is constitutive of prudence is essential

---

[101] This line is perhaps the best scriptural support for the common position that judging *per se* is not prohibited, but only vicious judging. After all, here Jesus enjoins precisely such removal of the brother's mote.

[102] Thomas Aquinas, *Summa Theologiae* II–II 60, 1 ad. 1.

[103] Thomas Aquinas, *Commentary on the Gospel of Matthew*, 636.

[104] Luther claims that what is decried in these verses is "self-centered [practical] wisdom." See *Sermon on the Mount*, 210. Once the term practical is added to explicitly qualify what must be the meaning of wisdom given the context, we see even in Luther how an inaccurate grasp of reality deforms one's ability to judge. Among contemporary biblical scholars, Betz most explicitly recognizes this connection between judgment and prudence when he claims: "The question is not whether one should abandon judging altogether; rather, the point is that good judgment is a necessary element in human relations, and that exercising good judgment is part of prudence." See *The Sermon on the Mount*, 487.

for good judgment. And these verses offer practical guidance for seeing more clearly in their injunction to remove one's own beam before turning to the mote of the brother.

Beyond the general importance of seeing well for the exercise of good judgment, these verses also provide some guidance as to what constitutes seeing well with regard to relations with others. In other words, these verses reflect the common virtue ethics affirmation of the importance of prudence for a virtue such as justice (and its activity, such as judging), but they also further specify what constitutes virtuous activity, in this case judgment. That contribution is labelled here "consistency in standards of judgment." As Betz claims, "any verdict [in other words, judgment], in order to be rendered, must be based on the standards of justice. . . . [J]ustice requires standardization."[105] This consistency of standards of judgment is a theme that reverberates throughout the Sermon. It first appears in the fifth beatitude, "Blessed are the merciful for they will be shown mercy," suggesting the merciless will not. It reappears in an equally prominent place in the Lords' Prayer: "Forgive us our trespasses as we forgive those who trespass against us." This consistency is reaffirmed in the ensuing vv. 14–15, "For if you do not forgive your brother. . . ." Thus one point offered in 7:1–5 and the Sermon as a whole, and indeed a point that is common in treatments of justice, is that there must be a consistency in standards of justice. Though this might crudely be understood as raw reciprocity (in other words, you get what you give), the virtue-centered approach to judgment outlined above enriches how consistency of standards is best understood. Judgments are made on the basis of assessments of reality (hopefully prudential ones). Such judgments reflect and (in the language of virtue ethics) further ingrain or habituate such a vision of reality. Activity on the basis of how we see things further conforms us to that vision. Thus rather than a raw reciprocity imposed from without, affirmation of consistency of standards of justice is a recognition of how formative on us our activities are in not only reflecting but further ingraining that grasp of reality.

On this point, the Sermon as a whole is informative of a virtue ethics, and 7:1–5 should be read as part of this overall Sermon theme. The standard or "measure" which the Sermon and these verses invite us to adopt is God's generous and merciful standard. We are called to be "perfect" as our heavenly Father is perfect (5:48). And our heavenly Father sends sunshine and rain to the just and unjust (5:45). He providentially cares for all of his creation, and especially humanity (6:26, 30, and 33). And as will be seen in the next part, He gives good things to those who ask (7:11). Therefore "if God's generosity and mercy are his yardstick, by which he measures us, we

---

[105] Betz, *The Sermon on the Mount*, 491.

are as human beings under obligation, and we are also advised in the name of prudence, to do the same."[106] Hence we hear "as you judge so will you be judged, and the measure with which you measure will be measured out to you" (7:2). Not only do these verses and the Sermon as a whole affirm consistency of standards of justice, but they also enjoin a merciful and generous such standard as evident in our heavenly Father.

Before concluding this part, one final question should be addressed. The question is why God would ever mimic vicious human judgment. If persons judge without mercy, out of ulterior motives reflective of a self-centered vision of reality, why would our heavenly Father ever judge in such a manner? After all, each of the Sermon's affirmations of consistency in standards of judgment explicitly or at least implicitly claim that people will be subject to the same sort of standard that they adopt, even if it is merciless (5:7), unforgiving (6:15), or judgmental in the negative sense (7:2). Augustine asks this question well: "Can it be, then, that if we give expression to a judgment that is rash, God will also judge us rashly? Or if we shall measure with an unjust measure, that in God's case too, there is in store an unjust measure by which it shall be measured to us again?"[107] The question is rhetorical of course, since Augustine does not think God can be so degraded. He answers it by saying that one who issues rash judgment suffers more from that act than the one who is judged. Though this brief answer can again be read in a raw reciprocity manner, a virtue-centered approach to morality might offer some illumination.

It was noted above (not only in this part but also Chapter 3) that intentional activity, based on a grasp of the way things are, is formative on us, since it conforms us to that grasp of the way things are (whether an accurate one or not). The Sermon and these particular verses enjoin us to adopt a generous and merciful approach to reality that in the case of relations with others is oriented toward their amendment. This is all in imitation of our heavenly Father. Obviously one need not adopt and act in accord with this approach to reality that is reflective of who God is. We not only can unduly prioritize temporal goods as people of no or little faith do, but we can also treat others in a manner that is self-centered, competitive, and merciless. Yet just as good action is constitutive of happiness and shapes a person's character accordingly, life in accord with such a (godless) vision of reality is also formative, or really de-formative. Therefore, as suggested by Augustine, it is not the case that God adopts an unjust measure. As "perfect" God could never do so. Rather in cases where we reject mercy and thus are not shown mercy (5: 7) or fail to forgive and thus are not forgiven (6:15), we are merely being subject to the consistent standards of (in this case in-justice) that we

---

[106] Betz, *The Sermon on the Mount*, 491.
[107] Augustine, *On the Lord's Sermon on the Mount*, II.18.62.

have willingly adopted, standards that permeate and de-form our characters. Thus in these verses and the Sermon as a whole, we find consistent standards of justice to be a central theme. This crucial theme is better understood with the resources of virtue-centered approach to morality not only through the affirmation of the importance of prudence for other virtues such as justice, but also through the crucially formative impact that our grasp of reality has on our actions and our very selves.

In summary, these first verses of this section prohibit judgment that is not oriented toward the amendment of the brother. The merciful standard or measure of justice that would prompt virtuous judgment (fraternal correction) is a reflection of who God is and who we are invited to be. What must be avoided is the "self-centered wisdom" that leads to hypocrisy. The passage thus continues the theme of the previous sections (and indeed Chapter 3) in enjoining single-minded devotion to God. Whatever standard is adopted in our relations with others (that includes but presumably extends beyond judging) will be applied to ourselves in large part due to its formative impact on our characters. Though primarily concerned about judging and relations with our brothers, these verses rely on the importance of seeing rightly, and enjoin the integrity that comes from seeking first the kingdom, a seeking that in turn transforms the manner of one's judgment.

B. RELATIONS WITH OUTSIDERS IN MT 7:6

The sixth verse of Matthew 7 represents one of the most challenging verses to interpret in the gospels, if not beyond.[108] The basic meaning, as was the case with the eye as lamp of the body passage, initially seems straightforward. As Guelich says, "One simply does not waste something of value on an inappropriate and undeserving object."[109] But this ready interpretation raises three immediate questions. First, what "of value" is being referenced here? The tradition of commentary and contemporary biblical scholarship is nearly univocal in asserting the missionary context of this verse. It is about sharing the gospel (or not, as it were) with others.[110] Second and

---

[108] In the words of Betz: "There is at present no consensus about the original text, the original meaning, the source, and the origins of later interpretations given to the saying" (*The Sermon on the Mount*, 494). Further, "By simply transmitting the saying as it was, the evangelist did not spell out the intended meaning; perhaps he did not know it himself" (*The Sermon on the Mount*, 499). Both he (*The Sermon on the Mount*, 494) and Luz recognize that this has led to the verse serving as a "playground for Aramaists" (Luz, *Matthew 1–7*, 418), though both eschew the value of retrieving some more transparent meaning of the verse in that pre-Matthean language.

[109] Guelich, *The Sermon on the Mount*, 376

[110] For a rare alternate view, see Stassen & Gushee who claim this verse is about not placing one's trust in unholy things or people, but rather in God (7:7–11). See *Kingdom Ethics*,

more problematically, who are the "inappropriate and undeserving objects," referenced by the pejorative terms "dogs" and "swine"? Biblical scholars commonly open their treatments of this passage with a survey of the numerous interpretations that have been offered in answer to this question.[111] The tradition of commentary offers a variety of answers, including: the ungodly and unchaste who are resistant to change,[112] attackers and despisers of the truth,[113] heretics,[114] or those with hardened hearts.[115] Contemporary interpretations by biblical scholars include viewing the verses as referring to heretics,[116] apostates,[117] moral laxists,[118] or in such a general way as to include all of the above and more.[119] Despite an initially apparent meaning of 7:6, interpretations by commentators over centuries are quite splintered as to specifics.

The latter broad interpretation of 7:6 as to the "who" question (all of the above and more) is affirmed here with some support from the context of Mt 7:6. It may seem obvious to seek an answer to this question through context. Yet as noted above, a common assumption in the history of interpretation of this verse is that there is no structural context for these verses that might aid interpretation in a case such as 7:6.[120] There are some who see 7:6 as connected to 7:1–5, usually in a mitigating manner. Davies and Allison claim

---

457–59. Some begin with an interpretation about sharing the gospel, but also note possible application to the sacraments. See, for example, Thomas Aquinas, *Commentary on the Gospel of Matthew*, 639.

[111] See, for example, Betz, *The Sermon on the Mount*, 494–96; Luz, *Matthew 1–7*, 418–19; Davies and Allison, *Matthew: A Shorter Commentary*, 106

[112] Chrysostom, *Homilies on Matthew*, XXIII.3, 196.

[113] Augustine, *The Lord's Sermon on the Mount*, II.20.68.

[114] Aquinas, *Commentary on the Gospel of Matthew*, 639.

[115] Calvin, *On the Harmony of the Evangelists*, 349.

[116] Betz, *The Sermon on the Mount*, 500   [117] Guelich, *The Sermon on the Mount*, 377.

[118] Davies and Allison, *Matthew: A Shorter Commentary*, 107.

[119] See Luz, *Matthew 1–7*, 419–20: "That which is holy is for the holy ones!" Luz says the passage can be used in a "manifold way, for the protection of the gospel, of the perfect law, of the ecclesiastical *communio*, of heavenly wisdom, of baptism, of the Eucharist, against the Gentiles, heretics, mockers, immoral children of the world, or ordinary believers." See also Davies and Allison in *Commentary on the Gospel of Saint Matthew* for their claim that the terms here are best understood not in reference to certain groups of people, but as "general terms of contempt" (675).

[120] Calvin claims "It is unnecessary to repeat oftener, that Matthew gives us here detached sentences which ought not to be viewed as a continued discourse. The present instruction is not at all connected with what came immediately before it, but is entirely separate from it" (*Harmony of the Evangelists*, 349). Luz claims, "I propose not to interpret the logion at all in its Matthean context. Matthew was a conservative author; he took it over from his tradition because it stood in his copy of Q" (*Matthew 1–7*, 419). Betz cites Luz approvingly (*The Sermon on the Mount*, 494). Even Guelich, who offers a more constructive interpretation of 7:6 as corresponding to the sixth petition of the Lord's Prayer, claims with regard to context that "there is no obvious one" in 7:1–11 (*The Sermon on the Mount*, 377).

that while 7:1–5 counsels against excessive severity, 7:6 is against laxity.[121] In the closest interpretation I have found to that offered here, Luz claims with regard to 7:6 (in relation to 7:1–5) that it reveals "there are limits to brotherliness."[122] As noted above, the claim here is that Mt 7:1–11 contains a triplet of sayings each concerning relations with others. As hinted at by Luz, whereas 7:1–5 concerns relations with one's "brothers," 7:6 offers guidance in relating to outsiders. This may of course include any or all of the specified outsiders listed above, and so with interpreters like Luz I contend this verse may apply to manifold types of people.

The third and most challenging question concerns why Jesus warns his audience not to give what is holy to these people. Once again the immediate answer is obvious and stated. The dogs and swine will turn and tear you to pieces and trample what is holy underfoot, respectively. But why is that to be avoided? A second common assumption in the history of interpretation of 7:6 is identified and contested here. The assumption contested here is that what is holy ought not be given to those for whom it is inappropriate, as Luz says, for the "protection" of what is holy.[123] This sense of the need to protect what is holy and even to protect those disciples who proclaim it is especially evident in the writings of Luther and Calvin.[124] This is in some sense understandable since the verse itself says "lest they trample them underfoot and turn and tear you to pieces." Yet doesn't the Sermon itself reiterate that those who spread the good news will suffer (e.g., 5:10, 5:11–12)? Just chapters later in Matthew's gospel Jesus claims He sends out the disciples like sheep among wolves.[125] Why the sudden concern here for self-preservation?[126] And as to the profaning of what is holy, the Sermon itself notes how our heavenly Father sends good things to the just and unjust alike (5:45). And just chapters later we hear Jesus tell the parable of the sower, where the good seed lands on all sorts of ground (13:1–23). Why the sudden concern to "protect" the gospel? A concern for self-preservation of the disciple, and/or protection of the gospel from the unjust seems incongruous with the evident missionary intent of Matthew's gospel.[127] Nonetheless clearly there is

---

[121] *The Gospel According to Saint Matthew*, 674. While noting this more common read of 7:6 "qualifying" 7:1–5, Thomas Bennett offers a novel interpretation whereby 7:6 reinforces 7:1–5. See "Matthew 7:6 – A New Interpretation" *Westminster Theological Journal* 49 (1987): 371–86, at 383–84.

[122] Luz, *Matthew 1–7*, 419.

[123] Luz, *Matthew 1–7*, 419.

[124] Luther, 225; Calvin, 350.

[125] See 10:16. Luther actually references this verse at the start of his treatment of 7:6 (*The Sermon on the Mount*, 223).

[126] Far more common in Matthew's gospel are the warnings against hypocrisy and the salt losing its taste.

[127] Guelich struggles with this question as well, noting that though most interpret the dogs and swine to reference Gentiles, this seems incongruous with the clear missionary injunctions of Matthew (*The Sermon on the Mount*, 354).

some warning here not to "give what is holy to the dogs or cast your pearls before swine." The question remains, why not?

Given the overall context of 7:1–11 as guiding our relations with others, it is maintained here that Mt 7:6 is counseling disciples how to engage those "on the outside," whether dismissive or even aggressive, not for the disciple's own protection nor that of the gospel, but for the sake of the outsiders themselves. The concern is that offering what is holy to those who (for whatever reason) are not ready to accept it, will only provide an occasion to further solidify their intransigence or opposition, which is no service to those people themselves. This interpretation is hinted at in Patristic commentary. Chrysostom observes that in giving what is holy to such persons "nothing results, beyond greater mischief to them that are so [ill] disposed when they hear."[128] We see here concern more for those recipients than for the disciples or the gospel itself. Something similar is said by Augustine: "by revealing things which they to whom they are revealed are not able to assimilate, they may do more harm than if they had completely and always concealed them."[129] The sense here is clearly that those sharing the message may do more harm to the recipients (not that the things revealed do harm).

This interpretation has the benefit of ameliorating the harsh description of those "on the outside" as dogs and swine by revealing that Jesus is enjoining his disciples to serve these very people in their handling of "what is holy." Of course, this interpretation does not wholly eliminate that challenge of the verse; after all, the outsiders are still swine and dogs. Yet this is a problem that extends beyond this verse in Matthew (e.g., 15:26–27). Nevertheless, the main benefits of this reading of Mt 7:6 are, contrary to two common assumptions in biblical scholarship, establishing its context in Mt 7:1–11 and re-establishing its continuity with the evidently missionary (rather than self-preservation) concern of the Sermon and Matthew's gospel. This second of the three sayings in 7:1–11 continues the focus on relations with others, and in continuity with 7:1–5, enjoins that one's relations with others (in 7:6 with outsiders in particular) be oriented for the good of the other. A measure or standard is proposed, presumably akin to that with which God regards us, which is compassionate and oriented toward the restoration of right relationship based on justice and mercy.[130]

---

[128] Chrysostom, *Homilies on Matthew*, XXIII.3, 197. See also XXIII.3, 198 where Chrysostom worries that in sharing what is holy with such people will they themselves be . . . the more damaged."

[129] Augustine, *The Lord's Sermon on the Mount*, II.20.67. Augustine goes on to spill the most ink in his interpretation of 7:6 explaining when and how not sharing what is holy with such people constitute lying and when it does not.

[130] Recall that the beatitudes were aligned in Chapter 1 with different virtues and parts of the Sermon. As will be further explained below, this part of the Sermon is helpfully read in the context of justice, and the corresponding beatitude is the fifth, "Blessed are the

C. RELATIONS WITH GOD IN MT 7:7–11

The third saying in this part of the Sermon concerns asking, seeking, and knocking, with the assurance that we will receive, find, and have the door opened. In these structurally balanced verses, we have a threefold injunction and assurance, vivid metaphors, and a stark explanation and assurance.[131] Jesus enjoins his disciples to ask, see, and knock, with an assurance that God will respond (7:7–8).[132] There are then two metaphors about parents giving good things (bread, not stone and fish not a snake) to their children (7:9–10).[133] The concluding verse uses the metaphors to explain the opening injunctions, saying "if you then who are wicked, know how to give good gifts to your children, how much more will your heavenly Father give good things to those who ask him?" (7:11).[134] For the purposes of this

---

merciful." These verses, along with passages such as the unforgiving servant (18:21–35) and the workers in the vineyard (Mt 20:1–16) help establish consistent standards of judgment and mercy as key descriptors of the kingdom of heaven and thus central themes in Matthew's gospel.

[131] There is extensive research in contemporary biblical scholarship on the structure of these verses, as well as their origin including their relationship to their parallel in Lk 11. In addition to the mainstay scholars whose work is consistently relied upon here (Betz, *The Sermon on the Mount*, 501–4; Luz, *Matthew 1–7*, 420–21; Guelich, *The Sermon on the Mount*, 356). See also Dale Goldsmith, "'Ask and It will Be Given . . . :' Toward Writing the History of a Logion" *New Testament Studies* **35** (1989): 254–65. Goldsmith's account of textual origin and development is contested in Jerome Murphy O'Connor, "The Prayer of Petition (Matt.7:7–11 and parr.)" *Revue Biblique* **110**.3 (2003): 399–416.

[132] Though v. 8 makes no explicit mention of it being God who answers/allows to find/opens, that is the near univocal presumption in the tradition of commentary. See, for example, Guelich, *The Sermon on the Mount*, 357; Luz, *Matthew 1–7*, 421; Davies and Allison, *The Gospel According to Saint Matthew*, 679. (For a distinct view see Betz, *The Sermon on the Mount*, 504, though even he recognizes the text can also refer to eschatological judgment. His position is addressed in more detail below.) As to the rationale for why there are three verbs used, and why they are these verbs, contemporary biblical scholarship regards the presence of three distinct verbs simply as an indication of urgency. (Guelich, *The Sermon on the Mount*, 378; Luz, *Matthew 1–7*, 421; Davies and Allison, *The Gospel According to Saint Matthew*, 682; Strecker, *The Sermon on the Mount: An Exegetical Commentary*, 149; see also Calvin, *Harmony of the Evangelists*, 351.) Earlier commentators commonly proposed significance to the set of three verbs. For examples of this, see Augustine, *The Lord's Sermon on the Mount*, II.20.71; Aquinas, *Commentary on the Gospel of Matthew*, 642; Luther, *The Sermon on the Mount*, 230–31.

[133] Once again, contemporary biblical scholarship commonly finds no significance in the content of the two metaphors here, bread and fish, other than their ubiquity in everyday life at the time of Jesus. For an example of an earlier commentator who does ascribe significance to the two metaphors, see Aquinas, *Commentary on the Gospel of Matthew*, 645–46. We also have here another example of *a minore ad maius*. See Calvin, *Harmony of the Evangelists*, 352; Guelich, *The Sermon on the Mount*, 359.

[134] Much as 6:8 ("your heavenly Father knows what you need before you ask") provides an occasion in the tradition of commentary to address the question of why it is necessary to pray, 7:11 provides a comparable occasion to address the issue of unanswered prayer. Luz provides a helpful overview of various strategies in the tradition to answering that

chapter, the following two points are important, and they concern the context and content of these verses.

First, how are these verses properly understood to fit into this part of the Sermon? Perhaps reflective of the common view that the verses 7:1–11, and really 6:19–7:12, are not intentionally structured, many biblical commentators do not examine these verses with attention to how their relationship to their immediate context is illuminating.[135] Other commentators do attend to the importance of immediate context. To counter the assumption that these verses are unconnected to those that precede and simply reflect Mathew's "messy amalgram," Davies and Allison claim 7:7–11 offers assurance of God's care after preceding "instruction" (7:1–6), comparable to the way "instruction" of 6:19–24 is followed by similar assurance (6:25–34).[136] Guelich interprets 7:7–11 in line with his view of this part of the Sermon explicating petitions of the Lord's Prayer, with these verses serving as the end of an *inclusio* (with 6:8).[137] I offer a different argument as to the place of these verses in their immediate context. These verses serve as the third of a set of sayings describing relations with other persons, relations which are transformed in light of the central injunction to "seek first the kingdom." After verses on relations with our brothers (7:1–5) and then those on the outside (7:6), this passage addresses our relationship with God. Though this claim about the context of 7:7–11 in relation to 7:1–6 is not present in the tradition of commentary, the claim that these verses concern our relationship with God is univocal.

Second, what do these verses have to say about that relationship with God? I claim they continue the focus on "seek first the kingdom" that unifies 6:19–7:11, but also further advance how that injunction is lived. We saw in 6:19–24 the importance of the last end and its impact on everyday activities. In 6:25–34 we saw how the last end was not something impersonal, but rather our heavenly Father, a God of provident gratuity. We saw again there how such knowledge transforms our activities with regard to temporal goods. In a similar way we have seen how in 7:1–11 our relations with others are

---

question. He is correct that it is most common in the tradition of interpretation to explain reasons why prayer may not be heard, since evidently not all prayers are answered. (For examples of this dynamic from authors treated here, see Aquinas, *Commentary on the Gospel of Matthew*, 642; Chrysostom, *Homilies on Matthew*, XXIII.4, 198–99; Guelich, *The Sermon on the Mount*, 358 and 378; Davies and Allison, *The Gospel According to Saint Matthew*, 680.) Against that broad consensus Luz claims that any limitation on what the Father provides or to whom "contradicts the scope of the text" (*Matthew 1–7*, 421 and 423).

[135] Recall the above referenced disavowals of the importance of context for interpreting Mt 7:6 by Calvin (*Harmony of the Evangelists*, 349), Luz (*Matthew 1-7*, 419), and Betz (citing Luz approvingly in *The Sermon on the Mount*, 494).

[136] Davies and Allison, *The Gospel According to Saint Matthew*, 677, 625–27.

[137] Guelich, *The Sermon on the Mount*, 377.

transformed by "seeking first the kingdom." In 7:7–11 the transformation of our relations with others reaches a climax, if you will, for two reasons.

First, here we have attention to that highest, most all-encompassing relationship, namely, our direct relationship with our heavenly Father. Though interpretation of this passage as concerning prayer is nearly univocal in the tradition, Betz offers a unique interpretation that actually supports the point made here. Betz claims that only the concluding verse 7:11 explicitly references our heavenly Father. Therefore, the preceding four verses, and especially the injunctions and assurances about asking, seeking, and knocking, are actually a "recommendation [that] pertains first of all to a general approach to life, an approach based on the assumption that one can trust life as good." Contrary to skepticism, "the SM [Sermon on the Mount] holds that it is more prudent to encounter life without suspicion. . . . Experiences among humans, as well as with God, bear this out. This is the message."[138] Betz thus recognizes the passage is about God, but is primarily about a general approach to life. Though (contra Betz) I interpret all five verses as concerning God, Betz's claim is a helpful of reminder how our relationship with God (as final end) is one that permeates all areas of our lives and thus will indeed engender a distinct "general approach to life."

Second, these verses not only address that highest, all-encompassing relationship with our heavenly Father but also enjoin direct, personal communication with God. Whereas earlier verses in this section of the Sermon attended to how faith in God as our heavenly Father impacts our activities with regard to temporal goods and relations with human person, these verses exhort the audience to not only trust in but also relate to a God of provident gratuity. Indeed, the threefold injunction to ask, seek, and knock is most commonly interpreted as providing a sense of urgency as to the importance of this relationship and our active participation in it.[139] It was noted in the previous section how the metaphors of the birds and lilies need not be interpreted to neglect human activity with regard to temporal goods, so long as a "managerial complex" that implicitly denies our creatureliness is avoided. Here, too, we see an evident role for human activity, and in this case with regard to direct communication to our heavenly Father. Thus there

---

[138] Betz, *The Sermon on the Mount*, 507. Betz is clearly influenced by Goldsmith, "'Ask and It Will Be Given,'" 254–65.

[139] As to urgency, see Guelich, *The Sermon on the Mount*, 378; Luz, *Matthew 1–7*, 421; Davies and Allison, *The Gospel According to Saint Matthew*, 682; Strecker, *The Sermon on the Mount: An Exegetical Commentary*, 149; and Calvin, *Harmony of the Evangelists*, 351. Certain commentators in the tradition underscore the sense of perseverance exhorted in these verses, particularly through the difficulties of discipleship. See Augustine, *The Lord's Sermon on the Mount*, II.20, 71 and 73; Chrysostom, *Homilies on Matthew*, XXIII.4, 198–99. The sense that the "add" here is our active participation is offered here as an expansion of that common point in the literature.

is an air of climax to these verses. Guelich describes these verses as the fitting conclusion of this section of the Sermon (6:1–7:12) focusing on our "vertical" relationship with God.[140] Though that structural view of the Sermon as focusing on our "horizontal" relations with others (Mt 5:21–48) and then our "vertical" relationship with God is not endorsed here, Guelich's view does underscore how these verses play a culminating role at least in this section of the Sermon.

CONCLUSION

Before more constructively bringing into greater relief the way that this section of the Sermon is helpfully read in light of the virtues of prudence and justice, this conclusion examines Mt 7:12, which itself serves as a concluding verse in the Sermon. I first examine the various ways that 7:12 serves as a conclusion before proceeding to how this section of the Sermon relates to prudence and justice.

In line with the argument of Section 3 that 7:1–11 concern relations with other persons, 7:12 is a fitting conclusion to that theme.[141] This is especially true given the prominence of the theme of consistency of standards of judgment in this section, in particular 7:1–5. That consistency is stated baldly in 7:12: "Do to others whatever you would have them do to you." Consistency of standards of judgment is a bedrock of justice, the virtue aligned here with Mt 7:1–12.

Yet the judgments (which entail standards of judgment) of justice are also matters of prudence, as seen above mainly through the work of Thomas Aquinas. This supports the way that 7:12 also plays a concluding function in the larger section 6:19–7:12. These verses in the Sermon are commonly lumped together by default due to the obvious structure of the preceding and succeeding verses, as addressed above. This chapter argues that there is indeed an internal cohesion to 6:19–7:12. In that structure, where 6:25–34 with its vital "seek first the kingdom" (6:33) is surrounded on both sides with a triplet of sayings (6:19–24 and 7:1–11), 7:12 stands out structurally as a concluding verse. This structural observation is supported substantively. Augustine observes it when he claims that 7:12 harkens back to "the eye that has been cleansed and made single," a clear reference to 6:22–23.[142] Being fully integrated in light of our heavenly Father as our last end, with the

---

[140] Guelich, *The Sermon on the Mount*, 360 and 378.

[141] Recall Davies and Allison treat 7:1–12 together under the title "Treatment of One's Neighbor" (*The Gospel According to Saint Matthew*, 667–92).

[142] Augustine, *The Lord's Sermon on the Mount*, II.22.76. Recall Augustine examines 6:1–7:12 in the context of the sixth beatitude on the "clean of heart," since all of those verses enjoin single-minded devotion to God rather than hypocrisy or disintegration. The sixth beatitude is aligned with prudence in Chapter 1.

consistency of standards of judgment that is vital to that integration, is a theme that unites 6:19–7:12 and indeed is integral to the "law and the prophets."

That leads to a third and final way that 7:12 serves a concluding role in the Sermon. Contemporary biblical scholarship is univocal in observing the way that 7:12 harkens back to the beginning of that "main part" (5:17–7:12) of the Sermon, namely, 5:17–20. The primary reason is the *inclusio* formed by reference to "the law and prophets" in both 5:17 and 7:12. As Luz claims, this latter verse serves as a "summarizing accumulation of the entire main part, 5:17–7:11."[143] Given the similarity of this verse to the second part of the love commandment, 7:12 is commonly interpreted together with that love commandment.[144]

There is extensive scholarship on various questions concerning the "Golden Rule," none of which can be addressed here due to the enormous scope of those questions.[145] Yet having noted how contextualized Mt 7:12 is within the Sermon on a variety of levels, and with consideration to the content of that verse, one question briefly considered here exemplifies convergence between the Sermon and a virtue-centered approach to morality.

The previous paragraphs make it clear how embedded or contextualized Mt 7:12 is within the text of the Sermon, on a variety of levels. Yet how is this compatible with the fact that 7:12 offers ethical guidance that is not only accessible to all, but virtually omnipresent in moral reflection across time periods and cultural milieus? Biblical scholars commonly note how consonant this verse is with various moral traditions before and contemporary with this verse, and also how it has served as a locus for common moral reflection in the centuries since.[146] How can one and the same verse be

---

[143] Luz, *Matthew 1–7*, 430. See also Betz, *The Sermon on the Mount*, 518; Guelich, *The Sermon on the Mount*, 360 and 379; Luz, *Matthew 1–7*, 425; Davies and Allison, *The Gospel According to Saint Matthew*, 685, affirming also the concluding roles for 6:19–7:11 and 7:1–11.

[144] See Mt 22:39–40. For more on this connection see: Guelich, *The Sermon on the Mount*, 380; Davies and Allison, *The Gospel According to Saint Matthew*, 686; and, especially Luz, *Matthew 1–7*, 430 and 432.

[145] Such questions include, among others: the origin of the text; the (in)significance of positive versus negative formulation; the possibility of a retaliatory interpretation and thus its compatibility with Mt 5:38–42; and, the possibilities of doing evil to both one's self and the other.

[146] See especially Betz, *The Sermon on the Mount*, 510–16. But see also Davies and Allison, *The Gospel According to Saint Matthew*, 686–88 and Luz, *Matthew 1–7*, 426. It is noteworthy that the International Theological Commission's 2009 (2013 in English) text, *In Search of a Common Morality: A New Look at Natural Law*, uses the Golden Rule as the basis of its survey of convergences across moral traditions in Chapter 1. See John Berkman and William C. Mattison III (eds.) *Searching for a Universal Ethic: Multidisciplinary, Ecumenical and Interfaith Responses to the Catholic Natural Law Tradition* (Grand Rapids, MI: Eerdman's, 2014). The document relies on the negative formulation from Tobit 4:15 ("And what you hate, do not do to anyone . . ."). For more

so contextualized in the Sermon, and so readily applicable and present across traditions? Put differently, is the moral guidance offered in 7:12 part of and only fully comprehensible within a fully Christian theological vision of discipleship given its content in the Sermon, or is it accessible to all without that theological context and therefore not distinctive to Christianity?

The short answer is, both. We have here another occasion where the Sermon presents a fitting opportunity to pursue a perennial question in moral theology, namely, the distinctiveness of Christian ethics.[147] That endeavor cannot be undertaken here, but it should be noted that this is a question that appears in contemporary biblical scholarship.[148] For instance, Luz poses the question of whether or not this verse indicates in Matthew a "slackened eschatology."[149] This is not exactly the same question as that of a common morality. But Luz' related question is whether or not the verse "blunts" the more robustly theological ethic of the Sermon with ethical guidance that is easily detached from that context. Luz says the verse makes application of Jesus's ethic especially at the political level more "plausible in the world."[150]

Another example of a contemporary biblical scholar addressing this question in the context of Mt 7:12 is Betz, who examines Paul Ricouer's interpretation of this verse in conjunction with the love command as presenting an ethic based on an "economy of abundance." Against interpretations of the Golden Rule that regard it either as an egotistical/utilitarian principle, or as a leftover from Judaism that Jesus's teaching ultimately "dispensed with," Ricouer claims "one must interpret the Golden Rile in accordance with an

---

on the significance of the positive formulation in 7:12 as distinct from the negative, see Betz, *The Sermon on the Mount*, 510–16.

[147] For a recent examination of this question in Catholic moral theology in light of the International Theological Commission document on natural law, see John Berkman and William C. Mattison III, "Introduction," 1–23 in *Searching for a Universal Ethic*. The case is made there that the document rightly tries to emphasize both the universally accessible character of moral theology and its fullest expression in Jesus Christ, a balance reflected in the first and last chapters of that document, respectively, and indicated in this Introduction by the use of the terms "common morality" and "natural law," respectively.

[148] What is actually more noteworthy is how little attention this verse garners in the classic commentaries, as indicated by brief treatments found in Chrysostom (*Homilies on Matthew* XXIII.6, 202); Augustine (*The Lord's Sermon on the Mount*, II.22.74–76); Aquinas (*Commentary on the Gospel of Matthew*, 648); Luther (*The Sermon on the Mount*, 235–41); and Calvin (*Harmony of the Evangelists*, 355–56). This seems to be a clear reflection that these authors where not nearly as occupied as post-Enlightenment thinkers with the question of a common morality.

[149] Luz, *Matthew 1–7*, 431.

[150] Luz, *Matthew 1–7*, 432. We see here the connection of two perennial issues with regard to the Sermon, namely, its feasibility (indicated by "plausibility") and its accessibility (since a post-Enlightenment assumption is that it is more "plausible" if not dependent on robustly theological claims)

'economy of abundance,'" a "supra-ethical, cosmic and quasi-theological process by which human beings experience life in its totality as an abundant gift requiring a concurrent response of generosity."[151] While Betz affirms Ricouer's interpretation as corrective of a certain read of 7:12 as incongruous with Jesus's overall ethic, he nonetheless claims Ricouer does not adequately consider the Sermon's theological context as indicating "God's generosity dispensed through nature. The SM [Sermon on the Mount] does not attempt to separate theological and philosophical ethics."[152]

Both of these contemporary biblical scholars address how the guidance of the Golden Rule is only fully understood in its theological context in the Sermon, and yet how it can indeed be accessible to and applicable to those who do not grasp that theological vision. Betz does not reject Ricouer's reading, but places it in broader theological context. Luz claims this broader accessibility of the Golden Rule indicates the compatibility of natural law and the gospel.[153] Yet he goes on to say that the Golden rule is "radicalized by the Sermon on the Mount" such that "It is only the gospel which really (gilds) the Golden Rule."[154] In both of these scholars' work we see an effort to maintain both the broader accessibility and applicability of the Golden Rule, and also its full theological context in the Sermon and beyond.

Obviously neither of these scholars "solves" the perennial issue of the distinctiveness of Christian ethics. But it is noteworthy both that 7:12 provides a ready segue into this perennial issue in moral theology, and that even the work of contemporary biblical scholars attests to the importance of this issue in interpreting Mt 7:12. What can a virtue-centered approach to morality add to that endeavor? A main theme of this chapter has been the importance of how we see things for the ability to act well, with regard to temporal goods and in our relations with others. A (hopefully accurate) grasp of the last end and temporal goods, and (hopefully consistent) standards of judgment, are necessary for our practical decision-making including relations with others. This is true on a "natural" level, evident in the importance of prudence and justice in classical ethical thought. Yet it is also true on the supernatural level, where faith in our heavenly Father, a God of provident gratuity, transforms our practical decision-making by providing a more

---

[151] Betz, *The Sermon on the Mount*, 514. For the language of "dispensed with" and "replaced" see 512. Betz, like Ricouer, rejects the prominent thesis of Albrecht Dihle from 1962 that Jesus's teaching is part of a development in antiquity away from a retaliatory morality, and thus the Golden Rule "may not represent Jesus's authentic teaching" (*The Sermon on the Mount*, 513).

[152] Betz, *The Sermon on the Mount*, 514.

[153] See *Matthew 1–7*, 428: "The Golden Rule is in harmony with the natural law, which law and gospel both presuppose."

[154] Luz, *Matthew 1–7*, 430. The latter quote is taken by Luz from R. Reuter, "*Die Bergpredict als Orientung unseres Menscheins heute*" *Zeitschrift für evangelische Ethik* **223** (1979): 84–105, at 103.

complete grasp of how we see things so as to act well. A theological account of virtue, say that of Thomas Aquinas, provides the resources for explaining the continuity between "natural" ethics and a robustly theological one, even while recognizing the distinctiveness of the latter. To use Thomas Aquinas's terminology, the virtues of prudence and justice can be "acquired" (in other words, natural) but can also be "infused," meaning made possible only by God's grace and orienting us to do activities accessible to unaided reason in a manner transformed by the supernatural end of those activities.[155] The analyses of scholars like Luz and Betz can be augmented by that virtue analysis.

That brings us to concluding point of this chapter, namely, the alignment of these sections of the Sermon with the virtues of prudence and justice. Recall this chapter began with the claim that the seemingly scattered sayings of Mt 6:19–7:12 are actually united by the central verse "seek for the Kingdom of God and his righteousness" (6:33). This verse indicates the importance of a proper grasp of the last end for how we act. The first six verses examined in this chapter address the character and function of the last end, and its impact on practical decision-making. The central verses 6:25–34 extend those first verses by explaining that and how faith in our heavenly Father transforms our engagement with temporal goods. What unifies 6:19–34 is the claim that a proper grasp of how things are enables one to act well with regard to those activities. That theme continues in 7:1–12, but with particular application to our relations with others (insiders, outsiders, and even God). There we learn how faith in our heavenly Father enables us to relate well to others. Thus the verses addressed in this chapter are about making good decisions with regard to goods accessible to unaided reason, and relating well with others. Those are precisely the virtues of prudence and justice, respectively.[156]

Yet as evident throughout the chapter, in another sense these verses are about the impact of faith in our heavenly Father on how we do those activities. Are they thus about faith on the one hand, or prudence and justice on the other hand? The short answer is both. The immediate activities described herein are those of prudence and justice. Nonetheless, the prudence and justice enjoined herein is transformed by faith in our heavenly Father. Thus to use Thomistic categories, we have in these verses accounts of

---

[155] The key texts of Thomas Aquinas on the distinction between the acquired and infused virtues are *Summa Theologiae* I–II 63, 2–4 and II–II 23, 7. See also *Disputed Questions on Virtue* q. 1 (on the virtues in general) aa. 9–10.

[156] I note above that concern for temporal goods and judging are both activities that require specification to be done virtuously. They are neither prohibited *in toto* nor permitted in whatever form they occur. In a sense these are the paradigmatic acts of each section (6:19–34 and 7:1–12), and the paradigmatic acts of prudence and justice, respectively. Something similar can be said for the verses 6:33 and 7:12, which can be seen as summation verses for 6:19–34 and 7:1–12 on prudence and justice, respectively.

infused prudence and infused justice. Those virtues have as their objects activities that are accessible to unaided reason (in other words, without faith).

Nonetheless, the broader context of faith, or put differently the supernatural final end of those activities provided from the perspective of faith, changes how those activities are done from the perspective of the acting person. This makes them continuous with "natural" instantiations of such activities, yet nonetheless distinctive. This is a point that is made squarely in a Thomistic account of virtue ethics. But as should be evident from this chapter, it is not at all one foisted on to these verses. The points stated explicitly in the last paragraphs using the language of virtue ethics are points that have been made throughout this chapter, relying on the tradition of commentary and contemporary biblical scholars. The terminology of virtue ethics clarifies such interpretation. And the content of the verses corroborates and further specifies the more formal virtue ethics claims. And thus in these verses 6:19–7:12 we have once again exemplified convergence between the Sermon on the Mount and a virtue-centered approach to morality, here with regard to prudence and justice in these verses in particular.

5

HOPE AND THE LIFE OF DISCIPLESHIP IN MATTHEW 7:13–29

Enter through the narrow gate; for the gate is wide and the road broad that leads to destruction, and those who enter through it are many.

How narrow the gate and constricted the road that leads to life. And those who find it are few.

Beware of false prophets, who come to you in sheep's clothing, but underneath are ravenous wolves.

By their fruits you will know them. Do people pick grapes from thornbushes, or figs from thistles?

Just so, every good tree bears good fruit, and a rotten tree bears bad fruit.

A good tree cannot bear bad fruit, nor can a rotten tree bear good fruit.

Every tree that does not bear good fruit will be cut down and thrown into the fire.

So by their fruits you will know them.

Not everyone who says to me, 'Lord, Lord,' will enter the kingdom of heaven, but only the one who does the will of my Father in heaven.

Many will say to me on that day, "Lord, Lord, did we not prophesy in your name? Did we not drive out demons in your name? Did we not do mighty deeds in your name?"

Then I will declare to them solemnly, "I never knew you. Depart from me, you evildoers."

"Everyone who listens to these words of mine and acts on them will be like a wise man who built his house on rock.

The rain fell, the floods came, and the winds blew and buffeted the house. But it did not collapse; it had been set solidly on rock.

And everyone who listens to these words of mine but does not act on them will be like a fool who built his house on sand.

The rain fell, the floods came, and the winds blew and buffeted the house. And it collapsed and was completely ruined."

When Jesus finished these words, the crowds were astonished at his teaching,

for he taught them as one having authority, and not as their scribes.

Though the conclusion of this book is reserved for the centrally placed Lord's Prayer, the verses treated in this chapter conclude the Sermon itself. These final verses of the Sermon of the Mount (7:13–29) combine with the opening verses (5:1–16) to bookend what is commonly referred to as the "main part" (5:17–7:12) of the Sermon. Thus, it is unsurprising that the opening and closing sections of this book address common themes. Chapter 1 examined the opening verses in the context of happiness, and there I argued that the beatitudes depict activities in this life that are rewarded because they are constitutive of the eternal happiness that is the kingdom of heaven. The central claim of that chapter, one that reverberates throughout all chapters of this book, is that there is continuity of activity between eternal happiness and the life of greater righteousness to which Jesus exhorts us here and now. This chapter makes a related claim about such continuity of activity, one that is foreshadowed by the final beatitudes on the suffering that accompanies the life of discipleship. All three passages in this final part of the Sermon address not only how our actions in this life are related to our ultimate destiny, but also the difficulties of living in this life in a manner that is directed toward the kingdom of heaven, including some ways that our activity can lead away from eternal happiness.

There is a dire tone to these closing verses in the Sermon, marked by stark alternatives, recognition of the commonality of the wrong alternative, and also the dire consequences of that wrong way. These verses parallel 5:1–16, but they have a different emphasis.[1] The opening of the Sermon is an exhortation to a life that is attractive and consoling. The focus is on Christological happiness (5:3–9), and – even as there is recognition of the suffering entailed in discipleship in this life (5:10–12) – being a Christological community of salt and light (5:13–16). These concluding verses make the same points, but with the opposite emphasis. There is assurance of eternal life (7:13), good fruits in this life (7:17–18), and perseverance through trials (7:25). There is a focus on Christ, eschatological judge (7:21–3) and the rock whose "words" (7:24) throughout the Sermon constitute the path to

---

[1] See Warren Carter and John Paul Heil, *Matthew's Parables, The Catholic Biblical Quarterly Monograph Series* 30 (Washington, DC: Catholic Biblical Association, 1998). Carter and Heil see the 7:13 injunction as an inclusion along with the 5:20 injunction (that is, conditional – "*unless* your righteousness exceeds that of the Pharisees and the teachers of the law ") (*Matthew's Parables*, 27). Carter and Heil further note a parallel:

Doing the will of the Father in heaven is thus synonymous with doing the greater righteousness necessary to enter into the reign of the heavens (5:20). Every tree "doing" good fruit to avoid the destroying fire (v 19) now becomes every person doing the will of the heavenly Father (v 21) that Jesus revealed throughout the sermon. (30)

See also Betz, The Sermon on the Mount, 567. See also Peter Rhea Jones Sr. "On Rock or Sand? The Two Foundations (Matthew 7:24–27 and Luke 6:46–49)," *Review and Expositor* 109 (Spring 2012): 233–49, at 234.

life (7:14).[2] There is ecclesial guidance for the community to recognize false prophets (7:15) upon whose teaching the Church "endures" like a house built on sand (7:26) and also guidance not to become such false prophets (7:21–23).[3] But most prevalent is the breadth of the road to destruction (7:13), the destiny of trees bearing bad fruit into the fire (7:19), the fruitless longing of some to enter the kingdom of heaven (7:21 and 23), and the complete ruin of those who hear but do not do the words of Jesus (7:27). These concluding verses of the Sermon do indeed bookend and parallel the opening verses but offer a more ominous tone emphasizing the difficulties of the narrow path and the ways that people deviate from it.

In line with the method of this book, Mt 7:13–29 is examined here with the questions and concerns of virtue ethics in mind so as to better understand these verses. These verses, in turn, further illuminate a virtue-centered approach to morality. In this chapter, the virtue of hope and one of its vices, presumption, are particularly important for convergence of this section of the Sermon and virtue ethics.

The chapter proceeds in two sections. Section 1 examines the three passages in this section of the Sermon to explore how the verses offer, in the context of difficulties, an account of the relationship between acts in this life and eternal destiny, one that unsurprisingly is labeled here intrinsically continuous. Part 1 examines the biblical terms "enter," "fruit," and "wise" in order to establish the biblical basis for such continuity. Part 2 draws on the resources of virtue ethics, particularly the virtue of hope, to augment these verses' account of that relationship between actions in the life and eternal destiny. Section 2 focuses on the discontinuity between actions in the life and eternal happiness. This is not to suggest there is no intrinsic relationship between activity in his life and destiny in the next for those who face destruction. Their actions are indeed continuous with that destiny, though reminiscent of the hypocrites in Chapter 3 that continuity is not oriented toward eternal life. Part 1 draws on the resources of Thomistic virtue ethics to describe how the vice of presumption derails one's journey toward eternal life. There is surprisingly little on presumption in this tradition, and so Part 2 demonstrates not only how a grasp of presumption helps us better understand 7:13–29, but also how these verses further illuminate the insidious ways that presumption thwarts the attainment of eternal life.

---

[2] There is a wealth of commentary on the "rock" of 7:24, and in particular whether it refers to Christ (e.g., Augustine, *The Lord's Sermon on the Mount*, II.25.87; Thomas Aquinas, *Commentary on the Gospel of Matthew, Chapters 1–12*, 671; and Luz, *Matthew 1–7: A Commentary* [454]) or to Peter, and by extension the Church (Betz, *The Sermon on the Mount*, 564; Guelich, The Sermon on the Mount, 404).

[3] See Betz, *The Sermon on the Mount*, 567 for the parallel between 5:13–16 and 7:24–27 (and 7:21–23) based on the common ecclesial focus. See also Paul Minear, "False Prophecy and Hypocrisy in the Gospel of Matthew," in *Neues Testament und Kirche*, ed. Joachim Gnilka (Freiburg: Herder, 1974), 87–88.

I. CONTINUITY OF ACTIVITY BETWEEN THIS LIFE AND OUR ETERNAL DESTINY: THE VIRTUE OF HOPE

The final verses of the Sermon on the Mount undoubtedly address the relationship between our actions in this life and our eternal destiny. As noted above, in this way they are reminiscent of the Sermon's opening verses on the beatitudes with a Christological and ecclesiological emphasis on continuity between activity in this life and the next. These verses not only supply a stark exhortation that is a fitting ending of a sermon meant to be lived rather than simply heard, but they also exemplify the thesis of this book regarding the convergence between the Sermon on the Mount and a virtue-centered approach to morality.

A. THE CHALLENGE OF LIVING THIS LIFE TOWARD ETERNAL LIFE

This first part begins with an examination of the structural coherence of these closing verses of the Sermon. The features of the different passages that generate that coherence warrant further attention to the relationship between our activities in this life and our destiny in the next. This part closes with examination of biblical scholarship on certain terms in this section, an inquiry that points us toward the virtue of hope examined in the following part.

Contemporary biblical scholars consistently note the internal coherence of Mt 7:13–27.[4] There are three distinct passages grouped together: 7:13–14; 7:15–23; and 7:24–27.[5] Though there is some discussion over whether 7:15–23 is indeed one unit, most treat it as such, not only in recognition of Matthew's penchant for triads, but for substantive reasons addressed in Section 2 below.[6] Luz helpfully summarizes the common features of these three passages. First, each passage contains stark contrast: wide versus narrow gate or

---

[4] Though the Sermon may be said to end with Mt 7:28–29, these are concluding verses on Jesus's authority and relationship to the crowds, forming an *inclusio* with Mt 5:1–2. For brief treatments of each of these, see Chapter 2 as well as Section 2 of this chapter.

[5] Scholars commonly address the many evident parallels between these verses and Luke's gospel, as only v 15 is exclusive to Matthew. This of course prompts discussions of Q and source criticism speculation. For examples of this, see Guelich, *The Sermon on the Mount*, 383; Betz, *The Sermon on the Mount*, 520; and Ulrich Luz, *Matthew 1–7*, 432–3. Davies and Allison in *The Gospel According to Saint Matthew* recognize the Q parallels but are more guarded in their assumptions of Q as the origin of 7:13–14 (694–96). For a fascinating analysis of the relation of Q to Mt 7:24–27, including attention to different forms of flood in both Mt and Luke, see Luz, *Matthew 1–7*, 451.

[6] For this view of 7:15–23 being one unit, see Luz, *Matthew 1–7*, 432 and 439–40; Guelich, *The Sermon on the Mount*, 384–85 (including a review of twentieth-century biblical scholarship, before concluding "Matt 7:13–27, therefore, though a complex of sources and themes, comes together as a related unit rather than a as a series of disparate admonitions"); and Davies and Allison, *The Gospel According to Saint Matthew*, 693–4. For a rival structure which separates 7:15–20 and 7:21–23, but perhaps to preserve the triad includes 7:24–27 oddly in the conclusion, see Betz, *The Sermon on the Mount*, 520. On the importance of triads, see Davies and Allison, *The Gospel According to Saint Matthew*, 693: "From the first to the last, Matthew has built his inaugural sermon around triads."

road; good versus bad fruit and doers of the Father's will versus doers of lawlessness; and the house built on sand versus rock.[7] Second, all three passages "are concerned with the final judgment."[8] Third, as noted above, while the possibility of a positive outcome is evident in each of the three it is clearly the negative that "predominates."[9] This is what engenders that ominous tone. Fourth and perhaps most importantly for this chapter, despite the overall lack of commands or injunctions (*pace* 7:13), there is a clear call to action in these verses that resounds even if only implicitly. It is particularly obvious in the second and third passages that the audience is called to be not only hearers but doers of Jesus's words.[10] As Guelich begins his analysis of these verses, "This concluding section of the Sermon with its final admonitions calls the audience to hear and respond to the teaching of the Sermon."[11] This recognition reverberates throughout the tradition of commentary, as seen in John Chrysostom's treatment of 7:24–27 with which he closes his Homilies on the Sermon:

> Conscious therefore of all these things, both the present, and the future, let us flee from vice, let us emulate virtue, that we may not labor fruitlessly and at random, but may both enjoy the security here and partake of the glory there: unto which God grant we may all attain, by the grace and love towards man of our Lord Jesus Christ, to whom be the glory and might forever.[12]

---

[7] Luz claims like many such texts in Judaism (Deut 30, Lev 26) the sermon ends with the presentation of stark alternatives. See Luz, *Matthew 1–7*, 452. Davies and Allison, *The Gospel According to Saint Matthew*, 699, say this is not naïve simplicity:

> Now such antitheses should not be thought to implicate our evangelists in a simplistic outlook – as though for him everything was black or white. Rather, the stark alternative that appear so often in the first gospel drive home the important lesson that one must choose clearly and unambiguously.

> For more on the constancy of this choice (rather than a simplistic view of its necessity just once), see Luz, *Matthew 1–7*, 437.

[8] Luz, *Matthew 1–7*, 432. Though with regard to 7:24–27, Betz claims that "[t]he text intends to speak of this world, without excluding the eschatological dimensions" (*The Sermon on the Mount*, 566). Davies and Allison say life here is eternal life, which is the kingdom of heaven (*The Gospel According to Saint Matthew*, 697 and 699).

[9] Luz, *Matthew 1–7*, 432. See also Betz who says this passage makes clear that failure is possible and that the path is arduous and requires perseverance (*The Sermon on the Mount*, 526). Davies and Allison note that "constricted" may in fact be better translated as "way of tribulation" which would echo passages like Mt 5:10–12 (*The Gospel According to Saint Matthew*, 700).

[10] Scholars consistently note that "these words" (7:24) refer to the whole of the Sermon on the Mount. See, for example, Minear, "False Prophecy and Hypocrisy in the Gospel of Matthew," at 84.

[11] Guelich, *The Sermon on the Mount*, 383.

[12] Chrysostom, *Homilies on Matthew* given here are from Jaroslav Pelikan, ed., *The Preaching of John Chrysostom*.

And as Augustine puts it succinctly, "no one makes positive of what he hears and perceives save by action."[13]

Therefore, it is clear in contemporary biblical scholarship and the tradition of commentary that this final section of the Sermon is a unified set of passages that concerns final judgment and "eternal life."[14] That future good (if indeed eternal life be attained) is possible though far from assured. Prescinding the question of the relative proportion of those lost and those saved, these passages at the very least indicate the difficulty of the path to life.[15] This results in the portentous tone. It also invites reflection on the virtue of hope which concerns the future possible (but difficult) good, an ultimate destiny very much related to our activity in this life. Though attention to hope will be reserved for the following part of this section, these three passages can be examined for contributions they make to an understanding of the relationship between our current actions and our eternal destiny.

A clear point of this section of the Sermon is that the one's activity now determines one's final destiny. Reminiscent of Chapter 1, that prompts inquiry into the nature of the relationship between our activity now and that final destiny. In that chapter, I argued for an intrinsic understanding of that relationship, such that what qualifies a person for eternal happiness is not only activity (rather than some state of affairs in which one finds oneself) but also activity that is continuous with and thus constitutive of eternal happiness. What if anything do these verses at the end of the Sermon contribute to that argument? In what follows, I examine some key terms in these verses to claim that this section not only affirms it is human activity that qualifies one for happiness but also at the very least suggests (even if not demonstrates) that such activity is intrinsically related to one's eternal destiny.

Starting with the third saying in this section, we read that one who listens to these words *and acts on them* is like a wise man who built a house on rock

---

[13] Augustine, *The Lord's Sermon on the Mount* II.25.87.

[14] Davies and Allison, *The Gospel According to Saint Matthew*, 699. See also Allison Trites "The Blessings and the Warnings of the Kingdom (Mathew 5:3–12; 7:13–27)," *Review and Expositor* 89 (1992): 179–96, at 191, where she claims that the term "life" in 7:14 is eternal life, "which comes from a right relationship to God through Christ."

[15] It is common in treating these verses to consider what they say about the relative number of people who attain eternal life. The first passage states that few do, while "many" follow the road to destruction. Similarly, the second pericope states that "many" come to Jesus and say "Lord, Lord" but are sent away. Luz notes that "many" is a unifying term in this section (*Matthew 1–7*, 432). Are we to take from this that only a few will be saved? That question cannot be treated in any depth here. While it may be tempting to draw this conclusion from the use of "many" here, Davies and Allison claim this text is inconclusive given the commonality of hyperbole in such texts, and that "many" is also used by Matthew to refer to those for whom Jesus is a ransom (Mt 20:28) or who come from east and west (Mt 8:11) (*The Gospel According to Saint Matthew*, 699–700).

which then survives calamity. They key term here is wise man, or *phronimos*.[16] For those conversant in the terminology of virtue this term leaps out in its importance. The virtue *phronesis*, commonly translated prudence or practical wisdom, is at the heart of the life of virtue. As recalled from the previous chapter, it is the virtue of good practical decision-making with regard to temporal goods. We now hear that the prudent person, who not only hears the words of the Sermon but acts according, presumably with infused prudence as described in the previous chapter, endures calamities.[17] As noted above the assumption among commentators is that this refers at least in part to eternal life, and thus prudence leads to eternal life. Thus in these final verses we have a clear statement that activity – hearing *and doing* "these words" of the Sermon – qualifies one for eternal life. Hearing and doing these words makes one like a prudent person who builds a house well.

A further note is warranted on the simile between the *phronimos* and the successful builder of houses. In the tradition of virtue ethics, a good craftsperson, for example, someone who builds a house well, need not be prudent. Although prudence is like a skill in that it entails making choices to achieve an end well, there is an important difference between prudence and skill. A skill, or "art," can be possessed even if the one possessing it is not a good person. The excellence of the craftsperson "resides" in the product made rather than in the person. So one can be a good homebuilder even if a scoundrel. But the prudent person's excellence "resides" in his or her self.[18] Thus it is interesting that the person in 7:24 who builds their home well is described as prudent. But given the context, the reason is clear. The analogy of house building is illustrative, but given the passage's emphasis on being doers not just hearers of the word, the "project" here is not a house or any such artifact but rather one's own life. Like an effective builder who constructs a sturdy home, the person who hears and acts on Jesus's words in the Sermon builds a life that is lasting, which as recalled from Chapter 4 is one of the traditional characteristics of true happiness.[19] Just as the builder has an accurate grasp of building material (or in this case the topography best suited for a foundation) and acts accordingly, the prudent person living the Sermon

---

[16] For more on this term in the New Testament, see "φρόνιμος" in *Exegetical Dictionary of the New Testament* (vol. 3), eds. Horst Balz and Gerhard Schneider (Grand Rapids, MI: William B. Eerdmans, 1993), 439–40.

[17] Echoing a consistent claim of virtue ethics, Betz claims both "word" and "deed" are required for prudence (*The Sermon on the Mount*, 558).

[18] See Thomas Aquinas, *Summa Theologiae* I–II 57, 3 and 4. See also Aristotle, *Nicomachean Ethics*, vi.4 and 5.

[19] In *Homilies on Matthew*, John Chrysostom connects these verses (24–27) with eternal happiness and virtue. He comments on 24–27 that "What can be happier than this type of life [lived by the wise man of 7:24]? For this, not wealth, not strength of body, not glory, not power, nor ought else will be able to secure, but only the possession of virtue" (XXIV.3, 219).

also acts in accordance with an accurate grasp of the way things are. That vision of reality is reflective not only of a God of provident gratuity as discussed in the previous chapter but also of the Lord Jesus who is judge as seen in the preceding verses.

Thus, it is clear that activity, indeed the activity of infused prudence, qualifies one for eternal life according to Mt 7:24–27. But is there continuity of activity with that state of eternal happiness? That is not addressed in this third passage of this section of the Sermon. However, it should be noted that in the tradition of virtue, habits (such as prudence) are qualities that qualify a person even when not being acted on in any given moment.[20] In the Thomistic tradition of virtue ethics, a cardinal virtue such as prudence is possessed in heaven, and thus inclines one to activity that while clearly different from activity in this life is also continuous with it, given the continuity of the virtue possessed.[21] Though we have now progressed beyond the immediate sense of the biblical text, the use of the term *phronimos* invites such reflection.

While the explicit language of classical virtue ethics is not as obvious, the second passage in this section of the Sermon also affirms the importance of activity for human happiness. This is obvious from Jesus's own words: "Not everyone who says to me, 'Lord, Lord,' will enter the kingdom of heaven, but only the one who does the will of my Father in heaven" (7:21). Doing the Father's will, "on earth as it is in heaven" as seen in the following chapter, is what qualifies one for the kingdom. But of course this is not necessarily an affirmation of continuity between such qualifying activity and eternal life. That connection is clearer in the metaphor of the trees producing fruits.

Given the context of 7:15–20, the trees clearly represent different sorts of people, the fruits of whom may be used to discern whether or not someone is a false prophet, a wolf in sheep's clothing: "by their fruits you will know them" since good trees produce good fruits and bad trees produce bad fruits.[22] What may be less obvious due to the horticultural analogy is that the fruits (in either

---

[20] See Thomas Aquinas, *Summa Thelogiae* I–II 49, 1 and 3.

[21] For Thomas Aquinas's mature thought on this question, see *Summa Theologiae* I–II 67, 1; Thomas Aquinas, "On the Cardinal Virtues," 241–77 in E. M. Atkins and Thomas Williams, eds., *Disputed Questions on Virtue* (Cambridge: Cambridge University Press, 2005), art. 4. Reflection on this question is a staple in the tradition since its treatment by Peter Lombard. Though see also Augustine, *On the Trinity* (New York: New City Press, 1991), XIV.12.

[22] On the scriptural motif of using trees to represent people, see Betz, *The Sermon on the Mount*, 530. See also Warren Carter and John Paul Heil, *Matthew's Parables*, 29n11, citing J. M. Nützel, "δένδρον, ου, τό," in *Exegetical Dictionary of the New Testament* (vol. 1), ed. Horst Balz and Gerhard Schneider (Grand Rapids, MI: William B. Eerdmans, 1990), 285: "Most frequent in the NT is the usage of the tree as an image for the human being, illustrating the idea that a person's actions determine his or her value before God and thus determine his or her future."

case) are activities performed. Luz observes that while the term "fruit" can be used as an analogy in reference to the results or consequences of one's activity, it also rightly refers to acts themselves. He claims this is the better interpretation here.[23] Betz also claims the phrase "bear fruit" is best understood to mean "produce deeds."[24] Furthermore, the term "bear," which given the tree analogy may seem to indicate a pre-determined unfolding, can be accurately translated as "do" or "perform."[25] Indeed the Greek word used here to describe how trees "perform" (*poiei*) fruits is the same as in Mt 6:1, translated "perform" righteous deeds.[26] Fruits, whether good or bad, are "performed." Biblical scholarship thus makes it clear that bearing fruit is an activity. "'Doing' good fruit to avoid the destroying fire now becomes every person doing the will of the heavenly Father (v 21) that Jesus has revealed throughout the Sermon."[27]

Even if this passage evidently links a person's activity to their eternal destiny, the relationship between that activity and eternal happiness need not be intrinsic if there is no continuity of activity between performing good fruit in this life and eternal happiness. For such continuity to be true, it would have to be that the fruit performed were constitutive of eternal life. Yet this passage does not state this explicitly. Nonetheless it does not preclude such an interpretation, and it even suggests it through the relationship between the tree and its fruit. The passage is emphatic, through repetition, of the fact that is not merely good or bad fruit that dictate's one's eternal destiny, but that good or bad fruit indicates whether the tree is good or bad: "every good tree bears good fruit, and a rotten tree bears bad fruit. A good tree cannot bear bad fruit, nor can a rotten tree bear good fruit" (7:17–18). While the fruit is clearly related to the tree, the two are not the same. While the passage says nothing of fruit the good trees continue to perform after the bad trees are thrown into the fire, reminiscent of the above reflection on prudence it is not unreasonable to assume the good trees continue to bear fruit, if not in the same manner as they did in this

---

[23] Luz, *Matthew 1–7*, 443. See also Davies and Allison, *The Gospel According to Saint Matthew*, 706. The tradition of commentary frequently addresses the question of whether or not these verses mean a person cannot change from being a bad tree (performing bad deeds) to a good tree (performing good deeds) or vice versa. The clear majority position is that these verses do *not* suggest an inability for a person to change. See, for example, Augustine, *The Lord's Sermon on the Mount* II.24.79 and Chrysostom, *Homilies on Matthew*, XXIII.3 (206–207). For treatment of this history in light of Gnosticism and Manicheanism, see Betz, *The Sermon on the Mount*, 530–31.

[24] Betz, *The Sermon on the Mount*, 553.

[25] See Carter and Heil, *Matthew's Parables*, 29, who use the phrase "do fruits."

[26] W. Radl, "ποιέω," in *Exegetical Dictionary of the New Testament* (vol. 3), 123–26. This term is the same as is used in 5:19 for "doing" the commandments (though the NAB translates it here as "obey").

[27] Carter and Heil, *Matthew's Parables*, 30.

life, at least in a way continuous with it.[28] In the terminology of Thomistic virtue ethics, habits are qualities that characterize (qualify) a person, and the type of quality possessed is intelligible by the activity toward which it inclines one. If good trees are still rightly called good in eternal happiness, they perform some sort of activity, activity continuous with good fruit in this life since it is the same good tree.[29]

Turning now to the first of the three passages in this section of the Sermon (7:13–14), what might biblical scholarship on these verses say about the relationship between activity in this life and one's eternal destiny? Two topics are worthy of note. First, the verb "enter" appears in 7:13 two times.[30] It is used with great commonality throughout the New Testament in a straight-forward locational sense, as when one enters a house, city, or synagogue. And thus this verse might be read as if providing directions to a location at which one hopes to arrive. But Carter and Heil note that the term can also have a more active sense. They point out that Jesus uses this term in response to the rich young man's question as to what to do (*poieso*) to inherit eternal life. Jesus responds in keeping the commandments he can "enter" into eternal life (19:17).[31] In colloquial English we commonly speak of "entering into" an event or experience, meaning not mere physical presence but active partici-pation. Thus, the term "enter" at least suggests activity leading to life, rather than a mere "happening upon" the narrow gate or road.

But even more important for this section is the tradition of reflection on the relationship between the gate and road metaphors in 7:13–14. A variety of views of the relationship between gate and road exist throughout the trad-ition and in contemporary biblical scholarship.[32] Is the gate an entry to a road? Does the road lead up to a gate? Is the gate passed though somewhere in the middle of passage down the road? While all of these views have adherents, the most common position is simply that these two metaphors are synonymous. Whether one imagine a gate or a road, there is a narrow, constricted way and gate on the one hand and a broad, wide way and gate on

---

[28] This point is suggested above in the references to the possession of the cardinal virtues after this life. Work is sorely needed in moral theology on the continuities and differ-ences between this worldly and eschatological activity.

[29] This passage is an obvious place to examine the fruits of the Spirit, a topic seriously neglected in moral theology today. Even as attention has begun to be given to gifts of the Spirit, attention to the Spirit's fruits lags. Though see Andrew Pinsent, "The Gifts and Fruits of the Holy Spirit" in *The Oxford Handbook of Aquinas*, edited by Brian Davies and Eleonore Stump (Oxford University Press, 2012).

[30] See H. Weder, "εἰσέρχομαι," in *Exegetical Dictionary of the New Testament* (vol. 1), 400–401. Luz claims "enter" is an important term for this section of the Sermon, appearing also at 7:21 and connecting these first and second passages in the section (*Matthew 1–7*, 432).

[31] See Carter and Heil, *Matthew's Parables*, 27.

[32] For a helpful overview of these positions, see Davies and Allison, *The Gospel According to Saint Matthew*, 697–98 as well as Luz, *Matthew 1–7*, 434–35.

the other hand.[33] One minority position noteworthy for this book given reliance on his work is that of Luz, who claims

> It is not so that the gate is conceived as the entry gate to the way. . . . Gate and way are not parallel, synonymous images. . . . Instead, the gate is at the end of the way, for one enters through the gate into life, i.e., into the kingdom of God in the eschaton.[34]

Why is attention to the relationship between gate and way important for the purposes of this project? Regardless of whether one adopts the majority position (images as synonymous) or that of Luz (the road leads to the gate), both approaches suggest an intrinsic connection between eschatological destiny and activity in this life. The image of the road suggests ongoing activity, such as travel.[35] Although one can be on or off a road, the image depicts passage down the road. A gate, however, connotes entrance. One is in or out. Both interpretations intricately intertwine activity and destiny. It may seem as if Luz does so potentially more extrinsically, as if one could travel the road to enter the gate and thus discontinue the activity of the road. But this is not his intent. He continues

> Thus Matthew did something that is quite characteristic of him when he supplemented the illustration of the gate with the illustration of the way. He lifted out the ethical aspect of eschatology and so placed righteousness next to the kingdom of God.[36]

Reminiscent of Chapter 1, here again we have ethics and eschatology bound together.[37] That connection is only more evident in those who assume the

---

[33] See, for example, Guelich, *The Sermon on the Mount*, 407. As he writes, "the two metaphors parallel each other as synonyms." See also Davies and Allison, *The Gospel According to Saint Matthew*, 698.

[34] See Luz, *Matthew 1–7*, 436. See also Betz, *The Sermon on the Mount*, 524 and 526, who says the gate is clearly to the kingdom of heaven.

[35] Betz repeatedly refers to the road as activity (e.g., *The Sermon on the Mount*, 523). For more on the road as a common metaphor for a way of life articulated by Jesus in the Sermon, see Guelich, who claims "the 'narrow way' itself and the 'constricted way' each connote Jesus's teaching as found in 5:3–7:12" (*The Sermon on the Mount*, 407). He claims this calls the disciple "to a life of discipleship to Jesus Messiah and the corresponding conduct that ensues from surrendering oneself to him and God's sovereign will that he came to proclaim and effect" (407). Luz also says "the difficult way . . . is the way of righteousness as depicted in the Sermon on the Mount" (*Matthew 1–7* 437).

[36] Luz, *Matthew 1–7*, 436.

[37] Luz could be read to separate ethics and eschatology if one takes "lifted out" and "placed . . . next to" to mean "separate from." That does not seem to be an accurate read of Luz's view of the relationship between ethics and eschatology, as addressed in Chapter 1. See Luz, *Matthew 1–7*, 245–46. Furthermore, the original German reads (see *Evangelium Nach Matthaus*, 398): *Matthaus hat also etwas fur ihn sehr Charakteristisches gemacht, als er das Bild des Tores durch das Bild des Weges erganzte: Er hat den ethischen*

gate and road are synonymous. In conclusion, a review of biblical scholarship over the term "enter" and especially the relationship between the road and gate metaphors suggests that the activity enjoined in this passage is intrinsically related to the destiny of eternal life.

What has this review of biblical scholarship on 7:13–27 yielded in contribution to a virtue-centered approach to morality? The three passages in this section all depict stark contrasts. They offer two different eternal destinies, ominously presenting the real possibility of eternal ruin. Contrasting ultimate destinies are presented to influence the audience's actions in this life. The key theme here that relates to a virtue-centered approach to morality is the relationship between activity in this life and our eternal destiny. This part of the Sermon treats that connection in a manner reminiscent of Chapter 1's claims about an intrinsic (as opposed to extrinsic) relation between activity now and eternal reward. These verses provide support for an intrinsic relationship between our activity in this life and destiny in the next, mainly through particular terms used in each of the three passages. I now turn to see what a virtue-centered approach to morality can contribute to understanding these verses, particularly through attention to the virtue of hope.

B. THE IMPORTANCE OF HOPE FOR ACTIVITY IN THIS LIFE

The previous part established that this final section of the Sermon addresses eternal destiny, offers a sharp contrast between two different destinies, and emphasizes that attaining eternal life is possible but not assured. Perhaps most importantly, these verses clearly establish a relationship between activity in this life and one's destiny in the next. The three passages in this part of the Sermon at the very least suggest an intrinsic connection between that activity in this life and our eternal destination. Prompted by these claims, in this part I turn to a Thomistic virtue ethics account of hope for analysis of the connection between our activity in this life and our eternal destiny.

In this part I first briefly describe the theological virtue of hope in a manner that will make quite evident why these verses are appropriately read with that virtue in mind. I then focus on how hope can be understood differently based on whether one has an understanding of our activities in this life and our eternal destiny as either intrinsically or extrinsically connected. I argue in favor of an intrinsic relationship, not only as a richer account of a moral life robustly informed by the theological virtue of hope, but also as a way to understand better these three passages in the final section of the Sermon.

> *Aspekt der Eschatologie herausgehoben und so gleichsam die Gerechtigkeit neben das Gottesreich gestellt."* "*Herausgehoben,*" translated above "lifted out" is better translated in this context as accentuated or emphasized, as when one "raises up" something for further inquiry.

In Thomas Aquinas's moral theology, "hope" can refer to a mere feeling, a virtuous (affective) activity, or a theological virtue.[38] Starting from the most basic level, the emotional response that is hope suggests a certain relationship between the person who hopes and the occasion (or "object") that prompts hope. Thomas Aquinas claims we hope for something that is good, future, possible, and not assured.[39] It should already be clear why hope is appropriate for these verses of the Sermon. According to Thomas Aquinas, one can feel hope toward a wide variety of things, even if that for which we hope does not in reality meet all of these four conditions. For instance, we may feel hope toward something that in reality is not good for us, or which in reality is not possible. We hope well, that is to say accurately or reasonably, when that for which we hope truly is good, future, possible, yet not assured.[40] In humans this occurs when our emotional response is governed by, or participates in, one's intellectual capacity, assuming what one grasps with one's intellect is indeed true.[41] Virtuous hoping is a stable inclination to the activity of reasonable hoping.

What is it for which all people hope? The consistent answer to this question in classical ethics is "to be happy." Complete happiness is what all people seek.[42] It is obviously good, and a future good since it evidently is not the case right now. It is also possible though certainly not assured. On this last point some thinkers of course disagree, asserting instead that complete happiness is not possible.[43] And even among those who affirm the quest for

---

[38] For other accounts of hope relied on here, see Josef Pieper, *Faith Hope, and Love*, trans. Richard and Clara Winston (San Francisco: Ignatius Press, 1997); William C. Mattison III, "Hope: A Virtue about the Next Life and for This One," in *Being Good: Christian Virtues in Everyday Life*, ed. Michael W. Austin and R. Douglas Geivet, (Grand Rapids, MI: Eerdmans, 2011), 107–25; Romanus Cessario, "The Theological Virtue of Hope (IIa IIae, qq. 17–22)," in *The Ethics of Aquinas*, ed. Stephen Pope (Washington, DC: Georgetown University, 2002), 244–58.

[39] Thomas Aquinas, *Summa Theologiae* I–II 40, 1 and II–II 17, 1 and 7; "On Hope," 217–239 in E. M. Atkins and Thomas Williams, eds., *Disputed Questions on Virtue* (Cambridge: Cambridge University Press, 2005), art. 1. See Robert Miner, *Thomas Aquinas on the Passions: A Study of Summa Theologiae, 1a2ae 22–48* (New York: Cambridge University, 2009), 215–30.

[40] This topic again provides occasion to examine the morality of the emotions, as occurred in Chapter 2. For particularly helpful treatments of this topic, see Cates, *Aquinas on the Emotions: A Religious-Ethical Inquiry* and Lombardo, *The Logic of Desire: Aquinas on Emotion.*

[41] For treatments of the continuity and difference between non-human animals' emotions and human emotions, see. Herbert McCabe, *The Good Life: Ethics and the Pursuit of Happiness* (New York: Bloomsbury Academic, 2005), 58–78.

[42] Augustine, *On the Way of Life of the Catholic Church*, 3–61 in Donald Gallagher and Idella Gallagher, trans., *The Catholic and Manichean Ways of Life* (Washington, DC: The Catholic University of America Press, 1966), i.3.4.

[43] For commonalities and crucial differences between interpretations of the human situation that occasions hope in Josef Pieper as distinct from atheist existentialists like Jean Paul Sartre, see Bernard Schumacher, *Une philosophie de l'espérance: La pensée de Josef Pieper dans le contexte du débat contemporain sur l'espérance* (Paris: Cerf, 2000).

happiness as something possible, the history of moral thought reveals enormously significant differences in what constitutes such happiness.[44] Indeed in the Christian tradition treatments of hope often provide occasions for reflections on the nature of happiness.[45] Nonetheless, at this point in the Sermon on the Mount, that answer has been made clear. Eternal life, happiness, is the kingdom of heaven as depicted in the beatitudes, delineated in the rest of the Sermon, and offered by and attained with the help of our heavenly Father.

Therefore, the highest sense of hope, where the future possible good sought is complete, is a theological virtue since it has God Himself as its object.[46] Hope has God as its object in a twofold sense. First God Himself is sought as (the "content," if you will, of) our eternal happiness. Second, God is sought as our help in attaining this complete good.[47] Given that this destiny of eternal happiness is only knowable, let alone attainable, with God's help, the virtue hope is an infused virtue, and like all theological virtues possible only with God's grace.[48] Hope is characterized by the essential features of all theological virtues, though it has a role distinct from the other two. It is like faith in being an infused virtue and having God as its object. Indeed, it relies on faith since only by some knowledge of God in faith can we hope for God. But whereas faith is a virtue of the intellect inclining us to know truthfully about God, hope is a virtue of the will inclining us to long for God as our complete happiness as well as our aid in attaining such happiness.[49] Hope is even more akin to charity, which is also an infused theological virtue of the will. But whereas by charity a person enjoys God for God's own sake under the mode of union, through hope a person longs for God as one's own complete fulfillment which is not yet present.[50] This is why a sense of difficulty is evident with hope. It is not that what is sought is in itself difficult. The difficulty is that it is not yet present, and though possible, it is not assured.[51]

---

[44] For one of the more famous attempts to categorize the vast number of possible visions of happiness, see Augustine, *City of God* (London: Penguin Books, 1972), XIX.1–11, esp. XIX.1.

[45] See Thomas Aquinas, *Compendium of Theology*, Book II (New York: Oxford University Press, 2009), ii.9.

[46] See Thomas Aquinas, *Summa Theologiae* I–II 62, 1 on how the theological virtues have God as object.

[47] See thomas Aquinas, *Summa Theologiae* I–II 17, 7.

[48] For a discussion of the various categorizations of virtue in Thomas Aquinas as well as their interrelations, see William C. Mattison III, "Thomas' Categorizations of Virtue: Historical Background and Contemporary Significance," *The Thomist* 74.2 (2010): 189–235.

[49] Thomas Aquinas, *Summa Theologiae* II–II 17, 7.

[50] Thomas Aquinas, *Summa Theologiae* II–II 17, 3 and 6 and 8.

[51] For more on whether or not with hope we know with certainly we are saved, see Thomas Aquinas, *Summa Theologiae* II–II 18, 4.

There are various ways that a person can hope poorly, and thus be characterized not by the theological virtue of hope but by one of its contrary vices. These are examined in the following section. For now, it suffices for these introductory remarks on hope to conclude that hope is an infused theological virtue whereby one longs for God as one's complete happiness and for God as one's aid in attaining that happiness.[52] It should be clear why hope is directly relevant to this section of the Sermon, which presents an eternal life as a future good that is possible but not assured. Hope is the virtue that describes how a person can long for that destiny well.

In the previous part it was clear that this part of the Sermon not only depicts a stark contrast in eternal destinies but also emphasizes the importance of human activity in relation to those destinies. Thus here I examine the resources of a virtue-centered approach to morality to address the question of how the virtue of hope influences our activities in relation to that ultimate destiny. Reminiscent of Chapter 1, I describe two types of such a relationship. But before turning to those, I briefly address an approach that is a non-starter.

Christians are oriented by the virtue of hope to long for eternal life as their ultimate destiny. One way of understanding how that inclination influences activity in this life is that it renders them irrelevant. Or more exactly, while properly religious activity in this life helps keep one focused on our eternal destiny, activities with regard to temporal goods have no relation to that eternal destiny. Sadly this grossly inadequate view of the relationship of hope to our activities concerning temporal goods has likely been prompted by Christians whose emphasis on religious piety completely suppresses any concern for, say, social justice. This criticism of Christianity has been made in more sophisticated form and has prompted responses in turn by Christians.[53] Thus at the outset of this argument such a view must be mentioned, if only to state how unsubstantiated it is in Scripture and the Christian theological tradition. Without even relying on obvious passages such as Mt 25:31–45 that clearly establish the importance of non-properly religious activities for one's eternal destiny, the very section of the Sermon under examination here emphasizes that one's eternal destiny is determined by

---

[52] Many of the references here to "one's complete happiness" can be read in a purely individualistic sense, as if salvation were simply for individuals. This would be a serious error since that fulfillment for which we long is a communal endeavor. See, for example, Pope Benedict XVI, *Spe salvi*, http://w2.vatican.va/content/benedict-xvi/en/encyclicals/documents/hf_ben-xvi_enc_20071130_spe-salvi.html, sec. 13–15.

[53] For examples of two such responses, see Eric Gregory, *Politics and the Order of Love: An Augustinian Ethic of Democratic Citizenship* (Chicago: University of Chicago, 2008); Dominic Doyle, *The Promise of Christian Humanism: Thomas Aquinas on Hope* (New York: Crossroad, 2011); and, David Elliot, *Hope and Christian Ethics* (Cambridge University Press, 2016).

whether or not one follows "these words" of Jesus throughout the whole Sermon, words that describe a life of discipleship focused on far more than properly religious activity. Thus in answer to the question, what does hope for eternal life have to do with how we act in this world with regard to temporal goods, the answer cannot be "nothing."

Two other possible ways of conceiving the impact of hope on our actions in this world with regard to temporal goods are presented here. They differ based on whether or not one affirms an extrinsic or intrinsic relationship between our activities in this life and the next. Recall from Chapter 1 and from above that an intrinsic relation is said to exist when human activity not only "qualifies" one for eternal life, but is in some part continuous with eternal life, which therefore also entails activity on the part of the person. In this view, virtuous or truly happy activity in this life is constitutive of, a foretaste of, a participation in, eternal life. Alternatively, an extrinsic relationship between our activity in this life and eternal destiny includes no such continuity of activity. That is not to say there is no relationship between activity in this life and one's eternal destiny. To the contrary, one must act in a certain manner in order to attain eternal life. But in the extrinsic view there is no continuity of activity between those qualifying actions and one's eternal destiny.

How hope, whose proper object is God and not temporal goods, impacts one's activities concerning temporal goods depends on whether one holds an extrinsic or intrinsic understanding of the relationship between those activities and one's eternal destiny. Consider first an extrinsic relationship. Can a person who affirms such an extrinsic relation possess hope? Absolutely. By hope they long for union with God as eternal life, and for God's helping attaining it. Thus the virtue of hope helps them to fix their gaze on eternal life as true happiness, and not be side-tracked by the goods of this life. They will follow the teaching of Jesus (for instance as offered in the Sermon) and the Church to attain eternal life, and can trust in God's help not only in entering the kingdom but even in "doing" the good fruits needed to attain it. Since this path is difficult, hope will help them endure.

This vision of hope based on an understanding of activities in this life and our eternal destiny as extrinsically related represents an honorable life. But note that one's activities may be sustained by hope as one endures with God's help, but hope does not shape the activities themselves. Since the activities and the destiny for which one hopes are not (by definition) intrinsically related for this person, hope can "do no more," if you will, than sustain one when the narrow path is difficult. After all, that for which one hopes bears no continuity of activity with this life.

How might the impact of hope on our activities concerning temporal goods differ when one regards those activities as intrinsically related to eternal happiness? In such a view, these activities are by definition continuous with one's eternal destiny. Though hope's proper object is God, hope more directly impacts temporal activities due to that continuity. Chapter 3 described how charity is called the form of the virtues in orienting temporal activities toward the supernatural end of friendship with God. What follows on hope is not intended to displace that distinct role for charity, or even equate the role of hope to charity. But unsurprisingly since both are virtues of the will, there is a commonality in how hope influences the activities of the moral virtues.[54] The thought of Thomas Aquinas on hope's regard for temporal activities can be of assistance here.

Having established that the proper object of hope is God as our eternal happiness, Thomas Aquinas considers whether or not one may hope for temporal things. His answer is reminiscent of his description of charity as form of the virtues. He confirms that "hope principally concerns eternal happiness," but also concerns other things as ordered to eternal happiness.[55] This claim is quite extraordinary not only due to Thomas Aquinas's insistence that the object of hope *qua* theological virtue is God ("uncreated being"[56]), but also given the pertinent scriptural text (Jer 17:5) that states "cursed is the one who places his trust in man." In this context, Thomas Aquinas's willingness to say we can hope in temporal goods is noteworthy.

Thomas Aquinas draws an explicit parallel here between charity and hope.[57] Both are properly directed toward God as object. But just as charity entails love of others in a manner referred to (or as Augustine says, "whisked along toward"[58]) God, hope can be directed toward things further ordered to God. In fact, the twofold object of hope results in two distinct ways this dynamic occurs in the case of hope. Hope's object is first God as our eternal happiness. Yet Thomas Aquinas claims we can hope in things other than God as long as they are ordered to God as eternal happiness. Examples might include being married, having children, a fulfilling job, or some successful performance. Though longing for any of these as one's complete fulfilment would be vicious, longing for true (albeit non-ultimate) goods as further ordered to God makes

---

[54] I avoid using the terms "in-form" or "trans-form," since these terms are technical ones best left to charity since the form is provided by the end, to which we are oriented by charity. It is hoped this initial exploration of how hope plays a distinct but similar function to charity (which alone is the form of the virtues) will prompt further scholarship on that topic.

[55] "*Spes principaliter quidem respicit beatitudinem aeternam.*" Thomas Aquinas, *Summa Theologiae* II–II 17, 2 ad. 2. The translation is mine. See also Thomas Aquinas, "On Hope," art. 1: "everything that is hoped is also ordered toward the ultimate, single thing for which we hope, which is to enjoy God." See also "On Hope," art. 4 "through this virtue of hope we hope not only for blessedness in the future but also for the other things that are ordered toward this."

[56] Thomas Aquinas uses this term in "On Charity," 105–93 in E. M. Atkins and Thomas Williams, eds., *Disputed Questions on Virtue* (Cambridge: Cambridge University Press, 2005), art. 3.

[57] For Thomas Aquinas's identification of this similar dynamic in both hope and charity, see "On Hope," art. 4

[58] Augustine, *Teaching Christianity* (New York: New City Press, 1996), I.22, 21.

perfect sense if there is continuity of activity between virtuous activity in this life and eternal life. Second, hope's object is God as aid in achieving eternal happiness. Thomas Aquinas claims we can also hope in people for such assistance, again as long as we recognize they are not the ultimate cause of eternal happiness:

> Just as it is not lawful to hope for any good save happiness, as one's last end, but only as something referred to final happiness, so too, it is unlawful to hope in any man, or any creature, as though it were the first cause of movement towards happiness. It is, however, lawful to hope in a man or a creature as being the secondary and instrumental agent through whom one is helped to obtain any goods that are ordained to happiness.[59]

Thomas Aquinas continues by saying we may pray to the saints with hope precisely in this second way. Again, given the text from Jeremiah claiming "cursed is the one who places his trust in man" this seems striking. However, assuming an intrinsic relationship between activity in this life and our eternal destiny, it becomes less surprising.

Thomas Aquinas does not of course use the term "intrinsic" to describe this relationship. But his claim about hope and its relation to activity concerning temporal goods makes it clear he affirms such a relationship. If there were no continuity of activity between the actions Jesus enjoins upon us for this life and the activity of eternal life, Thomas Aquinas could not affirm that we can hope in temporal goods as ordered to eternal happiness. We could only hope in eternal happiness and allow that hope to sustain us as we endured the performance of activity that is not continuous with eternal life. Yet by claiming we can actually hope in temporal goods as ordered to eternal happiness, and even hope in others as assisting us on that path, Thomas confirms continuity between activities concerning temporal goods and the activity of eternal life, enabling one to hope in the former as ordered to the latter.

A Thomistic understanding of hope therefore buttresses the previous part's claim about the intrinsic connection between activity that qualifies one for eternal life on the one hand, and eternal happiness on the other. This section of the Sermon is best read as affirming not only that our actions in this life determine our eternal destiny, but also that there is continuity between our activity here and that destiny. Before turning in the following part to examine impediments to eternal happiness, it is worth pausing to address the ramifications of this argument for the moral importance of hope. As seen in Chapter 3, when activity of a cardinal virtue is oriented toward the supernatural end of friendship with God by charity, that further orientation

---

[59] Thomas Aquinas, *Summa Theologiae* II–II 17, 4.

literally "trans-forms" the act, giving it a different formal object.[60] That is why charity has a privileged role as form of the virtues. Note the further end is not simply an addition to the immediate act, but shapes the meaning of that immediate act. Though hope does not provide the end of the activity of the cardinal virtues in the manner of charity, hope likewise impacts the immediate act and can be said to support the activities of the cardinal virtues. Consider some examples.

How does hope impact the activities of temperance? The person of hope enjoys pleasurable activities, but knows they do not offer complete happiness or fulfillment and so does not seek that in them. This would be true even if one had a view of activities in this life and complete happiness as extrinsically related. But assuming an intrinsic relation, hope has even greater impact on the activities of temperance. The hopeful person engages in these activities, all the while understanding how they are intrinsically related to their final destiny. Thus how they eat, drink, or have sex will only be in a manner that helps them continue on the journey toward union with God. In one sense, the person of hope is "detached" from the activity, not needing it since they know it does not constitute their complete happiness. But in another sense, it is the person of hope (and of course temperance) who can most fully enjoy the activity, because they do not expect it to "save" them, and it is engaged only in a manner that it serves as part of their journey toward union with God.

What does hope have to do with our relationships with others, which are first and foremost a matter of justice? Though examples are possible at the realm of social justice, consider here the example of romantic relationships. How does hope sustain a person's activities in such relationships granting an intrinsic view of the relations between activity in this life and the next? First and foremost, a person does not expect their romantic relationship to fulfill them completely. The relationship is part of their path toward union with God but only part of the journey and not the goal. The hopeful person is therefore in one sense detached, or put more colloquially, not as "needy" in the relationship. This is not because they are apathetic in the negative sense of uncaring and distant. To the contrary, the hopeful person is actually free to be engaged in the relationship, fully present in each moment, simultaneously knowing it need not meet the impossible demands of complete fulfillment, *and* that nonetheless the relationship is intrinsically related to their final destiny and not something simply to "endure" until that destiny is reached. The hopeful person also knows they have in the virtue hope the gift of God's grace to sustain them during those inevitable difficult times, whether they be failures on the part of the couple (neglect,

---

[60] Thomas Aquinas, *Summa Theologiae* I–II 63, 4.

cruelty, unfaithfulness, and so on) or unfortunate circumstances that befall the couple (sickness, job loss, death in the family, and so on). Ironically, by not desperately or idolatrously placing all of one's hope in a relationship, the person of hope is more free to love the other and find true (even if not ultimate) fulfillment in the relationship.

Further examples could be offered not only of temperance and justice but also other cardinal virtues. But the above examples suffice to make the point about hope relevant for this part. Hope is morally important not only in how it directs us toward God as our complete happiness and as our aid in attaining that destiny, but also in how hope qualifies us to engage in temporal activities that are oriented toward that happiness. Granting an intrinsic relationship between activity in this life and the next, hope as the proper orientation toward eternal destiny equips a person for how they perform activities in this life, even those that immediately concern temporal goods.

And this brings us full circle to Part One of this section on how the verses under examination in this chapter concern the relationship between our eternal destiny and activity in this life. There can be no question that these verses affirm such a relationship, more specifically whether or not we do (rather than merely hear) these words of Jesus. Yet I also argued in that part that the connection between activity in this life and the next can be labeled intrinsic since the verses at least suggest continuity of activity between this life and the next. In this second part of the section, I have attempted to buttress that argument with the resources of virtue ethics. I first argued that the virtue of hope is particularly relevant for these verses that concern a future and possible but difficult good. I then argued how the virtue of hope not only orients us properly toward our eternal destiny but also impacts our activities concerning temporal goods, especially granting an intrinsic relationship between activity in this life and the next. What has yet to be examined are ways contrary to hope that characterize activity in this life in relation to the next. That is the task for the following section.

II. LACKING CONTINUITY BETWEEN THIS LIFE AND ETERNAL HAPPINESS: THE VICE OF PRESUMPTION

The main contention of the previous section is that this part of the Sermon addresses the relationship between our actions in this life and our destiny in the next. There I mined both biblical scholarship and the Thomistic tradition on virtue to claim that these passages are best understood as describing an intrinsic relationship between our actions in this life and destiny in the next, and furthermore that the theological virtue of hope is particularly helpful in explaining how one's stance toward eternal happiness can influence one's activities with regard to temporal goods. Yet as was noted there, an ominous tone dominates these verses, since the failure to attain eternal happiness is depicted more often than its attainment. Thus these verses have much to offer on how and why people fail to attain eternal happiness. This section will once again review both the biblical scholarship and the Thomistic tradition of virtue, this time in opposite order, to analyze that failure of attainment, primarily with appeal to the vice of presumption.

A. THE THOMISTIC TRADITION ON PRESUMPTION

In this section, I deviate from the normal order of starting with biblical scholarship since there is so little in the Thomistic tradition on the topic at hand. I noted above how hope orients (one's will) toward eternal happiness, with resulting impact on one's activities concerning temporal goods. Human persons naturally find themselves in the precarious position of longing for true happiness, complete fulfillment. We are inchoately aware of its possibility as a future good, but its non-attainment in the present presents us with adversity, an arduous situation. Christians claim the virtuous response to this situation is hope. Yet there are also poor responses to that situation. Perhaps the most well-known response opposed to hope is despair. The person who despairs does not regard the attainment of complete happiness as possible, perhaps since they do not think it exists, or perhaps because they think it exists but is not possible for them due to their sinfulness.[61] It is easy to imagine how someone in despair is lacking not only in their regard toward eternal life, but also in their activities that could be further oriented to it. Thomas Aquinas notes that despair commonly entails an inordinate turn toward mutable goods.[62] For reasons that will be especially clear in the following part on the identity of people whom Biblical scholars say are "targeted" by these verses, despair is less relevant for this section of the Sermon.[63]

More relevant for 7:13–27 is the vice of presumption. Whereas despair opposes hope in denying the possibility of hope's fulfillment, presumption assumes – or really "presumes" – that fulfillment is assured. For this reason,

---

[61] See Thomas Aquinas, *Summa Theologiae* II–II 20, 2, for both of these possibilities.

[62] See Thomas Aquinas, *Summa Theologiae* II–II 20, 1 ad. 1. For more on despair, see Pieper, *Faith, Hope, and Love*, 113–23; Romanus Cessario, *The Virtues, or The Examined Life* (New York: Bloomsbury Academic, 2002), 48–50; and Schumacher, *Une philosophie de l'espérance*, 134–48. For more on how despair looks in "real life," see Paul Wadell, *Becoming Friends: Worship, Justice, and the Practice of Christian Friendship* (Grand Rapids, MI: Brazos, 2002), 119–38.

[63] It may be that those who travel the wide path in 7:13–14, or perhaps even those who hear but do not do Jesus's words in 7:24–27, are characterized by despair. I have no stake in denying that this vice can be a target of these verses, though both in the findings of Biblical scholars below as to the target of these verses, and due to the presumed continuity of the three passages and the more obvious target of 7:15–23, this section of the Sermon is examined primarily in light of presumption.

one twentieth-century Thomist calls it a "characteristically Christian vice."[64] It entails recognition of God as our eternal happiness. Yet, as with despair, there is something inordinate in the will for that happiness in one who is presumptuous. If despair is a failure to recognize the proper object of hope (attainment of God) as *possible*, presumption is a failure to recognize that object as *difficult*. There are two types of presumption, which correspond to the dual object of hope. First, one may presume that complete fulfillment is possible on one's own ability. This sort of presumption is described by another twentieth-century Thomist as "Pelagian" since it fails to recognize the need for God's help in attaining eternal happiness.[65]

Second, one may hold that complete fulfillment is possible, but fail to act now in the manner corresponding to such destiny by repenting of sin and turning away from inordinate reliance on temporal goods.

> Those who presume on God's merciful omnipotence want his sovereign goodness and forgiveness outside of the order that is established by the divine wisdom and justice. . . . In the final analysis, the one who presumes does not understand that God's plan for our salvation includes our complete interior transformation.[66]

In the language of this project, the presumptuous person yearns for and expects eternal happiness, but without acting in a manner that is oriented toward and indeed an initial participation in that happiness. Thomas Aquinas claims "Such like presumption seems to arise directly from pride, as though man thought so much of himself as to esteem that God would not punish him or exclude him from glory, however much he might be a sinner."[67]

In this connection to pride, we see continuity with certain claims made in Chapter 4. Here again we have an inadequate stance toward God that impedes a life of discipleship with regard to temporal matters. If the managerial complex as depicted in Chapter 4 is a lack of faith and a prideful effort

---

[64] See W. J. Hill, O.P., "Appendix 9: Sins against Hope: Despair, and Presumption," 175–79, in Thomas Aquinas, *Summa Theologiae XXIII: Hope*, ed. W. J. Hill (Cambridge: Blackfriars, 1966).

[65] Pieper, *Faith, Hope, and Love*, 126.

[66] Cessario, *The Virtues, or The Examined Life*, 51–52. See also Hill, "Sins against Hope: Despair, and Presumption," who claims that presumption entails "an expectation of what lies outside of God's power, not in an absolute sense, of course, but outside his power as it respects that order which in transcendent freedom he has imposed upon the existing pattern of things." It presumes "God can bestow eternal life without the prerequisite of righteousness" (179). This language of "prerequisite" can make our heavenly Father's requirement seem arbitrary, but when our activity in this life is understood as intrinsically related to our eternal destiny, the defective nature of presumption is more readily apparent.

[67] Thomas Aquinas, *Summa Theologiae* II–II 21, 4.

to control one's own and others' lives, presumption as depicted in these verses is a failure of hope and a prideful attempt to have eternal happiness on one's own terms. Echoing Thomas Aquinas in connecting presumption and pride, Josef Pieper claims presumption "is a lack of humility, a denial of one's creatureliness and an unnatural claim to being like God."[68] Unsurprisingly given the pride evident in it, Pieper claims presumption is an impediment to prayer. As will be clear in the next chapter, prayer is at the heart of the Christian life and the Sermon itself, so this claim that presumption impedes it is no small matter. As Pieper says, comparing presumption with that other sin against hope, namely, despair:

> Despair and presumption block the approach to true prayer. For prayer, in its original form as a prayer of petition, is nothing other than a voicing of hope. One who despairs does not petition because he assumes that his prayer will not be granted. One who is presumptuous petitions, but his petition is not genuine because he fully anticipates its fulfillment.[69]

This connection between pride and presumption proves helpful when examining some of the most challenging verses of this chapter, namely, 7:21–23, where those who say "Lord, Lord!" are dismissed by Jesus.

What conclusions relevant to this section of the Sermon can be drawn from this brief review of the Thomistic moral tradition on presumption? First, it is very clear that presumption is a vice of "insiders," or as Hills says, "a characteristically Christian vice." The presumptuous person is knowledgeable of and even in a sense seeks eternal happiness. But the vice entails a disordered will toward that happiness. Second, the Thomistic tradition articulates two distinct types of presumption based upon the dual object of the virtue hope. The presumptuous person can affirm eternal happiness as their goal, but fail to change how they live accordingly, pridefully assuming their own terms are those of salvation rather than what the Lord teaches. Even more evidently prideful is the presumptuous person who deems their own efforts adequate to attaining eternal life. In both of these cases, to continue a theme of this book, the presumptuous person's activities fail to be constitutive of eternal happiness, either by non-activity or activity that appears oriented toward it but in actuality is not. These claims point us to biblical scholarship on the verses in the Sermon considered in this chapter.

---

[68] Pieper, *Faith, Hope, and Love*, 127.

[69] Pieper, *Faith, Hope, and Love*, 127. As the translator of Pieper's work notes, Pieper prefers the German term *vorwegnahme* (anticipation) to the more common German term used for the Latin *presumptio*, namely *vermessenheit* (overconfidence). This quote indicates the sort of anticipation of which the presumptuous person is guilty (Pieper, 113n1).

B. FAILURE TO ATTAIN THE ETERNAL LIFE IN MT 7:13–27: GUIDANCE FROM BIBLICAL SCHOLARSHIP

What does the tradition of commentary on these verses as well as contemporary biblical scholarship contribute to a virtue-centered reading of the moral importance of these verses? Two topics are addressed consistently in this literature. First, commentators speculate as to the identity of the people referenced in these verses. Second, they reflect on the different ways that those who do not attain eternal happiness go awry. Both questions are relevant to all three passages in 7:13–27, but they are particularly important for the more complex 7:15–23.

Who are the people who fail to attain eternal life in these three passages? There are a variety of positions throughout commentaries on these verses, and there is attention to how those who go awry are described differently in the three passages that constitute Mt 7:13–27. These various views are reviewed here. But to offer the conclusion at the outset, the thrust of commentary on these verses affirms those who go awry are insiders, those who know the words of Jesus and may even in some sense seemingly act on them. By the end of the review, it will be clear how all of these people can rightly be called presumptuous, even as different types of presumption may be depicted in these verses.

Each of the three passages offers a slightly different explanation for why people can be headed for eternal destruction. The most obvious is the third passage in 7:13–27, where 7:26 describes a person "who listens to these words of mine but does not act on them." Here we clearly have someone who may be labeled an "insider" in that they are aware of Christ's teaching. Yet there is no corresponding action. The least specified of the three passages concerns those on the road "that leads to destruction," who are "many" (7:13). It is easy to suppose that the "many" are those outside the community, and indeed the "many" may include such people. But biblical scholars emphasize "the many" also include "Christians, members of the community."[70] Betz claims people on the broad road to destruction may travel it "knowingly or unknowingly," at least the former requiring familiarity with Jesus's words, and possibly even the latter (as seen below).[71] The most common reason given for identifying the "many" to at least include (if not be wholly constituted by) insiders is typified by Guelich who claims that the text "does not delineate who the *many* are by referring to any particular group. Their identity emerges from the warnings that follow in 7:15–27."[72] We turn now to 7:15–23, a passage whose more extensive description of those headed for eternal ruin we will see does not necessarily bring with it consensus as to their identities.

---

[70] Luz, *Matthew 1–7*, 437.   [71] Betz, *The Sermon on the Mount*, 525.
[72] Guelich, *The Sermon on the Mount*, 388.

The second and longest of the three passages enjoins the audience to beware of "false prophets," describing them as wolves in sheep's clothing. Though these descriptions in 7:15–16, as well as the haunting portrayal of those who cry out "Lord, Lord!" in 7:21–22, are more detailed than the preceding and succeeding passages, there are a host of interpretations in commentators as to their identities in the contemporary context (e.g., Zealots, Pharisees, Essenes, strict Jewish Christians, Paulinists, and Hellenistic antinomians).[73] Betz claims the ambiguity seems intentional, allowing future audiences to supply an answer relevant to their time.[74] He also claims the original audience likely knew exactly to whom this description referred.[75] Yet the ambiguity has given rise to a wide variety of speculation from commentators in ensuing generations. Guelich identifies the false prophets as legalist rigorists, "professing believers … who represented a rigorous Jewish-Christianity that stressed the strict adherence to the Mosaic law."[76] Yet Luz claims the most common position today is the exact opposite, namely, that the wolves represent Hellenistic antinomians.[77] Further back in the tradition a comparable variety of interpretations is evident. Augustine represents a common view that the wolves are heretics, who may live ascetically austere lives but who mislead others in their teaching.[78] John Chrysostom explicitly rejects this view (as he found in Irenaeus's and Tertullian's work) and claims the wolves are hypocrites, those who may teach accurately but whose actions ought not to be followed.[79]

What conclusion can be drawn from this great variety of interpretations as to the identity of the wolves in sheep clothing? One consistent claim about these people is that they are insiders. Thomas Aquinas offers a capacious reading of the passage noting that the false prophets are those who corrupt the people, whether by teaching or example.[80] But in any case he says they are superiors "in the Church."[81] As Davies and Allison put it, they are "almost certainly Christians."[82] Thus in these verses we have warnings about people

---

[73] For this list, see Luz, *Matthew 1–7*, 441–2. For helpful overviews of various answers, see also Davies and Allison, *The Gospel According to Saint Matthew*, 702 and Betz, *The Sermon on the Mount*, 534. See also David Hill, "False Prophets and Charismatics: Structure and Interpretation in Mt 7, 15–27," *Biblica* 57.3 (1976): 327–48.

[74] Betz, *The Sermon on the Mount*, 534.

[75] Betz, *The Sermon on the Mount*, 535. See also Luz, *Matthew 1–7*, 442.

[76] Guelich, *The Sermon on the Mount*, 408.

[77] Luz, *Matthew 1–7*, 442, citing the origin of this thesis in G. Barth ("Matthew's Understanding of the Law," 159–64) and even further previously Bacon (*Studies*, 348).

[78] Augustine, *The Lord's Sermon on the Mount*, II.24.78.

[79] Chrysostom, *Homilies on Matthew* XXIII.8 (205).

[80] Aquinas, *Commentary on the Gospel of Matthew, Chapters 1–12*, 657. I label the read capacious since he seems to intend "by teaching or example" to include heretics and hypocrites, respectively.

[81] Aquinas, *Commentary on the Gospel of Matthew, Chapters 1–12*, 654

[82] Davies and Allison, *The Gospel According to Saint Matthew*, 702.

who are aware of and purportedly seek eternal life as offered in Jesus's words, but are in actuality heading for eternal ruin.

Before examining why they are headed to destruction, it is worth noting that these verses are not only *about* people on the inside but are also *addressed to* people on the inside. Reminiscent of Chapter 3 on hypocrites and Chapter 4 on those of "little faith," Jesus's audience here is aware of Jesus's words of eternal life. As Guelich says regarding these verses,

> [T]he summons comes as an exhortation not as an initial invitation. It reminds the disciples that Jesus' ministry demanded an active response that by virtue of its very nature was not a once-and-for-all decision.[83]

Jesus exhorts the audience as insiders not to become the sort of insiders depicted so frequently in these verses, who purport to seek eternal happiness yet in reality are oriented away from it.

The task now is to determine the way or ways that people are oriented toward eternal ruin, which of course is related to their identity. What lacks in these people? One way they lack is rather straightforward. What all have in common is that they do not act on the words of Jesus. But why not? As most evident in 7:26, they are people who hear but do not do these words of Jesus in any recognizably sense. The people depicted in 7:26 do not perform acts that seem to respond to Jesus's words but in actuality do not. They simply do not act on Jesus's words. Such people are also surely included in 7:13. In fact, that passage gives some suggestion as to why people might not act on Jesus's words that they have indeed heard. Commentators consistently note that the sizes of the road (constricted) and gate (narrow) offered in these verses reference not only the relative number of people who choose each, but also the difficulty of traveling the road to life constituted by Jesus's words.[84] As Guelich explains, "the contrast in size … connotes the relative ease and difficulty corresponding to the respective gates and ways that make the exhortation in 7:13 a necessary in the first place."[85] The road to destruction's width therefore suggests ease. Additionally, Davies and Allison even suggest this width reflects the classic virtue ethics claim that there are far more numerous ways to live in vice than there are ways to live virtuously.[86]

---

[83] Guelich, *The Sermon on the Mount*, 406.

[84] Davies and Allison, *The Gospel According to Saint Matthew*, 697; Guelich, *The Sermon on the Mount*, 386; Betz, *The Sermon on the Mount*, 526. This is a common occasion in the tradition to address how the path to eternal happiness could be understood as difficult, along with how this passage related to Jesus's assurance that his yoke is easy and his burden light (Mt 11:30). See Chrysostom, *Homilies on Matthew*, XXIII.7 (202–204) and Augustine, *The Lord's Sermon on the Mount*, II.23.77.

[85] Guelich, *The Sermon on the Mount*, 387. Luz claims this "way to life is full of afflictions" and "the way to life means suffering for the sake of the faith" (*Matthew 1–7*, 436).

[86] Davies and Allison, *The Gospel According to Saint Matthew*, 697. See also Aquinas, *Commentary on the Gospel of Matthew, Chapters 1–12*, 651.

Thomas Aquinas claims something similar when commenting that this road is wide because the devil and his presumption are wide.[87]

This passing reference to presumption offers occasion to suggest a first way that the ominous warnings in these verses can be better understood in the context of presumption. In all cases of presumption, there is an inadequate recognition of the difficulty of that for which we hope. As noted above, presumption's two forms correspond to the twofold object of hope. One form of presumption is a failure to recognize eternal life as difficult to attain since it requires a way of life, though surely incomplete, that begins to instantiate eternal life through activity constitutive of it. Such activity is difficult in this life, due both to our own resistance to embrace it and the afflictions faced when one does embrace it. Thus this first form of presumption occurs when one who is aware of eternal life and what is needed to attain it presumes eternal life will be attained without living accordingly in this life. This seems exactly what is depicted in 7:13 and 7:26. For the second form of presumption, we turn to 7:15–23.

In the first and third passages on this section of the Sermon, the reasons why people are headed toward eternal ruin are quite evident, namely, through failing to heed Jesus's words. Yet the second passage is more challenging since the reasons that people are cast "into the fire" or summarily dismissed by Jesus are less obvious. After all, in some sense these people *do* heed Jesus's words. These verses concern people who do specific acts that seemingly follow Jesus's words, yet who nonetheless are oriented toward eternal ruin. With both the wolves in sheep's clothing in 15–20 and those who cry out 'Lord, Lord!" in 21–23 there is some lack. Those dressed in sheep's clothing "underneath are ravenous wolves" (7:15), and those who cry out "Lord, Lord!" in actuality do not do "the will of my father in heaven" (7:21). This commonality leads biblical scholars to treat these verses as one unified passage. Guelich claims the deeds of those in 7:22–23 are the sheep's clothing covering wolves.[88] Davies and Allison claim "the contrast between inward intention and outward appearance hold together 7:15–23 and recalls the 'hypocrites' of 6:1–18."[89] Thus once again we have discontinuity between people's actions and eternal life. Yet in these verses that discontinuity is different due to the outward appearance of activity in accordance with Jesus's words. How exactly are the actions of those in 7:15–23 lacking?

Turning first to 7:15–20, this passage concerns wolves in sheep's clothing and offers guidance on how to know they are truly wolves. Comparable to Davies and Allison's connection of this passage to 6:1–18, Thomas Aquinas

---

[87] Thomas Aquinas, *Commentary on the Gospel of Matthew, Chapters 1–12*, 651.

[88] Guelich, *The Sermon on the Mount*, 410.

[89] Davies and Allison, *The Gospel According to Saint Matthew*, 704.

remarks that the sheepskins of 7:15 are fasting and almsgiving.[90] He calls these people "simulators," a sin of which Thomas Aquinas says hypocrisy is one sort.[91] All hypocrisy entails disjointedness between the purported further point of some observable virtuous activity, and the actual further purpose of that activity. In the discussion of hypocrisy in Chapter 3, a distinction was offered between subjective and objective hypocrisy. With subjective hypocrisy, the hypocrite is aware of the disjoint between the outward appearance of their act and their true further goal. With objective hypocrisy, such disjointedness exists but the person is not aware of it. They in effect think they are truly doing God's will. If the false prophets are rightly understood (at least partly if not all) as hypocrites, what sort of hypocrites are they? The reference in 7:15 to their being "ravenous wolves" underneath suggests subjective hypocrisy, the knowingly wearing of sheepskins to cover up the ravenous wolf underneath. Thus, despite actions that outwardly appear to heed Jesus's words, we have here people clearly not doing the Father's will.

Before turning to those in 21–23, some attention is warranted to the text's assumption that false prophets are readily identifiable by their fruits. After all, as Augustine notes, acts that may be sheep's clothing for wolves may be the true heeding of Jesus's words for others.[92] How can acts that are seemingly the same be recognized as different in reality? It should be recalled from Chapter 3 that the fact they are indeed different is evident once one considers intentionality and the perspective of the acting person. The observer's perspective can access much about an act, but not everything. That said, what the passage enjoins here is that the true nature of such acts be observed ("by their fruits you will know them . . ."). How is that possible?

Here a virtue-centered approach to action is very helpful in supporting what traditional commentators have offered. For instance, John Chrysostom claims that the identity of the wolves eventually becomes clear since they do not bear toils well and thus the sheep's clothing ceases.[93] Similarly, Thomas Aquinas affirms the wolves cannot maintain this appearance for long. He counsels observing what people do suddenly, or what they do during affliction, or what they do when they cannot attain what they seek or once they attain it.[94] These bits of guidance for spotting wolves underneath sheep's clothing all presuppose a relationship between acts and habits "underneath," and assume that while people can perform acts that hide their true character, their character will be evident at certain more revelatory moments. Thus in 7:15–20 we have clear hypocritical disjointedness between people's acts and

---

[90] Thomas Aquinas, *Commentary on the Gospel of Matthew, Chapters 1–12*, 656.
[91] Thomas Aquinas, *Summa Theologiae* II–II 111, 2.
[92] Augustine, *The Lord's Sermon on the Mount*, II.24.80.
[93] Chrysostom, *Homilies on Matthew*, XXIII.8 (205).
[94] Thomas Aquinas, *Commentary on the Gospel of Matthew, Chapters 1–12*, 659.

their true character, a disjointedness difficult but possible to identify, an identification made easier by a virtue-informed understanding of the relationship between a person and his acts.

Turning to 7:21–23, we face the most difficult verses in this chapter. We know the activity of the people referenced in these verses is importantly lacking since they are dismissed, and since they are said not to perform the will of our heavenly Father. But here as in 7:15–20, we have the performance of good acts, and in this case acts that are done explicitly in Jesus's name. Furthermore, there seems to be none of the subjective hypocrisy suggested by the image of a ravenous wolf donning sheep's clothing since in this case the people seem genuinely surprised at not attaining eternal life. Thus, they call out – in a phrase that should give pause to all believers – that haunting "Lord, Lord!" How exactly is the outwardly impressive activity of these people – including prophesying, driving out demons, and doing mighty deeds – actually lacking?

This vexing question is too commonly ignored or poorly addressed in biblical scholarship. Carter and Heil note simply that such people do not do the will of the Father, but they no offer no explanation of why not.[95] Luz claims the criterion at judgment is "practice," but he fails to explain what lacks in the performance of mighty deeds by those in 7:21–23.[96] Guelich's answer is also less than satisfactory. He claims the lack here is "a fundamental failure to recognize and do God's will that shows itself in the breakdown of relationships between individuals."[97] Betz comes a little closer to the position offered here by acknowledging that the acts of these people are indeed miraculous and even seem to be given power by Jesus's name, but claims they carry no eschatological reward since they are not accompanied by righteousness.[98] The danger here is that Jesus's dismissal may seem arbitrary, as if the acts of these people were good other than lacking some arbitrary quality that garners entrance to the kingdom. Yet here a virtue-centered approach to morality can be of great help in avoiding such an interpretation of what lacks in these peoples' acts. Two answers are offered here as to why those in 7:21–23 fail to attain eternal life. The first builds on a claim present in the tradition of commentary (and mentioned in contemporary biblical scholarship) about what lacks in these people, namely, charity. The second answer speculates as to what is present in such people, namely, the vice of presumption. In both cases, I rely on the tradition of Thomistic virtue ethics but also corroborate these claims from the text of these three verses.

Davies and Allison hint toward the first virtue-centered answer offered here by saying, with mention of Chrysostom, that 7:21–23 is commonly read in conjunction with 1 Cor 13, where deeds performed without charity are

---

[95] Carter and Heil, *Matthew's Parables*, 31.   [96] Luz, *Matthew 1–7*, 444–50.
[97] Guelich, *The Sermon on the Mount*, 410.   [98] Betz, *The Sermon on the Mount*, 550.

dismissed as nothing.[99] This is exactly Thomas Aquinas's interpretation of these verses. He surveys and dismisses previous positions on this question, such as that these people lie about their actions, or that these people were once good but went bad. Thomas Aquinas says there is no accusation by Christ of falsehood, and He even says "I never knew you" (7:23) indicating the actions were never good.[100] Comparable to Betz's view mentioned above, Thomas Aquinas grants that that these people did apparently perform miraculous actions. Yet he claims they must have been performed based on a greater grasp of natural causes rather than from supernatural causality. Thomas Aquinas claims, reminiscent of 1 Cor 13, that such acts surely lack charity, which is the distinguisher of true miracles and supernatural causality.[101] Indeed, he claims that such actions may have been done in Jesus's name, but not done in the Spirit.[102] And as recalled from Chapter 2, the new law that animates life in Christ is the grace of the Holy Spirit through faith in Christ, our (created) participation in which is charity.[103]

The strength of Thomas Aquinas's answer to the question of what lacks in the actions of those described in 7:21–23 is that he affirms that these people in fact performed "mighty deeds," but he also gives an account of how these deeds, though mighty, were themselves lacking. Unlike Betz who identifies the lack not in the acts themselves but in their failure to be accompanied by righteousness, Thomas Aquinas's view identifies a lack in the seemingly good acts of those who cry out "Lord! Lord!" Yet how is this evident in the text itself?

Perhaps fittingly since this final section of the Sermon bookends the opening verses with the beatitudes, these verses contain some of the more Christologically important texts in the Sermon. The Sermon's final words emphasize Jesus's authority, "for he taught them as one having authority and not like their scribes" (7:29). We also encounter Jesus as eschatological judge at the time of judgment: "many will say to me on that day …" (7:22).[104] There is also perennial discussion among commentators over whether Jesus is the "rock" upon which the wise man builds his house (7:24).[105] But less commented upon in a Christological manner is the dismissive phrase "I never knew you" (7:23). This line receives scant attention in the tradition

---

[99] Davies and Allison, *The Gospel According to Saint Matthew*, 729.

[100] Thomas Aquinas, *Commentary on the Gospel of Matthew, Chapters 1–12*, 667.

[101] Thomas Aquinas, *Commentary on the Gospel of Matthew, Chapters 1–12*, 668

[102] Thomas Aquinas, *Commentary on the Gospel of Matthew, Chapters 1–12*, 667.

[103] On the new law, see Thomas Aquinas, *Summa Theologiae* I–II 106, 1. On charity as created, see *Summa Theologiae* II–II 23, 2.

[104] Despite his helpful scholarship on this part of the Sermon, Betz is surprisingly insistent that Matthew's gospel as a whole and the Sermon in particular do not present a robust Christology: "The figure of Jesus in the SM is not interpreted christologically but eschatologically" (554). This repeated claim is buttressed by denials of any soteriology (555) or ecclesiology (564) in the Sermon. These claims are not affirmed here.

[105] See n. 2 above.

of commentary.[106] Instead, contemporary commentators focus on the legal context of advocacy.[107] Yet the Christological importance of this passage seems to be its assumption not only that Jesus is present at the final judgment but that some sort of relationship to Him is necessary for eternal life. It is not a mere knowledge as in awareness, since the people of 7:21–23 do mighty deeds in Jesus's name. They clearly "know of" Jesus. What is suggested here is a greater knowing, as in a friendship.

As indicated above, 1 Cor 13 is commonly associated with this passage in Mt 7 due to their common theme of the inefficacy of seemingly good deeds. The association of these passages could be understood as a "one-way street," where the clearer 1 Cor 13 on the importance of love for accompanying good acts is appealed to in order to clarify the more opaque Mt 7. Yet this powerful phrase in 7:23 helps inform what is lacking in those without love in 1 Cor 13. A knowledge of Jesus the Lord, a relationship helpfully understood as friendship, is necessary to attain eternal life.[108] This friendship is called charity in the Thomistic tradition of virtue. Charity is the form of the virtues, supplying the final end of all activity oriented toward eternal life. From the perspective of the acting person, those in 21–23 lack charity, friendship with God. Thus their acts, though mighty, do not lead to that final end. The result is tragic. They perform mighty deeds, and even appear to have faith ("Lord! Lord!"). But given the absence of charity this faith is what is called in the Thomistic tradition "dead faith," an inert intellectual affirmation of Jesus as Lord without the charity that animates reverential knowledge.[109] This mention of the lack of both charity and living faith invites attention to hope, or lack thereof, which is the second answer offered here as to why those in 7:21–23 do not attain eternal life.

---

[106] See, for example, Chrysostom, *Homilies on Matthew*, XXIV.2 (216–17); Augustine, *The Lord's Sermon on the Mount*, II.25.84; Aquinas, *Commentary on the Gospel of Matthew, Chapters 1–12*, 669 and 667.

[107] See, for example, Betz, *The Sermon on the Mount*, 551 and Luz, *Matthew 1–7*, 445–6. See Guelich, *The Sermon on the Mount*, 401–402, on the connection to Ps 6:9.

[108] For an interesting linguistic analysis of the broken parallelism in 7:24–5 and 7:26–7, with a suggestion that this is done intentionally to supply a reverential connotation to how the winds "fall down before" the rock, see Gary Yamasaki "Broken Parallelism in Matthew's Parable of the Two Builders (7:24–27) *Direction* 33.2 (2004)143–49.

[109] For more on Thomas Aquinas's notion of dead faith, see *Summa Theologiae* II-II 5, 2 and 6, 2. See also Chrysostom, *Homilies on Matthew*, XXIV1 (215) who also describes dead faith with regard to this passage, though without using the term: "For surely [Jesus's] intention is to make out that faith is of no avail without works. Then enhancing it, he added miracles also, declaring that not only faith, but the exhibiting even of miracles, avails nothing for him who works such wonder without virtue." In the very next section, Chrysostom speaks of what is lacking with reference to 1 Cor 13 on charity. See *Homilies on Matthew*, XXIV.2 (216). After reference to 1 Cor 13, Chrysostom comes closest to the language of dead faith by describing these workers of mighty deeds as people "without life suitable to their faith" (216).

My first answer to the question of what is lacking in those who cry "Lord! Lord!" builds upon a traditional connection of Mt 7:21–23 with 1 Cor 13, augmenting that connection with attention to 7:23b ("I never knew you"), to claim that these people lack charity and thus their observable mighty deeds are not actually "performing my father's will." My second answer focuses more on what their actions are rather than what they lack. Drawing on both the resources of virtue ethics and the biblical text, I suggest we have here an example of presumption.

Presumption is always a failure of hope by its inadequate response to the difficulty of hope's twofold object. First, one can presume that attaining eternal life does not require the often difficult changes in one's activity necessary to lead to, indeed even to constitute an initial participation in, eternal life. We saw this with regard to 7:13–4 and 7:24–7. But second, one can also presume in failing to realize the need for God's help in that attainment. Such people presumptuously think they can secure eternal life on their own by their actions.[110] This is the "Pelagian presumption" described above in the words of Pieper. Such presumption is evidenced in the verbal exchange narrated by Jesus in 7:21–23. Jesus makes his opening claim about the need to do His Father's will, and not simply say "Lord! Lord!" He then narrates how many will come to Him on that day and remind Him of their mighty deeds in His name. These words suggest a sort of claim on God that the required acts have been done, and thus reward should be received.[111] Yet more than externally observable mighty deeds are required. The performance of these acts without the animating friendship can only mean the acts are done to secure for one's self the eternal life to which they can lead.[112] While Chapter 4 depicted the "managerial complex" with regard to temporal goods, we see here in 7:21–23 the presumptuous absurdity of a managerial complex with regard to eternal life. The people depicted here are incredulous at Jesus' words, demanding a reward they deem they have earned. The reward they seek is the notion of reward decried in Chapter 3, namely, one that is earned on one's own and places God under obligation. Therefore, we have in these verses not simply people who are petulant or misguided as they perform acts that are mighty and good.

---

[110] See Thomas Aquinas, *Summa Theologiae* II–II 21, 1. Recall n. 64 above on Pieper's claim that this sort of presumption is "Pelagian" (*Faith, Hope, Love*, 126).

[111] See Betz, *The Sermon on the Mount*, 549: "the reason for this . . . is to express a quasi-legal client relationship. The protestors take the experiences [prophesy, exorcism, miracles] to be evidence of a legal obligation on the part of Jesus."

[112] Chrysostom describes the lack of such animation thus: "But though they marvel because they are punished after working such miracles, yet do not thou marvel. For all the grace was of the free gift of him that gave it, but they contributed nothing on their part, wherefore also they are justly punished, as having been ungrateful and without feeling towards him that had so honored them as to bestow his grace upon them though unworthy" (*Homilies on Matthew*, XXIV.2, 215–16).

Although their acts are good from an observer's perspective, from the perspective of the acting person these acts are vitiated as they are performed with an eye toward laying a claim on God for eternal life.[113]

This does not of course mean that attaining eternal life entails no activity in this life. Indeed, the whole point of the Sermon and the verses in this chapter is the necessity of such activity. But what leads to eternal life is charitable action in friendship with God, hopeful action relying on God's grace for help, not presumptuous action that attempts to bind God and secure eternal life as something under one's control. Betz is right that the verses 7:21–23 can be seen as a sort of climax to the Sermon.[114] Certainly Mt 6–7, and arguably the entire Sermon, is addressed to insiders.[115] Along with the rest of this final section of the Sermon, verses 7:21–23 concern that most insidious of insider vices, presumption. These verses may even concern a type of presumption where one is so (self-)deluded as to no longer see that one is relying on one's own saving efforts rather than the grace of God. These verses are truly haunting and should give pause to any believer, or "insider." Yet despite their mighty deeds these people are rightly dismissed by Jesus. Their actions are vitiated by their presumption, rendering them – despite their "mighty deeds" - truly "evildoers."

CONCLUSION

In certain chapters of this book, I turn in the conclusion to explicitly connect the preceding analysis with one of the theological or cardinal virtues. That is obviously unnecessary here since the whole chapter is dependent on the

---

[113] Some attention to whether or not the people in 7:21–23 might be victims is in order. Betz for instance claims that the people in 7:21–23 are deluded by, indeed "victims of," the false prophets in 7:15–20. The discussion from Chapter 3 of objective hypocrisy might also be relevant. Recall objective hypocrisy is when there is disjoint between people's righteous deeds and their further goal without subjective awareness of that disjoint. Given the seemingly sincere cries of "Lord! Lord!" might these people be inculpable victims? As indicated in Chapter 3, I am less convinced by the possibility of objective hypocrisy as the term "hypocrite" seems to indicate knowing duplicity. Even if such disjointedness were present and yet not known from the perspective of the acting person, that would seem better handled as a case of what traditionally has been called erroneous conscience, which can of course still be culpable. That this would be the case should those in 7:21–23 be sincere seems indicated as even Betz calls those in 7:21–23 "*self*-deluded" (*The Sermon on the Mount*, 540). My own read of 7:22 as indication of presumption also militates against a claim of objective hypocrisy.

[114] Betz, *The Sermon on the Mount*, 540. This claim is reflected in Betz's unusual structure for the verses treated in this chapter. Perhaps to make 7:21–23 the literal climax, he posits a triadic structure of 7:13–14, 7:15–20, and 7:21–23, adding 7:24–27 to the concluding 7:28–29.

[115] See Chrysostom, *Homilies on Matthew*, XXIV.3 (217), on this passage as concluding Jesus's explanation of "diverse kinds" of "pretenders," starting with those who "for display fast and make prayers. . . ."

conceptual resources of virtue ethics, and in particular the virtue of hope and one of its key vices, namely, presumption. A hope-based analysis is apt for Mt 7:13–29 since these verses in the Sermon concern a future good that is possible but not assured; indeed, they concern the ultimate future possible good.

In Section 1, I drew on Thomistic virtue ethics on hope to explain how hope can inform our activities with regard to temporal goods, especially granting an intrinsic understanding of the relationship between our activities in this life and our eternal destiny. I also argued that certain terms in the Sermon text support such an intrinsic understanding of that relationship. In these senses, the verses addressed in this chapter are "hopeful," not merely in the technical sense but in the colloquial one, as they encourage the audience to live a life of discipleship oriented toward, and indeed an initial participation in, eternal happiness.

Yet as explained at the start of this chapter, the predominant tone of these verses is more ominous. More prevalent at the close of the Sermon are those headed for eternal ruin. Here is where the resources of a virtue-centered approach to morality can be most illuminating. Those depicted in these verses (and indeed the audience of these verses) are "insiders," already acquainted with the path of discipleship articulated by Jesus ("these words of mine"), including in the Sermon itself. Therefore an analysis based on presumption such as that of Section 2, while innovative in its explicit use of that terminology, is clearly at home in these verses. A Thomistic account of presumption helps clarify the various ways that one can go awry on occasions of hope. These ways are evident in the closing verses of the Sermon. The future calamity portended in these verses seems intended to "astonish," as it did Jesus's hearers in the crowd (7:28). But more than astonish, these closing verses are surely intended to prompt decisive activity, the life of discipleship depicted throughout the hundred or so preceding verses.

6

A VIRTUE ETHICS APPROACH TO THE LORD'S PRAYER IN MATTHEW 6:7–15

In praying, do not babble like the pagans, who think that they will be heard because of their many words.
Do not be like them. Your Father knows what you need before you ask him.
This is how you are to pray: Our Father in heaven, hallowed be your name,
your kingdom come, your will be done, on earth as in heaven.
Give us today our daily bread
and forgive us our debts, as we forgive our debtors;
and do not subject us to the final test, but deliver us from the evil one.
If you forgive others their transgressions, your heavenly Father will forgive you.
But if you do not forgive others, neither will your Father forgive your transgressions.

A chapter on the Lord's Prayer/Our Father could not be a more fitting way to conclude this book on the Sermon on the Mount and virtue ethics. These verses are of course surrounded by those treated in Chapter 3 and must be understood in that context, let alone the broader context of the Sermon, Matthew's gospel, and Jewish piety and cultic acts. Yet there is indeed something central about these verses, warranting distinct and in this case climactic treatment in a book on the Sermon on the Mount from a virtue ethics perspective. That centrality is not only a structural claim but a substantive one, and it is a claim reiterated in both classical and recent commentaries.

The Lord's Prayer is absolutely foundational in the history of Christian life, be it in liturgy, commentary, sacramental preparation and catechesis, preaching, and so on. Tertullian famously called the prayer a "summary of the whole gospel."[1] Augustine audaciously claimed that "if you go over all the

---

[1] See Tertullian, *On Prayer*, found on pp. 41–64 in trans. Alistair Stewart-Sykes, *Tertullian, Cyprian, Origen on the Lord's Prayer* (Crestwood, NY: St. Vladmimir's Seminary Press, 2004), 42.

words of holy prayers, you will, I believe, find nothing which cannot be comprised and summed up in the petitions of the Lord's Prayer."[2] Aquinas called it "the most perfect of prayers,"[3] and Bonaventure said that despite its brevity it "contains in itself all prayer and everything to be asked for."[4] St. Theresa exclaims in her *Way of Perfection*, "I marvel to see that in so few words everything about contemplation and perfection is included."[5] The current *Catechism of the Catholic Church* calls it the quintessential prayer of the Church and uses it to structure the fourth pillar on prayer.[6]

This affirmation of the enormous import of the Lord's Prayer is evident also in contemporary scholarship. In a rather uncommon approach for a contemporary biblical scholar, Guelich regards the verses of the Lord's Prayer as governing the structure of the ensuing section, Mt 6:19–7:11. He aligns each petition with several verses leading up until the summary in Mt 7:12.[7] Luz has an even more striking interpretation of the role of the Lord's Prayer in the Sermon. He finds in the Sermon a chiastic structure, with parallel sections preceding and succeeding the Lord's Prayer. "[The Sermon on the Mount] is built symmetrically around a center, namely, the Lord's Prayer (6:9–13). The sections before and after the Lord's Prayer correspond to each other."[8] He concludes of the Sermon, "The Lord's

---

[2] See Augustine's Letter 130 (to Proba), 12.22, 183–99 of Boniface Ramsey, ed., Letters 100–155 II/2 (New York: New City Press, 2003).

[3] Thomas Aquinas, *Summa Theologiae* II–II 83, 9. See also *Catechism of the Catholic Church*, 2763.

[4] Bonaventure, *Commentarius in Evangelium Sancti Lucae* XI.8, *Opera Omnia* (Quarrachi: Typographia Collegii Sancti Bonaventurae, 1882–1902). Tomus VII.279: "*Quamquam sit brevissima, continet in se omnem orationem et omnia postulanda.*"

[5] St. Theresa of Avila, *Way of Perfection* (Westminster, MD: Newman Bookshop, 1948). This text is cited in Paul Murray, O.P., *Praying with Confidence* (London: Continuum, 2010), 4.

[6] *Catechism of the Catholic Church*, 2776.

[7] Alignments of sections of the Sermon with other sets are not of course unprecedented. Perhaps most famously, Augustine claims the (seven) beatitudes govern the entire remaining part of the Sermon. Yet these claims are far less frequent in contemporary biblical scholarship. See Guelich, *The Sermon on the Mount*, 307: "the importance of the Lord's Prayer her will become even more evident when we observe its serving as the structural outline for the selection and arrangement of the material that follows in the Sermon up to 7:12." See also 320: "The Lord's Prayer offers the structural outline for what otherwise appears to have no obvious ordering principle [in other words, 6:19–7:11]."

[8] Luz, *Matthew 1–7*, 211. For a chart of this schema, which is difficult to present in prose but striking as a chart, see 212. See also Betz, *The Sermon on the Mount*, 373 for the centrality of the prayer in 6:1–18 and the entire Sermon.

The sections of the chiastic structure (where first corresponds to last, second with second to last, and Lord's Prayer at the center) are: 5:1–2; 5:3–16; 5:17–20; 5:21–48; 6:1–6; 6:7–15; 6:16–18; 6:19–7:11; 7:12; 7:13–27; 7:28–8:1a. (Note the exclusion of Mt 6:7–8 and 14–15 in the quote in the text; these could be listed as an additional chiasm.) Luz's structure accords well with the structure of this book (though it is not the impetus for it): 5:1–2; 5:3–16 [Chapter 1]; 5:17–20; 5:21–48 [Chapter 2]; 6:1–6 [Chapter 3]; 6:7–15 [Chapter 6]; 6:16–18 [Chapter 3]; 6:19–7:11; 7:12 [Chapter 4]; and 7:13–27; 7:28–8:1a [Chapter 5].

Prayer is its central text," and it is evident in context that the term "central" is used structurally as well as substantively.[9]

One final (and less intrinsic) reason is offered here to justify this distinct and climactic treatment of the Lord's Prayer in this concluding chapter of the book. Moral theology and Christian ethics have for too long neglected the importance of prayer, worship, and sacrament in the moral life. There are a variety of explanations for how this division between the moral life and spirituality/prayer has arisen, and that narrative cannot be treated here.[10] Though not the primary task of this book, I do hope to contribute to the reintegration of morality and the other sub-disciplines of theology. Other sections of this book on, for example, Christ, the Church, and the sacraments have hopefully pointed toward a richer integration of morality with systematic and sacramental theology. It is similarly hoped that by concluding with a climactic chapter on the Lord's Prayer, the book can also contribute to the reintegration of morality on the one hand and prayer and spirituality on the other.

All that said, this climactic treatment of the Lord's Prayer as the heart of the Sermon is warranted based simply on the central thesis of this book, namely, that the text of the Sermon on the Mount is fruitfully read in light of, and in turn further illuminates, a virtue-centered approach to morality. The central claim of this chapter is that the Lord's Prayer can be accurately understood as a request for the seven foundational virtues of the Christian life: the three theological virtues and the four cardinal virtues. Given the importance of the Lord's Prayer (and commentaries on it) in the Christian tradition, this argument is an enormous boon toward the argument of this book on the confluence of the Sermon on the Mount and a virtue-centered approach to morality. Previous chapters have at times contained structural analyses of portions of text in the Sermon that are suggestive of the virtues. Chapter 1 contains an alignment between beatitudes and virtues. Indeed, each of the previous five chapters has noted one or two virtues that correspond particularly well with that section of the Sermon. Yet the focus of all previous chapters was mainly on how the conceptual resources of this virtue can help us better interpret the verses in the Sermon, and then be further illuminated by those verses. This chapter also suggests a dynamic of convergence and alignment. But its main task is rather baldly establishing the legitimacy of an alignment between the petitions of the Lord's Prayer and the seven virtues.

The chapter proceeds in two sections. Section 1 contextualizes the thesis within the Christian tradition by surveying how Christians for millennia have

---

[9] Luz, *Matthew 1–7*, 213. See also 372: "The basic understanding and the constant use of the Lord's Prayer have led to the fact that there is hardly a Christian text which has had greater effect in piety, worship, instruction, and dogmatics."

[10] The one most influential on this book is that of Servais Pinckaers, O.P. See *La Vie Selon L'Esprit: Essai de théologie spirituelle selon saint Paul et saint Thomas d'Aquin* (Luxembourg: Éditions Saint-Paul, 1996), 33–38.

understood the Lord's Prayer. This section prepares the reader to see in what ways the interpretation of the Lord's Prayer in Section 2 is a seamless continuation of a long tradition, and in what ways it is more innovative. Section 2 then offers a constructive interpretation of the Lord's Prayer with its petitions aligned with the virtues, and then more broadly explores how the prayer contributes to certain common questions and concerns of virtue ethics.

Before proceeding, repetition of a caveat applicable to this book as a whole is in order, especially here since the Lord's Prayer is so fundamental in the Christian life. I am certainly not claiming that one *only* understands the Lord's Prayer truthfully through the lens of virtue employed here. As commentators have consistently stated, the Lord's Prayer invites a plenitude of interpretation. My more modest claim here is that given the centrality of the Lord's Prayer (and the Sermon on the Mount) in the Christian life, it is not surprising that there are important convergences between the prayer and the virtues if it is the case (as virtue ethicists would avow) that virtue offers a helpful lens through which to understand the life of Christian discipleship.

This caveat presents an opportunity to return to the Introduction's claims about the methodology of this book, an appropriate task here given both the argument of this chapter and its function as a conclusion for the book as a whole. This caveat echoes an abashed self-consciousness throughout this book about alignments of parts of the Sermon with other sets or groupings in the Christian life. Yet barging through that hesitancy is a persistent instinct that such parallels signify something beyond numerological fixation or aesthetic appreciation. As noted in the Introduction, there is a deeper wisdom here about the unity of truth as grasped in faith. The *Catechism of the Catholic Church* describes the "analogy of faith" as the "coherence of the truths of faith among themselves and within the whole plan of Revelation." It affirms that the "mutual connections between dogmas, and their coherence, can be found in the whole of the Revelation of the mystery of Christ."[11] In light of this fundamental "coherence" and "mutual connections," this chapter does not simply identify some interesting commonalities between the petitions of the Lord's Prayer and the virtues. Nor does it simply narrate an intellectual history of interpretation of the Lord's Prayer in order to situate the interpretation offered here. Rather it points toward the "beauty and spiritual power" in the illuminating convergences between the Sermon and virtue that "discloses a richness of meaning" in both and evidence the fundamental unity of the truth.[12] As this chapter proceeds with a more detailed analysis, it is hoped this broader significance is kept in mind.

---

[11] *Catechism of the Catholic Church*, 114 and 90, respectively. I am deeply indebted to Patrick Clark for pointing me to these passages.

[12] These phrases are credited, respectively, to Patrick Clark and David Elliot, to whom I also owe a debt of gratitude for helping me articulate the methodology of this project.

I. FOUR CONSISTENCIES (AND A LACUNA) IN THE HISTORY OF COMMENTARY ON THE LORD'S PRAYER

Commentaries on the Lord's Prayer began less than two centuries after Christ, and now number in hundreds if not thousands.[13] The purpose of this first section of the chapter is to identify some important commonalities of these commentaries, which will place the more constructive work of the second section in historical context. Far from an exhaustive survey of the history of interpretation of the Lord's Prayer, this section identifies four consistencies in the tradition of commentary: focusing on the prayer's petitions; numbering those petitions; grouping those petitions; and aligning the petitions with other groupings relevant to living the Christian life in order to better understand both the prayer and a life of discipleship. The section concludes by identifying a surprising omission in that history of interpretation of the Lord's Prayer.

A. COMMENTING ON THE PETITIONS

All commentaries on the Lord's Prayer address the different petitions in the prayer. That the prayer is making requests is more evident to English-speakers in the later petitions given the use of the imperative mood ("Give us ... ," "Forgive us ... ," "Lead us not ... ," and "Deliver us. ..."). But commentators have universally noted that the three clauses dealing with God's name, God's kingdom, and God's will are also petitions, a fact easily missed in English, since the imperative is not used and thus the grammatical construction indicating a request is less evident. Nonetheless, the nature of these first three as petitions is evident in attending carefully to their grammatical construction. The verbal mood of the first three petitions is not indicative, as might be assumed in the absence of the imperative. We are not *stating* that God's name is hallowed, His kingdom comes, and His will

---

[13] Nowhere have I found an attempt to number these commentaries. For evidence of the sheer number of commentaries on the Lord's Prayer, see Morton Bloomfield, *Incipits of Latin Works on the Virtues and Vices 1100 A.D.–1500 A.D.* (Cambridge, MA: Medieval Academy of America, 1979), which lists the opening lines of texts (known in 1979) simply from these four centuries. Though it does include some repetition, it lists over 1,200 incipits on the *Pater Noster*. There are well over a hundred works on the Lord's Prayer treated in some level of detail in the research of Kenneth W. Stevenson and Jean Carmignac, both of whose books proved invaluable for this chapter. See Stevenson, *The Lord's Prayer: A Text in Tradition* (Minneapolis, Fortress Press, 2004) and Carmignac, *Recherches sur le "Notre Père"* (Paris: Éditions Letouzey & Ané, 1969). Tertullian's commentary, written approximately 200–206, is widely regarded as the earliest such commentary (Stevenson, *The Lord's Prayer*, 30). For more on the Lord's Prayer in North Africa in the early Church, see Michael Joseph Brown's *The Lord's Prayer through North African Eyes* (New York: T & T Clark International, 2004).

is done. We are praying *that* it be the case, hence the use of the subjunctive in languages such as French, Latin, and even English. That the English is in the subjunctive is seen by the use of "be" in petitions one and three. This may be commonly assumed to be an archaic form of the verb form "is," akin to the continued use of "art" and "thou." But it is actually a necessary grammatical formulation, as the subjunctive of the verb "to be." Thus the first three clauses express the sense of petition through the use of the (in this case, jussive) subjunctive, while the last four employ the imperative. All of the verbs in Greek are aorist imperative, revealing that the first three petitions are indeed petitions.[14] The verb forms in the original Aramaic are obviously only speculation.[15] In sum, the Lord's Prayer consists of petitions, and commentators have universally examined the prayer as such.

B. NUMBERING THE PETITIONS

It is widely recognized that there are seven petitions in the Lord's Prayer. However, this observation is far from universal.[16] In the earliest Latin commentaries (Tertullian ca. 200 and Cyprian ca. 252[17]), in Greek commentaries in the East (from Origen's ca. 234[18] commentary onward) and in Protestant discussions of the Lord's Prayer (beginning with John Calvin[19]), the last two petitions are treated together as one, rendering a total of six petitions.[20] But in a long tradition beginning with Augustine, followed by hundreds of medieval commentaries, and continuing today particularly in Catholic circles, seven petitions are recognized in the Our Father.[21]

---

[14] For a helpful treatment of the grammar of the petitions, see Raymond E. Brown, "The Pater Noster as Eschatological Prayer," 217–53 in his *New Testament Essays* (Milwaukee, WI: Bruce Publishing Co., 1965). I am grateful to Barrett Turner for pointing out to me that the sixth petition, "lead us not into temptation," is actually in the negated aorist subjunctive, which has the same sense as the aorist imperative.

[15] For an example of such speculation, see Ernst Lohmeyer, *The Lord's Prayer* (London: Collins Publishing, 1965), 27–29.

[16] Stevenson's historical overview continually attends to the number of petitions identified by authors of commentaries. See his helpful summary, *The Lord's Prayer*, 222. See also Carmignac, *Recherches sur le "Notre Père,"* 312–19 for a specific discussion of this issue.

[17] For Cyprian's commentary, see *On the Lord's Prayer*, 65–93 in trans. Alistair Stewart-Sykes *Tertullian, Cyprian, Origen on the Lord's Prayer*. On its dating, see Stevenson, *The Lord's Prayer*, 32.

[18] See Origen's *On Prayer*, pp. 95–214 in trans. Alistair Stewart-Sykes *Tertullian, Cyprian, Origen on the Lord's Prayer*. On the dating see Stevenson, *The Lord's Prayer*, 35.

[19] See John Calvin, *Institutes of the Christian Religion* III.xx.35, 183–84 in trans. Henry Beveridge *Institutes of the Christian Religion* (Grand Rapids, MI: Eerdman's, 1981). Note that Luther maintains there are seven petitions; see Stevenson, *The Lord's Prayer*, 160.

[20] See also Hans Dieter Betz for a contemporary biblical scholar example of counting six petitions (*The Sermon on the Mount*, 405).

[21] For contemporary examples, see the *Catechism of the Catholic Church* 2803–2854 and Pinckaers, *Sources of Christian Ethics* 155–158. See also Servais Pinckaers, O.P. *Au Cœur*

The variance in the number of petitions is actually even more complicated than even this divergence suggests. Authors such as Tertullian and Cyprian saw what are called here the sixth and seventh petitions as distinct, even while treating them as one petition.[22] And Augustine, the apparent originator of the seven petitions tradition, seems to have equivocated on the number of petitions. For instance, in sermons thought to be written ca. 410–412, Augustine treats the sixth and seventh petitions together.[23] Catholics after the Reformation have generally maintained there are seven petitions, though Carmignac claims an increasing number of twentieth-century Catholics number the petitions as six.[24] There is a thorny Greek grammatical question at the root of this variance, concerning the conjunction ἀλλά.[25] Carmignac claims there is little hope of definitive resolution on grammatical grounds. But he rather directly claims that given the symbolism of the number seven and how scripturally based the Lord's Prayer is, it would be surprising for the Our Father to be divided into only six and not seven petitions.[26] Perhaps this is what led some authors who number six petitions to treat the prayer in seven parts by counting the opening invocation "Our Father who art in heaven."[27] Regardless, the point for the purposes of this essay is that there is a long and prominent tradition of numbering seven petitions in the Lord's Prayer. Indeed, the variance over the relationship between the last two petitions may further substantiate the interpretation offered here, for reasons explained below.

C. GROUPING THE PETITIONS

Commentators have consistently divided the petitions into subgroups. The oldest and perhaps most common subdivision is found in Tertullian and

---

de *L'Evangile: Notre Père* (Saint-Maur: Editions Parole et Silence, 1999), 39–40. See also Pope Benedict XVI, *Jesus of Nazareth* (New York: Doubleday, 2007), pp. 128–68. Finally, see Robert Guelich as an example of a contemporary biblical scholar who counts seven petitions (*Sermon on the Mount*, 311–312).

[22] See Tertullian, "On Prayer," VIII, 48 (Stewart-Sykes, Alistair, et al, *On the Lord's Prayer*, Crestwood, N.Y: St. Vladimir's Seminary Press, 2004); Cyprian, "On the Lord's Prayer," 84–85 (Stewart-Sykes, Alistair, et al, *On the Lord's Prayer*, Crestwood, N.Y: St. Vladimir's Seminary Press, 2004). See Carmignac, *Recherches sur le "Notre Père,"* 312 for how others authors treat the sixth and seventh petitions.

[23] See Augustine, Sermon 57.10 56.18–19 These are found at 114 and 105, respectively, in. Edmund Hill, O.P., trans., *Sermons III (51–94)* (New York: New City Press, 1991).

[24] Carmignac, *Recherches sur le "Notre Père,"* 314. He also notes one Catholic from 1572, Jansénius, who counts six petitions.

[25] See Betz, *The Sermon on the Mount,* 411–12 for an overview of this issue. He counts six petitions despite recognizing on the basis of New Testament and Jewish parallels that "vs 13b could and actually did exist traditionally as a separate petition" (412).

[26] Carmignac, *Recherches sur le "Notre Père,"* 315.

[27] For an example of treating the prayer in seven parts, but with the invocation and seven petitions, see Tertullian "On Prayer," 2–8.

Augustine, who distinguished the first three petitions from the remaining ones.[28] Both of these Latin Fathers saw the first three petitions as concerning heavenly or eternal things and the remaining petitions as concerning earthly or temporal things. Both note the division is not hard and fast, as if the two groups had nothing to do with each other. Yet authors such as these, and later ones such as Bonaventure,[29] notice that the first three directly concern God ("Thy name," "Thy kingdom," Thy will"), while the later petitions concern worldly matters (bread, trespasses, temptation, evil).[30] Once again, it should be noted that this sub-grouping is not univocal. For instance, Luther understands the first three petitions as spiritual, the fourth as material, and the last three as concerned with deliverance form evil.[31] Interestingly enough, although Aquinas consistently affirms Augustine's 3 – 4 eternal/temporal grouping, he never uses it as his own primary principle of grouping the petitions in the various groupings he employs throughout his works.[32] Nonetheless, once again the basic point stands that sub-groupings are common, and a division between the first three and the remaining petitions has extensive precedent.[33]

D. ALIGNING THE PETITIONS WITH OTHER GROUPINGS

Finally, following in a tradition inaugurated by Augustine, many commentators on the Lord's Prayer have aligned the different petitions with some other organizing structure. Note this claim may be related to, but is distinct

---

[28] See Tertullian, "On Prayer," 6: "But how gracefully did divine wisdom draw up the order of the prayer that, after heavenly petitions on the name of God, the will of God, and the Kingdom of God, it should also provide a place for earthly needs" (46). See Augustine, *The Enchiridion on Faith, Hope, and Love* (Washington, DC: Regnery Gateway, 1961), cxv (132–33): "[I]n the evangelist Matthew the Lord's Prayer seems to embrace seven petitions, three of which ask for eternal blessings and the four remaining for temporal").

[29] See Bonaventura, *Expositio Super Regulam Fratrum Minorum* III.3 (Quarrachi VIII.407): "*Cum autem subdit: Sanctificetur and so on, oratio subiungitur, quae in septem petitionibus continetur, quarum tres primae pertinent directe ad Dei honorem, quatuor sequentes ad petentium utilitatem.*"

[30] This division is also evident in the number of contemporary commentators who distinguish (in both Matthew's and Luke's petitions) between the "you" or "thou" petitions on the one hand and the "we" petitions on the other. See Raymond Brown, "The Pater Noster as Eschatological Prayer," 238. See also Joachim Jeremais, *The Prayers of Jesus* Naperville, IL: Alec R. Allenson, Inc.: 1967), 98–104; Davies and Allison, *The Gospel According to Saint Matthew*, 594; Luz, *Matthew 1–7*, 369; Betz, *The Sermon on the Mount*, 375–76.

[31] See Martin Luther, *The Sermon on the Mount*, 160. There is precedent of this claim in Anselm of Laon; see Stevenson, *The Lord's Prayer*, 124.

[32] See below for an in-depth discussion of Aquinas's different groupings of the petitions throughout his corpus.

[33] For another contemporary example of this, see Leonardo Boff, *The Lord's Prayer: Prayer of Integral Liberation* (Maryknoll, NY: Orbis Books, 1983).

from, the previous claim about division into subgroups. Although many have sub-divided the total number of petitions, some have aligned them with another (generally seven-fold) grouping. The most famous example is Augustine's alignment of the petitions with the seven gifts of the Holy Spirit as well as the beatitudes.[34] Carmignac[35] and Stevenson offer examples of commentators who have aligned the petitions with one or even more of the following: the gifts of the Spirit, the beatitudes, the seven deadly sins [the petitions would be antidotes to those], orders of Church ministry, Jesus's seven last words from the cross, stages in spiritual growth, and even the seven days of the week.[36] It should be noted that there are often changes in the orderings of groupings, as when Amalar of Metz in the early ninth century initiated a tradition of inverting Augustine's alignment of petitions and gifts of the Holy Spirit, an ordering continued with authors such as Anselm of Laon and Hugh of Amiens.[37] In sum, there is ample precedent in the tradition for aligning the petitions with other groupings important to life in the Spirit.

E. A LACUNA: ALIGNING THE PETITIONS WITH THE THEOLOGICAL AND CARDINAL VIRTUES

Of particular interest in this chapter are alignments of the petitions with the seven virtues of the Christian life. In his list of different groupings historically aligned with the petitions, Carmignac mentions virtues, but unlike each of the other alignments listed, he offers no substantiating footnote.[38] Stevenson mentions five commentators from the twelfth and thirteenth centuries who parallel the seven petitions of the Lord's Prayer with virtues. The *Allegories on the New Testament* attributed to Hugh of St. Victor (likely composed by his colleague Richard of St. Victor) treats several different virtues in its discussion of the petitions, but it offers no specific alignment.[39] The

---

[34] Augustine, *On the Lord's Sermon on the Mount*, I.4, 11–12.

[35] See Carmignac, *Recherches sur le "Notre Père,"* 387.

[36] For an example of several of these at once, consider not only Augustine on gifts and beatitudes but Hugh of Amiens on gifts, beatitudes, and orders of Church ministry. See Stevenson, *The Lord's Prayer*, 126.

[37] See Stevenson, *The Lord's Prayer*, 124–36. This inversion (or, more accurately, this undoing of Augustine's inversion of the order of gifts in Isaiah 11) is not adopted by all after Amalar, as seen in the case of Thomas Aquinas who follows Augustine's ordering.

[38] Carmignac, *Recherches sur le "Notre Père,"* 387. When he mentions seven virtues, he even specifies "the theological and cardinal virtues," which mirrors the interpretation offered in the second section here. But again, he cites no historical example of this.

[39] Stevenson mentions this text at 123. The text, *Allegoriae Novum Testamentum - Liber Secundus*, is found at PL 175:763–89. For an example of the more fluid associations of virtues and petitions, see how the opening invocation "Our Father" is aligned with benevolence and reverence (PL 175:768).

remaining four scholastics do indeed align the seven petitions with seven virtues. But in each case, the virtues are actually the beatitudes, or rather, the qualities of people described in the first half of each beatitude: poverty of spirit (in other words, humility), meekness, mourning, yearning for justice, mercy, cleanness of heart, and peacefulness. In none of these cases where an author intends to align the seven petitions with the seven virtues are the virtues the three theological and four cardinal virtues.[40]

A text that comes close to aligning the seven petitions of the Our Father with the theological and cardinal virtues is the contemporary *Catechism of the Catholic Church* itself, which simply mentions faith, hope, and love with regard to the first three petitions but never explicitly aligns them with particular petitions or mentions the cardinal virtues.[41] There is also, however, a text that was suggested to me that explicitly aligns the seven petitions with the three theological and four cardinal virtues: J-F Bonnefoy's *Le saint-esprit et ses dons selon saint Bonaventure*, which aligns the petitions and virtues (along with gifts and capital sins, among others) in a manner reflective of St. Bonaventure's thought.[42] However, as is clear from Bonnefoy's chart, Bonaventure never offers this alignment himself; Bonnefoy presents his own constructive alignment as compatible with Bonaventure's thought.[43] Furthermore, the alignment

---

[40] See Bonaventure (d. 1274), *Expositio Orationis Dominicae* 5 (Quaracchi VII.653): "*Septem virtutes sunt contra septem vitia, videlicet paupertas spiritus contra superbiam sive inanem gloriam, mansuetudo contra iram, luctus contra invidiam, sitis iustitiae contra acediam, misericordia, contra avaritiam, munditia cordis contra gulam, denique pax contra luxuriam.*" See William Durandus (d. 1296), *Rationale Divinorum Officiorum* IV.xlvii.10: (Corpus Christianorum Continuatio Mediaeualis 140: 504–579, at 508): "*Septem vero virtutes sunt hee: paupertas spiritus, mansuetudo, luctus, esuries iustitie, misericordia, munditia cordis et pax.*" For dating see Stevenson, *The Lord's Prayer*, 123–38. See Gunther the Cistercian (d. 1220), *De Oratione, Jejunio, et Eleemosyna* PL 212:171–205 at 172, where he does not list the seven all together but notes their connection to the beatitudes: "*Septem etiam dona Spiritus sancti quae prophetia enumerat, et septem virtutes quae in Evangelio memorantur, et septem beatitudines quae ipsis virtutibus applicantur.*" (References to each of the seven are given during successive treatments of each petition.) See Stephen of Auten (d. 1189), *Tractatus de Sacramento Altaris* PL 172:1303–1308, at 1304: "*Septem sunt virtutes: humilitas, pietas, compunctio, justitia, misericordia, munditia, pax sive tranquillitas.*"

[41] See *Catechism of the Catholic Church*, 2806. In fact, in 2803 and 2805 different bases of alignment are suggested.

[42] I am grateful to Gregory LaNave for pointing this text out to me. This text references two more texts, which seem by their title to do something of the sort done by Bonnefoy. They are Le P. Louis-Th., *Les opérations du Saint-Esprit dans les âmes*, 1896, and Mgr. Amédée Cure, *L'Oraison dominicale. Ses rapports avec les sept dons du Saint-Esprit, les sept péchés capitaux, les vertus théologales et cardinales et les béatitudes*, IV vols., 1895–1906. I was unable to obtain either text.

[43] In fact, Bonnefoy seems to do with Bonaventure something of the sort mentioned below with Aquinas. Namely, Bonnefoy seems to constructively suggest a Bonaventurian alignment of petitions and virtues based on texts where he aligns each of those grouping with a third group.

between petitions and virtues offered by Bonnefoy is different from that offered here.[44] In conclusion, the number of occasions in the commentary tradition where specific virtues are mentioned in the context of the petitions of the Lord's Prayer is miniscule, especially considering the breadth of that tradition of commentary. On the basis of this research, I cautiously conclude that that there is no prominent example in the tradition of aligning the seven petitions with seven virtues in the manner outlined here.

This is rather surprising. It is not only surprising due to the massive amount of commentary on the Lord's Prayer and various ways authors have aligned the petitions with other groupings. It is also particularly surprising that Thomas Aquinas does not adopt such an alignment, given that Aquinas organizes his entire treatise on specific moral theology according to the seven virtues. Indeed, within that work Aquinas consistently aligns virtues with the gifts of the Holy Spirit and with the beatitudes. In that same work, he acknowledges and affirms Augustine's alignment of the petitions on the one hand, and the gifts and beatitudes on the other.[45] The transitive property would seem to dictate that Aquinas would make the connection between the seven virtues and the petitions. But nowhere in his work does he do this.[46] The same may be said of contemporary Thomists, including Servais Pinckaers, O.P. who wrote extensively on Aquinas's alignments and who even wrote a book on the Our Father.[47]

There is no obvious explanation for why Aquinas and contemporary disciples, such as Fr. Pinckaers, have not aligned the petitions with the virtues. One possibility is that the use of the transitive property to align

---

[44] Bonnefoy's alignment of the virtues and petitions, in order of the petitions, is: temperance, justice, prudence, fortitude, hope, faith, and charity. As will be seen below, this is different from the alignment offered here.

[45] See Thomas Aquinas, *Summa Theologiae* I–II 83, 9.

[46] The closest Aquinas comes to aligning the virtues with the petitions is in his *Commentary on the Gospel of Matthew*, where he mentions the three theological virtues but all in conjunction with the salutary "Our Father in heaven" rather than any particular petitions. See *Commentary on the Gospel of Matthew*, 584.

[47] Pinckaers writes extensively on the virtues, gifts, beatitudes, and petitions. But like the Angelic Doctor, he connects the petitions with the gifts and beatitudes, and virtues with the gifts of beatitudes, but never the virtues with the petitions. See *Sources of Christian Ethics*, 155–58. On 158, Pinckaers claims that "The order of the petitions follows the structure of the *Prima Secundae*: the relation between God's ultimate end and all that is ordered thereto. ... The Lord's Prayer expresses the desire that impels us toward the divine beatitude as our ultimate end. It dominates our entire moral life." Here Fr. Pinckaers affirms that the Lord's Prayer "dominates our entire moral life" and is thus unsurprisingly reflected in the structure of the *Prima Secundae*. Yet he never aligns sections of the latter with petitions of the former. While certainly not denying his claim that the Lord's Prayer orders all our desires in a way reminiscent of the *Prima Secundae*, the parallel of the seven petitions with the seven virtues used to structure the *Secunda Secundae* seems even more obvious, though it is surprisingly unmentioned by Fr. Pinckaers, even in his *Au Coeur de L'Evangile: Notre Père*, cited above.

virtues and petitions on the basis of how Aquinas himself aligned the gifts with each of these groups simply does not work. First, Aquinas assigns two gifts to the virtue faith and none to the virtue temperance, thus preventing a neat alignment. Second, while both of his alignments between the petitions and gifts/beatitudes on the one hand,[48] and between the virtues and gifts/beatitudes on the other, seem to "work" in terms of the content of each of the groups aligned, connecting the petitions and virtues using the transitive property results in an alignment in which the meaning of the virtue aligned with each petition does not appear reflective of the content of that petition.[49] Since presumably Aquinas would respect the order of the petitions as given in the Lord's Prayer given their source, an alignment of the petitions to the virtues "through" the gifts, ordered by the petitions, would look like this:

Hallowed be thy name	Fear of the Lord	Hope
Thy Kingdom come	Piety	Justice
Thy will be done	Knowledge	Faith
Give us this day . . .	Fortitude	Fortitude
Forgive us our trespasses . . .	Counsel	Prudence
Lead us not into temptation	Understanding	Faith
Deliver us from evil	Wisdom	Charity

In this chart, the virtues are aligned to the petitions "through" the gifts, as Aquinas in different places aligns each grouping of seven to the gifts.[50] Besides the omission of temperance (and double inclusion of faith), the problem with this schema is that the meaning of each virtue is not at all obviously reflective of the meaning of the petition to which it corresponds above. Furthermore, Aquinas at times indicates the importance of the order of theological and cardinal virtues, an ordering that is wrecked in the above alignment.[51] Therefore, the above alignment is *not* the alignment endorsed here.

To conclude this first section of the chapter, there is an extensive history of commentary on the Lord's Prayer. In this tradition, the prayer is always

[48] Here Thomas Aquinas follows Augustine directly, without the inversion of order that had become common in the twelfth century. See *Summa Theologiae* II–II 83, 9 ad. 3.

[49] The transitive property states that "if A = B and B = C then A = C." One reason using this property on the petitions, gifts, and virtue may not "work" is that the relationships between each pair are not relationships of equality, but rather ones of correspondence in some ways. So it is quite possible that the ways different pairs correspond will not be reflected in new pairings set up by the transitive property.

[50] It is just such an alignment of two groupings "through" another that Bonnefoy may be doing with Bonaventure's work. Though note he arrives at a different alignment, with the petitions corresponding to temperance, justice, prudence, fortitude, hope, faith, and charity, respectively (*Le saint-esprit et ses dons selon saint Bonaventure*, 220–21).

[51] For the significance of the order of the theological virtues, see Thomas Aquinas, *Summa Theologiae* I–II 62, 4. For the cardinal virtues, see *Summa Theologiae* I–II 61, 2–4. Discrepancies in Aquinas's work as to the order of the cardinal virtues are treated below.

addressed according to its petitions, which commonly (though not uni-vocally) number seven. The petitions are also commonly sub-divided, and there is strong precedent for grouping them into the first three and latter four. Furthermore, alignment of seven petitions with another group of seven is also common, though it has been done in many different ways. Finally, despite the commonalities in the tradition noted here, there is a surprising lacuna as to aligning the seven petitions to the three theological and four cardinal virtues, an omission that is particularly surprising in the Thomistic tradition. These conclusions serve to contextualize the second section, and more constructive contribution, of the chapter. With these conclusions in mind, it should be clear in what ways the claims below are a natural continu-ation of a long tradition, and in what ways they are surprisingly without precedent.

II. THE LORD'S PRAYER AND THE VIRTUES: AN ILLUMINATING CONVERGENCE

The thesis of this chapter is that the seven petitions of the Lord's Prayer can be aligned with the seven foundational virtues of the Christian life, namely, the three theological and four cardinal virtues. This second section proceeds in two parts. First, how can the seven petitions of the Lord's Prayer be aligned with these seven virtues in such a way that the alignment helps shed light on both the virtues and petitions? Second, how does this alignment reveal that the Lord's Prayer both addresses and helps answer questions about the moral life from the perspective of virtue ethics?

A. SEVEN PETITIONS AND SEVEN VIRTUES

The goal of this part is to examine each of the petitions individually and explore how the particular petition reflects and further illuminates one of the seven main virtues of the Christian tradition. Again, the claim here is neither that each petition offers an exhaustive understanding of one of the virtues, nor that each petition only makes sense in reference to its corresponding virtue. The more modest claim here is that in most cases there is a strikingly clear correspondence between each petition and a virtue and that we can better understand both the prayer and the virtues by looking at them in relation to each other.[52] Given the genre of this book, what follows is neither

---

[52] Aquinas offers some reflection of how aligning two groups can be helpfully illuminative but should not be taken as a reduction of one such entity to the other, or as a claim that one of the entities aligned or cannot also be somehow reflected in other members of the group with which they are aligned. See his *Commentary on the Sentences* in *Scriptum super Sententiis Magistri Petri Lombardi*, vol. 3, ed. Maria Fabianus Moos (Paris: Lethiel-leux, 1929–1947), III d. 34, q. 1, a. 6: "*Et sic per proprietatem non potest fieri reductio*

an extended spiritual reflection on each petition, nor even a thorough historical analysis of how each petition has been commented on in ways commensurate with the interpretation offered here. Rather, the task here is briefly to state why each petition is aligned with the virtue it is, and then to offer a couple of examples of how that interpretation reflects claims made by commentators in the tradition (even though these latter do not explicitly align the petitions with virtues).

A brief word is in order on method since this chapter relies on authoritative thinkers in the tradition of commentary on the Lord's Prayer. The method adopted here is similar to that used in Chapter 1 with regard to the beatitudes but with an important difference. The difference is that the thought of Thomas Aquinas will be more central here than in Chapter 1. I rely most on his thought, and on the thought of those who precede him and whom he explicitly references in his work.[53] Beyond the practical reason for this limitation of sources given the enormous amount of material on the Lord's Prayer, there is also a substantive one. Thomas Aquinas offers his most extensive treatment of morality in the form of analysis of the seven virtues, three theological and four cardinal. Though he does not align the petitions with the seven virtues in the manner offered here, the constructive proposal offered here is particularly suitable to Aquinas's thought given his reliance on those virtues and his (Augustine-inspired) willingness to align

---

singulorum donorum ad singulas petitiones; quia ea quae in diversis petitionibus postulantur possunt pertinere ad unum donum et e converso; sed per appropriationem quandam, inquantum singulae petitiones habent aliquam similitudinem cum singulis donis, sicut et de beatitudinibus dictum est."

[53] Thomas Aquinas examines the Lord's Prayer extensively in five texts in his *corpus*. They are given here in chronological order, according to Jean-Pierre Torrell, O.P., *Saint Thomas Aquinas, Vol 1: the Person and His Work* (Washington, DC: The Catholic University of America Press, 1996), 332–58. (Note there will be closer attention to dating, with years provided, below.) *Commentary on the Sentences* III d. 34, q. 1, a. 6; *Commentary on the Gospel of Matthew* 583–602; *Summa Theologiae* II–II 83, 9; *Homilies on the Lord's Prayer*; *Compendium of Theology, Book II* (New York: Oxford University Press, 2009). Note that the *Compendium of Theology* remains unfinished, as Aquinas died before completing it. It is structured in three sections, each corresponding to a theological virtue, akin to Augustine's *Enchiridion*. Reminiscent of this latter book, Aquinas's book two, on hope, treats that topic through an examination of the Lord's Prayer. Aquinas died after finishing only his discussions of the first two petitions. Note there is no mention in this text of any alignment of the seven petitions with the seven virtues, even though as seen below what we have of his commentary seems to warrant such alignment. As for Aquinas's Patristic sources on the Lord's Prayer, the works explicitly mentioned in the above Thomistic texts and referenced here are: Augustine's *On the Sermon on the Mount*; Augustine's *Enchiridion*; Augustine's *Letter 130* (to Proba); Gregory of Nyssa's *On the Lord's Prayer*; Cyprian's *On the Lord's Prayer*; John Chrysostom's *Homilies on Matthew*; and Jerome's *Commentary on Matthew*. In his *Catena Aurea* on Mt 6:9–13, the sources Aquinas cites that are used here (and not already listed) are: Augustine's *On the Gift of Perseverance* and Cassian's *Collections*. (Critical edition citations to Aquinas's source texts are given as they are referenced.)

different sets within the Christian tradition. That said, since as with Chapter 1 I claim the argument here is consonant with traditional interpretations of the petitions even if they do not explicitly offer this alignment, on occasion other authors are referenced, particularly those after Aquinas, to corroborate the claims of this part.[54]

> Our Father, who art in heaven, hallowed be thy name. (FAITH)
> Thy Kingdom come, (HOPE)
> Thy will be done, on earth as it is in heaven. (LOVE)
>
> Give us this day our daily bread, (PRUDENCE)
> And forgive us our trespasses, as we forgive those who trespass against us. (JUSTICE)
> Lead us not into temptation, (TEMPERANCE)
> But deliver us from evil. (FORTITUDE)

1. "HALLOWED BE THY NAME": FAITH After the opening invocation "Our Father who art in heaven," the first petition reads "hallowed be thy name." God's name reveals who God is,[55] or as Aquinas says, a reference to "God in Himself."[56] What is being asked for here? Commentators consistently claim it is not *that* God's name be holy, since this is clearly already the case. It is that what is holy in itself be recognized as such *by us*.[57] This first

---

[54] Reminiscent of Chapter 1, I appeal for contemporary Catholic thought to the work of Fr. Servais Pinckaers, O.P. cited above and Pope Benedict XVI's treatment of the Our Father in his *Jesus of Nazareth*, 128–68. I also on occasion reference Reformation thinkers. References to contemporary biblical scholarship found throughout this book and even earlier in this chapter continue. I have also found particularly helpful the Patristic commentaries of Origen and Tertullian available in English in the Stewart-Sykes translation cited above. Though Thomas Aquinas serves as an anchor for this analysis, there are a significant number of other sources employed.

[55] The fact that God's name is a representation of God's identity is a point made consistently in the tradition of commentary (though surprisingly not emphasized by Thomas Aquinas). For an extensive treatment of this point, see Origen, *On Prayer*, 24. He offers several Old Testament examples of where God's "name" stands for the reality of who God is. Tertullian offers several Johannine examples of this point in *On Prayer*, 3, to which could be added the end of Paul's Christological hymn at Phil 2:10. For contemporary examples of this point see Pope Benedict XVI, *Jesus of Nazareth*, 142–144 and Guelich, *The Sermon on the Mount*, 310.

[56] See Thomas Aquinas *Summa Theologiae* II–II 83, 9: "*Deum in seipso*." Note the next word in this quote is *diligimus*. Aquinas treats this petition as an example of *loving* God in Himself, which is different from the point made here about the priority of faith. Yet Thomas Aquinas is well aware of the ways faith is a prerequisite of love. See I–II 62, 4, as well as Michael Sherwin, O.P.'s *By Knowledge and by Love* (Washington, DC: The Catholic University of America Press, 2005), esp. 152–63. He is also insistent that one's final end is best possessed primarily through an act of the speculative intellect, which faith is in its essence (I–II 3, 5; II–II 4, 2 ad. 3). Indeed, in his *Explanation of the Lord's Prayer*, in *The Catechetical Instructions of St. Thomas Aquinas* (New York: Jospeh Wagner, Inc., 1939) he mentions the virtue of faith in his treatment of the invocation: "*God dwells in the devout through faith.*"

[57] Thomas Aquinas, *Commentary on the Gospel of Matthew*, 585: "that is the name that is always holy, should be held holy among men ... for by this God's glory does not

petition is asking that who God is, as represented by God's name, be "hallowed," or reverenced by people. This is exactly what the virtue of faith enables people to do. Aquinas recognizes that faith enables people to know who God is in a manner inaccessible without God's gift of grace.[58] Far from simple knowledge of who God is, the virtue of faith is a reverential knowledge, involving not only an intellectual grasp of what is true about God (though it is primarily this) but also a loving desire of that "object" as good.[59] The knowledge of the virtue of faith is thus a "hallowing," as opposed to the knowledge of the demons who "believe and yet shudder" (James 2:19).[60] Furthermore, as the first word of the Lord's Prayer reminds us, the virtue of faith is not simply an individual but rather a communal, an ecclesial,

---

increase but our recognition of it." See also his *Explanation of the Lord's Prayer*, petition 1 where the claim is made twice. This point is not only ubiquitous throughout the history of commentary, but it is also recognized by Aquinas as made by many different people throughout his work. In his *Commentary on Matthew*, he attributes it to both Cyprian and to John Chrysostom. See Chrysostom's *Homilies on Matthew* XIX.7, 139–140 in Jaroslav Pelikan's *The Preaching of Chrysostom* (Philadelphia, PA: Fortress Press, 1967). See also Cyprian's *On the Lord's Prayer* 12 (73). In Augustine's *De dono perseverentiae* 4 (PL 45:996–997), cited in the *Catena Aura*, the same claim is found. See also two works referenced by Aquinas concerning the Lord's Prayer, though not on this particular point: Augustine's *On the Lord's Sermon on the Mount* II.5.19 and Gregory of Nyssa *On the Lord's Prayer* 2, p. 49 in Hilda Graef (trans.) *St. Gregory of Nyssa: The Lord's Prayer and The Beatitudes*, Ancient Christian Writers No. 18 (Westminister, MD: The Newman Press, 1954). For treatment of this question in contemporary biblical scholarship, see Betz, *The Sermon on the Mount*, 389. He claims it is inconclusive as to who is the "agent" of the hallowing, though he also holds the strange view that the firth three petitions are reminders of God's need" (378–79). Guelich takes a decisive position as to this being a petition asking for we humans to hallow God's name (*The Sermon on the Mount*, 378–80). Even more decisive is Luz, who claims that such an interpretation of the petition seeking that *we* hallow God's name is substantiated by comparison to Jewish parallels (378–80).

[58] In Thomas Aquinas's unfinished *Compendium of Theology*, the entire treatment of the first petition concerns knowledge of God, which is very imperfectly attained through reason and which God has revealed through salvation history, most perfectly through Christ. Given his focus here on humanity's knowledge of God, and even his distinction between reason and what is revealed, it is astounding that the word "faith" never appears in the chapter (8) on the first petition. This virtue seems most relevant to Aquinas's point in this chapter. Perhaps he refrains from mentioning faith to honor the overall structure of his work which, reminiscent of Augustine's *Enchiridion*, is organized by the three theological virtues with faith (and a treatment of the Creed) governing the first of the three parts.

[59] See Thomas Aquinas, *Summa Theologiae* II–II 2, 1; 4, 1–4. For God as the "object" of the theological virtues, including faith, see I–II 62, 1 and 2. For contemporary biblical scholarship recognition of how this hallowing is reverential knowledge, see Guelich, *The Sermon on the Mount* for how "honor, glory awe, and obedience belong inherently to God" (289) and thus this petition entails "the petitioner's desire and commitment as one of his own to live toward that end" (310).

[60] See Thomas Aquinas, *Summa Theologiae* II–II 5, 2 for Aquinas's treatment of this passage in the context of the theological virtue faith.

endeavor.[61] The first petition is thus aptly understood as a prayer for the virtue of faith, or an increase in faith, in us.[62]

2. "THY KINGDOM COME": HOPE The second petition reads, "thy kingdom come." The kingdom of heaven, according to Thomas Aquinas, describes that state of affairs where all is happening according to God's will.[63] It is a state of perfect justice,[64] or as Chrysostom notes, the redemption for which all creation groans (Rom 8:22–23).[65] In the second petition, one prays that this come to pass.

What does this have to do with hope? Reminiscent of the previous petition, commentators consistently observe that with these words the petitioner is not simply praying *that* God reign (since this is clearly already the case), or even that the fullness of God's reign arrive. For this reign is not simply a state of affairs in which people ("hopefully") one day find themselves. It is a state of affairs in which people participate.[66] Thomas Aquinas calls the kingdom of heaven "the happiness of the saints."[67] Thus the prayer is that God's kingdom come *in us*.[68] The person with the virtue of hope,

---

[61] Aquinas makes this point in his *Compendium of Theology* II.5. There he cites Cyprian, *On the Lord's Prayer* 8 (CCSL 3A:93–94) and John Chrysostom as making the same point. His citation of Chrysostom is actually the *Opus Imperfectum* (XIV) of Pseudo-Chrysostom, though the same point is made in John Chrysostom's *Homilies on Matthew* XIX.6. See also *Commentary on the Gospel of Matthew*, 584, where Aquinas claims we say "our" Father not only to distinguish our sonship (by adoption) with that of Jesus, but also due to the communal or ecclesial nature of the prayer.

[62] A prayer for faith is particularly fitting given the context in Mt 6. As seen in Chapter 4, the importance of faith for temporal activities is addressed in contrast to both those of no faith (the pagans) and those of little faith. Both 6:1–18 and 6:19–34 concern both people of no faith ("gentiles") and those who do not live their faith well ("hypocrites" as well as those of "little faith").

[63] See *Explanation of the Lord's Prayer*, petition 2: "for a kingdom ("regnum") is nothing other than a government ("regimen"). That will be the best government where nothing is found contrary to the will of the governor." Contemporary biblical scholar Guelich describes the kingdom in a comparable way, as "the final consummation when God's sovereign rule will be established over all" (310).

[64] See *Explanation of the Lord's Prayer*, petition 2: "This kingdom is greatly to be desired for three reasons. (1) It is to be greatly desired because of the perfect justice that obtains there."

[65] See John Chrysostom, *Homilies on Matthew* XIX.7.

[66] See *Explanation of the Lord's Prayer*, petition 2: "Hence, when we pray, 'Thy kingdom come,' we pray that we might participate in the heavenly kingdom and in the glory of paradise."

[67] See *Compendium of Theology* II.9: "*Therefore, we also call the blessedness of the saints the kingdom of heaven*" (228). This chapter of Aquinas's *Compendium* is an oft-overlooked jewel on ultimate happiness, and perfect companion to I-II 1–5. See also Augustine *On the Lord's Sermon on the Mount* II.6.20: "Then will the happy life be made altogether complete in the saints for eternity" (trans mine; see CCSL 35:110: "*Deinde beata uita omni ex parte perficietur in sanctis in aeternum*").

[68] See Cyprian *On the Lord's Prayer* 13: "Just as we desire that his name be hallowed among us, we ask that the Kingdom of God be known to us." See also Augustine, *On the Lord's*

equipped with the knowledge of faith, longs to possess that ultimate happiness that is God's kingdom. This person yearns to participate in the kingdom primarily by one day entering into it, but also by longing for it virtuously in this life, before it is fully possessed.[69] That virtuous longing for God as one's ultimate happiness – and the only possible way we achieve that happiness – is hope.[70] Aquinas comes closest to naming it as hope when he claims that the second petition is a willingness to enjoy God's glory.[71]

3. "THY WILL BE DONE": LOVE The final petition of the group that represent the three theological virtues is "thy will be done, on earth as it is in heaven." What is asked for here is rather straightforward: that God's will be done on earth just as it is in heaven. What is God's will? Commentators consistently claim it is God's will that all are saved, often citing 1 Tim 2:4.[72]

> *Sermon on the Mount* II.6.20, where he claims: "As if God were not even now reigning on earth and has not been doing so since the world was created! 'Come,' then, must be taken to mean 'may it be manifest to men.'" Aquinas says of this petition "may the reign of sin be destroyed and you, Lord, reign over us; for when we serve justice then God reigns" (*Commentary on the Gospel of Matthew*, 586). Despite ascribing clear human agency to "hallowing" and "will be done" of petitions one and three, neither Luz nor Guelich addresses agency on the part of humans for petition two.

[69] Thomas Aquinas claims that the final good of ultimate happiness can be possessed, albeit imperfectly, even in this life through hope. See *Summa Theologiae* I–II 5, 3 ad. 1 (where he cites Rom 8:24, "by hope we are saved") and 11, 4 ad. 1 and 2.

[70] For more from Thomas Aquinas on hope, and in particular its twofold object, see *Summa Theologiae* II–II 17, esp. 17, 4. See also II–II 19, 1 and his *Disputed Question on Hope*, art. 1.

[71] See Thomas Aquinas, *Summa Theologiae* II–II 83, 9: "Now our end is God towards Whom our affections tend in two ways: first, by our willing the glory of God, secondly, by willing to enjoy His glory. The first belongs to the love whereby we love God in Himself, while the second belongs to the love whereby we love ourselves in God. Wherefore the first petition is expressed thus: 'Hallowed be Thy name,' and the second thus: 'Thy kingdom come.'" Despite his aligning the first two petitions with different ways of loving God (which correspond to *amor amicitiae* and *amor concupiscientiae*; see I–II 26, 4). Aquinas's language here on petition two strongly evokes his thought on hope. Reminiscent of his distinction between charity and hope (I–II 62, 4; II–II 17, 6), he claims in II–II 83, 9 that the second petition pertains to love not of God simply, but "to the love whereby we love ourselves in God.

In one sense it is unsurprising Aquinas's language here is so evocative of hope. After all, he follows Augustine's *Enchiridion* in describing the Lord's Prayer as exemplary of the virtue hope when Aquinas writes his own "enchiridion," the *Compendium of Theology*, which he, too, organizes by the three theological virtues and in which he examines the Lord's Prayer under hope. Granted, he looks at all the petitions of the Lord's Prayer in the book on hope. But the treatment of the second petition, which is precisely where Thomas Aquinas's death ended work on this treatise, is particularly apt for a discussion of hope as it is a depiction of the ultimate happiness for which people long. It is striking that Thomas Aquinas never calls attention to a special affinity between the second petition and the virtue hope in either his *Summa Theologiae* or the *Compendium of Theology*.

[72] See *Explanation of the Lord's Prayer*, petition 3: "The Lord, therefore, wills that men have eternal life." Interestingly enough, Aquinas does not cite 1 Tim 2:4, but rather Jn 6:10.

Once again, this is not something that simply happens to us, but something in which we participate. As Cyprian says quite clearly

> "Let your will be done in heaven and on earth." We say this not so that God might do what he wishes, but that we should be able to do what God wishes. For who stands in the way of God to prevent him from performing his will?[73]

Therefore, the real question is how is God's will fulfilled in us? Here Augustine is very clear. "Thus 'they will be done' is rightly understood as 'let obedience be given to your precepts.' . . . For the will of God is being done when His precepts are being obeyed."[74] From here it is but a small step to see how the third petition represents the virtue of charity. Particularly in the Johannine tradition, charity is identified with keeping God's commandments.

> Whoever has my commandments and observes them is the one who loves me
>
> (Jn 14:21).

> If you keep my commandments, you will remain in my love
>
> (Jn 15:10; cf. 1 Jn 3:24).

> In this way we know that we love the children of God when we love God and obey his commandments. For the love of God is this, that we keep his commandments. And his commandments are not burdensome
>
> (1 Jn 5:2–3).

In this petition we are asking God to infuse us with charity so that we may live the commandments, which Christ Himself repeatedly summarizes as *agape* or *caritas* (Mt 22:34–40; Mk 12:28–34; Lk 10:25–28). This love of God and our neighbor in God is precisely what the infused theological virtue of charity enables us to do.[75]

(Yet see *Commentary on the Gospel of Matthew*, 586, cited below.) Cassian, whose work on the Lord's Prayer Aquinas cites in his *Catena Aurea*, cites 1 Tim 2:4 in the context of the third petition and claims God wills that all are saved. See *Conferences* ix.20 (CSEL 13:268–69). See also Gregory of Nyssa's *The Lord's Prayer*, 59.

[73] Cyprian, *On the Lord's Prayer* 14 (75). See also Aquinas's *Commentary on the Gospel of Matthew*, 586: "And note that he does not say your will be done as: may God do our will, but rather: may his will be fulfilled through us which 'wills all men to be saved' (1 Tim 2:4; 1 Thess 4:3)." One again contemporary biblical scholarship corroborates the claim here that (at least part of) what is petitioned here is that we humans are made able to do God's will. See Luz, *Matthew 1–7*, 380 and even Betz, *The Sermon on the Mount*, 392. Both of these scholars appeal to Jesus's words in Mt 26:42 about the Father's will being done to say that clearly what is sought is help for us to go God's will.

[74] Augustine, *On the Lord's Sermon on the Mount* II.6.21. See also *Explanation of the Lord's Prayer*, petition 3: "the will of God for us is that we keep His Commandments" (151) and "When we say 'Thy will be done,' we pray that we may fulfill the Commandments of God."

[75] Gregory of Nyssa actually mentions charity in conjunction with this petition. In discussing how the will of God dispels all in man that is contrary to that will, he claims "the

It is most fitting that this is the final petition of those representing the theological virtues. As addressed below, this completes an ordering of the theological virtues that matches Aquinas's understanding of that order. But more germane to charity is the phrase "on earth as it is in heaven." This phrase may seem to be simply a climactic conclusion to the previous lines, but it is actually most properly a reference to love, and therefore appropriately placed in the third petition.[76] For as important as faith and hope are in this life, they "pass away" in the next one as we see God "face to face" and experience full union with God. There is no need for faith or hope then; but love remains.[77] Love is the very meaning of existence "on earth as it is in heaven." In commenting on this petition, Aquinas claims, "Hence you cannot go there unless you are made heavenly. And thus he [Jesus] adds 'your will be done,' i.e., make us imitators of the heavenly ones."[78] Though Aquinas does not mention charity here, it is difficult to think of a more apt term for what describes heavenly life.

4. "GIVE US THIS DAY OUR DAILY BREAD": PRUDENCE   One of the dangers of aligning two groups together and grafting them on to each other as related and illuminating is that the effort is always in danger of being "forced," driven more by the desire to align two groups (in this case of seven) neatly than by whether or not their content is really related. Yet despite the lack of alignment of the seven petitions with the seven virtues in the history of commentary, the alignment as presented here is surprisingly *not* forced. The fourth petition, however, "Give us this day our daily bread," appears at first glance to be an exception. What does this have to do with prudence? A look at the tradition of interpretation of this verse reveals that prudence is not so foreign an imposition after all.

We must first ask what is meant by bread. This is unsurprisingly a prominent issue in the commentary tradition.[79] Does "bread" refer to literal

---

supreme good of charity will expel a whole catalogue of opposing evils from the soul" and "the whole hoist of such evils is wiped out by a charitable disposition." See *The Lord's Prayer*, 59.

[76] See Stevenson's *The Lord's Prayer*, 223 where he claims that despite noteworthy exceptions (such as Origen, Meister Eckhart, and the *Catechism* of the Council of Trent) the "overwhelming" consensus in the commentary tradition is that this phrase refers solely to petition three. For this view in contemporary biblical scholarship see Guelich, *The Sermon on the Mount*, 291.

[77] See Thomas Aquinas, *Summa Theologiae* I–II 67, 3, 4, and 6.

[78] *Commentary on the Gospel of Mathew*, 586.

[79] There are of course others, most notably the meaning of what St. Jerome translated in the Vulgate as *supersubstantialem*. That question is not addressed here. For a helpful overview, see Carmignac *Recherches sur le "Notre Père,"* 121–43 for an (inconclusive) survey of the tradition as to the meaning of the Greek word *epiousios*.

material bread, or does it have a spiritual meaning?[80] Thomas Aquinas is representative of the broad current of the tradition in affirming both meanings. Citing Augustine's *Letter 130* (to Proba), Aquinas claims that in a material sense, "bread" refers not only to actual bread but also to all necessary sustenance for bodily life.[81] As for its spiritual sense, its most obvious meaning is the Eucharist, an interpretation Thomas Aquinas recognizes and even holds as paradigmatic for all spiritual interpretations of "bread."[82]

Yet Aquinas claims bread also has other spiritual meanings. In his *Explanation of the Lord's Prayer*, Aquinas claims bread also refers to the Word of God, citing Mt 4:4 that "man does not live by bread alone, but by the Word of God."[83] In his *Commentary on Matthew*, Aquinas claims the word can be taken to mean "the bread of wisdom."[84] Is it unreasonable to understand this as *practical* wisdom, or prudence? Not at all, according to Aquinas and Augustine, for two reasons. First, both saints affirm that bread in this sense refers to observing God's commandments, or precepts. Aquinas claims "he eats who keeps the commands of wisdom: 'my food is to do the will of him who sent me' (Jn 4:34)."[85] Indeed, Augustine, after acknowledging that bread can mean material bread or the Eucharist, reveals his preference for interpreting bread in this third sense, as "meditating on and living the divine precepts."[86] Second, both affirm that "this day" (*hodie*) is a reference to this

---

[80] See Carmignac *Recherches sur le "Notre Père,"* 143–91 for an historical overview of this question.

[81] Thomas Aquinas, *Summa Theologiae* II–II 83, 9 and *Commentary on the Gospel of Matthew*, 589–592. For another example of this claim in the tradition, see Cyprian, *On the Lord's Prayer* 18 ("*Quod potest et spiritaliter et simpliciter intellegi.*") where he claims, "'Give us this day our daily bread.' This may be understood both spiritually and literally" (78). See also Augustine's *On the Lord's Sermon on the Mount* II.7.25–27, cited below. See also Gregory of Nyssa, *On the Lord's Prayer*, 70. Luz oddly claims that "bread" should not be understood to extend to other necessities of life (*Matthew 1–7*, 383), but Betz (*The Sermon on the Mount*, 399), Davies and Allison (*The Gospel According to Saint Matthew*, 610) and Guelich (*The Sermon on the Mount*, 293) affirm the contrary.

[82] See Thomas Aquinas, *Summa Theologiae* II–II 83, 9, as well as *Explanation of the Lord's Prayer*, petition 4. Aquinas is far from alone in understanding "bread" as the Eucharist. For instance, see also Cyprian, *On the Lord's Prayer* 18 (78) as well as Augustine, *On the Lord's Sermon on the Mount* II.7.25–27. Jn 6 is consistently cited in these passages.

[83] Aquinas, *Explanation of the Lord's Prayer*, petition 4.

[84] Aquinas, *Commentary on the Gospel of Matthew*, 592.

[85] Aquinas, *Commentary on the Gospel of Matthew*, 592. In very virtue-centered language he goes on to claim, "These divine precepts now are bread, for they are ground with a certain difficult, by considering and doing, but afterwards they will be a drink, for they will refresh without difficulty."

[86] Augustine, *On the Lord's Sermon on the Mount* II.7.27. The reference to both meditating and observing, like Aquinas's considering and doing in the previous note, is evocative of prudence, which is not simply a knowledge of how to act well but rather a putting of such knowledge into action. For helpful overviews of prudence see Josef Pieper, *The Four Cardinal Virtues* (Notre Dame, IN: University of Notre Dame Press, 1966) and Daniel Westberg, *Right Practical Reason* (Oxford: Clarendon Press, 1994).

life.[87] Aquinas repeatedly references "temporal goods" in this section of his *Commentary on the Gospel of Matthew*,[88] and Augustine does the same, even starkly claiming that "this food is now called daily since it is finished during this temporal life, during its passing, waning days."[89]

It is now more clear how this fourth petition can be understood as a prayer for prudence. Prudence is the virtue that enables one to see things truthfully so as to act well in worldly matters. Commentators such as Augustine and Aquinas have understood "bread" to refer to the wisdom needed to act well in daily life.[90] In this petition, one thus asks for that quality, or virtue, by which one possesses precisely such practical wisdom. Finally, the prevalence of references to Jn 6 in these commentaries reminds us that this practical wisdom is found most perfectly through Christ, the Word made flesh and Bread of Life (Jn 6:35), who identifies himself as the way, the truth, and the life.[91]

5. "FORGIVE US OUR TRESPASSES": JUSTICE "Forgive us our trespasses, as we forgive those who trespass against us" is simultaneously an enormously important, and yet perhaps the least commented on, petition in the Lord's Prayer. As evidence of the latter, consider that it is given only thirteen pages in Carmignac's magisterial survey of writing on the Lord's Prayer, less than any other petition.[92] As evidence of the former, it is the only petition that Christ in effect "repeats" at the conclusion of the prayer (Mt 6:14–15).[93] Here is a perfect example of how the quantity of treatment of a matter need not reflect its importance. The best explanation for the degree of treatment is that the meaning of the petition is straightforward. It is also quite obviously about justice.

---

[87] I am grateful to Daniel Westberg for helping me to see this point more clearly.

[88] Aquinas, *Commentary on the Gospel of Matthew*, 593.

[89] See Augustine, *On the Lord's Sermon on the Mount* II.7.27.

[90] Indeed, even when Aquinas is examining "bread" in a material sense, he refers to it as aiding a person to act well and as instrumental in service to virtue. See III *Sent.* d. 34 q. 1 a. 6: "*Aliud est organice ad virtutem serviens, sicut temporalia subsidia quibus homo ad bene operandum juvatur; et hoc pertinet ad quartam petitionem qua dicitur:* Panem nostrum quotidianum.

[91] For an example of contemporary biblical scholarship that interprets "bread" in 6:11 in a spiritual sense as "bread of life" (citing Jeremias), see Davies and Allison, *The Gospel According to Saint Matthew*, 610.

[92] See Carmignac, *Recherches sur le "Notre Père*," 222–235.

[93] Of all 100+ verses in the Sermon on the Mount, these two verses are given least direct attention in this book. They are not addressed in Chapter 3 and yet only mentioned here in Chapter 6 as a recapitulation of petition five. Reminiscent of the paucity of attention given in the commentary tradition to petition five, the lack of extensive analysis of 6:14–15 should not be taken as indication of the lack of important of the theme of those verses. Indeed those two verses emphasize a crucial theme from Chapter 4, namely, consistency of standards of justice. For more on that topic and its relation to 7:1–5 as well see Guelich, *The Sermon on the Mount*, 313.

What does the fifth petition have to do with justice? Betz notes that this petition is about human relationships, "including our relationship with God." He describes the wording of the petition as the use of "business language to interpret what otherwise would be called sins."[94] It describes the restoration of relationships, the resolution of debts, in our relations with others and with God. This has everything to do with justice, which is the virtue that inclines one to right relations with others, to give others' their due.[95] The forgiveness sought in the fifth petition is the reestablishment of right relations after some disruption. Therefore, in this petition we are praying that the order of justice (*ius*) be restored, that rights be reestablished between us and God, and between us and other people.[96] Reminiscent of Chapter 4 (and echoed in 6:14–15), restoration of justice entails consistent standards of judgment. Thus, as with the theological virtue petitions above, we are not simply praying that something happens *to us*, but also that we participate in that reestablishing of right relations, in part by adopting a merciful standard of judgment. The possession of the virtue justice makes this possible.

6. "LEAD US NOT INTO TEMPTATION": TEMPERANCE The last two petitions are treated quite similarly in the tradition of commentary, whether the commentator sees them as one (two-part) petition or as two distinct petitions. When examining the sixth petition, "Lead us not into temptation," Thomas Aquinas and those whose work he draws on are concerned primarily with one point. They emphasize that this petition cannot be taken to mean that we never be tempted, not primarily because it is "unrealistic" but mainly because it is clear from the Scriptures that God allows us to be tempted.[97]

---

[94] Betz, *The Sermon on the Mount*, 402. Aquinas also discusses the petition in the context of remission of sin. See Thomas Aquinas, *Summa Theologiae* II–II 83, 9 and *Commentary on the Gospel of Matthew*, 596. See also Augustine who, in his commentary on this petition, points his reader back to his examination of the nature of punishment in the context of the fifth antithesis (Mt 5:38–42). See *On the Lord's Sermon on the Mount* II.8.29, where he refers the reader back to i.19.56–1.20.68. Notably for this book's connections between justice and mercy in Chapter 1 (5:7) and Chapter 4 (7:1–5), Betz also notes the importance of mercy in this dynamic of re-establishing justice (403).

[95] For more on the nature of justice for Thomas Aquinas, see *Summa Theologiae* II–II 58. See also Betz, *The Sermon on the Mount*, 402 for an explicit discussion of this petition in the context of justice. Betz even employs the traditional definition of justice as *suum cuique* in his interpretation of this verse.

[96] There is a consistent question in the tradition as to the strength of the conjunction "as." Stevenson (*The Lord's Prayer*, 15) notes the different approaches to this question among Gregory of Nyssa, Thomas Aquinas, and John Calvin. Related to this is the common appeal by commentators to the story of the "unforgiving servant" from Mt 18:21–35. For examples of this see Cyprian, *On the Lord's Prayer* 23 and John Chrysostom, *Homilies on Matthew* XIX.9.

[97] See *Explanation of the Lord's Prayer*, petition 6 for Aquinas's treatment of the ways God *does* try us (in accordance with Deut 13:3), and yet does *not* tempt us (in accordance with James 1:13). Though he does use the term "prove" or "try" (*probat*) for the former, he also

As Aquinas says, "To be tempted is human, but to consent to it is diabolical."[98] As indicated in this quote, the strategy generally employed to make this point is noting that the prayer says "lead us not into temptation," rather than "let us not be tempted." Aquinas claims, "we do not ask not to be tempted, but not to be conquered by temptation, which is to be led into temptation."[99] He does not use the language of "consent to temptation" here as he does in his work on the Lord's Prayer, but the basic sense is the same. Aquinas cites Augustine to specify more precisely the different ways we may be "led into" temptation (rather than simply tempted) when he says we pray here for three things: not to be without divine help in resisting temptation, not to consent to its deception, and not to give in to its affliction.[100]

What has any of this to do with temperance? Temperance is the cardinal virtue whereby our desires are moderated reasonably, specifically with regard to sensual pleasures (of touch), but more generally to include all desires.[101] Similarly, "temptations" can refers to all sorts of desires, though perhaps the sensual temptations which are most proper to temperance especially come to mind.[102] A connection to sensual pleasures was particularly clear to Augustine who, though he does not use the term temperance, says

> What else does one say who says, "Remove from me the desires of the belly, and let not the desire for intercourse lay hold of me" (Sirach 23:6), but, "Lead us not into temptation"?[103]

Both temptation and temperance can also be taken more generally to refer to temptations other than those which are properly sensual. Furthermore, the claim that this petition is a request for temperance fits perfectly into the commentators' concern that the petition means *not* that we be not tempted, but that we not be *led into* temptation. For possessing the virtue temperance does not mean one never encounters temptation. Rather, it enables one to encounter and even at times enjoy pleasing entities in a moderate

---

uses "tempt" ("*Sic tentavit Deus Abraham*"), and so the question is not resolved simply with different terminology. For treatment of this issue in the context of 6:13 in biblical scholarship, see Luz, *Mathew 1–7*, 384–5; Guelich, *The Sermon on the Mount*, 294–297; and, Betz, *The Sermon on the Mount*, 406–11.

98 See *Explanation of the Lord's Prayer*, petition 6: "The reason is that it is human to be tempted, but to give consent is devilish."

99 See Thomas Aquinas, *Summa Theologiae* II–II 83, 9, See also *Commentary on the Gospel of Matthew*, 598.

100 See III *Sent* d. 34 q.1 a.6: "et ne nos inducas, *in qua, secundum Augustinum petimus ne deserti divino auxilio alicui tentationi vel consentiamus decepti vel cedamus afflicti.*" There is no reference to a text of Augustine in this text, but this basic quotation is found in Aquinas's *Catena Aurea* on Mt 6:13, attributed to Augustine's *Letter 130*.

101 See Thomas Aquinas, *Summa Theologiae* II–II 141, 2 and 4.

102 In treating this petition, Betz raises the point that temptation is born of human desire (*The Sermon on the Mount*, 407).

103 See *Letter 130* (to Proba) 12.22.

and reasonable manner in accord with one's station in life. The temperate person is indeed not "led into temptation" even when faced with tempting situations.

7. "DELVER US FROM EVIL": FORTITUDE What are the evils from which we pray to be delivered in the seventh petition?[104] Aquinas and his sources consistently make two points about the nature of this evil. First, the "evil" named in the petition is (or at least includes) evil that is already present.[105] Second, it refers to both punishment and also afflictions in general. In his work on the Lord's Prayer, Aquinas says that since the previous two petitions concern sin and temptation, he'll speak here of other evils, such as adversity and afflictions of this world.[106] How are we to be delivered from such evil? In this same work, Aquinas claims God "delivers" us from evil only rarely by preventing evil from happening to us. Far more common are other ways God delivers us, which include consoling us in affliction, bestowing good things on those afflicted, and directing the evils of our trials and temptations toward our own good.[107]

What has any of this to do with fortitude? Fortitude is the cardinal virtue by which we are able to endure or resist obstacles that impede us from living in accordance with reason.[108] The brave person is able to face afflictions and adversities well. Reminiscent of Aquinas's claims about how God grants deliverance, this is quite often achieved not simply by removing the difficulty at hand, but rather by enduring it.[109] One is brave and has been delivered from evil when evils experienced are overcome, or at least one is not overcome by them. Hence in the seventh petition as one prays for deliverance from evil, one is indeed praying for fortitude.

[104] For a discussion of the historical and linguistic issue of whether this petition should read "evil" or "the evil one," see Carmignac, 306–312. See also Betz, *The Sermon on the Mount*, 411–413 and Luz *Matthew 1–7*, 385.

[105] This is especially evident in III *Sent.* d. 34 q. 1 a.6 where, as seen below, the last three petitions are grouped together as removing impediments to the active life, and this seventh refers to present evils (as opposed to the past evil of the fifth petition and future ones of the sixth). Even though Aquinas adopts this chronological grouping of the last three petitions in no other work, he still recognizes that this seventh petition is about present evil. See Aquinas, *Commentary on the Gospel of Matthew*, 599 where he claims that the evil here refers to "evil past, present, and future, guilt and punishment, and from every evil." See also Augustine, *On the Lord's Sermon on the Mount* II.9.35. Betz also attends to chronology but claims the last three petitions concern the present, past, and future, respectively *The Sermon on the Mount*, 405.

[106] See *Explanation of the Lord's Prayer*, petition 7: "But since we have already mentioned sin and temptation, we now must consider other evils, such as adversity and all afflictions of this world."

[107] See *Explanation of the Lord's Prayer*, petition 7.

[108] See Thomas Aquinas, *Summa Theologiae* II–II 122, 1 and 2.

[109] See Thomas Aquinas, *Summa Theologiae* II–II 122, 6 on endurance as the chief act of fortitude. For more on this point see also Josef Pieper, *The Four Cardinal Virtues*, 126–33.

This is the alignment presented here between the seven petitions of the Our Father and the seven foundational virtues of the Christian life. In most contexts, it would be appropriate to spend proportionally far more time on the richness evoked by these petitions and the virtues they suggest. But given the setting in this book, this more schematic presentation is offered, with the hope that it will be further developed in the future in other settings and by other theologians. I now turn to the task of identifying further ways that the Lord's Prayer converges with a virtue-centered approach to morality.

B. READING THE LORD'S PRAYER IN THE CONJUNCTION WITH THE VIRTUES: IMPLICATIONS FOR VIRTUE AND THE CHRISTIAN LIFE

In this final part of the book's concluding chapter, I turn to examine ways that the Lord's Prayer contributes to a virtue-centered approach to morality. As with the previous part, this analysis will be necessarily brief. But as in other chapters of the book, it is readily evident how striking the correspondence is between these verses and a virtue-centered approach to morality. I address four topics that directly concern these verses: the ordering of petitions and virtues, the grouping of these petitions, the importance of the infused moral virtues, and the age-old question of the relationship between happiness and virtue.

1. ORDERING OF THE PETITIONS AND VIRTUES The order of the petitions generally corroborates how the virtues have been ordered in the Christian, and especially Thomistic, tradition. The foundations of the life of Christian virtue are the three theological virtues, which are fittingly placed at the opening of the prayer. Aquinas affirms that faith is first among the three theological virtues as to the order of generation, since "it is by faith that the intellect apprehends the object of hope and love."[110] But of course love has also been consistently affirmed as both the form of the virtues and the one theological virtue that endures in the next life. And so it is given a climactic place at the conclusion of the first three petitions, and as noted above, even amended with the decisive "on earth as it is in heaven."[111] Thus the wording of the Lord's Prayer not only reflects primacy of and proper ordering among the theological virtues in the tradition, but it also ascribes an appropriately climactic place to the virtue of love.[112]

---

[110] See Thomas Aquinas, *Summa Theologiae* I–II 62, 4.

[111] For the claim about love as form of the virtues, see Thomas Aquinas, *Summa Theologiae* II–II 23, 8. See also Chapter 3.

[112] For the place of hope in between faith and love, see Thomas Aquinas, *Summa Theologiae* II–II 17, 7 and 8 as well as I-II 62,4.

The cardinal virtues have been presented in Christianity with more variation as to their order.[113] But the Thomistic tradition follows strains of Greek thought in consistently affirming this order: prudence, justice, fortitude, and temperance. Prudence is placed first since it is a virtue of the intellect, and directs the moral virtues.[114] Justice is next, since it is a virtue of the appetite, but the rationale appetite or will. Aquinas generally lists fortitude next, and then temperance. This is reflected in his ordering of the cardinal virtues in the *Secunda secundae* and explained in passages where he describes the irascible appetite (governed by fortitude) as participating more in human reason than the concupiscible appetite (governed by temperance).[115] Yet the differences between the capacities governed by temperance and fortitude are far fewer than between the sensitive appetite on the one hand (including both temperance and fortitude) and the intellect (prudence) or the intellectual appetite (justice) on the other. Indeed, at times in his work, Aquinas switches the order of temperance and fortitude, something he does not do with the other two cardinal virtues either in relation to each other or in relation to temperance and fortitude.[116] In sum, the ordering of the virtues presented here as aligned with the petitions of the Lord's Prayer (prudence, justice, temperance, and fortitude) largely respects the ordering of the cardinal virtues in the Thomistic tradition. Where it deviates from the most common ordering (fortitude then temperance), there is not only precedent for the different ordering but also a reason for the variation. Indeed, the fact that the virtues of temperance and fortitude both govern the passions explains not only why their ordering in relation to each other is variable but also why these two virtues could be treated together under one petition, as represented by the six petition tradition of commentary since Tertullian.

2. GROUPING THE PETITIONS AND VIRTUES The Lord's Prayer is consistently divided in the tradition into two groups of petitions: the first three and the remaining four (or three, depending on the author).[117] This

---

[113] The scriptural mention of the cardinal virtues is found at Wisdom 8:7, where the order given is temperance, prudence, justice, and fortitude.

[114] Prudence is commonly called the "charioteer of the virtues," a metaphor traced back to Plato's *Phaedrus*. For more on the centrality of prudence in classical virtue ethics, see Julia Annas, *Morality of Happiness*, 73–84. For its central role in directing the other virtues, see Thomas Aquinas, *Summa Theologiae* I–II 58, 4.

[115] For an example of this, see Thomas Aquinas, *Summa Theologiae* I–II 46, 5. For another example of Aquinas listing the four cardinal virtues in this way, see *Disputed Question on the Virtues* q. 5 ("On the Cardinal Virtues") a. 2.

[116] See examples of this at Thomas Aquinas, *Summa Theologiae* I–II 61, 2, 3, and 4.

[117] Stevenson, *The Lord's Prayer*, 221 notes that despite different groupings offered throughout history, "they all distinguish between the opening petitions (addressed to God) and later petitions (about our needs)." That this is somewhat overstated is revealed just by

division is suggested in the very grammar of the petitions, as noted above.[118] In explaining this difference, Thomas Aquinas and his sources consistently differentiate the two groups in the manner described by Augustine:

> Accordingly, in the Evangelist Matthew the Lord's Prayer seems to embrace seven petitions, three of which ask for eternal blessings, and the remaining four for temporal; these latter, however being necessary antecedents to the former. For when we say, "Hallowed be thy name: Thy Kingdom come: They will be done in earth, as it is in heaven . . . " we ask for blessings that are to be enjoyed forever; which are indeed begun in this world, and grow in us as we grow in grace, but in their perfect state, which is to be looked for in another life, shall be a possession for evermore. But when we say, "Give us this day our daily bread: and forgive us our debts, as we forgive our debtors: and lead us not into temptation, but deliver is from evil," who does not see that we ask for blessings that have reference to the wants to this present life?[119]

Thomas Aquinas recognizes and affirms this grouping in the *Summa Theologiae* when he explicitly refers to Augustine's *Enchiridion* and claims in reference to the first three petitions that "these three petitions will be perfectly fulfilled in the life to come; while the other four, according to Augustine, belong to the needs of the present life."[120] Interestingly enough, despite recognizing Augustine's eternal/temporal distinction here and in other texts,[121] Thomas Aquinas frequently groups the seven petitions otherwise, in fact in varying different ways that seem to display a clear trajectory of development.[122]

---

looking at Thomas Aquinas's differing ways of dividing the petitions, presented below. But cases like his are exceptions that prove the rule. The two group division is consistent in the biblical scholarship used here: Betz, *The Sermon on the Mount*, 396; Guelich, *The Sermon on the Mount*, 309–315; Davies and Allison, *The Gospel According to Saint Matthew*, 607.

[118] See Section 1's treatment of the use of both subjunctive and imperative in Latin-influenced languages. Note that in Greek the first three petitions are also grammatically distinct in the use of the passive. I am grateful to Barrett Turner for this point.

[119] See Augustine, *Enchiridion* CXV. For this English translation, see *The Enchiridion on Faith, Hope and Love* (Washington, DC: Regnery Gateway, 1961). Augustine makes basically the same claim in his *On the Lord's Sermon on the Mount* II.10.36–37.

[120] Thomas Aquinas, *Summa Theologiae* II–II 83, 9 ad. 1.

[121] In his *Explanation of the Lord's Prayer*, petition 4, Aquinas again affirms the distinction between the first three petitions from those that follow.

[122] Though space prohibits a full account of development in Thomas Aquinas's corpus as to the grouping of the petitions, the main lines of that development can be signaled here. In III *Sent.* D. 34 q. 1 a. 6 (dated by Torrell, 332 in the 1250's), Thomas Aquinas claims the first two petitions concern the contemplative life, and the final five the active life. The latter group is further divided into two petitions (3 and 4) requesting what assists the active life, and three petitions (5, 6, and 7) seeking the removal of what impedes the active life. Thus there is a clear 2–2–3 grouping. In the *Secunda secundae* of the *Summa Theologiae* (dated by Torrell, 333 in 1271–1272), Aquinas no longer employs the contemplative/active distinction. But his grouping is still best described in II–II 83, 9, as it is in

Nevertheless, the point for our purposes is that the petitions themselves, in their grammar and in their content, exhibit a ready division between the first three and next four with the first three concerning eternity (although begun in this life) and the last four concerning the needs of this life. This grouping is evident in the tradition of commentary.

This division perfectly reflects the distinction between the theological and cardinal virtues in Thomas Aquinas's thought, not simply in the numbers of each (three theological and four cardinal) but also in the content of the two different categories of virtue. For Aquinas, the theological virtues have God's very self as their object.[123] They govern activities which concern God directly (believing in God, hoping for God, loving God and one's neighbors in God)

the *Sentences*, as 2–5 and more specifically as 2–2–3. The first two petitions concern humanity's end itself, who is God. The rest concern what is directed to that end. Petitions 3 and 4 direct humanity to that end by their nature, since they concern what is useful to that end. Petitions 5, 6, and 7 direct us to the end accidentally by removing impediments to the good. This is a development from *Sentences* given the absence of contemplative/active language. It is also clear how the middle group of two petitions could easily be grouped with the first two rather than the last three. This is exactly what happens, in *Commentary on Matthew*, 585 (dated by Torrell, 339 "with high probability" to 1269–70) and even more clearly in *Explanation of the Lord's Prayer*, petition 7 (dated by Torell, 358 in 1273). In these texts, Aquinas employs a 4–3 grouping, or more specifically 1–3–3. The prayer contains all we ought to desire, which for Aquinas always means both what we ought to desire and what we ought to avoid. There are four things we desire, the first petition being the glory of God and the next three petitions being things from God as they concern ourselves. Then there are three things to be avoided (petitions 5, 6, and 7), and these are correlated to petitions 2, 3, and 4 as impediments. Aquinas claims there is no contrary to the glory of God (first petition). (Note that the unfinished *Compendium of Theology* contains no grouping of the petitions.)

The *Commentary on Matthew* presents an issue of authenticity and perhaps even dating. As for the former, Torrell notes that the 1951 Marietti edition contains inauthentic passages interpolated throughout. In fact, he cites the commentary on the Sermon on the Mount as one such example. However, he says "the interpolated passages extend in Matthew from 5:11 to 6:8 and from 6:14 to 6:19 (lects. 13–17 and 19), nos. 444–582 and 603–10 in the Marietti edition" (339). The fact that Torrell conspicuously omits listing from his list of interpolated passages Aquinas's commentary on Mt 6:9–13 (the text of the Lord's Prayer), which consists of nos. 583–602, is taken here as an affirmation of the authenticity of that part of the commentary, and thus it is treated here as such. The English translation used for this book makes note of this state of affairs and uses the Marietti edition for the verses on the Lord's Prayer.

As for dating and the immediately relevant issue of grouping petitions, Torrell dates this commentary "with high probability" (339) in 1269–70. However, Aquinas's grouping of petitions in this text (585) follows the *Explanation of the Lord's Prayer* treatment exactly. The texts on the groupings of petitions thus show clear development from the *Sentences* through the *Secunda secundae* as a sort of middle ground, ending in the *Commentary on Matthew* and *Explanation of the Lord's Prayer*. Yet Torrell's dating of the *Commentary on Matthew* does not match this development. No explanation is offered for this here.

[123] See Thomas Aquinas, *Summa Theologiae* I–II 62, 1 and 2. See also *On the Virtues in General* a. 12.

which are begun in this life but brought to perfection in eternity. The four cardinal virtues concern temporal activities accessible to unaided human reason: practical decision-making, relations with others, facing difficulties, and engaging in sensual pleasures.[124] The claim that the petitions concern both eternal (heavenly) and temporal (earthly) matters is directly reflective of Aquinas's distinction between the theological and the cardinal virtues. Of course, all commentators want to maintain that these two groups should not be dichotomized. For instance, Augustine claims that what is requested in the first three is begun in this life, and that the temporal necessities of the final four prepare one for eternity.[125] This leads to a third observation.

3. THE PRIMACY OF INFUSED VIRTUE IN THE PETITIONS Despite the neat division between the first three and last four petitions, the Lord's Prayer importantly affirms the unity of the Christian life, a life that is both directed toward (and indeed even a foretaste of) a supernatural destiny of union with God, and yet still firmly embedded in worldly existence in time and space. That this is the case with the first three petitions and their corresponding theological virtues is readily evident. What is sought in the first three petitions, and is made possible for humanity in the three theological virtues, is only perfectly possible in the next life but it is begun in this one.[126] Yet the same is true of both the last four petitions and the four cardinal virtues. In a simple sense, as Augustine notes, these four are needed in order to attain eternity. But it should also be noted that while directly concerning temporal activities accessible to unaided human reason, the cardinal virtues are only perfectly possible with God's grace. In praying the Lord's Prayer, one simultaneously recognizes both that God does help people with their temporal activities and that such grace is needed in order to do them perfectly.[127] In the

---

[124] See Thomas Aquinas *Summa Theologiae* I–II 62, 2: "the object of the intellectual and moral virtues is something comprehensible to human reason." See I–II 61, 1 where Aquinas explains how the four cardinal virtues "cover" the moral and intellectual virtues that engage the human will.

[125] *On the Lord's Sermon on the Mount* II.10.36–37.

[126] Readers of Thomas Aquinas will immediately protest, with appeal to *Summa Theologiae* I–II 67, 3 and 4, that faith and hope do not remain after this life. This is true. However, though the theological virtues faith and hope do not endure, the knowledge and possession toward which they incline a person are achieved. This renders the knowledge no longer faith and longing for possession no longer hope, but by reason of completion or achievement rather than removal or failure. And of course charity does remain (I–II 67, 6), and this distinction of charity is signified in the prayer by the "on earth as it is in heaven."

[127] For more on this claim, see Thomas Aquinas, *Summa Theologiae* I–II 63, 3 on the need for the infused moral (or cardinal) virtues. See also the Conclusion of Chapter 4.

Lord's Prayer, not only the first three but also the final four petitions are made possible by God's grace and direct one ultimately toward one's supernatural destiny even while directly concerning matters of this life. Thus, the very format of the Lord' Prayer is an "argument" for both the existence of the infused moral virtues and indeed the primacy of the infused (rather than acquired) moral virtues.[128]

4. THE RELATIONSHIP BETWEEN HAPPINESS VIRTUE IN THE PETITIONS Fourth and finally, the Lord's Prayer takes a stand on an age-old question in virtue ethics concerning the relationship between happiness and virtue. Is happiness achieved by the possession of virtues (as the Stoics claimed), such that the attainment of happiness not be subject to the capriciousness of luck or other factors beyond the wise person's control (such as health or external goods)? Or is genuine happiness something that in important ways happens *to* us, in a manner not fully achieved by possessing the virtues? Reminiscent of Aristotle's wrestling with this thorny question,[129] and especially Augustine's famous categorization of the multitude of possible answers to it in the opening pages of *City of God* XIX, it is clear from the Lord's Prayer that the answer is a both/and. As evident from the opening pages of this book, full happiness does not simply happen to us, given the capacities we possess as creatures in the image and likeness of God. Reminiscent of the Thomistic (and Aristotelian) claim that happiness is an activity, the happiness for which we pray in the Lord's Prayer is something in which we participate.[130] How it is lived out in this life (as a very participation in the next) is described in Chapter 1 on the beatitudes. Hence in the Lord's Prayer, we pray not simply that certain things happen (to us), but that we become people who are equipped to enjoy true happiness, namely, persons with the theological and cardinal virtues.

While the Lord's Prayer reveals that happiness requires a change in the petitioners (in other words, the possession of the virtues), it is also evident

---

[128] For more on the common neglect of the infused cardinal (or moral) virtues, see Romanus Cessario, O.P., *The Moral Virtues and Theological Ethics*, 2nd ed. (Notre Dame: University of Notre Dame Press, 2009), 165–72; Romanus Cessario, O.P., *Introduction to Moral Theology* (Washington, DC: The Catholic University of America Press, 2001), 200ff; Servais Pinckaers, O.P., *The Sources of Christian Ethics* (Washington, DC: The Catholic University of America Press, 1995), 178–81; Michael Sherwin, O.P., *By Knowledge and By Love* (Washington, DC: The Catholic University of America Press, 2005), 170–75; Angela McKay, "Prudence and Acquired Moral Virtue" *The Thomist* **69**.4 (2005): 535–55; Robert Miner, "Non-Aristotelian Prudence" *The Thomist* **64**.3 (2000): 401–22.

[129] See *Nicomachean Ethics* I.8–11.

[130] See Thomas Aquinas, *Summa Theologiae* I–II 3, 2. There Thomas Aquinas cites *Nicomachean Ethics* I.13.

from the prayer that the yearning for happiness from which the supplicants' words are born is not satiated on their own power. The petitioners are asking through God's grace to be granted the virtues. Furthermore, though the words of the petitions do request changes in those who utter the prayer (represented by the virtues), those who pray also ask God that certain things happen not only in them but in the world outside of them: that the kingdom come, thy will be done, that their bread is given, their trespasses be forgiven, and that they be delivered from evil. Hence the possession of the virtues alone, even the infused virtues, is not constitutive of the full happiness sought in the Lord's Prayer. This full happiness is the redemption for which all creation groans (Rom 8:22–23). For humanity it is a participation in the divine nature (2 Pet 1:4) requiring, but not constituted by, the possession of the theological and cardinal virtues.

In conclusion, given the prominence of depicting the fullness of life in Christ by reflecting both on the petitions of the Lord's Prayer and the seven virtues, it should not be surprising to find an alignment between those groupings. In this chapter, I hope that the historical inquiry of Section 1 has delineated how the constructive work of Section 2 is both historically grounded and yet interestingly new. This chapter serves as the perfect conclusion to this book on the convergences between the Sermon on the Mount and a virtue-centered approach to morality. In the Lord's Prayer at the heart of the Christian life, we find a very ready alignment with the seven virtues. Again in accord with the thesis of this book, we find that a virtue-centered approach to morality helps us better see the meaning of the verses at hand, and that the Scripture further illuminates a virtue-centered approach to morality. This chapter is a fitting conclusion to that overall thesis. But even more importantly, I hope that the rudimentary reflections in this chapter on the petitions in light of the virtues can nourish the lives of discipleship of the faithful who utter this prayer and endeavor to live out the virtues, both to know and to enjoy the happiness to which all are called as constituted by union with the God of Jesus Christ.

NAME INDEX

Allison, Dale C., 5, 7, 13, 21, 26–8, 34, 38–9, 41–3, 51, 54–8, 62, 64, 66, 69–71, 74–5, 77, 80, 88, 98, 103, 106, 111, 113, 115–16, 121–2, 125, 128–9, 133, 135, 140–2, 144–5, 151, 163, 167–9, 174, 177, 179, 184–6, 192, 195–9, 207–9, 212–14, 228–32, 258–9, 265

Ambrose, 11, 13, 26–7, 29, 31, 41–2, 44, 46, 49

Annas, Julia, 19, 23–4, 104, 123, 145, 165–6, 264

Anscombe, Elizabeth, 3, 123

Aquinas, Thomas, 1–2, 7, 12, 22–4, 26–32, 35–6, 40–2, 44–6, 48–50, 52–3, 55–6, 58–9, 65, 67, 69, 71, 73, 75–6, 80–1, 85, 88, 91–3, 95, 97–101, 105, 120, 122–8, 131–2, 136–7, 139, 143–7, 150, 155–9, 165, 167, 169, 171–2, 178–9, 185–6, 188, 192, 198, 200, 202, 206, 211, 228, 230–1, 234, 239, 245–6, 248, 251–4, 258–60, 264–6

Aristotle, 1, 10, 18–19, 22–4, 37, 76, 126, 147, 165, 167, 210, 268

Arnold, Duane W.H., 155

Augustine, 1–2, 10–13, 18, 20, 22, 26–7, 29–35, 40–2, 45, 48–9, 51, 54, 57–8, 65–7, 69–71, 73, 75, 80–1, 84–5, 88–9, 91–3, 95, 99–100, 102, 104–6, 110, 122, 125, 128, 147, 150, 155–7, 159, 165, 167, 169–70, 172, 178–9, 184, 186, 190, 192, 194, 197–8, 206, 209, 212, 217, 220, 228–9, 231, 234, 238–9, 243–5, 248–9, 251, 253–6, 258, 261–2, 265, 267–8

Austin, Victor Lee, 148

Barron, Robert, 98–9, 114

Benedict XVI. *See* Pope Benedict XVI

Betz, Hans Dieter, 1–2, 7, 13, 18, 20, 26–8, 38–9, 41–3, 48, 50–1, 53, 55–6, 62, 64, 69, 78–80, 86, 88–9, 98, 103, 105–6, 111, 117, 121–3, 125, 128–31, 135–6, 140–1, 143, 145, 150, 152, 157, 162–4, 168–71, 174, 177, 183–5, 188, 190–2, 195, 197, 199–202, 205, 207, 210–12, 214, 227–9, 232–3, 235–6, 239, 243–5, 253, 256, 258, 260–2, 265

Beveridge, Henry, 243

Birch, Bruce C., 3

Boff, Leonardo, 245

Bonaventure, 239, 245, 247, 249

Bonhoeffer, Dieterich, 1–2, 28–9, 31–4, 36, 49, 185

Bonnefoy, J-F, 247, 249

Bowlin, John, 179

Boxall, Ian, 66, 77

Brawley, Robert, 3

Bright, Pamela, 155

Brink, J.N. Bakhuizen van den, 132

Brock, Stephen L., 138

Brown, Michael Joseph, 242

Brown, Raymond E., 243, 245

Brown, Warren, 57

Burridge, Richard, 3

Bushlack, Thomas, 179

Butera, Giuseppe, 70

Calvin, John, 12–13, 30–4, 36, 49, 84, 162, 171–2, 185, 187, 192–3, 195, 200, 243, 260

Capizzi, Joseph E., 79

Carmignac, Jean, 242–4, 246, 258–9, 262

Carter, Warren, 175, 205, 211–13, 232

Cassian, 251, 256

Cates, Diana Fritz, 70, 216

Cessario, Romanus, 47, 216, 224–5, 268

Chan, Yiu Sing Lucas, 5

Charette, Blaine, 129–31, 133, 136, 141–4

Chenu, Marie-Dominique, 105

Chrysostom, John, 11–13, 26–7, 29, 35, 41, 65, 75, 83–4, 99, 105, 111, 122, 171–2, 187, 194, 200, 208, 210, 212, 228–9, 231–2, 234–6, 251, 253–4, 260

Cicero, 10, 19, 30

Clapp, Rodney, 153

Clark, Patrick, 15, 57, 241

Cloutier, David, 3, 6, 82, 120, 123, 152, 185

Crawford, David, 138

TERM INDEX

activity, 8–10, 12–13, 17, 23–5, 27–37, 39–40, 43–5, 47,
    50–2, 58, 63, 66–7, 72–91, 97–101, 117, 124–6,
    131–42, 145–6, 149–50, 154–7, 159, 166,
    176–83, 185, 187–90, 197, 205–7, 209–23,
    225–6, 230–2, 234–7, 268
  active life, 42, 45, 262, 265
  continuity of, 24, 28–9, 33–4, 43–4, 50, 58, 77,
    99–101, 117, 135, 205, 211–12, 219, 221, 223
adultery, 50, 69, 71–2, 76–7, 106, 126, 158, 168
  lust, 49, 63, 69–73, 76, 90, 105–6, 111, 168
almsgiving, 121–2, 124–8, 136, 139–40, 146, 152, 154,
    156–9, 162, 172, 231
anger, 31, 49, 63, 68–73, 76, 90, 105–6, 108, 111, 113,
    186
antitheses, 7, 9, 15, 47, 55, 58, 63, 67–90, 101–18, 142,
    144, 157, 174, 208, 260
appetite, 32, 50, 264
  appetitive power(s), 32, 50, 104, 145, 147
  concupiscible appetite, 48, 106, 264
    desire, 20, 23, 32, 48–51, 104–11, 113–14, 117–18,
      143, 148, 165, 248, 253–4, 261, 266, *See* sexual
      desire
  irascible appetite, 49, 108, 264
    aggression/spiritedness, 49, 104–5, 107–14, 117
  rational (intellectual) appetite, *See* will
  sensitive appetite, 264
apprehension, 107, 173, 175, 177, 180, 183, 187
  apprehensive power(s), 104, 145, 147
art, 210
asceticism, 82, 152
authority, 11–13, 58–9, 112, 114–16, 144, 148–9, 174,
    207, 233
aversion, 48

beatific vision, 45
beatitudes, 4–5, 7–9, 12–59, 63, 102, 114, 117, 134, 136,
    145, 149, 167, 194, 205, 207, 217, 233, 239–40,
    246–9, 251, 268

beauty, 15, 111, 241
body, 101, 159, 163, 169–74, 181, 191, 210
bread, 99, 195, 245, 252, 257–9, 265, 269

charity, 11, 46–7, 51–2, 76, 120, 154–60, 164, 177, 217,
    220–2, 232–5, 248–9, 255–7, 267
  agape, 256
  amor amicitiae, 255
  amor concupiscientiae, 255
  caritas, 256
  love, 49–52, 54, 65, 75–6, 78, 87–90, 104, 109,
    118, 147, 155–60, 167, 169, 172, 177, 186,
    199–200, 208, 220, 223, 234, 247, 252, 255–7,
    263
    love of enemy, 63, 73, 78, 88–9, 109, 156
chastity (evangelical counsel), 82
Christology, 9, 18, 55, 59, 116, 233
church, 11, 37, 40, 55–9, 63, 66, 82–3, 88, 92, 94, 98–9,
    102, 111–13, 115, 148, 154, 206, 219, 228,
    239–40, 242, 246
circumcision, 96, 112
clean of heart, 34–5, 42–3, 45, 47, 51, 168, 172, 198
command(s), 39, 47, 62, 65, 75, 78, 80–1, 83, 86–90,
    103, 110, 158, 172, 200, 208, 258
  commandment(s), 39, 52, 54, 81–3, 85, 93, 103,
    162, 199, 212–13, 256, 258
community, 55–7, 59, 109, 112–13, 145, 151–4, 176,
    205, 227
consequentialism, 24
contemplation, 15, 36, 42, 45, 111, 239
  contemplative life, 42, 45, 265–6
Council of Jerusalem, 92
counsel, 81, 86, 249
  evangelical counsels (counsels of perfection),
    65, 80–2, 177, *See* chastity, obedience,
    poverty
covenant, 66–7, 69, 72, 74–8, 80, 82, 84, 89, 97–9,
    113, 115–16

273

SCRIPTURE INDEX

Scripture texts in this work are taken from the New American Bible, revised edition © 2010, 1991, 1986, 1970 Confraternity of Christian Doctrine, Washington, D.C. and are used by permission of the copyright owner. All Rights Reserved. No part of the New American Bible may be reproduced in any form without permission in writing from the copyright owner.